Your people will be my people

THE RUTH KHAMA STORY

SUE GRANT-MARSHALL

PROTEA BOOK HOUSE
PRETORIA
2018

Your people will be my people: The Ruth Khama story
Sue Grant-Marshall

First edition, first impression in 2018 by Protea Book House
PO Box 35110, Menlo Park, 0102
1067 Burnett Street, Hatfield, Pretoria
8 Minni Street, Clydesdale, Pretoria
protea@intekom.co.za
www.proteaboekhuis.com

EDITOR: Rentia Bartlett-Möhl
PROOFREADER: Carmen Hansen-Kruger
COVER DESIGN: Hanli Deysel
COVER IMAGE: Margaret Bourke-White, The LIFE Picture Collection / Getty Images
BOOK DESIGN AND LAYOUT: Ada Radford
TYPOGRAPHY: 11 on 14 pt Dante MT Std

Printed by **novus print**, a Novus Holdings company

ISBN: 978-1-4853-0889-8 (printed book)
ISBN: 978-1-4853-0890-4 (e-book)
ISBN: 978-1-4853-0891-1 (ePub)

"Where you go I will go, and where you stay I will stay. Your people will be my people and your God my God. Where you die I will die, and there I will be buried."

Ruth 1:16–17

Table of contents

Dust and decades

This is the story Ruth Khama told me thirty-five years ago after her husband, Sir Seretse Khama, president of Botswana, died. I wrote it on a portable mechanical typewriter, beloved by journalists before the digital age.

It's now finally being published due to an extraordinary coincidence, serendipity, call it what you may. Two things happened, in the same month, in December 2016.

The major movie, *A United Kingdom*, about Seretse and Ruth was launched. So was a richly historic book, *The Thirstland Trek*, by author, publisher and Protea Bookshop owner, Nicol Stassen.

I saw *A United Kingdom* at Hyde Park Corner in Joburg, where Ruth and I often had coffee together. So many years had passed that it was with a sense of surrealism that I sat down in the theatre on the day it began showing in South Africa. At the end the multiracial audience rose spontaneously to its feet, clapping, cheering and even crying.

I was stunned. Here was Ruth, who had become like a second mother to me, being recognised along with Seretse – from Hollywood to New Zealand – for their courage, their tenacity, their refusal to be broken by a world riveted by race divides.

In Exclusive Books upstairs lay *The Thirstland Trek*, a book about Boers journeying to Angola through the then Bechuanaland Protectorate. I called Nicol Stassen saying I wanted to interview him for my newspaper, *Business Day*, and for my "Reading Matters" show on Radio Today.

During our interviews, I kept asking him about the Great Khama III, and he queried my interest in the visionary Bamangwato chief.

"I lived with his grandson, Seretse, and his family in Botswana," I explained. As we talked it emerged that I had written a book on Ruth decades earlier.

"But I've not seen it," exclaimed the avid historian.

"It was never published," I responded.

"Well, I would like to have a look at it," said Nicol.

I whirled back home, and soon my family was searching the house for the manuscript – of which I had one copy left. I sent it to Nicol and had almost forgotten about it when some weeks later he contacted me, saying he was keen to publish it.

Overjoyed, I began to hunt for all my notebooks, twenty-two files crammed with research, the tape recordings and books I had been given by my parents' Botswana friends. They were safe at the top of a cupboard, thick with dust, draped with cobwebs and fortunately not chewed by fish moths. We spluttered and choked as we carefully hauled them down.

As I've worked my way through them again in the past eighteen months, Ruth, who has always had a place in my heart, has taken up even more space in my mind as I hear her voice and debate issues with her.

I had to make a call about adding updated material about other personalities in this book. I decided to keep to my original text – focusing on Ruth.

And so, three decades on, here is her book.

Sue Grant-Marshall
Johannesburg
September 2018

Meeting Ruth

I was a baby when Ruth and Seretse Khama came to live in the same pretty, hilly Bechuanaland Protectorate village of Serowe to which my father, Peter Cardross Grant, had been posted a year earlier.

Seretse was the chief designate of the biggest and most powerful tribe in the protectorate, the Bamangwato. My father was an assistant district commissioner.

It was August 1949 and one tumultuous year later the British Government banished the Khamas, arguably the most famous couple in the world back then, to England.

Their crime? Seretse was black, Ruth was white.

They had married in the same year that white South Africans elected a government which decreed that sex and marriage between black and white people was a crime. You could be jailed for it. They called their law apartheid.

Soon three countries – Britain, South Africa and Bechuanaland – were reeling with angry words, telegrams, unofficial dispatches and urgent ambassadorial meetings as the marriage between a British woman and an African chief-in-waiting became a battleground.

The Khama couple lost the war, their union shot full of holes because their skins were of different colours. The British decided it was not expedient to allow a mixed-race couple to live on the borders of a powerful country where unmitigated white was lawfully right.

The brave couple was exiled, and Seretse's birthright extinguished, until in 1956 he and his uncle, Tshekedi Khama, both renounced their right to the chieftainship. Consequently, Ruth and Seretse were allowed to go home to Serowe.

Fast forward to the early 1960s when my father was district commissioner of Gaborone, the designated capital of soon to be independent Botswana. My parents renewed their acquaintance with Ruth and Seretse, and us four Cardross Grant children became friendly with the four Khama children. I was a teenager at the time and, at my father's request, I had been allowed out of boarding school in Johannesburg, not only for the celebrations but because there were not enough women to attend the Independence ball.

I wore a pale powder blue satin evening dress that my mother Mary Cardross Grant and I had sewn on her hand-operated Singer sewing machine, and my mother taught me to waltz.

As Ruth Khama danced past me, one elegant shoulder bare, her auburn hair glowing and unusual eyes sparkling, every nerve cell in her body must have been murmuring, "We've done it."

She would have attracted attention at any swish dance in London or Washington. Here in Gaborone, a town newly carved out of virgin thornbush to be a capital city, the country's first lady was mesmerizing. Her extraordinarily pale skin was emphasised by the rich redness of her ball gown, and her slender gracefulness drew many an eye.

Near us was Princess Marina, who had granted the former Bechuanaland Protectorate its independence on behalf of Queen Elizabeth II of Britain. To my delight Sir Seretse asked me to dance, and as we did, I reflected on the triumph the celebrations must have been for him and Ruth.

I rushed home at midnight, jumped on to my sister Jane's bed and, bouncing up and down breathlessly, told her that I had danced with the new president.

After Seretse's death in 1980, his young widow Ruth agreed I should write a book about their life, but for once from her perspective. "I want my story told," she wrote from the Khama farm outside Gaborone.

And so we met over a period of three years, and I taped our interviews and made notes about her life and stories.

One of these stories concerned my parents. In 1949, as Seretse showed his new bride the village of Serowe where he'd spent his early formative years, she was aware there were other English women of similar backgrounds to her own. One was my mother who had grown up in Chiswick, West London, only twenty-five kilometres away from Ruth's home in Blackheath, a suburb in South London. Like Ruth, my mother had been evacuated to the British countryside in World War II, had never left England before moving to Bechuanaland, had never lived in African villages nor listened to women singing at night around the fires outside their mud huts. They would have shared much over a cup of tea and indeed, my father refused to bow to the British administration's order that Ruth be frozen out of (white) society or "sent to Coventry" as the English say. For the Colonial Office in London had decided to make life for Ruth as miserable and isolated as they could in the hopes that she would run home to her comfortable, warm-hearted mother Dorothy.

But my principled and kind father would not countenance such cruelty even at the risk of insubordination. "Please invite Ruth to tea and make her feel at home," he suggested to my mother. "And so she did," Ruth told me on one of the many weekends I spent with her on her farm, outside Gaborone, when I was interviewing her for this book. "But our tea date never happened," Ruth paused, "because that is the day I gave birth to Jackie. But I never forgot your parents' kindness." I was astonished when Ruth told me the story, for my parents had never mentioned it.

I loved the weekends I spent with her on the Khama family farm. As I lay in bed on my first night there and heard the screech owl calling, the cry of the jackals and the intense rhythm of the cicadas, my childhood flooded back. I was "home" again in the country of my birth, one I love with a passion.

In between our interviews I flew to London, journeyed north to Scotland, through much of England and spent time in The National Archives Public Record Office doing research. I often drove through Botswana to Serowe, Mahalapye and Palapye as well as to Gaborone. I also travelled throughout South Africa to listen to the stories of my parents' and Ruth's retired generation.

I finished writing this book just weeks before my daughter Amy's birth. But the publisher who had loved the book experienced financial problems and others here and in England said readers would not be interested in it. Ruth was as devastated for me as she was for herself, for we had grown close over the years. "So much work, Sue," she exclaimed. I investigated self-publishing but we both rejected it, for not only was it prohibitively expensive, but back then it was considered "vanity publishing".

Once it was clear my book on her would not be published, Ruth and I saw each other less often, but from time to time she came to stay with us in our Johannesburg home.

One day in September 1999 she rang me to suggest we have tea at Joburg's Hyde Park Corner, where we spent hours chatting as I caught up on her and her family's life. Thereafter we met often when she came to Joburg for cancer treatment. She stayed with us, making my family chuckle when she asked if she needed to "dress for dinner".

When we were out together, nobody, except for a few waiters, recognised the slender woman with one pale blue eye and one green. She'd pat the back of her head, a gesture that became familiar to me, and cleared her throat, touching her lips with her fingertips. "It's catarrh, I must keep off sugar," she'd say. She never lost her British way of speaking and although she did try to learn Setswana, she gave up, telling me she was always too busy to do so.

We became close as we sat chatting alone after dinner in our home one night, my husband having retired for the night and my daughter Amy asleep in bed. We'd chat late into the evening, and she spoke increasingly of her hopes for her children and confided in me the seriousness of her illness. "Sue, this cancer is terrible," she'd say. "So many people are afflicted with it."

My sister Annie was ill with cancer in London at the time. She and Ruth had a couple of chats on the phone and they'd talk about who was doing what in London and chuckle together.

Ruth also spoke to my stroke-affected mother in Cape Town. She was kind and concerned, and when I was overcome with sadness, she'd put her arms around me and soothe me.

I didn't realise how ill she was, subsumed as I was in my sister's dying days, and she kept her own precarious state of health from me. I was with my mother in Cape Town when I got a cell phone message from her one day, saying, "Sue, I am not doing well. I'm struggling."

It was typical Ruth understatement.

Busy with my mother, who had lost the power of speech, it was a few days before I returned her call.

By then she had been hospitalised before being allowed to go to her son Tony Khama and his family's home. He allowed me to speak to Ruth on condition I alone did the talking, which I did, trying hard not to weep when we said goodbye. She died on 22 May 2002.

Her funeral in Gaborone's cathedral was a huge one. I drove with members of the Khama family behind her cortege through the capital, its streets lined with mournful crowds.

Back home in Johannesburg, after a violent hailstorm, unusual for winter, the sky that evening was a surreal and fiery red. Just like the young Ruth's hair, I mused. As the light faded I felt her direct gaze, heard her soft musical laugh and the clearing of her throat.

Days later she was laid to rest beside Seretse in the Khama family graveyard on a hilltop overlooking Serowe. There they are united for eternity.

ONE

The end of an era

The melancholy strains of "The Last Post" echoed through the hills and valleys of the vast, mud-hutted village of Serowe, and for the tens of thousands of mourners the lonely sound heralded the end of a tumultuous era in their lives. Many sobbed uncontrollably in the brilliant winter sunshine as the body of the first president of Botswana, Sir Seretse Khama, was laid to rest in the graveyard, hewn from granite, of his illustrious forebearers. The hilltop cemetery with its imposing view over the village, over the undulating terrain to the great plains beyond, also overlooked the heart of Serowe, the tribal meeting place known as the kgotla, which nestled below it. And in that kgotla (pronounced khot-la) were packed so many people that they flowed through it and up the slopes of the sacred hill behind.

President Kenneth Kaunda of Zambia cried openly, dabbing at his face with his famous white handkerchief, and President Julius Nyerere of Tanzania struggled to control the moisture welling in his eyes. The wintry breeze tugged playfully at the black skirts of the choir members, who sang at the graveside, and microphones carried the bitter-sweet sound from the hilltop to the mourners on the surrounding hills and in the kgotla below.

During that emotion-charged scene, the slim, white-faced widow in her heavy black veil and dark glasses was such a picture of controlled composure that her family, relatives and friends marvelled. Ruth, Lady Khama, had lost the man she adored and for whom she had suffered and given up so much. His death meant the end of life as she knew it, for the exalted status of first lady of the land was also taken from her. Despite this overwhelming sense of bereavement, she stood erect, her shoulders straight, a model of dignity.

Grief had streaked her copper hair with white, and her widow's weeds hung on a frame that had been comfortably covered. The previously robust woman now had an air of fragility about her, a porcelain, almost doll-like quality that aroused the fiercely protective instincts of those who loved her, and that included the 100 000 Bamangwato tribespeople amongst whom she had made her home so many years before when she married their chief designate.

Lady Khama was slightly taller than the average woman, but she appeared tiny, surrounded by her three strapping sons and her daughter. Struggling to maintain the composure they knew their father would have expected of them, the children managed, despite their own grief, to watch her with a tenderness and solicitude that even in half measure would have gratified mothers the world over. Her eldest son, handsome, moustached Ian, unconsciously straightened the shoulders that now bore the full weight of being head of the family and chief of the tribe, as well as being second in command of the Botswana Defence Force. His brothers, powerfully-built identical twins Anthony and Tshekedi, towered three inches above his six-foot frame. Jacqueline, the only daughter and the eldest child, had to battle the hardest of the children to maintain the stiff upper lip she had inherited from the British side of her family, for her father had been the rock to whom she had clung in her turbulent life.

Near Lady Khama stood her blonde, tall sister, Muriel Sanderson, who had also made her home in Africa and who had journeyed from Zambia to pay her last respects to the brother-in-law she had so loved. And close to Ruth, her face drawn with sorrow, was her sister-in-law, Naledi Khama, to whom the sudden death of her brother had come as a rude shock, as indeed it had to the entire mourning nation.

The 200 people chosen to go to that hilltop grave for the committal heard the voices of the choir echo amongst the granite boulders and carried by microphone to the nearby hills and valleys, from which tumbled the thatch-roofed village, somewhat like a miniature Rome.

"U le gona ke tlekwa ke thata, le khutsahalo ga e botlhoko," ("I fear no foe, with Thee at hand to bless; hills have no weight, and tears no bitterness,") sang the choir.

Officiating at the internment, in the true spirit of the multiracial nation that Sir Seretse had created, were two ministers, one black and one white, and both from different religions, for although Lady Khama was a staunch Anglican, her husband was noted for his non-denominational approach regarding church matters.

The presidential flag that had flown wherever Sir Seretse and Lady Khama travelled in the vast country of Botswana (which is slightly smaller than Texas and a little larger than France) was handed to the widow by the new president, Dr Quett Masire. With it passed another trapping of her exalted status, for the flag had hung in the gracious grounds of State House, at their farms on the Limpopo River, at their little thatched holiday home outside the capital of Gaborone, and in the rocky garden of what they considered to be their true home in Serowe.

Then came the time for the laying of wreaths, of which there were so many from all quarters of the globe, testifying to the international reputation of the deceased president, that the local district council had take them to the kgotla in lorry loads. The wreath that Lady Khama had asked a close friend to bring with her from Johannesburg in South Africa, and which had accompanied her husband's coffin wherever it went, was made of blue irises, white chrysanthemums and red roses in the shape of a cross. When Lady Khama dropped it into the granite grave, it landed perfectly in place.

The soil, which had inspired the name Seretse (red earth), thudded on to the coffin, and the sound hammered painfully at the widow's ears as she and the funeral party made their way from the stone-walled ancestral graveyard and down the gravel path to the kgotla below. The pallbearers, who had included the Khama family, Botswana cabinet members and local dignitaries, had carried the heavy coffin in teams of six up the steep path with difficulty. Every few yards they had stopped, and gently deposited their burden on a lion skin while the next team came forward. There was no particular significance attached to the skin, beyond the fact that it was one worthy of a chief and president, and that it was symbolic, for in the words of Seretse's sister: "They say a lion has two hearts – to kill and not to kill. They say a chief must also have two hearts, one of forgiving and one of killing."

The wintry sun was high overhead and it, combined with the heavy emotion, was taking its toll on the mourners who covered the hills near the kgotla and who filled the crescent-shaped expanse of stamped earth, surrounded by a crescent of wooden poles that comprised the tribal assembly. Those who could not fit into the kgotla where the main funeral service had been held, gathered on the sandy paths that twisted and wound their way around the huts. The vast crowd that filled the environs of the kgotla flowed like water in the mighty tributary of a river, inward to the heart of the village.

The women, strongly built from their years of sowing and harvesting crops, stood stolidly in the sun. Some wore brightly-coloured headscarfs on their heads, others draped shawls around their shoulders. Some hid their emotion by cupping their foreheads in their hands, others let the tears course down their cheeks as they stared blindly ahead of them. Old women, their legs covered by cotton skirts, sat in the dust while their men, some wearing World War II army greatcoats and an assortment of headgear ranging from woollen balaclavas to pith helmets and trilbies, sat on wooden folding stools close by.

The rheumy eyes of the old folk followed the graceful figure of the widow as she walked, surrounded by her family, back into the kgotla. Memories of the turbulent scenes that had taken place in that dusty meeting place crowded their thoughts. For it was there, under the great spreading camel thorn (mokala) trees, thirty-one years before, that the Bamangwato (also known as Bangwato), the largest tribe in the British Protectorate of Bechuanaland, had shouted their rejection of the white woman whom their chief designate had married in the cold, foggy island of England. The young man had listened to their angry voices denouncing his action, but he clung steadfastly to his English bride and returned to her despite their pleas.

But those denunciations had within months turned to shouts of acclaim for him in that same place under the mokala trees, when it was realised the tribe would lose their popular young leader forever if they did not accept his wife. However, by then, forces beyond their control had swung into action, and the fair-skinned young bride who had made her home amongst them was forced into exile with her husband by the British Government.

In the sad times that followed, the leaderless tribe drifted into chaos and confusion, and in that self-same kgotla they delivered one of the biggest snubs to a representative of the British Empire that pre-uhuru Africa had experienced. And in that sandy place they killed for the love of their leader. Yes, there were many old heads in that vast funeral crowd that remembered those troubled days, and their eyes followed the black-clad figure as they prayed that she would cope as bravely in this as she had in the other disturbed times in her life. "Dust to dust ..." – the words rang in the tired ears of a people for whom life is filled with sand and heat and dust. They shuffled through the brown powder, their hands gripping the wooden sticks they had carved for themselves, their shoulders covered by the greatcoats they had acquired while fighting for the freedom of the great British Empire.

Many of them had spent several nights sleeping in the kgotla, waiting to pay their homage to a man who had not only won their love with his gentle, direct ways, but who had reached international stature as a moderate leader who put democracy in his own country above all else.

When the news of his death was broadcast throughout the nation in the early hours of Sunday, 13th July 1980, the shattered people of Botswana, the landlocked country that is surrounded by the Republic of South Africa to the south-east and east; by Namibia to the west; by the Caprivi Strip to the north; and by Zimbabwe to the north-east, began to make their way to Serowe. They travelled by train, bus, car, lorry, bicycle and donkey cart, across the loneliest, most sparsely-populated territory in Africa. Many of them made their way through the vast Kalahari Desert, which covers three quarters of the country and is the home of the last remaining Bushmen, to reach the capital of the Bamangwato tribe and the home of the man they had always regarded as chief, although the British had prevented him from claiming his rightful title.

There had been some concern after the death of Sir Seretse that the tribe would make their way 300 kilometres to the south, to the Botswana capital of Gaborone, to camp on the great, green lawns that surrounded the gracious, white-washed State House. For it was Tswana custom, after a death, for a fire to be lit in the yard (garden) of the deceased, and for friends and family to keep watch there. Food was needed to feed the well-wishers, and therefore everyone in the surrounding area was expected to help by bringing along a gift of a goat, a bucketful of corn, wood for the fire, or a pail of water for cooking and washing up.[1] The idea behind this custom was to relieve the family of the deceased of the everyday drudgeries of life, so they can be free to receive the respects of callers, and also to provide support and comfort to the bereaved.

But the tribesfolk knew the heart of their leader had always been in his ancestral village, and so they settled down in the garden of his Serowe home and in the kgotla lit their fires, prayed, and waited for him to come to them. From the moment the Serowans heard of Sir Seretse's death, they began to get ready for the funeral. They graded the dust roads, filling in potholes and smoothing the rough, rocky patches that jar the spines of those who travel over them. They swept the pathways that weave between huts where hens cluck and squawk as they scratch the earth, looking for corn and grubs. They picked up all the sweet wrappers and Chibuku cartons – a commercially-made highly popular beer made from maize meal or sorghum.

And they trimmed the green rubber hedges known as tlharesetala, which now surround nearly every lolwapa (yard) and give those in an aeroplane the impression that Serowe is a green valley instead of the stark village, eaten away by soil erosion and goats, it actually is. Despite its bleak appearance, particularly in the dry winter months when the landscape is browned by sun and frost and dust is whirled continually by winds flinging it into the eyes and noses of the patient villagers, the traditional village of Serowe is attractive.

It derives its name from serowa, which is a small bulb, sweet to taste and eaten raw. At one time it grew prolifically in the area around the kgotla, and it is believed to look like the hill on which the Khamas are buried. The vast, tumbling, hilly village is surrounded by a ridge of low hills which make it a cohesive unit. This is what the Great Khama who founded the village desired. It was he, the wise grandfather of Sir Seretse, who welded many diverse minor tribes into the powerful Bamangwato, in much the same way his grandson was later to bring together the tribes throughout the country to make up the Botswana nation.

When Khama III, who gained fame throughout Britain for his statesmanship and Christianity, knew he was dying, he left instructions that he was to be buried in the granite rock above the kgotla, in the sacred hill on which no one is allowed to kill any living thing, be it human or animal. Thereafter the other members of the royal Khama family followed his example, and the hill became both a graveyard and a memorial to the greatness of the family.

It is Tswana custom that the grave is only dug the night before burial, usually at midnight, but because Sir Seretse's grave had to be blasted out of the granite, this custom was not followed. A custom that was followed, however, was the period of mourning that is observed after the death of a chief, during which the whole tribe abstains from their normal occupation. Therefore, after Sir Seretse's death the vast village was silent at night, and the customary noises of singing and chattering around the night fire and the shouting of children at play was stilled. There was also no shopping done and the village was emptied of the little groups who, having made their purchases, normally would exchange news and gossip in front of the trading stores.

The day before the funeral, the Botswana Defence Force aeroplane carrying the body of the president flew over the ridge of low hills and touched down on the small landing strip several kilometres to the east of the village. Lady Khama and her children who had accompanied the coffin, draped with its presidential flag on top of which was her personal wreath, followed it on its slow journey to the kgotla. All along that seven-kilometre route of thick sand the tribe had gathered. Those who thought the swift death of their president due to cancer was all a bad dream, stared in shock and sorrow at the coffin.

Others cried silently, reaching out their arms towards the funeral cortege and reaching out with their hearts to the pale woman they called Makosi (mother of the chief) and Mohumagadi (the chief lady, or woman of importance).

Some of the tribeswomen ran all the way from the airstrip, alongside the cavalcade of cars to the kgotla in the heart of the silent, watching village. There was no stamping of corn, no making of beer. The men had ceased thatching their huts and the women smoothing their mud courtyards. Even the mischievous little herd boys, naked except for a loincloth, had stopped their wild rag-tag games during which they chased one another along the dusty paths that wound around the huts and through the entire village.

They gathered quietly at the kgotla and watched the coffin being carried inside the large hall that comprised the district council chambers. People had begun queueing early that morning to pay their last respects to their president, and soon the coffin was opened, and the patient people began to file past it and look for a last time at the face of the man that had nearly always smiled at them gently and with humour.

Lady Khama, her children, and her friends from Johannesburg, drove away from the kgotla and through the village up the hill, dubbed Nob Hill because in colonial times the British administration officials and their families had lived there, and along the road to the end of the hill where the Khama house stood in its imposing, isolated splendour. There were no huts there, and the closest brick bungalows were about a kilometre away. The house, painted in the Botswana Defence Force colour of dark green, marked the end of the road, which ran straight into the garden. From it there was a commanding and breathtaking view over the hills and valleys that comprised Serowe to the great plains beyond it.

The house was built on rock, and although Lady Khama had tried hard in the early days of their living there to wrest a garden from the unyielding terrain, she had given up the battle when they went to live in Gaborone when the country obtained its independence in 1966. Now camped on that rock were scores of people who, following custom, had come to keep watch over the house and family in their time of bereavement. As night fell, their fires glowed warm; little beacons of love and comfort in the desert climate. They spoke softly amongst themselves as they stirred their meat and porridge in the three-legged, cast-iron cooking pots they had carried up there with their blankets.

Amongst the many black faces was a white one, that of Roy Blackbeard, a childhood friend of the Khama children. The following day he would be the only white man to act as a pallbearer at the funeral. His father, Colin Blackbeard, who was minister of works and communications, had been the only white man to carry the coffin at the imposing state memorial service, complete with a twenty-one gun salute and pomp and ceremony earlier that day.

After Lady Khama and her children had finished dinner in the modern bungalow, they drove back down the hill to the council chambers to say goodbye to the man they had all loved so dearly. As their car drew up, Lady Khama noticed the many hundreds of people camping in the kgotla, their sad faces and blanketed figures lit up by their fires. Even in that dark night, punctuated only by the brilliant stars that flare undimmed by city lights and pollution in the desert air, it was possible to discern the faint outline of the sacred hill and the granite graveyard where her husband would be buried the next day.

She hurried into the hall, shivering violently, for she hated the cold, and walked slowly and sadly around it, looking at the wreaths from princes, presidents, heads of state, acquaintances, friends and loved ones around the world. When her children had looked for the last time at their father, she went to say farewell to him. For a moment the sadness was washed away as she recalled his gentle, humorous ways, the teasing, and the practical jokes that had first attracted her to him.

In her garden the fires and blanketed forms reminded her of the time thirty years before when she had waited, a heavily pregnant woman, in her thorn-fenced bungalow for the British to allow her exiled husband to come home. She had been lonely then, ostracised by her own kind on Nob Hill for having married a black man and upsetting the status quo. But the tribe had flocked to the isolated bungalow, situated on the outskirts of the village, which her husband had made home for her, and had camped there, keeping watch over the social outcast they wanted for their queen.

Now some of those same faithful, trusted friends were keeping watch over her again during the first days after his death.

During the night the coffin was moved from the kgotla to the huge church made of dressed sandstone blocks that was built by the Great Khama in 1915, and which is so imposing that it is the dominant architectural feature of the large village. After breakfast, the Khama family was joined for prayers in the church by close friends, by the new Botswana president, Dr Masire, and by those heads of state who despite logistical difficulties had insisted on attending the Serowe funeral. These included Zambia's Kenneth Kaunda, Tanzania's Julius Nyerere and the King of Lesotho, Moshoeshoe II.

The kgotla service that followed the family prayers was a simple but impressive affair, with hymns interspersed with prayers, a lesson reading, a sermon and eulogies. The sermon was given in the national language of Botswana, Setswana, by the world-famous Kalahari missionary, Dr Alfred Merriweather, who had been both Speaker in the Botswana parliament and also the deceased president's doctor. The mild-mannered, white haired and bespectacled missionary chose for his text "Blessed are the Peacemakers", and his eloquent but well-modulated voice with its marked Scots accent carried to the tens of thousands listening intently in the kgotla and on the hillside.

Dr Merriweather spoke the words that had been used by Seretse in the same place, twenty-one years earlier, at the funeral of his uncle Tshekedi, whose angry and bitter rejection of his nephew's marriage had resulted in tribal discord and the eventual exile of both uncle and nephew.

"Let there be peace, Bamangwato," the dying uncle had said to his nephew who flew to be at his bedside in a London clinic in 1959. Seretse had repeated the words at his uncle's funeral in the same place where he was now to be buried, and the Scottish missionary did the same.

Peace had indeed come to the Bamangwato, and now Dr Merriweather used the words in a wider, national context when he spoke of how Sir Seretse had made peace for Botswana by uniting all the tribes, and the black and white people in that huge, impoverished country. He paid tribute to the task of reconciliation that Sir Seretse had set himself, and to the respect and love that his tolerance had created among the diverse people of the land.

The president had personally followed the text of what he preached, and he had never borne any bitterness towards those who had exiled him but had worked quietly and ably with the British administration officials in the winds of change that blew through Africa in the 1960s – winds that stirred the colonised continent's people who shouted for their freedom (uhuru) and sometimes killed for it.

But no liberation movement was necessary in the British Protectorate of Bechuanaland, and its peaceful moves to independence were due to a variety of reasons, one of them being the assurance that both black and white people gained from seeing a couple such as Ruth and Seretse at the head of their new state. It was ironic that the very reason the British Government had officially used to exile the couple from their home in 1950 – that of the mixed marriage causing tribal dissension – should in the end have been instrumental in helping to build Botswana into a peaceful, unified, and happy nation.

The real reason for the exile, and one that was only revealed some thirty years later by the release of secret documents, was British acquiescence to the South African Government's request that Seretse should not be recognised as chief while he had a white wife. Today the marriage, which lasted thirty-one years, is seen as a triumph, surviving as it did the efforts of two governments to break it up, and indeed surviving both prejudice and bigotry. It was one of the most romantic love stories of the twentieth century, and people all over the world were fascinated by the attractive woman who followed her husband to his tribal home, on the edge of the Kalahari Desert, in what Westerners then called "the Dark Continent".

Some of this history was recalled by the missionary doctor before he ended his sermon, and the funeral procession moved away from the kgotla and up the hill.

When the funeral was over, and the exhausted Lady Khama returned home, the Botswana Council of Women, of which she was president, streamed up the gently-sloping hill after her, wearing their distinctive uniform which depicts the country's national colours of blue, black and white. Blue represents the colour of water and means rain – "pula" – the giver of life. In Setswana, the word "pula" is also used as a greeting, meaning "may your crops be blessed." The colour black stands for the Batswana, and the white for the white people – the whole signifying peace and prosperity for all.

When the women reached the bungalow, they grouped quietly in front of it and sent word for their president, who appeared with her son Ian. Then they sang to her, in the rich, melodious, deep-throated manner for which they are noted.

They sang of their respect, sympathy and their affection for someone who had not merely gone to live amongst them as their chieftainess but had systematically and methodically thrown herself into improving their impoverished lives with her community work. And this she had done at a time when few other white women in the village did anything for their black counterparts. She taught them about hygiene and nutrition and first aid, she helped them build a community centre and a crèche, and her work is visible amongst them to this day. And so they sang, an outpouring of their devotion to the fragile, pale woman in black on that dusty, wintry day.

Friends and family who heard the singing said it was the sweetest and the saddest sound in the world. Some of the singers fainted and were quietly carried away by their fellows. Others wept, and those who did, left the group so that Lady Khama who was being so brave would not see their sorrow and be overwhelmed by it. When the singing was over, she made a speech – in English for she could not speak Setswana – and thanked those loving women for working for her and her husband, and said she hoped they would continue to work for their country.

Then the women left, making their customary gesture of respect, which is a small bobbing movement, rather like an abbreviated curtsey.

As they trudged the long distance down the hill and back to the kgotla, they carried the image of the former first lady of the land in their minds. They thought of the interesting mixture that she was – a modern, liberated and independent woman, and an old-fashioned, traditional wife. Much of her life was dedicated to the improvement and upliftment of women in the stark country where if the rains do not come, and often they do not, famine takes its toll.

Lady Khama recognised early on the conflicts that arise when a rural and poverty-stricken nation is faced with the totally different lifestyle that rapid urbanisation brings with it. She realised there was a need for daycare centres for the working mothers whose children could no longer be cared for by their grandparents who lived in remote villages. And mobilising the women of the country, she set to work to create an infrastructure that would ensure the harmony of family life.

Family was terribly important to her, and she and her husband set the nation an example by emphasising this with their own children. Her existence centred around her husband, he was the core and mainstay of both her life and that of their children, and this was the case despite her strong character and her tendency to dominate. Seretse was her *raison d'etre*, and a major portion of her astounding energy and considerable life force went into the almost continual nursing of her husband, who for much of his life was a sick man.

Their close and warm relationship fulfilled her life. Therefore, when the great funeral crowds dispersed in Serowe, the kings and presidents went back to their own countries, and she had to move out of State House, it left a great void and a tremendous emptiness and loneliness. And this new and altered life from which the pivot had gone was something with which she battled to come to terms years after her husband's death.

In the bleak, cold days that followed the funeral, the Khama children closed ranks around their mother, fiercely protective of her and deeply concerned for her well-being and happiness. She was constantly aware and grateful for this. But despite the love that surrounded her, and the respect and affection afforded her by the simple, loving and genuine people of Botswana, the great loneliness continued to well up inside her.

It is at such times that her thoughts returned to that grave carved into the granite rock, high above the Serowe kgotla, to the man whom she was a part of and around whom were centred the fascinating memories of her extraordinary and eventful life.

TWO

Ruth's early life

Ruth Williams was born on a freezing winter's day on the 9th of December 1923, into a conventional, typically English, middle-class home in a South London suburb. She was born in the same year that her future husband's wise and famous grandfather, Khama III, died in Serowe, the sprawling mud-hutted capital of his tribe, the British-administered Protectorate of Bechuanaland. The rejoicing at the birth of pretty little Ruth in the Williams household was in stark contrast to the mourning of the vast crowds of tribesmen at the death of one of Africa's great chiefs.

The birth and the death in such different worlds bear no relationship to each other, apart from the fact that they set in motion a train of events that were to culminate in a marriage that shook two governments and made world headlines for nearly a decade.

Naturally when George and Dorothy Williams took their second daughter home to their comfortable, double-storeyed house near the large heath from which their suburb derived its name of Blackheath, they had not the faintest premonition that one day their babe would marry the grandson of an African chief and leave the luscious isle of her birth to live in his dry, rocky village. Ruth's upbringing was so conventional, so middle class, that it is hard to conceive of anyone less likely to have defied convention and to have married as she did.

This will no doubt surprise many people, for at the time of her marriage, stories were rife about her upbringing in the seedy East End of London. Rumours that she grew up in a rough neighbourhood, with gangster-type friends, were popular. Administration officials from the protectorate who hoped that the marriage could be ended, by buying off what they imagined might be a chorus-girl type, were dashed when they met the intelligent, vivacious woman who clearly came from a respectable home. They soon discovered she wasn't some out-of-work actress, hanging around dance halls, waiting to catch a big fish – the rationale that was employed by a race-conscious world to explain how a white girl came to marry a black man.

The gossip and the rumours would have horrified the Victorian George Williams if he had bothered to listen to them, for he was very aware of his position in society and the community. He was a tall, ginger-haired man with a distinguished, military bearing which came from his years in the British army in India, and from his family which had a military background. He joined the army at the outbreak of World War I, and so loved India that he implored his fiancé, Dorothy Goode, to make their home there.

But the comfortable, fussy little Englishwoman, who had met the dashing George as a child when their families lived near each other in North London, was horrified at the very idea. She loved her London home, and refused outright to leave her native shores, a very different approach from that which her daughter would adopt in later years.

The problem of where they would live solved itself when George was invalided home with enteric fever and was warned that it would not be sensible for him to return to India as the fever could recur. His six-year engagement to his childhood friend ended in marriage in 1921, and their first child, Muriel, was born a year later.

"There is no doubt my father wanted a son, he would rather have had two boys than two girls any day," said Muriel. "He was a person who related far easier to men than he did to women, and I think that for a long time he didn't really know how to treat two daughters, although I think he came to terms with it. But I think that if he had had one or two boys, it would have been easier all round."

Mr Williams made up for his disappointment by giving his daughters nicknames. Muriel was Archie and Ruth was Bert, and the names stuck for years, although no one outside the Williams home knew of their existence.

"My father had a very strong personality, and he was a true Victorian. He liked to have his own way, and he thought that daughters, being women, were inferior to men," said Muriel. "I think he found it very difficult when Ruth and I grew up, and he found that we had minds of our own."

Deep-voiced Mr Williams, who was six feet two inches in his socks and had a large belly, known in England as a "public opinion", due to his love of good food and wine, was a stickler for routine. "Everything had to run like clockwork in our house – when we ate, did our homework, went to bed, and so on," said Ruth. "My mother was dominated by my father. We lived in an age when men did dominate women. He was a black and white person. He had a routine, and his routine wasn't to be interrupted."

Mrs Williams, who was small when compared with her large husband (she was the same height as Ruth – five feet, five inches), was a gentle, fair-haired woman who was the archetypal housewife and mother. "She was the easy-going one, always loyal to my father, always putting him first. He had the sort of job which meant he came home at varying times, and she always thought it was her duty to be there to welcome him," said Muriel. "She was always interested in what he did, and what we did too. She was the one who held the family together."

It was only in later years that Ruth and Muriel realised the influence that the quiet but determined Mrs Williams had on them, for from an early age she taught them to be tolerant of other people and of other ideas, as was she. Her tolerance was severely put to the test when Ruth married, but even then, she did not waver in her belief that she herself had chosen the man she wanted to marry, and that her daughters had the right to do the same.

In this she was very different from Mr Williams, with his definite ideas about life and particularly about mixed marriages. His six years in India had engendered in him a firm belief that people of different races should not mix, and certainly should not marry and have coloured children. But strangely enough, he did not convey these attitudes of his to Ruth and Muriel until it was too late, for although some of their earliest recollections are of the romantic tales of India which he spun them, they grew up unaware that their father was so dogmatic about mixed marriages.

The India he described to them was a magical one; of tigers and rajahs, of delicate English women who were sent into the hills to escape the wilting heat of the towns and plains, of the dashing army life with horse riding and pig sticking, and lively social fun in the officer's mess. "I'm not sure he didn't make up some of the stories," said Muriel. George Williams was very aware that the British Empire for which he had fought was a great and glorious one, responsible as it was for the welfare of millions and millions of people and ruling as it then did the sea routes of the world.

Ruth and her family were fortunate to live so near to the extremely large common of Blackheath, for it gave them a sense of freedom and of the outdoors that they all loved. The large old houses surrounding the heath had been fashionable in Victorian and Edwardian times when servants were plentiful and large establishments relatively easy to run. But after World War I servants were hard to come by, as factory work had given them a sense of independence and freedom as well as higher wages, and so these gracious old homes gradually fell into disuse until they were divided up into smaller houses.

It was one of these that George Williams managed to obtain on his return from India, and he immediately set about knocking down walls, adding a new bathroom, and generally sprucing it up. "He had it painted every year and liked it to look nice. He was very fussy about his property and his possessions," said Muriel. She attributes this to his six years as an officer in India, "where he had got used to a high standard of living. But because he nearly died and had to leave in such a hurry, he didn't bring home any Indian furniture and furnishings apart from a lovely Afghan carpet. I think he left a lot of his nice things behind because he thought he would return one day as a civilian."

The house-proud Mr Williams and his wife, whom Muriel describes as being "a slave to housework," made an indelible impression on Ruth, for when she grew up and managed several households at the same time, she ran them all with an efficiency and attention to detail that are not surprising when considering her early background.

The Williamses' house was one of about sixty on a small road in the village of Blackheath and was situated approximately one kilometre from the common. It was near a little village called Lea Green, which had a shopping centre, a couple of pubs and a cinema, and close by was the school that Ruth and Muriel attended, run by the Church of England. When they were babies, Mrs Williams would wheel them in their prams around the heath, and during weekends Mr Williams joined her, cutting a dashing figure in his smart jacket, jaunty cap and his walking stick. "He always wore a hat to work, he liked to look smart, and he was always very polite, raising it to acquaintances," said Ruth. When she and Muriel grew older, they joined their father in invigorating walks around the common, taking their black-and-tan mongrel called Fella along, whooping and racing around with him, in high spirits and filled with the joy of life.

One of Ruth's earliest recollections is of her parents' rowing oars in the upstairs passage of their home, near her bedroom. It was a mutual love of swimming, roller skating and rowing which had brought George and Dorothy Williams together, and Ruth's mother must have been pretty good, for she had captained a rowing team at the club nearby her childhood home in North London. George was also an extremely good horse rider, and Ruth inherited her parents' love of sport.

It didn't take Ruth long to realise that books took second place to her sporting activities. "I didn't particularly like school, apart from the sport, and I certainly am not one of those who say that my school days were the best days of my life," said Ruth.

By the time she had left primary school in Blackheath and gone to high school in nearby Eltham, Ruth had developed the strong personality and determination she inherited from her father, and which stood her in good stead on the sports field. She excelled in gymnastics, and played lacrosse, rounders, tennis and netball, often captaining her teams.

The bouncy, chubby little baby had grown into a red-haired, extremely fair-skinned, plump girl, who tore her way down the lacrosse field. "That's a gorgeous game," said Ruth. "There are no rules, no off-sides, nothing. Anybody can tackle you in any way they like. Girls used to be knocked out quite frequently, teeth used to come out, and I used to arrive home with a bruised head, and I couldn't eat or talk. Sometimes my mother wrote to the school, saying I shouldn't play anymore, but of course I did." And she added with relish, "Many schools didn't like to play lacrosse because it is so rough, and those of us who played it were such toughies."

Many people in later years were to complain about Ruth being "off-sides" in her choice of life partner, but she never played life by its social rules any more than she stuck to the few rules there were in lacrosse. This freedom of thought and spirit and her highly individualistic approach to life are interesting in view of her strict upbringing. Muriel was also an independent, strong-minded woman, and clearly their father's Victorian dictum that women existed solely to complement men backfired. It made them all the more determined to be people in their own right.

The two sisters were totally different. "Muriel was very thin, and I was very fat," chuckled Ruth, who took an interest in cooking from an early age, helping her mother in the kitchen. Mrs Williams was a good cook, turning out steak and kidney pie, bubble and squeak, roast beef and Yorkshire pudding – English dishes the family enjoyed. Ruth's interest in the preparation of food was to stand her in good stead in later years when her husband's poor health called for careful diets.

But the two sisters differed in other ways too. Muriel had a heart murmur, and was therefore precluded from playing sport, something that irritated her enormously for she too had the abundance of energy with which Ruth had been blessed. It left her with more time to concentrate on the studies that she enjoyed as much as Ruth detested them.

The two girls, one tall and fair-haired, the other shorter and red-haired, were close to their parents in spite of their strict upbringing. They were not allowed comics, there was no such thing as pop music in their lives, and the radio was not played at all unless it was time for the BBC news, or for a special programme that Mr Williams wanted to listen to. The nearby cinema was out of bounds, and it was only when they were well into their teens that they experienced the excitement of going to their first screen show.

But although Ruth's parents might have disapproved of the cinema, they were very fond of the theatre, and Mr Williams would make a great occasion of a visit to it, buying good seats in the first row of the stalls or in the circle. The sisters and their mother turned out in long evening dresses, Mr Williams wore a white tie and tails and hired a chauffeured car. He often took them out to dinner first, usually to a seafood restaurant because he was particularly keen on fish.

At Christmas they went to pantomimes, often accompanied by some of Ruth's many aunts and uncles, for both her parents came from large families. And although it was the era of the music hall, Mr Williams was not all that enthusiastic about it, considering it too bawdy for his young daughters.

It was an extremely secure, happy, comfortable and contented childhood, and although the two sisters were always very polite to their parents, never questioned parental authority, wore their hair neat and short as their father requested, and always tried to look tidy, they nonetheless had an enormous amount of fun as a family.

Mr Williams was a salesman for a tea and coffee firm, who worked his way up until he became the senior manager for London and the South (of England). He put in such long, hard hours that Muriel described him as being, "married to his job. I think Ruth and I have both absorbed a lot of that, we don't watch the clock, we work until we have finished what we are doing. He set us such a high example." But he also used the flexible hours at his disposal to be with his daughters, and particularly with Ruth as she grew up and the bond between them grew stronger.

He would take Ruth and Muriel to school by car when he could, saving them the cold tram or bus ride, and took them into the country on his working trips when this was possible. Ruth fondly remembers the country pub lunches, with the great sides of ham, turkey and pork, the large variety of salads, and the pickles and spices he had grown fond of in India. Mr Williams ate three hearty meals a day, "He loved his meat," said Ruth, and breakfast for him was not complete without a chop, a piece of liver or bacon.

"He was big, but he used to call me pud, short for pudding, I suppose because I was so plump," laughed Ruth, who clearly enjoyed tucking into good food as much as her father did. She came to enjoy seafood too, and it was a marvellous occasion for the family when a small barrel of oysters arrived, sent up by a friend of Mr Williams who lived on the Kentish coast. But his liking for eel, shared by his wife, did not extend to his daughters. Ruth was horrified at the way he would bring them still flapping and wriggling into the house and refused to help him cut them up. "It was revolting, because they were still alive, and would go leaping around the room." She was always so nauseated by the experience, she couldn't eat anything for some time afterwards.

"My father was moody, but he could be lots of fun. He liked company, he was very sociable, and so we did a lot of entertaining at home," said Muriel. "He loved giving us surprises, taking us out to shows and off to the seaside for the weekend. But he couldn't keep a secret, and he'd say, 'You wait until you know what I have in store for you', and then my mother would say, 'but that's a secret', and then of course we would die to know what it was," said Muriel. Mr Williams had a quick, clever sense of humour, although it could often be very dry, and it was not unlike that of the African chief who was to become his son-in-law. Dorothy Williams was a fun-loving person who without fail caught out both her daughters on April Fool's day every year.

George loved taking the family for excursions on the River Thames, and on a mild summer's day, Ruth's mother would pack a delicious picnic hamper and they would put on their hats and spend a lazy day in a boat, watching the tree-lined bank slip by.

Although Mr Williams wasn't particularly fond of swimming or lying about on the beach, an aversion Ruth inherited from him, he enjoyed taking the family for day trips to the Kentish and Cornish coasts. "We took the Channel ferry to France for the day, something we all loved. And strangely enough, we spent a day at Dunkirk the year before war broke out," said Ruth. "But father always wanted to spend hours sitting in restaurants, while we tried to interest him in buying French bread and cheeses and eating them by the sea," she said.

Her parents loved to go abroad for their holidays, usually to Europe, and they also enjoyed going cruising. They went up the Rhine, to the Norwegian fjords and to the Mediterranean. "My father loved the cruises, especially the ones in cargo ships that only took twelve passengers, and you had your own cabin and steward which made it all rather luxurious," said Muriel. "We didn't go with my parents, because they thought we wouldn't appreciate it, and although we didn't agree at the time, we could see later that they were right."

Ruth and Muriel usually spent these holidays when their parents were away either with their close-knit family, or they went fruit picking in the glorious British countryside which is what many children did then. Despite their large number of aunts and uncles, there were few cousins for Ruth and Muriel to play with, and consequently they received far more attention from their relatives than is normally the case. One of Ruth's aunts lived a most rural existence in Norfolk, complete with a well and pump from which they drew their water and an outside toilet, and the sisters used to enjoy the challenge of the somewhat spartan existence. In later years, Ruth was exasperated by people who queried her ability to live in an African village, pointing out that she was not entirely unacquainted with rough living.

Ruth's paternal grandmother and maternal grandfather lived within a few kilometres of each other in the North London suburb of Edmonton, and Ruth and her family would go over nearly every Sunday and have lunch with one or the other. "We were dead scared of my grandfather. He used to call my mother 'child', something I could never get over," said Muriel. He was of Welsh extraction, with a fiery Welsh nature, and was a domineering character whose word was law. An engineer, who had worked for an arms and ammunitions firm, he was fanatical about football. Ruth remembers with fascination how he used the salt and pepper sets to replay matches during their Sunday lunches.

"No one laughed or said anything, it was most serious," said Ruth. "Another thing he liked doing was saving the most difficult puzzles he could find in the newspaper during the week, and on a Sunday, he would say, "Now, I have a problem for you two girls," said Muriel.

The stunned and sometimes terrified looks on the two sisters' faces was enough to bring the doting aunts rushing to their aid. "Come on," they would remonstrate, "that's far too difficult for them."

Mr Williams was as dutiful a son as he was a father, for he would often drive to North London with his family to take his increasingly arthritic mother on outings. She was a gentle, loveable person, who kept chickens at the bottom of her garden, and always made a cake for tea.

It is memories like these which made up the happy childhood that Ruth so enjoyed, and which she said she took so much for granted, imagining that all children were as fortunate as she to have such a stable upbringing.

Someone who made an impression on her was a close friend of her father who was very wealthy. "I was friendly with his daughter, and one Christmas our fathers told us little girls to go and sing Christmas carols outside the door. When we had done so, they flung pennies at us, and we all roared with laughter," said Ruth. On another occasion, the men cut the slightly burnt legs off the Christmas turkey and flung them into the crackling log fire, saying that no one should eat black meat. A horrified Ruth displayed the tender conscience that later made her work so hard to improve the lot of her husband's impoverished nation. "What about the poor?" she cried, to their discomfiture.

A childhood memory both sisters treasured was of watching cricket from the upstairs window of their house, on balmy summer days and evenings. There were three fields behind the Williamses' house, all rented by London firms. "Our house was strategically situated on the long side, which meant we were right opposite the wicket. We sat either on the top of the roof of the gardening shed, which was attached to the house, or else at the back-bathroom window, watching the game," said Muriel.

As the children grew older, Ruth grew closer to her parents, while Muriel began to loosen the strong childhood bonds. "Ruth always said that when she grew up, she wanted to live in the same street as my mother, a sentiment I never agreed with," said Muriel. It is interesting therefore that Ruth's mother did eventually join her daughter and son-in-law in their African village home.

Ruth began to accompany her father on more of his working trips into the countryside, developing a companionable bond with him, despite his preference for male company and his wish that he had had sons. It was this strong attachment that made the break when Ruth's father refused to accept her marriage to Seretse Khama such an intensely painful and hurtful experience for them both.

Muriel, who said she was a lot like her father in many ways, used to argue with him (inasmuch as daughters could argue with Victorian fathers) about politics or religion. He used to tease Muriel about the church, in which she was particularly interested, and the two of them became so heated in discussions that Dorothy Williams came to dread them and would nervously try to change the conversation when she sensed what was coming.

Both Ruth and Muriel were church-goers all their lives, and more than that, very active members of their respective congregations. They attended services on most Sunday mornings and went to Sunday school in the afternoons.

"The latter was partly because my father used to like to have a sleep," said Muriel.

Religion had a profound influence on the lives of the two sisters, and Muriel's work for her church was later to result in the meeting between Ruth and Seretse and to take her to Geneva to work for the World Council of Churches.

It was therefore a very quiet and protected childhood that Ruth enjoyed, in which her parents, her church and sport were the main points of interest. The only club she and Muriel belonged to was the local Young Women's Christian Association (YWCA), where they played netball and badminton, and their evenings were spent quietly at home with their parents, doing their homework, playing cards or board games with them and very occasionally listening to the radio. Mr and Mrs Williams did not join clubs, although he was a Freemason, and so the Williamses' family did not play much of a part in the lively Blackheath community.

Ruth was to adopt a very different approach to life when she married and went to live amongst the Bamangwato tribe, for it was her community work amongst them which so endeared her to them.

It was into this contented, quiet existence, that the rumblings of war came in the late 1930s. Ruth remembers her father's grave face as the family gathered around the radio in the evenings to hear the news reports of Hitler's frightening cant, of the violence at his huge rallies, and of Jewish shops being looted and burnt down. At the time she was going through a personal crisis, trying to decide whether or not to continue battling with academic subjects in which she was not particularly interested.

After much discussion with her parents, she gave up the academic world and enrolled at the South East London Technical Institute for a two-year domestic science course. She was adapting to the change in schools and classmates, when World War II broke out, and the British Government, which believed that the Germans would concentrate their bombs on London initially, decided to evacuate all schoolchildren to the countryside.

Everywhere Ruth looked trenches were being dug in parks and shelters prepared. Bags of sand were piled up against buildings as protective measures and works of art were carefully removed. While across the Atlantic Americans, removed from the immediacy of war, were being captivated by Clark Gable and Vivien Leigh in *Gone with the Wind*, Britain prepared grimly for war.

On 1st September 1939, a bewildered, fifteen-year-old Ruth found herself on a station platform with her classmates and hundreds of other frightened schoolchildren. "It was all so sudden. I felt horror, absolute horror, at leaving my home and my family, we were all so close. I didn't know where I was going and whom I was going to be billeted on. I just wanted to stay where I was," said Ruth.

The memory of standing on that crowded platform, wearing a tag around her neck with her name and address on it, stayed with her her whole life, in the same way in which she described the pain of saying goodbye to both her parents and her sister. Muriel, who was still at Eltham, was not evacuated with Ruth, and as the train gave a warning toot and began to roll out of the station, Ruth's tears streamed down her face as she watched her parents disappear in a blur. Not for many years would she attain again the peace and joy of the settled existence she had accepted unquestioningly as her right when she was a child.

Ruth grows up fast

Ruth's traumatic parting from her parents was to be the first upheaval in a life that would be full of change from that moment on. In future years when people would ask Ruth how she managed to adapt to living in an African village and to cope with an entirely new way of life, so alien to the one she had known, she would answer that her life had been a series of changes and adaptations. Her ability as an adult to cope with difficult circumstances and to stick to a course of action once she had made up her mind, no doubt had much to do with her marvellously secure and contented childhood. It was a stable, seaworthy craft that George and Dorothy Williams launched upon the often turbulent waters that were to constitute Ruth's life.

As the train chugged southwards through the English countryside, the bright flowers and green leaves of summer were fading, and the chill in the air that foretold winter crept into the hearts and minds of the British people as they prepared for war with Germany. All over the country mothers kissed their sons and husbands goodbye as they marched off in their unfamiliar uniforms, and many families like the Williamses' were broken up due to the evacuation of schoolchildren.

Ruth was fortunate to be one of five children from her college whom eminent British barrister, Sir Edward Boyle, and his wife chose to live with them on their lovely estate, situated between Robertsbridge and Hursgreen in Sussex. Ruth found it a nerve-wracking experience alighting from the train, not knowing where she was to be billeted. After the children had been milling about for a while, it was with relief that she heard one of her teachers say: "You five, you go with Lady Boyle. Go and get into that car over there."

Sir Edward had a daughter and two sons, the eldest of whom became a Conservative Party member of parliament and was a good friend to the British prime minister, Mrs Margaret Thatcher, before he died in 1981. The Boyle family lived in a large and gracious English country house, set amongst rolling lawns and neat, gravel and tree-lined walks. Ruth and her classmates were placed in the chauffeur's cottage, which must have been a big one for it also accommodated two teachers who gave the five children their lessons there.

Muriel had been evacuated to the seaside town of Folkestone on Britain's south coast and was fortunate in being able to live with the family of a good friend of her father's. She enjoyed her time there, both because she loved her schoolwork and enjoyed her newfound independence. In this respect she differed greatly from Ruth who was horribly homesick and waited miserably for her parents' visits on alternate Sundays, for they had to divide their time between their daughters.

The family home was quiet and empty without the two lively teenagers, and the bond which had grown stronger between Ruth and her father as she grew older was evident from the way in which he would visit Ruth at her billet on his sales rounds and take her out to lunch. He sometimes motored a long way out of his set routine to do this and often took her to nearby Hastings, and over a meal told her about his family who came from that ancient town and who he believed derived their name from the conqueror who had landed there in 1066.

As the weeks passed, Mr Williams became increasingly alarmed by Ruth's health. She was suffering from severe anaemia, and her poor physical condition, which was in such contrast to the bouncing, sporty girl she had been, manifested itself in boils and in styes on her eyes. After discussions with her teachers and with Sir Edward and Lady Boyle, who had become fond of their evacuees in the couple of months they had spent there, George Williams took his daughter home to Blackheath. Ruth was confined to bed for about six weeks and was so debilitated that at one stage she had to be carried about.

Some of the remedies tried on her in addition to iron, were raw meat – she particularly liked raw kidneys – and Burgundy wine. Allergies which were to affect her at various stages of her life became apparent – she was allergic to sugar, coffee and chocolate. She also discovered that she had almost no sense of smell, a sensory defect that might have cost her her life twice in later years because she did not smell the smoke in her burning homes.

When Ruth had recovered somewhat, her parents decided she should not return to her billet. The equipment for teaching domestic science was, according to Ruth, not up to par due to the difficult teaching conditions, and besides, she was feeling weak and dejected and did not want to leave home again. The Luftwaffe had not yet begun its strafing, and Ruth therefore enrolled at the London Polytechnic, which was still operating in the city. But there again the classes were not quite what she was looking for, she told her parents, and so after a few months Ruth left and suddenly found herself free of any school ties. She never did complete her schooling, nor did she do the course in dietetics she said she was so keen on, and although her quick mind ensured that she did not suffer because of this lack of education, she would later regret that her education was disrupted by her illness and the war.

George Williams, with his Victorian approach to life and the role that females should play in it, probably had quite a bit to do with Ruth's decision not to continue with her schooling. "I can hear my father saying, 'a girl is, after all, only going to get married. She's going to become a cook and a mother, a housekeeper and teacher'," said Ruth. It is an attitude both she and Muriel resented.

For a couple of years after this, Ruth led what she subsequently felt was an aimless and drifting existence. But she could not pull herself out of it, which is not all that surprising, for severe anaemia is characterised by a lack of energy and, consequently, a lack of interest in life. As the months passed and the war escalated, Londoners began to suffer badly, for bombs were destroying lives, homes and offices. The insecurity this engendered in the already tense, nervous child, who was so close to her parents, made her even more determined not to leave them. But they worried about Ruth's uncharacteristic listlessness, and friends of the family rallied round to try and arouse her interest in some sort of activity outside the home. Eventually she went to work as a junior in a confectionary business that belonged to a friend of her father's. She was a welcome recruit, for the establishment, like so many others in the war years, was short of staff, and she turned her hand to almost anything, helping in the office and behind the counter.

One occasion Ruth did enjoy as she was recovering from the worst effects of anaemia, was a Freemason dinner her father took her to, which was probably the last of its kind until after the war. It was organised on a grand scale, which was possible as it was still the early stages of the war, and rationing had not yet begun to bite in Britain. As Ruth dressed in a long evening gown, complete with elbow-length gloves, her cheeks which were paler than ever due to her anaemia glowed with excitement. She had lost the weight which had characterised the plump, naughty schoolgirl, and she was growing into an attractive woman who was beginning to turn heads. Her copper hair gleamed, and her strange eyes, one of them brown and the other green, fascinated people. Spots of colour burned on her cheeks at the Freemason dinner as the many courses came and went – soup, fish, poultry, meat, dessert, cheese, fruit and coffee. Her father, imposing and distinguished in his white tie and tails, was proud of his lovely daughter.

But the war was closing in, and soon dinners and fun were forgotten. In May 1940 France was invaded and collapsed, and Britain caught the imagination of the world as her people set out from the south coast in every conceivable sea craft and snatched their men from under the noses of the Luftwaffe, who were strafing them as they huddled, trapped on the beaches of Dunkirk. Muriel and her schoolfriends in their south coast billet were considered far too vulnerable to remain there as the Germans pounded the coastline. They were only given a couple of days' notice before being put on to trains and sent to South Wales where they were billeted with coalminers who had suffered thirteen years of unemployment and were really poor, some of their families suffering from malnutrition.

The British Government paid for the billet, and the irony of people who had been receiving five shillings a week on the dole being given sixteen shillings to house schoolchildren, did not escape the intelligent and highly observant Muriel. She had matured fast, and the schoolgirl who adored her lessons, the school debating society and chess club realised that life was not wonderful for everyone. It was during this period in Wales that Muriel became a socialist and left the Anglican church to join the Congregational church. Her actions emphasised the different approach to life of Ruth and Muriel, for the former was politically conservative and enjoyed the High Anglican religion.

In London the bombing increased, and Ruth joined a fire fighting team. They worked in groups of six, and one of their tasks, if they saw an incendiary bomb coming down, was to warn the possible victims. Every street had a team, and everybody did their bit with the marvellous spirit of valour and comradeship that British Prime Minister Sir Winston Churchill, spoke of so eloquently in his broadcasts. "If an incendiary bomb set the curtains in a house alight, often the whole building went up, and then the house next door caught alight and so on," said Ruth. "You have a situation where the whole community is at risk, and therefore everyone pulls their weight." Ruth also worked with St John Ambulance, learning about first aid, and so was born in her the tremendous community spirit and sense of caring that was later to benefit the people of her husband's Bamangwato tribe.

Ruth also learnt to drive, and she put in long hours with a van distributing cups of tea for servicemen and women on gun sites, balloon sites or bridge guard points. She was fast regaining her formidable energy, and all her voluntary work aroused her interest in the services, but when she tried to join the Women's Auxiliary Air Force, she was told she was too young.

On 15th September 1940, disaster struck the Williams household. It was early evening, and Ruth was upstairs watching one of the many dogfights overhead during the Battle of Britain. Watching it with Ruth from the upstairs window of his house, was the youngest son of the family next door.

The two teenagers were discussing the battle from their respective windows, and how the war had changed their lives, when Ruth heard a scream and the house started to rock and tilt. "The scream was the bombs coming down, it was a dreadful sound, absolutely horrific." Her friend's house took a direct hit, and he was killed. Ruth was conscious of the dreadful sound of another bomb falling, and then the house on the other side of the Williamses' was hit too.

"I went rushing down the stairs, with the house heaving up and down at all sorts of angles, and bits of plaster and woodwork falling all about me. My sister, my parents and I huddled in the corridor until we heard the all-clear, and then we went outside and saw the house next door had been flattened. It was too awful." Ruth was so traumatised by the death of her friend that she resolved not to allow herself to become too attached to anyone during the war. And she stuck to her decision, "although it was very difficult at times due to the unnatural circumstances of war when you are thrown together with people more than normal, and everyone tends to get sentimental and romantic," said Ruth.

The Williamses were incredibly lucky that the bombs had fallen around them, but although their house was standing, all the windows had been blasted out, and the walls moved when they were touched. It was clearly unsafe, and so the family moved out and spent the rest of the night in the large underground cellar of a friend's pub, along with many other people who had lost their homes in the same way. They sat on beer crates, and those who couldn't sleep played cards until the dawn broke and they stumbled bleary-eyed with aching limbs into the grey sadness of London.

The family moved in with Ruth's grandparents in North London for a couple of weeks while George and Dorothy shuttled back and forth from north to south, looking for alternative accommodation. This wasn't easy at a time when many, many people were being bombed out of their homes. But George was a most determined man, and he found a nice ground floor flat in Lewisham, a few kilometres from Marble Arch and nearby Blackheath. Belmont Hall Court was small as blocks of flats go, and consequently there was a friendly, communal spirit amongst the people who lived there. The flat was modern, and in contrast to many of the gracious old London buildings, was well sprung and had good foundations. The area suffered an enormous amount of bombing during the war, but the Williamses' flat did not lose more than its windows. "There were bomb shelters attached to the flats which I ran to regularly, said Muriel, "but my parents ignored them. They didn't seem to have any nerves at all."

By November 1940, 4000 civilians had been killed and tens of thousands of Londoners had lost their homes as Ruth did. Many of them did not have homes again for the entire duration of the war. They made do as best they could in underground shelters or slept in bunks and hammocks in the tunnel-like passages of London's famous underground railway. "They were amazing people," said Ruth. "Night after night bombs screamed down, houses were hit, people lost all their possessions, their friends, their families. It was very, very depressing, and yet they struggled on." Firemen rushed valiantly from one seemingly uncontrollable blaze to the next, their eyes red-rimmed with exhaustion, and the weather was often so bitterly cold that the water froze in their hoses.

The night the East End was set ablaze by the German bombs, George Williams, worried about Ruth's grandparents, set out with her accompanying him to cross the River Thames and go north to see how they were. The dreadful flames that destroyed so much of the East End lit up the night sky, and when Ruth and George, having reassured themselves about the old folk, got back to the Thames, they found bridge after bridge closed as they tried to cross the river. Firemen who worked all through the night and the next day greeted Ruth's concerned eyes with ones that were raw from the heat and flames, and their clothes were filthy with smut. The sight of the homeless, sobbing quietly and helplessly, some of them too stunned even to cry, made such an impression on Ruth that the hardship she suffered in subsequent years seemed small in comparison. "One night an entire family, who were great friends of ours and who lived just down the street from us, were killed by a bomb," said Ruth.

In 1941, the year that Ruth decided to join the forces, the Germans met their first major defeat in North Africa; General Rommel was forced to retreat, and the Russians stopped the invasion of their country at the very gates of Moscow and Leningrad. Unknown to most of the Western world, Jews were being packed into cattle trucks and herded to their death in German extermination camps. In England, bravely holding out against the massive German onslaught, everything was rationed. Utility clothes became the vogue, cosmetics disappeared from shops as did stockings, and socks consequently became chic.

Ruth was seventeen years old when she volunteered, which she said gave her an advantage over those who were called up, for she was given some choice about where she could serve. Her father was keen for her to go into either the army (because he had been there and had contacts) or into the navy, where he had a friend who was a captain. Ruth, with an unexpected show of independence and possible teenage rebelliousness, decided to apply for the motor transport section of the Women's Auxiliary Air Force (WAAF). It seemed to her a glamorous section to be in, and the daring young pilots were the darlings of the nation. "It was exciting and fun to be in transport. We were so mobile, we didn't just stay on one station, and of course there were very few cars on the road in those days. We therefore had a sense of freedom, and you had a feeling of being on your own, and that is something I always liked," said Ruth.

George Williams, not used to being crossed by a woman and particularly his daughter, was most displeased. "Of course you'll join the army, I've got friends there and you'll have a commission," he said, and Ruth retorted, "No! I'm too young. I don't want a commission. I want to be irresponsible."

Ruth might have been a toughie on the lacrosse field, but during six weeks of square bashing, she developed such bad blisters on her sensitive feet that she ended up in the sick bay. "I told them it was no use making me march. But you know these people, they have to learn for themselves, and so I got blisters again. In the end they excused me from marching and even told me I could wear my own shoes," said Ruth, who was thrilled to escape the square bashing. "The whole idea of this sort of thing of course is that you learn to obey a command without arguing. I don't think I'm too much of a soldier," she said candidly, showing that independence of spirit which was to be such a thorn in the flesh of the British Government in later years.

Ruth did a three-month transport course, during which she learnt all about driving and mechanics and how to carry out minor vehicle repairs. During her four and a half years in the WAAF, Ruth was posted mainly to airbases in the south of England, first to Friston and then Beachy Head, and later on to Uxbridge, Gatwick and then London.

She considered herself lucky to have joined Fighter Command 11, the Battle of Britain group of pilots, and to have driven people such as the extraordinary and famous "Cat's Eyes" Cunningham around (so named because of his amazing ability to see at night). Ruth drove a variety of vehicles, ranging from cars to trucks, lorries, ambulances and vans. Sometimes she had to evacuate wounded pilots who crash-landed on the coast, an experience she found traumatic because she so often knew them. "They were young boys, babies, straight from school, and it was very tough to see them go off and know that some of them would not return. You would wait for the aircraft to come back, you knew it was long overdue, and just hoped they had landed somewhere else," said the woman, who was after all not that much older than some of the men she called babies.

Ruth considered the emergency landing at Friston, on the coast between Eastbourne and Brighton, hair-raising: "There was a sheer cliff and the sea rushed up at them as they came in low." The Germans also came in low in the early days, almost on the crest of a wave, to escape radar detection. The south coast, because of its position close to Europe, naturally took a hammering, and Ruth would see flying bombs being shot down and watch dogfights in the air as she drove around, carrying dispatches, ferrying propellers in huge trucks, or transporting staff. She found the work exciting and fulfilling, she was always a person of action who hated sitting twiddling her thumbs. She could not bear to be bored, and she certainly wasn't during the war as were some women who spent mind-numbing hours bent over assembly lines in munitions factories.

Sometimes it was too exciting, for example when she got lost in fog or mist, or when she didn't know where she was going because all the road and street signs had been taken down in case German pilots landed. But Ruth found it remarkable how well they got to know the unsignposted roads. She once took a route at night whilst taking dispatches from her base at Friston to a place on the other side of Brighton and learnt her way around so well in the dark that when she was asked to do it by daylight she lost direction.

Ruth worked long and arduous hours during the war, as did so many others, and for the first six months in the WAAF did not have any leave at all. It was 1942, the gloomiest year of the war, with Canadians dying in their thousands at Dieppe, and the Japanese invading Southeast Asia. RAF Fighter Command flew from dawn to dusk, and in an English summer this is a long day, often stretching from 4 a.m. to 10 p.m. Ruth, exhausted, sometimes used to lie under a tree in the field where the emergency landing strip was situated at Friston and go to sleep. One particularly tiring day, she fell into such a deep sleep that the sun moved across the heavens, taking the shade with it, and she woke with such severe sunburn that she was very ill indeed.

Friston, being such a small station, was a tight-knit unit, almost like a family. Ruth and about twenty other WAAF's lived in a lovely old gabled house near the cliffs, and although the latter was out of bounds, they would often sneak down it for a swim in the cove below. This came to an end when the house burnt to the ground, and for the second time in as many years, Ruth lost everything she owned. The WAAF's who were living there believed the house was haunted. "It was scary living there, until you got used to it," said Ruth. "I would hear these footsteps coming up the stairs and think it was one of the girls, and the steps would reach the top and then … silence … before my door would fly open, and nobody was there. Everyone who lived there experienced that. The officers who were on duty downstairs got the fright of their lives when a safe that nobody had been able to unlock just flew open one night."

The fire started in a room at the top of the house, which was never opened because no one could ever find the key. Ruth was almost alone in the house when it burned down, for everyone else was out rehearsing for a talent show, and she, having finished her part, returned home early. The fire had already started when she went to sleep, but having no sense of smell, she was unaware of it. She was woken by shouts of, "Fire, fire, all out, all out," and, opening her door, found smoke billowing into the hall. She grabbed a coat to cover her nightdress and raced down the stairs. The entire building was alight, nobody was allowed back in, and there they stood, watching the flames engulf their possessions, a desolate experience which was not to be the last in her life.

But the tension of the war years was broken by moments of intense fun and gaiety, and Ruth welcomed these, for she enjoyed a party as much as anyone. She was growing into a striking woman with the peaches-and-cream complexion for which English women are so famous, and which was highlighted by the glow of her red-gold hair. All kinds of men, but mostly pilots, paid her attention on jaunts to the pub and to parties. She was happy to flirt gently, but there it ended, and although she became good friends with some of her admirers, she never allowed romance to develop into a permanent relationship, so aware was she of the painful way relationships could end in war.

Ruth had a lively sense of fun, bunking out of station bounds at night, and on one occasion tearing through a village in an ambulance with her siren wailing, and roaring with laughter as people pulled over to the side.

She particularly loved ballroom dancing and had gone regularly to classes before the war put a stop to it. She was thrilled therefore when she was placed second in a large ballroom dancing competition held in Eastbourne where she was based while working at the Beachy Head radar station. Ruth had not planned to enter the competition and was helping a girlfriend stick on her number when the girl suddenly got cold feet and insisted Ruth dance with her partner. And although the two had never danced together, they took to the floor with scores of other couples. Watched by hundreds of people, Ruth forgot her fear after a while, and her trim, uniformed figure went confidently through the steps of the waltz, quickstep, foxtrot and tango. Eliminations knocked out the couples until there were only three on the floor and the air crackled with tension. Ruth's commanding officer, who was watching, was disappointed she came second, but to Ruth it was one of the highlights of her life.

Ruth's continuing closeness to her family was emphasised by the fact that she nearly always went home on her air force passes. "She would come home on leave every few months, and the toll that tension took of her nerves showed by the way she would sort of collapse, and sleep and sleep, and relax, and then back she would go again," said Muriel. Muriel had spent a year at home, not knowing what to do, when the forces turned her down because of her heart murmur. "Nobody ever wanted to take a chance on that in case they might have to pay me a pension for life," said the dejected and frustrated Muriel. So she worked in a bank, which she found boring, doing accounts and foreign exchange. She couldn't leave her job, due to the extreme shortage of skills resulting from so many men being away at war. She envied Ruth her lively and exciting life and felt, with all the young men away in the forces and her uneventful job she was missing out on a lot.

"I know of one place Ruth was working, where there were about six WAAF's and I've forgotten how many hundreds or thousands of air force men, and I think both the navy and the army was in the area. Ruth therefore had a pretty hectic social life, although being a WAAF driver could be really grim too," said Muriel. It was ironic that Muriel was not allowed to join, for she was an air raid warden, and with all the bombing of London, particularly the hard-hit South East London, she was often up all night, witnessing scenes every bit as tragic and horrific, if not more so, than the ones with which her sister dealt. Her air warden duty involved establishing where people were sleeping in a given number of houses, and if there was a direct hit she had to know whether it was necessary to dig beneath a pile of rubble. She also patrolled the streets, searching for unexploded bombs.

It didn't take Londoners long to develop the spirit of bravery and invincibility for which they became famous. Civilians were warned about air raids by signs flashing on in cinemas, and announcements were made in theatres and dance halls. But many people after a while simply disregarded them and carried on with what they were doing. One of the paradoxes of war is the love, warmth and friendliness it generates in a time of such pain, sorrow and destruction, and the feeling that there was no time to lose in living life to the full with death everywhere. London, despite the heavy pounding it took from German bombs, was so lively that American GI's were initially amazed by it.

But as the war dragged on, and the Germans unleashed weapons like the doodle bomb, life became progressively more grim. The bombs made a whining noise as they came in, followed by a deathly silence as the engines that powered them cut out, and then came the explosion. Ruth was in the radar section at Beachy Head when they first started coming over. "All the time the noise was going on, you knew you were all right. It was when the engine cut out that you started counting. If you reached five, you were all right. The waiting in the awful silence was the worst part," she said. She got through the war, as so many others did, by living from day to day. "There was no way else to live, you never knew if tomorrow would come."

It was during her time in the air force that Ruth first experienced racial discrimination, and the sense of outrage that people could be judged by the colour of their skins and not their characters, found expression for the first but certainly not the last time in her life. Despite her father's strong views about mixed marriages, he had never suggested to his daughters that they were superior or inferior, or that they should compare themselves with others in terms of pigmentation, class or wealth. "I think that this is a very strong point in his favour," said Ruth. The condescending airs, the derogatory and sometimes frankly abusive remarks made by some of the pilots to West Indians, who like people from many other British colonies had left their homes to help the British fight the war, surprised her. The post-war influx of West Indians, Jamaicans, Africans and Asians was still to come, and many English people, including Ruth, had not been in contact much with those of a different colour.

When she remonstrated with those who were being abusive, the ridicule was turned on her too. Scorn was reserved for her defence of a middle-aged West Indian father of eight, who worked as a ground crew member. "These

Englishmen hated to see white women even talking to a coloured man," said Ruth. But she was genuinely concerned about someone so lonely and far from home, who struggled to communicate with those around him, and so she continued in her strong-minded, determined manner to chat to the father of eight. On one occasion when she returned to the airbase from some leave, she was asked sarcastically if she had inquired about the welfare of her "boy-friend", and there was dead silence in the pub when she retorted, "I suppose not one of you had the decency to pass a civil word to him when I was gone?"

She thought a great deal about the war they were fighting to save the world from domination by an Aryan purist and fanatic. "I would get angry that people could be so beastly to others. After all, we were fighting a war against some crank who was exterminating people he didn't like. Was his prejudice a more extreme version of ours?" Ruth could not of course have imagined that one day she would learn from personal and bitter experience just how petty and extreme racial prejudice could be.

By the time the war began to draw to a close, she was growing tired of the regimentation and rules of life in the forces, and the glamour of which she spoke so glowingly in the early days was wearing off. The end of the war meant that fighting for the British came to a halt rapidly, yet some of the tough living conditions continued for many years, and although the end to the bombing brought intense relief, life did not return to normal for a long time.

Unmarried women were the last to be demobbed, and it was therefore a year after fighting ended before Ruth left the WAAF. She ended her duties at Group 11 headquarters in London, driving the staff around, something which she found interesting and enjoyable. "But it got to the stage where I could not face another demob party. Some of us were asked to stay on and were offered commissions, but I felt four and a half years had been enough for me." Returning to a civilian way of life was not as easy as some thought it would be after such a long period of regimentation, and Ruth soon missed the comradeship she had so enjoyed in the WAAF.

She had stuck to her resolve to form no permanent attachments, and she might well have been lonely if, due to the shortage of accommodation, she had not moved back home to the flat in Lewisham. Ruth did not get a job immediately. "I didn't know what to do. My schooling hadn't been completed, I wasn't qualified for anything, in fact I was qualified for absolutely nothing. I would have liked to continue with my training as a dietician, but the college hadn't started operating again." It was a demoralising time for Ruth, who felt she was in a state of limbo, neither in the forces and yet not a civilian, and although she realised many other people were experiencing the same sense of futility and listlessness, she did not know what to do about it.

It was at this time that a cousin of Ruth's who was working for the huge insurance and underwriter's firm of Lloyds, suggested she join it too, as they were looking for staff. "I thought about it a for a long time. I wasn't convinced that office routine was my line, but I decided to give it a try."

She was happy working there for the relatively short time that she did before she married Seretse Khama. Lloyds underwrote everything, from shipping to airlines, and Ruth worked on the foreign claims side as a confidential clerk to an underwriter. Her work involved a certain amount of accounting and calculation, and as mathematics had been one of the subjects Ruth had liked at school, she enjoyed her job.

In view of the work she did at Lloyds, the label "London typist" which the press pinned on her soon after news of her marriage hit the headlines, was incorrect. It is a minor point, but Ruth could not type, and she always got furious when people erroneously described her as a typist. It seems to have hit a raw nerve, or maybe it symbolised her antagonism towards those journalists whom she accused of writing "rubbish, absolute rubbish" about her down the years.

Muriel, who had been attending night classes in accountancy during the war, left the bank as soon as she could, and joined a firm of auditors. She too was living at home, and so George and Dorothy Williams who had often waved a sad goodbye to their daughters during the war, ended it with them both safely back in the nest.

FOUR

Seretse's tribe and his childhood

Seretse Khama was born on the 1st of July 1921 in his famous grandfather Khama III's lolwapa (yard) on the slopes of the kgotla hill in Serowe, then the largest village south of the equator. He was born two and a half years before Ruth Williams into a world that was unaware the 1920s was to be a decade noted for its art deco, jazz, fast living and wealth. For Serowe was attuned to the laws of nature and the seasons. The sprawling, mud-hutted village tumbled up and down pretty rock and bush-covered hills, and the rhythm of its life was governed not by fads and fashions, but by the rainy seasons, the time for planting and sowing, and the time for harvesting.

Seretse's birthplace was a small, tin-roofed, concrete-walled house with a veranda running along its front, and from this you could see over the kgotla – an expanse of stamped earth, sheltered by a crescent-shaped windbreak of wood poles. The kgotla was the centre of tribal life, where men gathered to listen to the chief and to perform their judicial and political duties. From the veranda of the house stretched an expanse of thatched huts to the twin hills of Swaneng on the outskirts of Serowe, where Seretse would one day take his English bride to live.

He was born into a world of peace and orderliness, where men, women and children had certain roles to play and certain tasks to fulfil. The men spent most of their day in the kgotla, sitting on their little fold-up stools, made of wood and riempie (animal hide). Their attire was Westernised, and ranged from suits to khaki shirts and overcoats, and they wore a variety of headgear, including woollen balaclavas and pith helmets which kept off the sun in summer and the occasional chilly wind in winter.

The women built mud huts and mud courtyards, decorating the walls of the courtyards with intricate patterns and constantly smoothing them with lovely round stones. Sometimes they thatched the huts, although that was the men's job, as it was theirs also to build windows and doors, and to erect the pole-and-rafter framework for the thatch, spacing it from the wall to prevent the spread of white ants.

Seretse came into the world at the time of year when Serowe bustled with people and activity. There were times when it was almost deserted, for the Bamangwato, as was the case with most Batswana, had three homes. The main one was in the village where they lived from about June to October. Then, when the rains came, the chief went to the kgotla and announced that the time for ploughing had come, and a great exodus ensued. The towing of oxen, the creaking of wooden wagons and the shouts of excited, naked little children filled the air. The rains brought life to everything, for out of the dust and dry bushveld burst wild flowers, lilies, wild hibiscus, amaryllis and acanthus. Acacia and mosetlha trees bloomed in white and yellow profusion, and the very air seemed alive with growth as insects, crickets, frogs, mosquitoes and snakes woke from their hibernation.

The lands to which Seretse accompanied his mother when he was a little child were within a couple of day's trek from Serowe, and the men, having helped the women to plough, would leave them behind to frighten the birds away and to ward off wild animals that might eat or trample their crops. As Seretse grew more steady on his sturdy little legs, he would help in these activities. The lands were located in blocks or zones, within which many families had their fields close together. They were used exclusively for cultivation, and cattle were not allowed to graze near them. The lands were situated as far away as sixty kilometres from Serowe to prevent the limited grazing near it being exhausted.

For the same reason, the cattle posts were placed even further away, on the fringe of the Kalahari Desert. These posts consisted of a borehole, a few crude huts, and kraals (circular enclosures made with thorn bushes), and there the men would tend to the animals by which a Mongwato (the singular form of Bangwato or Bamangwato) measures his wealth. Often young boys were left there to herd, while their sisters attended school in Serowe – at that time of year a village was populated by the very old and by girls.

The Bamangwato lived in a reserve, about 75 000 square kilometres in size. Khama III had welded many sub-tribes into one, making a total population of about 100 000, of which the original Bamangwato numbered about 20 000.

Although the Bamangwato were by far the largest tribe in Bechuanaland, they were a poor people, as were the other seven major tribes in the territory. They practised subsistence farming, growing sorghum, melons, beans, millet and groundnuts. The erratic and generally poor rainfall meant it was almost impossible to grow enough crops to store as provision for the many years when the rains did not come. Due to the limited scope for employment in Bechuanaland, the young men of the tribe travelled to the gold mines in the neighbouring Union of South Africa, where they remained for months at a time. It was into this world of constant movement and change, which was paradoxically an unchanging world with its strict tribal laws, traditions and family discipline, that Seretse spent his happy childhood.

He was the son of Sekgoma II and Tebogo.[2] Sekgoma was a sickly man who died when Seretse was four years old, and much of his poor health was due to his unsettled life, for he was driven into exile by his father, Khama III (or the Great Khama as he was called), for about seventeen years. He spent these years wandering from village to village with his people and cattle, before he was allowed home by his father. To understand the family background of Seretse and the colourful history of his tribe, we must go back in history, to the time when the Setswana-speaking tribes first moved into the area that came to be known as the British Protectorate of Bechuanaland, and which finally became the independent Republic of Botswana in 1966.

Setswana is the most widely dispersed language in southern Africa, spoken as it is by the predominant tribes in Botswana. It is generally accepted that the Batswana came from the north at the time of the tribal migrations into southern Africa, and that they settled first in what is now South Africa's North West and Free State provinces, then over the centuries spread in a broad belt across the middle of southern Africa, from Lesotho to Botswana.

The Tswana people, who have for centuries called themselves Batswana – people of the Tswana grouping of tribes – were referred to as Bechuanas during the colonisation of Bechuanaland, but I shall call them the Batswana. Tradition has it that the Batswana of southern Africa were a united people, but fragmentation has been a feature of their history, with different sections hiving off to a new locality where they would form a new tribe with their own chief.[3]

This intensified with the arrival of the Mfecane, or the "crushing", an eruption of tribal violence in the early 19th century, which the Zulus under Shaka inflicted on tribe after tribe in southern Africa. It scattered the Bamangwato in all directions, and the Batswana tribes were in total disarray. Fortunately for the Bamangwato, a strong leader, Sekgoma I, merged many refugees from the Mfecane into a stable tribe and united them around a capital at Shoshong, which is about seventy kilometres south as the crow flies from the present Bamangwato capital of Serowe. Land then was plentiful, rich in game, and the tribe settled down to a fairly peaceful existence as cattle breeders.

When the famous missionary, David Livingstone, one of the first white men to visit Chief Sekgoma, went to Shoshong in 1842, Khama III, who was to become famous in Britain for his wisdom, statesmanship and Christianity, was a little boy. He grew into a striking young man with sensitive, aquiline features and excelled both in athletics and in Bible study. Unlike his pagan and polygamous father, who despite Livingstone's persuasive manner remained adamantly pagan, the young Khama embraced the Christian faith. So did his brother Kgamane, and when they refused to participate in traditional customs such as bogwera (initiation) or in rainmaking, and when they continued to adopt European customs and dress, Sekgoma was outraged. He ordered Khama to take a second wife, and when this request was also refused, he set in motion yet another of the dynastic feuds which characterised the Bamangwato's royal family. The existence of the feuds is not surprising, for the polygamous chiefs had up to sixteen sons and several wives, each of whom lived in her own house, albeit in the chief's lolwapa, and if sons were not plotting against their father for the chieftainship, they were fighting with each other.

It is important to understand this dissension in the ruling family, for it led naturally to tribal disorder with different factions taking sides, and much was made of this by the British when there was such an uproar over Seretse's marriage.

Sekgoma tried everything from witchcraft to assassination in his efforts to dispose of his disobedient son, none of which worked, and eventually son and father ended up in a battle from which Khama emerged victorious. He was magnanimous in victory, however, and allowed his father back, only becoming chief when Sekgoma died in 1875.

After his installation, he immediately set about writing into tribal law the Christian tenets that would make his society a more compassionate one, and he retained the good he saw in the traditions and customs of the Bamangwato. He outlawed witchcraft, the payment of bogadi (bride price), the initiation ceremonies for men (bogwera) and for women (bojale). But an integral part of tribal life, that of the age regiments of Mephato, continued.

Khama III abolished bogwera because men were sometimes killed during rites that led up to the formation of a regiment. In its place, he instituted prayers and lectures. The men's regiments undertook tasks such as road, dam or school building, cleaning the village or collecting wood. The women's regiments thatched, collected water and did generally lighter tasks.[4]

Khama III also abolished the traditional killing of one twin as well as barbarous corporal punishment. He introduced prohibition about which he was fanatical. He enforced it strictly amongst his people and was in subsequent years much acclaimed for this by British temperance societies. He also introduced a law to protect big animals and certain big birds, and he moved the capital from Shoshong, where the ground water on which the Bamangwato were so dependent had virtually dried up, settling his people about 100 kilometres north-east of Shoshong, at Palapye.

Bessie Head, in her excellent book, *Serowe, Village of The Rain Wind*, writes:

> With Sekgoma I, the old order died a complete death, and with Khama, a new order was born, which was a blending of all that was compassionate and good in his own culture, and in the traditions of Christianity. An historian, Douglas Mackenzie, writing during the 1920s, observed of Khama, that he produced a history as yet unsurpassed anywhere in Africa.[5]

It is against this picture of benign and peaceful rule that we must look at the African continent in the 19th century, for naturally what happened directly affected its peoples, and this was particularly the case of the Bamangwato who found themselves caught up in the scramble by European powers to divide up the great continent. The latter were jockeying for position and trading claims in most parts of Africa. The British, the Portuguese and the Belgians were closing in on Bechuanaland to the north, the Afrikaners to the east and the south-east, the Germans to the west, and the British to the south. The colonial powers watched each other and worried about any expansionism that would threaten their interests, while the subjects of that expansionism were generally not given much thought at all.

Britain, being the great naval power she was in those glorious days of her mighty empire, was concerned that she should be in control of most of the seaports around the coast of Africa. She was concerned about German activity in South West Africa, and therefore, in March 1878, she annexed Walvis Bay and a coastal strip of about thirty-five kilometres surrounding it but limited her interest and responsibility to that small territory. Shortly afterwards, the Germans began their colonisation of the territory, and in 1884 Germany proclaimed its protectorate over the Namaqua-Damaraland coast.

In 1856 the Boers had set up the Zuid-Afrikaanse Republiek under President Marthinus Wessel Pretorius on the eastern border of Bechuanaland, and in 1868 some of them crossed into the Tati area, north of Palapye, to mine gold. Pretorius annexed it, despite Bamangwato protests to the governor of the British-ruled Cape to get rid of the Boers. However, the governor was not interested, and it was the Kimberley Gold Rush that saved the Bamangwato, for it diverted the interest of the invaders. But the Boers continued to filter in, and Khama, together with Chief Sechele of the Bakwena (the senior tribe in Bechuanaland) asked Queen Victoria for protection in 1876. It was a request that was met with no response.

The situation did not improve for the Bamangwato when Cecil John Rhodes arrived on the scene, for Bechuanaland was included in his expansionist dreams.[6]

His commercial company, the British South Africa Company, busy with its expansion in Mashonaland and Matabeleland was looking for a corridor to the north, and Bechuanaland was the only place for it. The fears of the Bamangwato that they might lose their lands went unheeded by the British until there was panic that President Kruger, by annexing Goshen in south-eastern Bechuanaland, might push his Zuid-Afrikaanse Republiek boundaries to the German border and thus exclude Britain for ever from the road to the north.

In 1884 Britain acted by sending as commissioner to British (southern) Bechuanaland the missionary and friend of the Bamangwato, John Mackenzie, and then Rhodes himself, while an expedition led by Sir Charles Warren cleared Bechuanaland of Boer invaders. Queen Victoria assumed power over the whole territory by Order in Council in 1885. But Khama's fears continued, for ten years later it was openly suggested that the protectorate be transferred to the British South Africa Company. In August 1895, Khama sailed for England with Chief Sechele of the Bakwena and Chief Bathoen of the Bangwaketse to protest against such a move. Khama's reputation as a God-fearing, law-abiding, superb administrator had preceded him. The British Government wasn't on his side, but the British public certainly was, for it packed the meetings he addressed throughout England and rushed to buy the book written by the missionary J.D. Hepburn, *Twenty Years in Khama's Country*.[7] A visit to Queen Victoria, who was clearly greatly impressed with Khama, combined with vigorous public support, had the desired effect, and two months later, on the 7th of November 1895, the chiefs reached satisfactory terms with the British Government.[8] It is ironic that Khama's grandson would one day also appeal to the British people for their support in his battle to end his exile and return to the Bamangwato.

Mary Benson in her book, *Tshekedi Khama*, writes:

> Under the Queen's protection the Chiefs would rule their own people much as before. The Queen's officer who would receive orders through the Secretary of State and the High Commissioner in the Cape, would try cases involving death and involving white men or natives of other tribes, and would hear appeals in serious cases.
>
> The Chiefs would give up a strip of land in the east for a railway, and boundaries for their respective countries would be defined. In response particularly to Khama's urging, a ban was placed on the "white man's strong drink". Their fears of the British South African Company finally evaporated with the fiasco of the Jameson Raid in 1895, when the company was told that, "in view of recent occurrences in South Africa, the matter must stand over for the present." At last the British Government firmly established its protection over Bechuanaland. The new Protectorate was three times the size of Britain, but sparsely populated and poor. The government appointed a Resident Commissioner, with headquarters in Mafeking (situated in the Cape Colony), and Resident Magistrates for the eight tribal areas and the small pockets of white settlement on the Protectorate's borders. Bechuanaland, by becoming a British colony, had saved itself from being divided up between the Germans, the Boers and the British South Africa Company.[9]

When Khama returned to his people from England, he was a happy man, but that happiness was clouded by his son Sekgoma's behaviour, for in his absence the young man had made laws of which he disapproved. Sekgoma chafed under what some people have described as the autocratic rule of Khama, and the result of this was the exile of Sekgoma for many years. He had flouted the dominant rule in Batswana society, that of complete submission to parental authority – an authority that was drastically enforced. He was banished about the time that Khama moved his tribe again, for the surface water at Palapye was becoming scarce, and he decided on resettlement at his cattle post in Serowe (forty-seven kilometres away) where there were two running streams. In 1902, the wagons were piled high, and the Bamangwato followed their chief to their new home.

Shortly after the move, in September 1905, Khama's fourth wife Semane (his first two died and he divorced the third) gave birth to a son Tshekedi (which means "clarifier").

Such was Khama's impressive reign that stories about his wisdom and foresight are remembered clearly by the descendants of his contemporaries.[10]

While he welcomed traders settling amongst his tribe, he stuck strictly to his rule that land belonged to the Bamangwato and could not be sold. The stores therefore were built on stilts to emphasise the leasehold and were made of wood and iron that could be easily dismantled. He would not allow the traders to live or work clustered together and dispersed them amongst his people. He paid his accounts once a year, when he walked into a store, deposited a bag of gold sovereigns on the counter and invited the trader to take his due.

There was very little this astute chief did not know about what was going on in his territory. A large bird called a pow was royal game, and a trader, Arnold Johnston, with whom he was friendly, shot one of these birds some distance from Serowe when returning from a trip to an outlying store. By the time he reached the kgotla to explain his misdeed, Khama knew of it and was waiting patiently, long sensitive fingers flicking his fly whisk as he sat. The trader was forgiven on condition he cooked the bird and gave a leg to the chief.

Mrs Johnston's wife wore a plain gold brooch with a ruby in it that Khama admired, until one day he noticed that it was missing, and on inquiry was told that it had vanished from her home. Khama's law about stealing was enforced so strictly that people who lived in Serowe did not bother to own house keys.

It took him three years, but Khama eventually tracked down the brooch and returned it to Mrs Johnston, an old trader's wife who wished not to be named, told me when I visited Serowe.

The chief had a dignity and a style that were the subject of much comment, and his lean, erect figure riding around the village on a white horse was as much admired as it was feared. He loved his horses, and always took great care of his animals – people knew when it was his wagon passing, for his team of oxen were always of one colour – either black or tan.

Khama died in his Serowe kgotla home in 1923, after fifty difficult and demanding years as chief. He has been described as the most outstanding African of his time; as a man whose life benefited not only the Bamangwato but Bechuanaland as a whole, and who obtained for that country the territorial unity it possesses today.[11]

After Khama's death, the respect he commanded was so great that for at least three days no one spoke. People streamed in from their lands and cattle posts, and thousands attended his funeral. He was buried on the granite hill overlooking the kgotla in Serowe, and his son Sekgoma erected a monument there, inscribed with the Biblical words, "Righteousness Exalteth a Nation". On top of the large tomb is a bronze duiker, called a phuti (pronounced pooti), which is the tribal emblem.

The legend[12] goes that three brothers, Ngwato, Kwena and Ngwaketse, broke away from the main Tswana tribe, and for a while Ngwato remained attached to his eldest brother, Kwena, and shared the Bakwena totem, the crocodile. But then they started fighting, and Ngwato was forced to flee. He took refuge in a clump of bushes with Kwena's followers hot on his heels. They knew he must be near and began to search in the thicket for him. They were on the point of discovering Ngwato when the small buck, the phuti, burst from the bushes. "Look," they cried, "there was a phuti inside the bushes, Ngwato can't be there, he has escaped," and they left him. Ngwato gathered his followers together and formed the Bamangwato, which adopted the phuti as its emblem. Thereafter the term was also used in describing the chief. The phuti on Khama's tomb was sculpted by well-known South African artist Anton van Wouw, and it was unveiled by the Prince of Wales in 1924.

Seretse was only two years old when his grandfather died, and his father Sekgoma, who had returned from exile some years before, became chief. Sekgoma had become reconciled with his father in 1916 and had married a woman of whom Khama approved and who produced two children, a daughter, Naledi, and Seretse.

In the two years that followed Khama III's death, Sekgoma, a tall, dignified and handsome man, ruled the tribe and set out to follow Khama's ideas on social reform. One of his main objectives was to build a hospital. The original outlay for it had been 700 pounds collected by the tribe for the Prince of Wales during his 1924 visit. The prince made the figure 1000 pounds from his own pocket and suggested it be used for the much-needed hospital.

Sadly, Sekgoma died before it was completed, but it was named after him, and one of little Seretse's first official functions was to lay the foundation stone.[13]

Seretse was four years old when his father died in 1925, and dynastic feuds and struggles followed his death. Finally, it was established that Seretse was heir apparent, and second in line was Khama's second son, Tshekedi. Due to Seretse's age, it was decided that Tshekedi should rule the tribe as regent until Seretse was old enough to assume his rightful position. Tshekedi, who was at school at Fort Hare in the Eastern Cape, was called back home before he had matriculated to take over the chieftainship, an act that upset him at the time, for he loved law and was planning to study it in Britain. He wept as he clambered off the train that took him home and away from his education.

But Tshekedi was not one for moping – he was a man of action and he certainly had plenty of that in his life. He was described as an African Napoleon, for he was short in stature compared with his father and brother, and he was intense, dynamic and forceful. He inherited his father's brain, but differed from him in his quick, almost nervous movements, for one of Khama's characteristics was his measured, thoughtful way of speaking. This his grandson Seretse inherited from him.[14]

Tshekedi's lengthy regency of twenty-three years was characterised by dispute and controversy, both within the tribe and with the British administration in the protectorate.

The structure of the tribe starts with the family group, which in Batswana society is a collection of households, living together in their own hamlet. Families live in wards, which are under the authority of a headman who acts as an intermediary between the ward members and the chief. A Batswana town is really a collection of small villages, each village being the habitat of a ward. A kgotla is a meeting place, and a family can have a kgotla, so can a ward. Then there is the main kgotla of the tribe, the chief's kgotla, where all the important announcements are made, where the regiments are called up, and where serious cases are tried.[15]

When Tshekedi assumed the mantle of chieftainship,[16] he was determined to follow in his famous father's footsteps and to continue with his programme of taking the best of tribal custom and tradition and amalgamating it with the attainment of the white man's skills in an effort to improve the tribe. In later years, Tshekedi was to be described as "this great African" by Sir Winston Churchill, and by other people as a progressive and able administrator who was fiery, dominant, coldly aloof and at times puritanical. A Whitehall official who had many dealings with him described him as the perennially angry young man of the Bamangwato.

Education was Tshekedi's main priority. He called out the age regiments to build schools, including a controversial secondary school at a place called Moeng, which was situated in a beautiful but remote valley. The backbreaking work that went into the clearing of the site and the erection of the building caused intense resentment against Tshekedi, for the regiments were not paid.

He also had dams and roads built, grain silos, and a water reticulation system installed, and his energetic figure darting from one project to the next was a familiar sight.

But Tshekedi's enthusiasm for these projects, worthy as they were, was not generally shared by the Bamangwato, who found the severe, Spartan way of life that they entailed too burdensome.

The first major controversy in Tshekedi's life occurred shortly after he was installed as regent, and it could have cost him his life. It involved the Ratshosa family, the head of which was of royal lineage, angered by Tshekedi's action in abolishing the Regency Council which had been an administrative measure until he took over as regent. They had seen it as a means of extending their influence, and it wasn't long before some minor quarrel between Tshekedi and the Ratshosas ended in court, before the chief's kgotla. The Ratshosas were sentenced to corporal punishment when they initially failed to appear for their case. This humiliation enraged them, and two of the Ratshosa brothers escaped from the kgotla, ran for their guns, and fired on Tshekedi, grazing him but wounding two headmen. They were sentenced to ten years imprisonment, and several members of the family were banished by Tshekedi, who also ordered the burning down of their stone and concrete houses.[17] This strong action of his had repercussions later when the British curtailed the power of the chiefs.

One of Tshekedi's first disputes with the British administration arose over a mining concession granted by Khama III to the British South Africa Company. Tshekedi was informed that the original concession had been approved by the British Government, and when he was advised to sign it, he refused and took legal advice from a lawyer in the Cape, Douglas Buchanan, who was to prove a valuable ally to Tshekedi in his contentious life.

Tshekedi sailed for England to see the secretary of state about the mining concession, and a new one, drawn up in 1932, was so advantageous to the tribe that the British South Africa Company soon abandoned it. The question of mining in the Bamangwato Reserve was to crop up frequently over the years, and Tshekedi's handling of it showed a skill and competence for which he was admired.

While he was in England, he also obtained an assurance that the British Government would not hand over the protectorate to the Union of South Africa without first asking the Batswana's opinion. The question of the incorporation of the three high commission territories (Bechuanaland, Basutoland and Swaziland) into South Africa was a highly contentious one, causing great unease and insecurity amongst the tribes. Sir Peter Fawcus, resident commissioner of Bechuanaland, told me in his retirement in an interview at his Scottish home that Tshekedi's greatest service to the protectorate was his campaign in the 1930s against transfer, which attracted sympathetic public attention in Britain.

The Ratshosa affair led indirectly to British reforms of the tribal administrative and judicial system. In the early 1930s the British Government felt it was necessary to investigate a change in the method of governing Africans in the Bechuanaland Protectorate, and a commission of enquiry appointed in 1931 also looked into the control of tribal funds, the chief's use of age regiments, and generally at ancient tribal law and custom.

How were the British administering the territory at this stage? Mary Benson in her biography of Tshekedi Khama explains that ultimate responsibility for the government of the high commission territories lay with the Queen of England and the British Parliament, acting through the secretary of state for the Dominions. The latter delegated power to the high commissioner for the territories, who until 1928 was also governor-general of South Africa.[18]

This was an ambivalent situation according to Benson, for when the two offices were separated, the high commissioner both supervised the territories and represented the United Kingdom in the Union Government on its annual migrations between the seat of administration in Pretoria and parliament in Cape Town.

The chief or native authority was supposed to have a large measure of independence albeit taking advice from the resident magistrate.

However, the chief's powers were being gradually curbed, and the high commissioner had the power to depose or banish chiefs. District commissioners – magistrates – heard cases involving whites and cases where the death sentence could be imposed. They were supposed to be closely involved with the life of the tribe and were the authority on its activities.[19]

In 1931, the resident commissioner made it known that the British Government was considering introducing reforms to local government. Two draft proclamations put before the Native Advisory Council (consisting of chiefs and tribal representatives) for their consideration were criticised by Tshekedi as an encroachment on native law and custom, and when they were enacted the following year, he challenged their validity in court. The young chief of the Bangwaketse, Bathoen II, who was to be such a staunch friend of Tsheke-di's in the furore over Seretse's marriage, supported the court action, but they lost their case, and with it some of their chiefly prerogatives.

The greatest drama in Tshekedi's life before Seretse's marriage occurred in 1933, when Tshekedi was accused of flogging a white man in his kgotla.[20] The young chap in question had stepped over the line that in those days divided whites from blacks. He was keen on a Mongwato girl and had assaulted a black man in his ardour. He chose to go before the kgotla rather than the district commissioner and was sentenced by Tshekedi to a flogging. There is some dispute as to whether he was formally flogged, or simply beaten by tribesmen indignant at his behaviour, but the result was the same as far as race-conscious whites in South Africa and Southern Rhodesia were concerned: a black man had struck a white one.

The resultant uproar was such that the acting high commissioner, who was also commander in chief of the Royal Navy in Simon's Town, Admiral E.R. Evans (Evans of the Broke), rushed in a naval detachment with 300 soldiers and marines and armed with three ships' guns to put down this "insurrection" on the edge of the Kalahari Desert.

The farce assumed new proportions when one of the guns was aimed throughout the hearing (held under a canvas canopy in an official's garden in Palapye) at the passive Tshekedi's head. And the comic opera continued the next day when the navy, dragging the guns through the thick sand that consti-tuted the road between Palapye and Serowe, got bogged down, and the friend-ly Bamangwato had to help drag the guns out. The judgement was handed down by the admiral, attired in the finery expected of a man in his position, on the open parade ground in Serowe.

The show of force required a naval salute as the admiral mounted the dais, and as the guns boomed out, the Bamangwato, who had been assembled neat-ly behind a white line a discreet distance from the dais, threw themselves face down in the sand. Embarrassed officials motioned them to stand, which they did, amazed that their huts and they themselves were still in one piece. But the next volley found the tribe flat on their faces again.

After these trying moments, the admiral sentenced the bareheaded Tshe-kedi to banishment in Francistown, 210 kilometres to the north of Serowe. Tshekedi was also suspended from the office of chief and told he could not communicate with the tribe.

After the admiral had been driven away, the white population of Serowe, including the parents of the flogged boy, filed past Tshekedi to shake his hand and to tell him how sorry they were about his punishment and how they looked forward to his return.

The case made world headlines. Letters poured in for Tshekedi and included a request to name a tobacco company after him. Many letters, filled with sympathy and photographs, were from British girls.

But the incident embarrassed the British, and after two weeks of exile, Tshekedi was taken to the Cape, where he was handed a telegram from the English king, announcing the termination of his suspension and banishment. This was done in view of Tshekedi's abandoning any claims to the right to try "a European".[21]

Seretse was twelve years old at the time of this incident and was at school in the Union of South Africa. He wasn't particularly happy there, for he missed Serowe, his playmates, and his uncle whom he had come to regard as his father. He had been orphaned at the age of ten when his mother Tebogo died, and Tshekedi had taken him to live with his family in the large Victorian house which Khama III had built between the rocky outcrop of Serowe hill and the kgotla. The house had a corrugated iron roof, and during the violent summer storms, Seretse would lie awake in his bed at night, listening to the rain thundering down. The gardens and houses of other members of the family were laid out nearby, and Seretse knew the house well, long before his mother's death, for it was only a few metres away from his birthplace, and it is Bamangwato custom for children to spend time with various members of the family.

Seretse spent his childhood in his mother's picturesque house, in Tshekedi's kgotla house, and in another house belonging to his uncle which was situated on the other side of the kgotla hill, near the homes and offices of the district commissioner. Tshekedi's second home was as gracious and Westernised as the first, with a large brick chimney, a veranda supported by wooden poles, and large Victorian sash windows. A stockade fence surrounded the lovely house, and syringa and flame lily trees adorned the garden.

Seretse's love of hunting was fostered when as a young boy he would ride on horseback with his uncle, friends and relatives, to the cattle posts, and in those days the country teemed with animals, ranging from lion to elephant and buck of various kinds. He enjoyed sitting around the fire at night, watching its sparks flashing into the clear night air, hearing the lowing of the kraaled cattle, and listening to the men talk about tribal affairs and about their history, customs and traditions. As he settled down to sleep, under the night sky he so loved, he gazed up at the brilliant stars, which, polished by the dry desert air, twinkled down at him.

It was on these trips that the greatest interest of his life, cattle farming, was fostered. In years to come, when he was president, he was never happier than when he was out in the flat, open country of his birth, inspecting his cattle and deciding on some new form of stock control or breeding.

As a little boy, he sometimes went with his mother to the lands and saw the extremely hard work of ploughing, sowing and reaping, and helped to chase away the brilliantly coloured birds such as the shrike and lilac-breasted roller, that are a feature of Botswana.

In Serowe, he tore happily around the village, playing with both his tribal friends and the sons of traders. Whoever they were, they were all conscious of one thing; their playmate was of royal extraction, he was the future chief. His position was drummed into him both by Tshekedi and his mother and, when she died, by Tshekedi's wife. He learnt to accept the deference of his future subjects, about his place in tribal life, and what was expected of him. As he grew older, he sometimes watched his uncle dispensing justice in the sandy, stockaded kgotla and began to ponder his own position as chief and, being an extremely intelligent child, began to wonder what would happen if he was a bad chief.

But when he was young, these were half-formed thoughts. He was more concerned with chasing dassies and shooting birds with his young playmates. The Serowe dam, about ten minutes' walk through the village from his kgotla home, was a favourite haunt, for the boys would race along the wall and paddle in the water, watching the cattle meander slowly down to drink. Seretse was a mischievous child, on one occasion stealing food from his aunt's three-legged black cooking pot as it stood over the fire and racing away with his friends before the loss was discovered.

His mother had a hard time trying to discipline him, for he was a great favourite of Tshekedi's and got away with exploits that others did not.[22]

In the evenings, after supper, the men sometimes went back to the kgotla to chat around the fire, the air rich with the smoke from aromatic wood they had chopped up. The women sang around the fires in their courtyards, and little girls danced, while boys played rag-tag amongst the huts. When the villagers heard lions roaring nearby, it often meant that livestock was being poached, and the next day a party would set out to hunt them.

The school in Serowe was run by wise, gentle Tsogang Sebina, who told me before his death that the young Seretse was a lively, naughty boy in class too. "He didn't like anybody looking at his exercise book when he was working. He used to say, 'teacher, they are copying from me'," said Mr Sebina in the flawless, beautifully articulated English that he spoke far better than many who call themselves English.

It was he who was given the task by Tshekedi of accompanying the six-year-old Seretse who was suffering from tonsillitis to hospital in Johannesburg, along with the "royal retinue" as one Johannesburg newspaper described it, of secretary, personal attendant and nurse. In future years Seretse would return to this city as the gravely ill president of his country for medical care.

Seretse's status was never forgotten, not even by his playmates who also came from the royal family and were usually his cousins. One of his friends, Lenyletse Seretse, later to become Botswana's vice-president, recalled that custom did not allow anyone to eat from the same plate as royalty. He was doing just this one day, when Tshekedi noticed and asked who he was, and Seretse replied that they were friends. The royal status was equally evident at the South African schools he had attended, especially those run by the London Missionary Society which had converted his grandfather to Christianity and whose churches filled the protectorate.

But although his status set him apart, he never showed by any word or deed that he was to be chief, and the friendly, gentle and considerate manner that was his hallmark in later years, first manifested itself at boarding school. Seretse was a big chap, with a broad chest, and muscular arms and legs, for he enjoyed sport. He was of average height at five foot, eleven inches, and his features were typically African, for he did not inherit the aquiline looks of his grandfather. The humour for which he was so loved and for which he later became famous developed at a young age, and his eyes and his lips always seemed to have a smile lurking there, although he was also a serious young man.

He was at school at Lovedale in the Eastern Cape when he fell ill, and Tshekedi was so concerned about his health that he sent him to Cape Town for treatment of what was thought to be bronchial catarrh. After a series of tests, doctors suggested he had tuberculosis, and he was sent home to recuperate for a year in the dry Serowe climate. He was thrilled, for he spent much of his time out at his beloved cattle post, and his tuition continued under the extremely competent Tsogang Sebina.

It was while Seretse was at Tiger Kloof Mission Station near the South African border town of Vryburg that he contracted severe pneumonia. When he heard the news, a distraught Tshekedi hired a car and a nurse to accompany a Bechuanaland Protectorate medical officer, who rushed to the bedside of the dangerously ill seventeen-year-old. The popular Seretse, who had fallen ill after a football match, soon recovered. He completed his Junior Certificate, and then with his Bamangwato friends, Gaositwe Chiepe and Goareng Mosinyi, he matriculated at Lovedale.

Gaositwe, later to become Botswana's minister of mineral and water affairs, told me that Seretse tried to hide his royal status as a Khama at Lovedale, so that he would not be set apart from his colleagues. His plan, not surprisingly, didn't work, and on one occasion, he was panic stricken when he was recognised at a public concert, and people began shouting, "We want to hear the voice of the chief."

He whispered to Gaositwe, "What shall I say?" and she wisely replied,

"Say, 'Hello. Now you have heard my voice, and it is just like anybody else's voice.'"[23]

After he had matriculated in 1941, Seretse went to Fort Hare, the university attended by so many African leaders, situated in the Eastern Cape Ciskei town of Alice. Seretse graduated with his Bachelor of Arts degree in 1944, at a time when his future wife was tearing around the war-torn British countryside as a transport driver in the Women's Auxiliary Air Force.

The following year, Seretse was at the University of the Witwatersrand, when Tshekedi and the tribal elders decided that it was time he took over the chieftainship. Seretse had misgivings about directly assuming the position and said that he wanted to work under his uncle for two years before taking over the reins of power. His ambivalence about the chieftainship, his questioning of the wisdom of hereditary as opposed to elected leadership, troubled him deeply at this time, and he wanted both a breathing space and to further his education. It is not clear whether he was already entertaining at this early stage the conviction he held much later, that the time of chiefs was past, that Africa had outgrown them.

When Seretse said he wanted to read law at a British university (which had been Tshekedi's original ambition) the regent called together the tribal elders for their opinion on the matter, and they acceded to Seretse's request, as did high commissioner Sir Evelyn Baring. Tshekedi's lawyer, Douglas Buchanan, therefore arranged for Seretse's admission to Balliol College at Oxford University.

Seretse set sail for England in August 1945, and on the same boat were two young men, Brian Nkonde and Sfile Thileshe, with whom he became fast friends. Tshekedi went to see his nephew off at the Cape Town docks, and as the band played and people threw streamers from the ship, the uncle's eyes misted with emotion and pride at his "son's" brave step. How could he possibly have guessed it would be the last time he would view Seretse with such unquestioning love, and that the vessel was carrying him into stormy waters that would batter them both in coming years.

Seretse took a little while to settle into university life in the strange country and climate, amongst people he found so different from the warm and friendly ones back home. But once he began playing rugby for Balliol (under a South African captain) and became noted for his boxing ability, he felt more at home. However, his academic career was fraught with problems that were not of his making.

He was supposed to read law, but soon after his arrival, he was persuaded by his academic adviser, Sir Reginald Coupland of All Souls College, to change to politics, philosophy and economics. Sir Reginald felt this would provide a broader-based education for the young man from Africa, but his suggestion was met with absolute dismay by Tshekedi. On 26th November 1945, he wrote a sensible letter to Seretse, "My dear Sonny ... I feel doubtful whether English politics would be of practical help to you in South[ern] Africa, because our political conditions are very different indeed."[24] Tshekedi was following his lawyer's advice, for no one knew better than Buchanan how much the regent had had to rely on him for legal advice before he could act in certain matters.

Seretse accepted Tshekedi's advice, and in his reply, telling his "father" so, he mentioned how very homesick he was feeling. He added sadly, "I hope I will not continue to make as many mistakes as I have made up to now."[25] He must have been feeling very low indeed at that stage.

There was dismay all round the following year when Seretse, due to mistakes made by Balliol in the post-war reorganisation of Oxford, was not allowed to sit for his exams. Seretse was extremely peeved and understandably so, at the waste of time and money, and in June 1946, he wrote to Tshekedi, suggesting that he should concentrate on becoming a barrister, and that the best place for this training was in London, and not at Oxford. He was most concerned at his lack of professional training, and wrote, "If I were to lose my position for some reason or other as chief, or my country was annexed to the Union of South Africa, economics or politics cannot help me very much in the Union."[26]

The threat of incorporation into South Africa was a very real one, and it clearly worried Seretse as much as it did his uncle.

Sir Reginald in a letter to Tshekedi took note of Seretse's desire to leave Oxford and study in London, and he emphasised to the regent the social and intellectual advantages of college life. These he wrote, "cannot be obtained in the scattered world of London."[27]

He concluded, "If his advisers decide ... he should go to London, so be it, but I think it would be a real mistake."

In the troubled years ahead, Tshekedi must often have thought of Sir Reginald's words, for they were prophetic ones for the regent.

FIVE

Ruth meets Seretse

There have been many extraordinary stories of how Ruth met Seretse. Some have claimed it was at a sleazy dance hall where black men went to pick up white girls; others had Ruth working as some sort of ministering angel to seamen in British ports, although how a Londoner was supposed to meet an African chief studying law in a Liverpool or Bristol seaman's club is hard to imagine.

It is also incorrect. Ruth met Seretse through the church, a missionary society, the London Missionary Society to be exact. But before we look at that meeting through the eyes of Ruth and her sister Muriel, let us look at the kind of life Ruth was leading at the time, and the world in which she was living.

Ruth had been demobbed about halfway through 1946 into a world that struggled to start anew. Refugees, displaced people and demobilised soldiers were trying to return to what had once been a home and was now often a pile of debris from which remnants of families had fled. Worldwide, more than sixty million people had died, and many more had been maimed, both physically and mentally. About 70 000 British civilians lost their lives. England had a massive deficit and rationing continued.

But life returned slowly to normal as museums reopened, concerts and especially the cinema became popular again. Britons and Europeans began to catch up on the entertainment they had missed, and they flocked to see Lauren Bacall and Humphrey Bogart in *To Have and Have Not*, based on the novel by Hemingway. Charlie Chaplin's parody of Hitler, *The Great Dictator*, was a great success, and audiences were thrilled to see plays such as Eugene O'Neill's *Long Day's Journey into Night*. They read Ernest Hemingway's *For Whom the Bell Tolls* and listened to Gershwin's *Rhapsody in Blue*. Musicals were a powerful attraction, particularly *Oklahoma*.

In 1946 a Labour government under Clement Attlee was in power, busy paving the way over the next few years for introducing the welfare state, the National Health Service, and the nationalisation of the railways and of the coke, gas and electricity industries. The Conservatives had gone into the election of July 1945 full of confidence, for led by Churchill they held 432 seats out of 615 in the House of Commons. In one of the most surprising upsets in modern political history, the Conservatives were however lamentably defeated at the polls. It was the first time that Britain had elected a Labour government outright, and many people were stunned.

One of those shattered at the Conservative defeat was George Williams, for he was a staunch Tory, although he was never involved in party work. The Labour win upset his belief in the might of Britain and the British Empire. And the riots in India as that continent agitated for its independence must have shaken the stern traditionalist to the core.

Muriel, who was a committed socialist and who worked as the youth secretary for the local missionary society, was interested in, and could understand, the stirrings of revolt by the colonies against their masters. She had always argued politics and religion with her father, but as he grew older and more set in his ways and beliefs, she spoke with newfound knowledge. Their exchanges grew more heated, and Dorothy Williams came to dread them.

Ruth had never been particularly interested in politics, apart from being a Conservative because her father was one. She was far more interested in her ballroom dancing, ice skating and horse riding. At twenty-three years of age, she was a most attractive young woman. She wore her copper hair brushed off her face with a parting on the left, and it tumbled in curls on to her shoulders. She followed the fashion for fuller and longer skirts, higher heels and accentuated waists. The plump, sports-mad schoolgirl, who had become a listless anaemic, emerged from the war an independent, fairly self-assured woman, who was mindful of her father's strictures, but nonetheless had a strong will of her own.

Ballroom dancing was her first love, and she went to classes in Blackheath, nearby her Lewisham home. She had got the senior bronze medal and was working hard towards the silver medal, which entitled her to teach dancing, when she met Seretse. She also went ice skating with a group of her friends to the select Queen's Club in Bayswater, the gracious upper-class district near Hyde Park. She loved waltzing on ice and was good at it. Although she said she was never much good at horse riding (she went to a riding school in Blackheath), she always compared herself with Seretse, who was almost born in a saddle, a horse being the major form of transport when he was a boy.

Riding was one interest she was able to continue with when she went to Serowe. But foreign countries were the last thing on her mind back then, as she rushed from work each evening with either her riding clothes, her skates or her ballroom dancing shoes. Life was full, she seldom had an evening free, and when she did there was usually some young man who danced attendance on her, although if he got serious or hinted at marriage, she would warn him off. She was still not interested in a serious relationship, for the tension of the war years had left its scar.

Muriel, meanwhile, was working in a predominantly male world, that of auditing, and she found life at Deloittes, the chartered accountants, stimulating. There were only five women out of 500 on the audit side, and she loved learning about accounts and taxation. Her lifelong interest in Africa, its peoples and politics, was awakened when as youth secretary of the local missionary society in Lewisham she was asked to take charge of one of the Bible study groups and found herself at a young people's missionary conference in Hayward's Heath, Sussex, in 1946. Muriel was also an attractive woman, she had reached her full height of five foot, ten inches, was blonde, big boned and serious. Her interests included classical music and plays by Chekhov.

Her Congregational church had always asked missionaries to address it during its missionary weekend, but the one Muriel attended departed from tradition. Two young men from Northern Rhodesia (now Zambia), Brian Nkonde and Sfile Thileshe, who were studying law, history, economics and social work, spoke instead.

Muriel was fascinated by their descriptions of life in Africa and learnt during the discussion groups that the two had come over on a ship from South Africa with other students, and that they were living in a hostel, Nutford House. It was situated near Marble Arch and sponsored by the Colonial Office. Students from all over the world, Africa, India and the West Indies, stayed there, and swapped stories about their peoples, customs, history, problems and political aspirations.

In time, many of those students would become heads of state, presidents, prime ministers, attorney generals and so forth. But in 1946 the real influx from the colonies had not begun, and many of the students were lonely, surrounded by an alien culture, and dismayed by the cold and dismal climate.

Muriel also discovered that some of the students were living in her home suburb of Lewisham. She invited them to her church, which raised some congregants' eyebrows for they weren't sure about socialising with black people.

Muriel had no doubts on that score, and it wasn't long before she was being invited regularly to dinner at Nutford House, where her friendly and approachable manner was much appreciated.

Seretse arrived at the hostel about midway through 1947. He had been lonely in England, for when he first went to Oxford, away from the warmth and love of his extended family circle and from people who knew all about his illustrious background, he felt isolated. Tshekedi and his lawyer Buchanan were aware of this, and they contacted friends in England so that Seretse was invited to their homes, and on his own initiative he worked as a farmhand in Northumberland during one vacation. Once he began playing sport, however, his social status altered, and by the time he left Oxford, he was enjoying the social life.

London seemed huge and unfriendly by comparison, although he soon cheered up when he found his shipboard friends, Nkonde and Thileshe, at Nutford House. But it is important to understand the enormous difference between the natural warmth and friendliness that characterises African tribal life from the reserved, rather withdrawn approach to life of the English. If there had been lots of young black girls in London then, as there are now, it is possible that Seretse might not have met Ruth or fallen in love with her.

Muriel met Seretse on one of her visits to Nutford House, and she was struck immediately by his lively intelligence, his tremendous sense of humour and his presence, for although he never told people he was soon to be chief, and in fact disliked it intensely when mention was made of this in conversation, he nonetheless had the bearing and dignity of a chief. In later years, people would remark that when Seretse walked into a room, they were aware that here was a man, a chief, a big person. He didn't set out to create this aura, it was just there.

At twenty-six years of age, Seretse was striking, with his broad shoulders and strong rugby thighs, his humorous, sloe-shaped eyes and his broad smile. He was studying law at the Inns of Court, learning about British politics and way of life and enjoyed meeting people from cultures different to his own. It was a time too, in which he was appraising his future chieftainship, for one of Seretse's lifelong characteristics was his dislike of clubs, sects, clans and tribalism. He had an extremely broad and balanced view of life, which was not fettered or blinkered by group identities based on race, religion or culture.

Muriel asked Seretse and his friends to tea one afternoon, for Ruth could bake marvellous cakes, but he stayed behind in London, saying it was too hot to move in the trying English heatwave. And so it happened that his friends met Ruth before he did, and returned with glowing accounts of her, pointing out how much the two of them had in common, and when they next met Ruth, they expounded on Seretse's finer points. It was a few months after Muriel had met him that she was invited to a dinner dance at Nutford House, and she asked Ruth to accompany her.

By then Seretse had heard about Ruth's many admirers, and she had been told of his popularity. His friends kept saying, "You must meet Ruth, you have so much in common." Ruth said later, "When you are continually told you really should meet so and so, your immediate inclination is not to do so."

The first meeting with Seretse was inauspicious. Both had heard too much of the attributes of the other, and being of such independent natures, this had given rise to a certain antagonism and tension. Ruth puts it more strongly, "He was the rudest man I had met, not bothering to rise when I entered the room, something I was not accustomed to." This was totally uncharacteristic of the extremely polite and courteous Seretse, but she did not know that, and he found her dance card filled, and no opportunity to talk to her after their initial greeting. They thought each other most conceited. "I was not charmed. I didn't know what it was that we were supposed to have in common," said an indignant Ruth later.

Nonetheless, she thoroughly enjoyed the evening, finding the other students great fun to meet. She was naturally vivacious, witty and amusing, and she loved a party.

After that initial meeting, the couple met each other again, at social functions at Nutford House, on outings to the theatre, to jazz clubs, for they both loved jazz, and to restaurants. These were group outings, and then one evening Seretse invited Muriel and Ruth to accompany him to the London Palladium to see his favourite group, The Inkspots. Three or four months after their first meeting, Seretse took Ruth out to dinner alone, and a mutual attraction became apparent. "I liked him at that stage, I wouldn't have gone out with him otherwise," said Ruth. She wasn't quite so appreciative of his culinary tastes, for he was partial to curry, and had discovered a little restaurant off Shaftesbury Avenue famous for it. Ruth, too polite to say anything then, picked her way through the dishes, eating little. Sometimes Charles Njonjo, who became a lifelong friend of Seretse's and who was later also to marry a white woman and to become Kenya's attorney-general, accompanied them to dinner or the theatre.

At that stage, Ruth had no idea what a chief was, she was bewildered when his friends jokingly addressed him as one. But she wouldn't admit this to Seretse, and his friends later explained his background to her.

In those early meetings, Ruth talked about the war and her work as a transport driver in the WAAF, and Seretse began to tell her about his country and the people who lived there. Ruth did not know, as was the case with most Britons, where Bechuanaland was. She had never heard of it. Its size, 581 730 square kilometres in area, which makes it a little larger than France, stunned her. Seretse told her about the sparse rainfall which often meant starvation for the Batswana, about the Kalahari Desert which covers more than four fifths of the country, and about the terrific heat which can result in temperatures of forty degrees Celsius and more. He talked about the country's flat features, few hills, no mountains to speak of, and the unchanging vegetation, but through the realistic description ran the thread of love for his vast country.

There were living at that time in Bechuanaland 300 000 black people and 2300 whites, and the latter ranged from British administration officials such as district commissioners, agricultural and veterinary officers, policemen, doctors, post office staff, nurses and teachers, to traders and farmers. Many of the whites came from South Africa, were Afrikaans-speaking, and some of these people were the descendants of the trek boers. One such group, the Thirstland Trekkers, wanted to head across the Kalahari to Angola in the time of Khama III, and he warned them it was suicidal. But with their contempt for the black man, they disregarded the wise old chief, and many died of thirst in the barren wastes.

Those who struggled back settled in villages on the edge of the Kalahari Desert, and one of those was Serowe, which was situated, as most of the Bechuanaland villages were, to the east of the country, near the north-south railway line, which ran from the Cape to Northern Rhodesia. Bechuanaland resembled a sand-filled basin. On its east were low hills that faced the Limpopo River, and on the west was the Kalahari Desert, home of the last surviving Bushmen. Nine tenths of the country was covered by savannah; bush savannah in the south and tree savannah in the north. People who traversed the country by train regarded it as the most boring part of their long journey and pulled down the green blinds to shut out the intense heat and glare.

It was undoubtedly a hard country in which to live, both for the tribesmen who depended on the erratic rainfall for food, and for the whites who suffered in the terrific heat and struggled to maintain their civilised existence in remote villages with few amenities to make life comfortable. A typical village would include anything from 400 to 20 000 tribespeople, a couple of traders with their stores, a garage, post office, hospital, butchery, church, jail and the British administration offices and homes. Less than half a dozen white families lived in some villages whilst bigger ones contained up to 100 families.

There were three tiers of social strata. There were the black people, with whom very few whites mixed with the exception of the missionaries; then there were the traders, blacksmiths and garage owners who were generally Afrikaners; and finally the British administration officials and their families. The latter two groups mixed to a lesser or greater extent depending on the community, although the difference in education, background, and consequently interests did not usually result in close friendships between them.

Bechuanaland was divided into tribal reserves, Crown land and the Tati Concession. Five tribal boundaries were defined shortly after the country became a protectorate, and most of the remainder of the country became Crown land (that is, belonging to the Crown). Inside the reserves each tribe used its land freely without any fear of conquest; no white person could own land or carry on business of any kind without first having obtained the consent from the chief and the tribe. The Tati Company, which had its origins in the 1860s gold rush in the Francistown area, owned a vast stretch of land in the north-east of Bechuanaland. It leased and sold farms to white settlers.

The sheer size of the territory and its sparse population (a square kilometre for each inhabitant) resulted in a fairly lonely and isolated existence for the whites who relied a great deal on one another for company. At weekends they would travel for hundreds of kilometres along often extremely sandy or badly corrugated roads that twisted through the bush, to play cricket or tennis matches and to enjoy a party. British officials were transferred from one village to another every few years, which resulted in people right across the vast territory getting to know each other well. It was not uncommon for them, tearing along the dirt tracks for kilometres on end without seeing another soul, to stop in the middle of the road when they recognised the people in a passing car and have a social chat.

White families in Bechuanaland generally regarded it as a man's country. White men left their wives alone for days on end as they went on official trips into the bush, or hunted amongst the teeming herds of wildebeest, hartebeest, springbuck, kudu and the considerable numbers of lion and elephant.

Their wives baked cakes in heavy black ranges stoves heated with wood and took their children and their nannies to bridge and tea parties. There was no electricity, and drums of water heated by a wood fire in what were called donkey boilers provided baths. Paraffin pressure lamps that gave off a continuous hissing sound provided light, but also attracted clouds of insects. Charcoal coolers were used as fridges until paraffin ones arrived. Water-borne sewage was virtually unheard of, and long drops (deep pits sprayed with chemicals) or bucket latrines were the order of the day.

Life was easy on the one hand, for cheap labour provided servants for even the poorest family, but this was offset by the loneliness, intense boredom, stifling heat and lack of any form of entertainment. For some women the snakes, spiders and scorpions that lived in many of the rambling old houses were a constant nightmare. If someone fell sick and the hospitals with their fairly limited facilities could not cope, it meant a desperate dash hundreds of kilometres to the south to Mafeking or Johannesburg, or north to Bulawayo or Salisbury.

In my parents' time white babies were often born by the light of an oil lamp, and in remote areas were christened in the dining room during a pastoral visit. All fresh milk was boiled, but white people mostly used powdered milk. Often water had to be boiled too. The heat was so intense that meat was sold and eaten, tough as it was, on the same day, although many of the traders' wives could roll up their cotton sleeves and single-handedly cut up a bushbuck from which they made biltong.

After a hard day's work, white men would stomp in from the bush or office, covered in sweat and dust, shout for their bottle of brandy or gin, and settle down for what many people jokingly referred to as the "main occupation". If you didn't have a sundowner, you were considered a little odd, and alcoholism and cirrhosis of the liver were widespread and caused considerable concern.

When the rains came, the lessening of tension was tangible, and the dry, dusty countryside would bloom with wild flowers; frogs struck up their croaking chorus, joined by cicadas, beetles and crickets; and mosquitoes intensified their nightly bombing raids.

Women wrestled gardens from the sand and stone, while their husbands grew vegetables; and woe betide the person who left open the garden gate for goats and mules to wander through and eat the hard-won produce. Most of the water came from boreholes and rainwater tanks and occasionally was carted in drums from the river or a dam.

Seretse, in the first few months of meeting Ruth, gradually conveyed to her a picture of his harsh, but fascinating country. The contrast between the rainy, fog-ridden, densely populated British Isles, and the dry, sparsely populated Bechuanaland Protectorate could not have been greater, and it intrigued Ruth.

Her interest could not be shared by her father, for neither she nor Muriel dared tell him that she was seeing a black man. Mr Williams, whose views on mixed marriages and people with dark skins were commonplace in the 1920s – in fact the reverse was regarded as eccentric – had not changed his outlook in the 1940s. He might have told his daughters romantic tales about rajahs and tiger hunts, but that was where it stopped. He was horrified when Muriel joined the missionary wing of the local Congregational church, for in Ruth's words, "He was one hundred percent anti the London Missionary Society." And in Muriel's, "He was, I regret to say, a racist." It was a great surprise to both of them that he had kept his strong views to himself, until Muriel began to talk about missionaries and the students she was meeting. The upshot of that was Mr Williams's stern warning that social mixing with the students was not allowed, although he could not very well stop Muriel's work with them.

"You can belong to the London Missionary Society," he said to her, "but don't ask me for a penny for them." Mrs Williams, on the other hand, with her tolerant attitude, became the confidante of both girls, and she was soon told about Seretse, a secret the three kept from George.

It is indicative of the dominant position held by Mr Williams in his home that, even at the ages of twenty-three and twenty-four, his daughters, who had after all fought fires, saved people from death and seen others die, were so aware of his attitudes that they did not talk at all about their social activities with black people. They believed the resultant fuss and their mother's distress regarding the uproar would not be worth it, so they kept quiet, opting instead for what they called an unstressed, peaceful life.

In retrospect, they both felt that maybe they should have brazened it out and told their father, but in the early days Ruth and Seretse's relationship was a casual one. True, Seretse did drop the odd remark that an outsider might have construed as being serious, for example, at their second meeting he jokingly introduced Ruth to a friend as his future wife.

"But he would have been horrified if I had taken him seriously," said Ruth, "for at that time, casual, flirtatious talk was the mode. Today relationships seem to be so instantly intense and serious, but then, and particularly with Seretse, talk was light-hearted and fun. That suited me, for I didn't want serious involvement. There was plenty of opportunity to be serious, but I wasn't interested."

It was a little while later, during a conversation which turned to children, that Seretse, taking Ruth's slender white hand and placing it next to his large black one, said, "Our children will be somewhere in between these two colours." Ruth did not respond in a serious manner, for Seretse's teasing, jesting manner was so much a part of him that many people did not know when he was being serious, and there were even some who did not believe that he could ever be serious.

He had a dry sense of humour, not unlike that of Mr Williams, and was able to wisecrack and play practical jokes with such a straight face that some people were quite put out.

Ruth and Seretse realised the depth of their feelings for each other when Seretse, on returning from a holiday, found that Ruth had been seeing other men. He was unhappy about this and told her so. She had never made a secret of her admirers, and for a while they stopped meeting. It is possible that this would have been the end of their friendship, if they hadn't bumped into each other again on the street one day and realised as their eyes met how deeply they did care for each other. Thereafter the relationship became serious, and about fourteen months after their first meeting, Seretse, who beneath the jocular exterior was deep thinking and sensitive, told Ruth that he would like to marry her.

He agonised over his proposal, made in June 1948, for when he made it, he told her that marriage was for life, and it was not something he intended to enter lightly. "It was something that he was very certain about, he never wanted a divorce or a separation. When he married, it had to be for all time," said Ruth. He hesitated a long time before he made his decision, for he knew his country, he knew Ruth's background, and he probably wondered how she would adjust to the change from her gay London life, to living in Bechuanaland, with its rural atmosphere and unsophisticated people and way of life. He probably guessed Ruth would be ostracised by the whites and wondered if she would be strong enough to handle this, for life in that vast country could be lonely at the best of times and simply miserable if you were a social outcast where personal contact helped to make life bearable.

The match between Ruth and Seretse seemed a most unlikely one. He was an African chief. It is true that he was sophisticated, Westernised, far more highly educated than the average Briton, but nonetheless, he was a man destined to rule a tribe living in the heart of Africa. He proposed to take a sophisticated, highly independent woman, who loved skating, dancing and the theatre, and integrate her into his tribe. How would the Bamangwato, who had in the past beaten a white man who made advances to a black woman, accept Ruth? What would they feel about having a white woman as a chieftainess? And what about the people of her own race, the British administration officials and their wives? They lived up on a hill in Serowe, deliberately apart from the villagers, clinging to their English heritage and culture with their silver cutlery and candlesticks, their pretty gardens, gloves and pith helmets. How would they regard such a marriage?

Then there was the third group in that village, the traders, many of whom were Afrikaners with their deep racial prejudice – what would their reaction be to such a marriage? There were also the problems of the Tswana language, culture and customs. Setswana is not an easy language to learn, and tribal customs were involved and intricate.

These difficulties were awesome enough without the added problem of their parents. Seretse was well aware from Ruth's vivid descriptions of her father of his attitude to such a marriage. He knew too that his dynamic, difficult uncle would be intensely displeased about the match, for he would not believe it was in the interests of the tribe, and they always came first as far as he was concerned.

The startling contrasts in their lifestyles and backgrounds also had a corollary in their own looks and personalities. Ruth was slim, fast-talking with quick movements, witty, fun loving, and very different from the slow-moving, plump and comfortable women of the Bamangwato. Seretse was big, powerfully built, highly intelligent, a deep thinker, someone who considered before he spoke, and then said only what he meant. He didn't react immediately to circumstances, which made him very different from the excitable Ruth.

They also held different views on politics and religion. "We didn't agree on either. If you don't have those things in common, usually you don't have a good marriage," commented Ruth. "Ultimately, we came together on the political scene, but never on religion." Seretse was non-denominational while Ruth was a High Anglican and determined to remain so.

She was politically conservative, and it was only when she met Seretse that she began to think about British colonial policy in Africa, although Bechuanaland was a protectorate administered by indirect rule. Ruth was typical of women of her age in not being interested in politics. It was her sister Muriel who was not typical in that area. But Ruth was not one to relinquish her ideas easily, and she and Seretse had some terrific political arguments. "Well, it was my fault we used to have them, because I used to overreact. You think you know everything when you are that age, when in fact you know nothing," she said candidly.

While there was much the couple did not have in common, there was quite a bit that they did. Both had had disjointed childhoods, although Ruth's until the war was stable and settled. But her evacuation, loss of her home, and four and a half years in the forces, had made her feel very unsettled. Seretse was orphaned at the age of ten – the year he went to boarding school – and he never really lived in Serowe for any length of time after that.

They had both been ill in their childhood, although Seretse's illnesses had been far worse than Ruth's. They both suffered terribly from homesickness, coming as they did from close, happy families, and Ruth's family structure was not unlike Seretse's. His extended family might have lived in the same village as he did, but Ruth's aunts, uncles and grandparents were very much a part of her childhood, often visiting her home.

What attracted Ruth and Seretse to each other in the first place, is a matter for conjecture. The aura of power and status, whether or not it is deliberately dispersed, is attractive, and Ruth consciously or not must have responded to it. Seretse, in common with many men, reacted to Ruth's good looks, her sense of fun, and her lively, outgoing personality. Apart from that, they simply fell in love. It was a love match, there is no doubt at all about that.

But the proposal, made in Seretse's deceptively casual manner during a meal at Nutford House, made Ruth's heart pound with its implications. She would have to give up her parents, her way of life, her friends and her country to live with the man she loved, for he made it quite clear to her that he did not intend returning to England. She had already by that stage given up a great deal in order to see Seretse regularly, for as their relationship grew in intensity, so her ballroom dancing, then her horse riding and finally her skating were thrown over for him.

She knew to a certain extent what lay in store for her in this unusual union. She had experienced racism late one night when she and Muriel were getting the train home from Charing Cross to Lewisham. They had been to a dance at Nutford House, and Seretse accompanied them to the station and was saying goodbye, when two men got into the compartment. Their anti-black feeling was unmistakeable, and a worried Seretse said he would go with them as far as Waterloo or London Bridge, to see if it made any difference. It did not, and the appalling talk of the men about nigger lovers, and what they would do with them, was nauseating.

Seretse therefore travelled all the way home with them, because he was frightened the men would alight at Ruth and Muriel's stop and beat them up if he left them. Muriel said afterwards she had no doubt there would have been serious trouble. "Less educated people always seem to feel more threatened by other races," she said. Seretse, having seen the sisters safely home, had to walk the ten kilometres or so back to Marble Arch, for at that time of night London's public transport did not run.

Seretse was seeing Ruth home on another occasion, for he never let them travel alone after that, when they nearly bumped into her father. They must have travelled down from London on the same train. As they approached the bus stop, Ruth whispered, "Look, oh for goodness sake, look, there is my father," and she pulled Seretse into the safety of a shop doorway. The military bearing of Mr Williams was unmistakeable. They waited for him to get his bus, and then hung around in the cold waiting for another, giggling at their narrow escape.

Ruth found the necessity for secrecy the worst part of their courtship, hating her duplicitous role and feeling torn between her love of Seretse and that of her parents, and knowing that it might end in heartache for them all. She didn't mind the mutters and stares, the odd looks that people shot at a mixed couple walking down a street or sitting in a restaurant.

All this flashed through her mind when Seretse asked her to marry him. She didn't answer him immediately, and he did not expect her to, knowing how seriously she would have to consider her reply. She went home to steak and kidney pie, for it was a Saturday (on Sunday there was the roast, on Monday bubble and squeak, rice pudding and custard), and she looked around her cosy home and wondered what on earth to do. She felt so overwhelmed by it all that she put the whole matter out of her mind, shelving it for a while. Muriel warned her that she should realise what an extremely difficult time she was in for, and as Ruth couldn't tell anyone else besides a close girlfriend, it must have been a fairly lonely decision.

The answer she would give Seretse did not come to her in a flash, for she had been thinking of it, albeit subconsciously, for a while. She had come to realise slowly that she wanted to be with Seretse wherever he was, and that she couldn't be happy living anywhere without him. But still she hesitated, for it was an awesome step, and it was Seretse who, a couple of weeks later asked her if she'd given his proposal any thought.

Seretse was not the first person to propose marriage to Ruth, but he was the first one to whom Ruth said "yes". When she finally gave her answer, after agonising over it, she and Seretse didn't rush out and buy a ring as most engaged couples do. They decided to keep it a secret until they had settled on a wedding date.

Seretse, who was studying for his final law exams, found the time somehow to look for a flat, although it took him three long, difficult months to do so. British landladies were not all that happy to rent to a black person. Finally, Seretse and Ruth had to be content with a tiny bedsitter in Notting Hill Gate.

Seretse had suggested that they should marry before telling Ruth's parents and his uncle, but Ruth was too close to her family to do that. "I wanted to give them the benefit of the doubt, to give them an opportunity to accept my proposed marriage," she explained.

They set the wedding date for 2nd October 1948. Fifteen months after they had met, and three weeks before their wedding, Ruth told her parents about it. Her father's reaction was much worse than she had anticipated.

SIX

The marriage

Ruth put off her decision to tell her father about Seretse and their marriage until the banns were called at the pretty stone church she had chosen for the wedding, St. George's Anglican Church in Campden Hill.

When she returned home from work one evening, she made up her mind that she could put the moment off no longer and, with a voice stiff with tension, she asked her father if she could talk to him alone. She had told her mother a little while earlier that she was going to marry Seretse, and Mrs Williams had closed her eyes in silent anguish, for she was torn between her loyalty to her husband and her concern at the unhappiness he would feel and her belief that her daughter should marry the man she loved.

Muriel and Mrs Williams waited nervously in the kitchen while Ruth and her father sat in the lounge. If they had expected a violent scene with shouting, none was forthcoming. In a sense it was worse, for Mr Williams, who was absolutely shattered by the news of which he did not have the faintest inkling, responded with a cold, icy anger. When Ruth blurted out her intention, he sat bolt upright in his chair, staring at her in horror and amazement, his senses screaming at him that this could not possibly be true. His darling, vivacious daughter was going to marry a black man, someone he'd never heard of in his life. His golden-haired lovely, who waltzed so gracefully and skated so beautifully, was going to live in an African village, amongst a tribe. It was ridiculous, quite out of the question, it must be a passing infatuation, he thought to himself. But she looked so resolute.

His deeply ingrained prejudice, so well hidden over the years, was spelt out painfully clear for Ruth. He was so opposed to mixed marriages, he said, that he would not talk to her again until she changed her mind.

"You can stay at home until you get married. After that you may not enter this home again as long as you are married to that man," he ordered. He did not throw her out immediately, no doubt hoping that his shock, silence and terrible anger would induce her to change her mind before the marriage took place. Ruth, whose face was as white as her father's, realised that the painful encounter was over. She tried to persuade her father once more to meet Seretse, but he sat, face in hand, staring blankly down at the carpet, and shook his head.

She left him sitting there in his broken state and, tears streaming down her face, went to find her mother. It was the hardest thing Ruth had ever done in her life, and it was the heaviest blow her father had received in his. Indeed, it was one he never recovered from, for he became very ill afterwards and had a stroke as a result.

Muriel said later, "I don't think I have ever seen anyone as shocked as he was. It was as if Ruth had deliberately dropped down dead in front of him. He went out with my mother to the local pub, but he just sat there, staring ahead, saying nothing, he was so shattered." He later told his wife that he felt he'd been ganged up on by his family, but as Ruth pointed out, it was impossible to discuss anything with her father that they knew would displease him. Conversation was consequently always steered to safe topics. It was tragic, but Mr Williams had only himself to blame for his abysmal ignorance about what was going on under his nose. He had hoped that his daughters would marry the sons of his friends, and it is possible that if Muriel had said she was marrying Seretse, he would have been as angry as he was about Ruth, although not quite as stunned, for he was well aware of her missionary connections.

When Muriel tried to reason with her father about Ruth's marriage, he accused her of leading Ruth astray with her friends, and added, "Don't talk to me about the marriage. I know my views. I know my mind." Mrs Williams, her comfortable, housewifely demeanour reeling under the impact of this family drama, begged Ruth to change her mind. The emotional trauma suffered by the family brought tears to Ruth's eyes many years later, but she was as obdurate in her way as her father was in his. She had not taken lightly her decision to marry Seretse and, despite all the heartache and misery, she was not going to change her mind now.

For the ensuing three weeks, Mr Williams and his daughter passed each other silently in the corridor on their way in and out of the house. Most of the time Ruth tried to absent herself from the flat, leaving early and returning late. Mr Williams in his desperation went to see a lawyer to find out if there was any way in which he could stop the marriage and was informed there was not. Ruth's mother took the brunt of his anger, for he barely spoke to Muriel, and he bottled up his anguish to such an extent that he never mentioned a word of it to his friends.

"That was the worst part of it," said Muriel. "He thought that everybody would be so ashamed. He thought that he would lose all his friends. Even when the marriage hit the headlines and his friends naturally found out about it, he refused to discuss it with them." His fears of ostracism were never realised, and maybe that was the hardest thing of all for him to accept. Attitudes had begun to change, people had moved on, but he had not.

Muriel felt desperately sorry for her mother and, during weekends when Ruth was with Seretse, she went for long walks with Mrs Williams, encouraging her to unburden herself. Muriel was also a great support to Ruth. Once she had overcome her surprise at her sister's match and accepted it – although she had always wanted to go to Africa, her younger sister was going to get there first – she provided calm, sensible assurance. "Well, I would have done the same thing under similar circumstances. We both had the utmost confidence in Seretse, he was the sort of person you couldn't help trusting."

The pressure was mounting on Ruth. When she handed in her resignation to the firm of underwriters at Lloyds, she was asked to leave immediately once the reason for her resignation was known. She could only conject this was due to racial prejudice. She later discovered, as do so many young people who try to keep liaisons secret, that she and Seretse had been seen on buses, in trains and walking down the street by several of her friends.

Seretse had moved into the little bedsitter he had found for them both at number 10 Campden Hill Gardens in Notting Hill Gate. One evening towards the end of September, he had sat down with a heavy heart and nervous hand to write to his uncle Tshekedi to tell him about the marriage. It was a task he had postponed until the last possible minute, and his anxiety is plain to see in his missive.

It went:

> Dear Father, as I write this letter, I am no longer at Nutford House. By the time you get this letter, the hostel will be closed. At present I am living at a place which is near Nutford House. It is a flat; I pay four guineas weekly without food, gas and laundry etc. Ruth Williams and I have decided to get married next month. We well know the difficulties that await us. Her father disapproves of our marriage. She is going through a very trying time at her home for me; and she knows well the difficulties that await her at home in Serowe. The banns have

now been published. Pardon me, father. Please send me some money soon. I sincerely hope you will not be blamed for my action. Please do not try to stop me, father: I want to go through with it. I hope you will appreciate the urgency of my request for money. This thing, my marriage, will not please you, father, because the tribe will not like it; and I do not know what the tribe will say. At first, I meant to keep this news away from you until I was married; but then I thought that this would be wrong. I am ready to come home, father, when you want me, to work for the Bamangwato in such way as they may wish. I did not ask for your yes to my marriage, for I know you would not give it: I am sorry, father. Your loving son, Seretse.[28]

Tshekedi was hurt, angry and confused by Seretse's letter. He had been looking forward to Seretse's return, for he had been regent for twenty-three years and was hoping to play a less active role in the tribe on his nephew's return. The regent's mind reeled under the impact of the news.

What could Seretse mean by taking a wife without first telling him and the tribe? He was the future chief – how could he act so irresponsibly, went the thoughts of the angry uncle. And a white wife – as chieftainess! Tshekedi's heart pounded and his pulse beat a nervous rhythm as he sat in the cool Victorian house near the kgotla and tried to imagine a white woman doing the duties of a chief's wife. How would she, an English speaker, counsel the subjects who tramped vast distances on foot through the bush to discuss their problems with her? How would she possibly understand the customs and traditions of an African tribe? How could she work on the lands as the tribal women did?

In addition to all this, there were the implications of the recent National Party victory over Jan Smuts's United Party in the Union of South Africa to consider. Mixed marriages were to be made illegal under the new apartheid laws. It was a violently disturbed Tshekedi who responded to his nephew's letter.

Telegrams flew between the uncle, surrounded by tradition in his village home, and the Westernised, detribalised nephew in his tiny London flat. They were worlds apart.

Tshekedi's cable went:

Your proposal [is] more serious and difficult than you realise. It is [the] surest way of disrupting [the] Bamangwato Tribe. You seem to have forgotten your home is [in] south[ern] Africa, not England. Have made immediate arrangements for your immediate return. Get ready to leave [at] moment's notice. I shall only discuss your proposal personally after your arrival here. I repeat, your proposal [is] more serious and difficult than you realise. Question of support quite simple. Can be adjusted here.[29]

When Seretse received Tshekedi's reply, he was so alarmed by it that after a hurried discussion with Ruth, he advanced their wedding date. On Friday 24th September, the day Seretse received that telegram, he went to see the vicar who was to marry them, Dr Leonard Patterson, and his request for the wedding date to be advanced from 2nd October to the following day was granted, although the vicar was naturally not told the reason for the change. Seretse merely told him that he had to return unexpectedly to his country. The time of 1.30 p.m. on Saturday, 25th September, was agreed upon.

But a great deal was to happen before the next day. Seretse had written a note to Dr Roger Pilkington, a tall, friendly man with some fame as a geneticist, who was a director of the London Missionary Society, informing him of his wedding on the 2nd of October. He had known Dr Pilkington for some time, having stayed with him and his wife both when he was at Oxford and when he moved to London, and he regarded him as a good friend and confidant. Although they were on friendly terms, the doctor knew nothing of his relationship with Ruth until he received the note on Friday, 24th September. He telephoned Seretse immediately to ask him if he had the tribe's permission, and was alarmed to hear he had not, and even more worried to hear that the wedding had been brought forward to the following day. If Seretse had had the faintest idea of the reaction that his news triggered in Pilkington, he would have kept quiet.

Pilkington later wrote to Tshekedi, "I had seventeen hours in which to act." And he hit the panic button. Acting with him in an effort to prevent the marriage, was the secretary of the London Missionary Society, Mr R.K. Orchard, who also that fateful Friday received a telegram. It was from Tshekedi's legal adviser, Douglas Buchanan, who had asked his brother John Buchanan to take all possible steps to prevent the marriage. The cable ran:

Chief authorises me to urge you to take every possible and impossible step to prevent Seretse, 10 Campden Hill Gardens Notting Hill Gate, marrying English girl on 2nd October. Consult Dominion Office re immediate priority air transport for Seretse to Africa. Suggest caution parson who called banns. If Congregational contact L.M.S. (London

Missionary Society). If Church England contact Archbishop. Consider extraditing Seretse. Inform girl's parents of ostracism and misery awaiting her. Such marriage possible cause Seretse's deposition ... Please act immediately.[30]

Orchard reacted by telephoning Pilkington whose worst fears were confirmed by the call. The two worried men organised a meeting at the London Missionary Society's Mission House for 10.30 a.m. the following day (Ruth's wedding day) and to it they invited Douglas Buchanan's brother John (an Anglican parson who lived in England) and the Reverend A.J. Haile, who had worked in Serowe and knew the tribe well.

Roger Pilkington had an extremely busy Friday. He got his wife, who was very friendly with Seretse, to ring him and organise a meeting. The somewhat surprised but courteous young man agreed but pointed out that it would have to be very late that night as he had to see his fiancée home first. Despite his politeness, Seretse was suspicious, and would give the inquisitive Mrs Pilkington no details about Ruth, other than her name. Armed only with that, however, Dr Pilkington had succeeded by that evening in tracing the Williams family. He learnt with dismay from Ruth's mother of the quarrel between the young woman and her father, and realised they no longer had any influence on Ruth, and that he was dealing with a determined personality who was not going to be deterred even by strong parental censure. He asked Mrs Williams if he could speak to Ruth and was met with silence when he told her about the ostracism and misery awaiting her in Serowe. In desperation, he appealed to Ruth to read a statement containing the wishes of the tribe, which would be sent to her the next day, and to this she agreed.

It was late that night before the busy Pilkington got hold of the vicar, Dr Patterson. He informed the astounded parson in no uncertain terms that Seretse was not free to exercise his choice in marriage, and Dr Patterson was so taken aback at this surprising piece of news that he agreed to postpone the marriage. But the vicar was to change his mind often during the next fifteen hours, and he was later described by Roger Pilkington as "a reed shaken by the wind".[31]

Although it was after midnight when Seretse returned to his bedsitter, the doctor and his wife were not to be deterred from their course by the time, and they traipsed determinedly up the stairs. Nor did the lateness of the hour take any of the sting out of Dr Pilkington's words. Among other things Seretse was told that he was behaving in a disgraceful, cowardly manner, not worthy of one singled out to be the ruler of the Bamangwato tribe. The lecture went on until 4 a.m., and when the Pilkingtons left, they were under the firm impression that Seretse was ready to delay his wedding and head home for Africa and the tribe. They believed later that it was only Ruth's "intervention" the following day that changed his mind. Poor Seretse, he was a man under siege, for before he laid down his weary head that night, he opened a telegram from John Buchanan, also requesting an urgent meeting.

Ruth's wedding day was to assume the dimensions of a farce, although no one involved in it laughed or even smiled. Ruth woke that Saturday morning in the bedroom she shared with her sister with wildly mixed feelings, for although she was about to marry the man she loved, and without whom she could not envisage her future, she was leaving for the last time, and in such traumatic circumstances, a family she had cherished. Mr Williams hoped desperately as Ruth and Muriel's goodbyes to their mother rang through the autumn air that some miracle would restore his daughter to him and prevent her marriage, and he would have been amazed if he had known how close his wishes came to be granted that day.

Ruth and Muriel arrived at the bedsitter, unaware of the council of war being held at the LMS's Mission House. There, four men, Orchard, Buchanan, Pilkington and Rev A.J. Haile, connected in various ways to the church, puzzled and agonised over ways of preventing this church wedding. All four believed sincerely that they were acting in the best interests of Seretse and his tribe, and indeed, of Ruth. The phrase about the "misery and ostracism" awaiting her in Serowe rang in their ears. And so they drafted a letter to Ruth, in which they told her that the Bamangwato tribe was, "strongly opposed to Seretse's marriage to a European."[32] They urged her not to marry until Seretse had consulted his people about the matter.

A messenger went by taxi to the Notting Hill Gate flat to deliver the letter, and returned to report that Ruth, without opening the letter, had said that there was no reply. The dismayed men noted that it was 11.30 a.m. Time was running out. Pilkington again telephoned the vicar, for he had detected an air of indecisiveness in his voice during their conversation of the previous night. He told the vicar that it was hoped Ruth and Seretse would postpone the wedding of their own volition, but urged him yet again to do nothing until he had had a reply from Ruth, or until he telephoned him again at about 1 p.m.

However, back at the bedsitter, Ruth and Seretse had read the letter and decided to continue with their wedding. Muriel helped Ruth to put on a delicate, pale blue frock and hat she had bought especially for the day. She had discarded any ideas of traditional white, for only Muriel and a couple of friends were to be at the church. As they chatted and watched the clock tick around to 1 p.m., the time they had set for leaving for the church, they had no idea that four men were watching the time too, but with grim determination.

However, by 1 p.m. no further news had come through, and Dr Pilkington got back on the telephone to the vicar, asking him to telephone Seretse and tell him that he could not conduct the wedding that day. The vicar was asked to phone back immediately after he had notified Seretse of this decision, so that the four men would know how he had reacted to it.

And that is how Ruth and Seretse learnt to their shock and dismay, less than half an hour before their wedding that it was to be postponed. But they had not battled their way through a storm of parental disapproval to give up at the last minute, and they rushed around to the Patterson's flat to discuss the marriage with them. Said Mrs Patterson later: "We reasoned with him about his obligations and duties to his country. Miss Williams said that she had left her home. So, I offered her free hospitality in our home until matters were clarified. This she refused, so I issued my invitation to him … He refused but thanked me for my kindness."[33]

At this point, the vicar's telephone rang again. It was 1.20 p.m. and the men at the Mission were frantic to know what was going on. The vicar replied, somewhat defensively, that Seretse had come to see him, had demanded to be married as a free man, and that he (the vicar) was inclined to go ahead with the marriage, and Seretse would have to take the consequences of it. Dr Pilkington could not believe his ears. His was later to compare the events of the afternoon with a Sherlock Holmes detective story.

He impressed upon Dr Patterson the serious results of such action, to the extent that the vicar, looking for some way out of his moral dilemma, decided to temporise by asking for the consent of Sir John William Charles Wand, the bishop of London, to the marriage before he acted. This was accepted by Pilkington, but the three men (Buchanan had dropped out) were not taking any chances with someone who could be swayed as easily as they now believed the vicar could be, and they leapt into a taxi and raced to the church. They hung around, fully prepared to raise an objection to the marriage in the church. They intended to point out that the tribe's opposition to a marriage, about which it had not been consulted and to which it objected, constituted a legal objection.

Ruth and Seretse told the vicar they had no alternative but to agree to see the bishop, although they were both extremely angry and upset at the unexpected turn of events. A white-faced Ruth was on the verge of tears, Muriel was stunned and Seretse was now grimly determined to outwit the three men who wanted to prevent his marriage to the woman he loved.

And so, on that autumnal Saturday afternoon, making their various ways to an ordination service they had no interest in at all, at St Mary Abbots Church in Kensington were: Ruth and Seretse, Muriel, the Pattersons, Orchard, Pilkington and Haile. The latter trio had waited at the church until 2.15 p.m. before again ringing the beleaguered vicar, who said he was on his way to the bishop. Ruth was by then emotional and tense. Seretse tried to muster his usual laconic air for her benefit, but he was exhausted from a lack of sleep, and the tension of the last few weeks showed in his anxious face.

He and the two sisters were not to know that by the time they reached the ordination service, Orchard, Pilkington and Haile who had got there ahead of them, had signed a hurriedly written note, asking the bishop not to consent to the marriage, as it was quite possible that the tribe's non-consent at that stage did impose a legal barrier. It had been carried immediately to him, for as luck would have it, the bishop's chaplain was a friend of Dr Pilkington.

"As we walked into the church, I saw Mr Orchard coming out, and as I knew him, I thought to myself, how odd it was to see this man from my Congregational church in an Anglican one," said Muriel. "But it never dawned on me that he would go to such lengths to prevent the marriage, I was too naive and trusting. And so we waited for the service to end. The bishop then came to us, and was very, very abrupt and cold. Ruth was getting a little hysterical by then … well, who wouldn't under such trying circumstances? And he said something to me about doing what I could to help my sister, because there were disappointments involved in not getting married, and that was it! What bothered me, was that nobody seemed to care how Ruth was feeling or about her reaction."

It was, of course, an extraordinary episode, which did no credit to the Church of England, although the bishop later claimed when the incident was discussed in the House of Commons that he had merely followed his usual custom in dealing with the marriages of non-nationals, by telling the groom to get in touch with the Colonial Office.

Whatever the finer points of the matter, it was three dejected, miserable people who were turned away from that church, and Ruth, whose religion had always played such a big role in her life, did not go back to it for a long, long time afterwards. But Seretse was not a man who was easily beaten. He booked Ruth into a Bayswater hotel, and then the three of them went out to dinner with an old friend of Seretse's. After they had eaten a little and discussed the traumatic events of the day in detail, Seretse told Ruth of a new plan he had, and they all cheered up. Seretse was fully aware, with his knowledge of law, that there was no legal impediment to the marriage, and he decided that they would obtain a special licence from a registry office on the Monday and marry without the sanction of the church, in view of its refusal to give it to them.

That night, after kissing a weary goodbye, Ruth, Seretse and Muriel lay awake in their beds in different parts of London and pondered over the day's nerve-wrecking events. Ruth had made Muriel promise to tell her mother she was married, for she didn't want any more obstacles put into their already rock-strewn path.

"I had therefore to pretend to my mother about the wedding and the details, and it wasn't for years that she found out it wasn't on that Saturday after all," said Muriel. Mrs Williams said to Muriel, "Thank goodness you didn't tell me, because there was enough to go through at that time as it was, without having to worry about the whole marriage business." There is a sea of sorrow in those words.

"No further action was taken during the weekend, because we felt that it had been very harrowing and unpleasant for the two young people, and that it was best to leave them to cool off," reported Dr Pilkington later to Tshekedi,[34] in what sounds very much like a dispatch from the front, and no doubt he saw it all in pretty war-like terms. His affection for Seretse is clear in his letter, for he wrote, "He will, of course, be very angry that I was concerned in this business, and it is safe to assume that I have sunk for the moment from the position of his best friend to his worst enemy. I am not worried by this, however, for I know that his future and to a certain extent even that of his country, depended on our intervention, though I cannot expect that he will easily realise the good turn that was done to him on Saturday."

There was a great deal of letter writing going on in that weekend "lull". For one, the director of colonial students at the Colonial Office, John Keith, who had been contacted by the four men, thought that all registry offices should be notified of the possible marriage, and he wrote a note to his superior suggesting this line of action. Fortunately for Ruth and Seretse, it was a suggestion that the secretary for the colonies did not accept, and it was agreed that Keith would see Seretse on the Monday and persuade him not to take action until he had consulted his tribe.

Someone else who was busy with a pen that Sunday was John Buchanan, who wrote to his brother Douglas about his view of Miss Williams. He had gathered that she was a "respectable, not very intelligent girl, inspired possibly by a sort of proselytising zeal to improve relations between the native and the white. If this is true, she will possibly be more difficult to deal with than if it had been the case of a chorus girl or suchlike, when money would have talked possibly," he wrote. "I gathered it was Pilkington's view that neither Seretse nor the girl would be the least affected by money or economic outlook," he told his brother.

This was surely an extraordinary letter, suggesting as it does that Ruth might be brought off and the marriage prevented in this manner. And he was not the first person to write in such a way.

John Buchanan wondered what the future of Seretse in Britain would be if he gave up the chieftainship. How would he earn a living? He wrote to his brother, "How long could such a marriage last in this country (where just as I know so well in Northern Rhodesia) there is in theory no Colour Bar, but in practice!!" He concluded, "What possible hope have any children of such a marriage?"[35]

These were depressing and sobering thoughts indeed and reveal yet again the amount of prejudice that existed in Britain at the time. But Ruth and Seretse had decided to marry, fully aware of the odds stacked against them, and as Ruth said later, "The more opposition we encountered, the closer we drew to each other."

The astute Dr Pilkington realised that this was probably the case when he wrote to Tshekedi, giving him his view of the weekend's events. He also firmly believed that Ruth had persuaded Seretse to marry her after he had shown the young man, during his midnight call, the error of his ways. There were many people in the years to come who were to comment on Ruth's strong personality and will, but no one who really knew both her and Seretse well ever doubted that beneath his at times laconic exterior, was a person who knew his own mind. Seretse was so democratic in his outlook that he always listened to people before making a decision, but that certainly did not make him a reed in the wind.

On the Monday and Tuesday, following their abortive wedding day, Ruth and Seretse lay low. They had learnt their lesson well. A clear twenty-four hours had to elapse between application for a special licence and a marriage, so they took a train to the coast on the Tuesday and had an amazingly relaxing time under the circumstances, while the London Missionary Society, the Colonial Office, and the Commonwealth Relations Office tried to establish their whereabouts and future plans.

It was a very different outfit that Ruth wore to the Kensington High Street Registry Office on the 29th of September 1948. The beautiful blue frock had given way to a black barathea suit which nonetheless looked stunning on Ruth's trim figure and was possibly not as inconspicuous as she had intended it to be. They were the first couple married in the registry office that day, and the simple ceremony was attended by Muriel, a female cousin of Ruth's, and Charles Njonjo, Seretse's good Kenyan friend.

"We were all very highly strung, we felt like criminals," said Muriel.

"Everyone we saw we thought was someone trying to stop us getting married. I had become quite a nervous wreck by this time, quite neurotic, but determined to go through with it," said Ruth.

When the time came for the registrar to write down the profession of Seretse's father on the marriage certificate, Seretse said, "tribal chief". The registrar looked up in amazement. "What did you say?" And Seretse with his typical quickness of mind and his humour, said, "Oh, just put, gentleman farmer."

Ruth felt so weak with nervous tension that her voice had almost disappeared by the time she was asked if she was prepared to marry Seretse, and it came out in a squeak. But once the magic words, "I pronounce you man and wife," were delivered, the sense of relief was overwhelming. Laughing and joking, the party hugged and kissed each other, almost weeping with joy, and Ruth and Seretse held hands as if they would never let go of each other.

Muriel, who was late for work, dashed off to the office, and Ruth and Seretse set off for the city to have a celebratory lunch together. That evening they threw a party in their tiny bedsitter, managing to squeeze about twenty people into it. Ruth at last wore her pretty blue dress, and an aunt and some cousins were amongst the revellers. They had kept their marriage so secret that one of their student friends had no idea what the celebration was for until he saw the ring on Ruth's finger.

It was later that week that the London Missionary Society rang Muriel, to express their concern about Ruth's wellbeing, and to voice their distress that she had not been able to marry, and they offered the disappointed young woman their assistance through her sister.

"Look, you've left it a whole week, don't bother," retorted Muriel. And added, "Besides, they are married." She was both furious and terribly disillusioned by the behaviour of her church and the role it had played in trying to prevent the marriage.

Tshekedi was equally unaware of the marriage. Some days after the registry office ceremony, Seretse received another telegram from him. It went:

> You are apparently taking no notice [of] my strong objections to your marrying an English girl. I ask you [to] pay attention to what [the] Commonwealth Office advises you. Your obstinacy [can] only result [in] serious consequences [to] yourself. Have asked Commonwealth Office [to] arrange immediate return. On no condition can we agree to your marrying [an] English girl.[36]

Seretse, who was always both brief, and pertinent, answered: "Already married. Ready to return with wife."

Tshekedi was down, but not out:

> Formal signing of document in England does not constitute your marriage. As far as we are concerned, no marriage exists. Apparently you took my strong advice for [a] threat. We accept nothing short of dissolution of that marriage. Our decision [is] firm. Welfare of [the] tribe paramount in this case.[37]

Seretse cabled back: "Tribe and you [are] important to me. Suspension of allowances being felt. Suggest passage for two. Dissolution [is] unacceptable."[38]

It is obvious from these telegrams that relations between the two men were rapidly becoming strained, for Tshekedi was shattered at what he considered to be the flouting of both his and the tribe's authority, one of the cornerstones of Tswana tradition. Seretse on the other hand was determined not to be treated like a little boy.

There was only one ray of light in the darkness of all this parental disapproval and anger, as far as Ruth and Seretse were concerned, and that was Mrs

Williams. Dorothy said to her husband one day, fairly soon after the marriage, "You say you won't allow Ruth to come home, and that you won't see her. But there is no way that I can stop seeing her." And off the brave little woman went, to visit her daughter in her new home. Ruth met her mother with tears of joy and love, showed her proudly around the tiny flat, and made her a cup of tea.

Seretse met his mother-in-law for the first time shortly after that, at a fete held at Muriel's church at Lea Green, and they soon charmed each other, for Ruth's mother was the natural, gentle person she always was, and Seretse was his kind, polite and considerate self. It always amazed Muriel that Seretse, despite her father's total rejection of him, was always polite and respectful to him. He was able, in spite of the hurt and rejection, to understand how Mr Williams was feeling, to appreciate his point of view and his anger at the loss of his daughter. He even defended Mr Williams when Ruth and Muriel attacked him for his behaviour.

It was about the time of that fete that the London press caught up with Ruth and Seretse, and the first of many headlines, describing the marriage of "Black Chief to London Typist" appeared. The inaccurate label was to irritate Ruth for the rest of her life.

SEVEN

The tribe rejects Ruth

Ruth and Seretse had been married for less than three weeks when they were separated, and their marriage was subjected to the kind of tension and strain that would conceivably have broken up many of today's less committed relationships. Tshekedi continued his bombardment of letters and telegrams, urging his nephew to return to Serowe to discuss his future position with the tribe. Being the determined, vigorous personality he was, Tshekedi also approached the British administration in Bechuanaland, asking it to assist in getting Seretse to Africa by an administrative order.

And, putting on the pressure, he cut off Seretse's allowance, which was due by right to the chief designate from his father's estate. Seretse was keen to write his final Bar exams at the end of the year and to take his wife home to Serowe. But he realised after a while that there was no alternative but to go without her, in view of Tshekedi's stern opposition to Ruth going to Serowe until Seretse had faced his subjects.

Seretse confided in Ruth his fears about the reception he would get from the tribe, for he had not been home for nearly four years, he felt out of touch with his people, and he wondered what would happen if they rejected him. He worried about where he and Ruth would live if he couldn't take her home.

It was with great reluctance that Seretse finally agreed to leave Ruth behind, and he only did so after being given an undertaking from Tshekedi and the tribe, through the Commonwealth Relations Office, that he would be allowed to return to London if he wished to do so. It was an extremely apprehensive couple that kissed each other a sad goodbye in mid-October 1948. Ruth felt sure of Seretse's great love for her as she nestled in his arms. But who was to know how he would feel and how he would react when he saw the rocky hills and great plains of his country again and met the friends of his youth.

Ruth was having an extremely difficult time. George Williams would still not allow her to come home and refused steadfastly to see her. Muriel moved into the tiny bedsitter when Seretse had gone, to keep her sister company.

Number 10 Campden Hill Gardens was one of about a dozen bedsitters in an old house, and as Muriel soon found out, had only one bathroom, which was shared by all. This was not unusual in Britain then, but what caused Ruth great heartache, with her passionate attention to detail and cleanliness, was the fact that nobody, except for her and Seretse, took the trouble to wipe the bath after use. "He was the only black man in the house, and they talked about black people being dirty!" she exclaimed furiously.

The room they lived in contained two armchairs, a couple of beds that doubled as couches, a gas fire and a washbasin. The kitchen that led off this was big enough to turn around in but not much more. To get to the bathroom, they walked out on to the landing, and the one thing that did gratify Ruth was their room's position near the top of the house. Muriel was also under stress, for she had to divide her time between her job, Ruth, and her parents. She was particularly concerned about her mother, in view of Mr Williams's continued anger at Ruth's marriage. Nobody knew how to break the impasse. Muriel would rush over to Lewisham on a Saturday after work and take her mother out for a walk, have tea, and then go back to Ruth. It saddened her that her father still blamed her for Ruth's marriage. Ruth also met her mother regularly, either inviting her to the bedsitter or meeting her in a teashop in Blackheath. Otherwise she occupied herself as any young bride of that time was expected to, with shopping, cleaning and cooking, although not many women carried out their chores worrying about an absent husband, a wrathful father, and an uncle-in-law bent on destroying her marriage.

Tshekedi had already suggested to the British administration that Seretse be exiled for five years on political grounds until he gave up Ruth. It was even suggested, before Seretse decided to return to Bechuanaland, that he should be kept in England and be paid an allowance, like a remittance man. The irony of the latter was that the colonies were usually used by aristocratic British families for dumping their embarrassments, and not the other way around.

Later on, when Tshekedi was asked how he thought Seretse could "get rid of his wife" he said, "We felt it was a matter of negotiation. We did not think it could be done by law, but possibly with an explanation of the position in South[ern] Africa, with explanations to the parents of this woman and herself we might have got the couple to realise that the step taken was not in their interests."[39]

Tshekedi was later to complain bitterly that if the British had given him the support he needed during the early days of that marriage, to uphold both his and the tribe's authority, subsequent events would have proved less traumatic.[40] But the British view at that early stage was to maintain the strictest neutrality, so that it could never be said in the future that the government had influenced decisions in any way. The extreme irony of this will emerge later.

Seretse flew in to the Johannesburg airport of Palmietfontein on 22nd October. Tshekedi was not there to meet him, and he left the following day for Bechuanaland where he met up with two good friends from his childhood, Lenyletse Seretse and Gaositwe Chiepe. As they drove home to Serowe, along the thick sand roads, winding their way through dense thorn bush, so different from the plane trees and pavements of London, Seretse told them about his English wife, and laughed at the very idea that he should give her up. The trio arrived home in the early hours of the morning, as the cocks were crowing the village awake, and blue smoke from breakfast fires drifted up past thatched roofs.

Seretse was not to know that within a year the tranquil village would split in two, and families divide right down the middle as they would take sides in the uncle and nephew dispute. He made his way to Tshekedi's gracious Victorian home near the kgotla, and no doubt enjoyed surprising the man who always had everything under tight control with his sudden arrival.

Tshekedi, with his quick, nimble movements, clasped Seretse's outstretched hand, while his busy eyes searched those of the much taller, larger man opposite, and he thought to himself, why, why, why, did you have to spoil all my plans by marrying a white woman? He felt an enormous sense of responsibility for the tribe's welfare, and being the caretaker of the chieftainship, he could quite simply not begin to comprehend what he regarded as Seretse's totally irresponsible behaviour.

Uncle and nephew lived under the same roof for a while, and Seretse was taken to the kgotla where he sat with his uncle under the great mokala (camelthorn) trees, and was "shown" to the tribe, as was the custom. The thorny question of his marriage was not raised, nor was it proposed to be raised until he had had time to talk to his people and hear what they had to say about it.

One of the administration officials who was considered an authority on the traditions and customs of the Bamangwato, Mr G.E. Nettleton, thought Seretse looked cheerful and fit when he saw him, and learnt with interest that he was intending to write his law exams in December.[41]

He must have been surprised therefore to learn from Tshekedi that Seretse was moody, and on occasion burst into tears. Mr Nettleton deduced from this that Seretse was being told in no uncertain terms by Tshekedi that his marriage was not going to be allowed. The regent told Nettleton that his greatest fear was that Ruth, growing restive in Seretse's absence, would fly out, and he repeated his earlier request for her to be kept out of the protectorate. He also told Nettleton that if Seretse was to be chief, every possible means would be used by him to keep the young man from returning to England.[42]

The high commissioner, Sir Evelyn Baring's reply to this was that Ruth could not possibly be prevented from obtaining a passage out.[43] It was obvious at that stage that Baring was much opposed to the marriage, for anyone who lived in Pretoria, in the very heart of Afrikanerdom, as he did for six months of the year, could not help but be painfully aware of the abhorrence, even hatred, with which such marriages were regarded. He was much concerned the tribe would unconditionally accept Seretse as chief, but he did not act, hoping matters would be sorted out without outside interference.

Three big kgotlas were held during the course of the next eight months to decide what should be done about the marriage. The first of these was held about a month after Seretse returned, and it lasted for five days, from the 15th to the 19th of November 1948. Before describing the events that took place during it, it's important to understand how a kgotla or tribal assembly operated.

The kgotla met openly, and all adult men, even strangers, could attend and participate. Women at that time did not usually attend, although this was to change during the tribal dissension over the marriage. There was in theory great freedom of speech at the meetings, but in practice the fear of subsequent reprisals by the chief acted as a deterrent to free tongues. If during the debate opinion was so divided that the chief could not sum up and deliver a verdict, he could order the men to divide into two groups according to their opinions. The chief was strictly speaking able to override the wishes of his people, but in practice he seldom did so, because the cooperation of the tribe was essential for successful government, and if a chief acted contrary to public opinion, the result could be disastrous.[44]

The chief, whose prerogative it was to call a kgotla, sent his messengers days and sometimes weeks in advance to tell the headmen to inform their wards of the date of the meeting, for many came from afar, on foot along the twisting paths through the bush, on horseback, in trucks, on bicycles.

On the 15th of November they converged on the kgotla, wearing the odd assortment of clothes they often did, ranging from khaki to army greatcoats, pith helmets to trilby hats, some carrying walking sticks, others little stools. Many simply sat on the ground, and the 4000 present sat in a huge semicircle, facing Tshekedi and Seretse, who had near them their advisers and important relatives. That day these included the chiefs of three tribes. It was hot, and flies buzzed irritatingly around people's eyes. Goats bleated as they nibbled thorn trees nearby, and cattle lowed, the tinkle-tinkle of their cowbells drifting through the kgotla during the pauses in discussion. But the only people to notice these everyday sounds were the pressmen, to whom they were foreign.

Seretse felt a lonely man as he looked at that great sea of faces. He had moved out of Tshekedi's house before the kgotla, as their relationship had deteriorated. He had felt increasingly that the household, which included two visiting chiefs, Bathoen of the Bangwaketse and Sechele of the Bakwena, was against him.

Harsh words were spoken during the next four days, and they hurt Seretse. He was called a coward, told he ought to say outright that he did not want the chieftainship, that his heart was not with the tribe or his country, and that his father had been sent to wander in exile for having taken a wife without the tribe's consent. When the accusations were over, Seretse rose slowly to his feet, adjusted his sunglasses, put a hand in the pocket of his loose-fitting jacket, and looked slowly around the huge gathering. He then answered the charges against him honestly, admitting he was at fault for having taken a wife without proper announcement. "This is not custom, this is my fault and you reprove me for it, and you will judge me for it," he said. But he denied not loving his people, and he was able to say truly that he wanted to be chief, for there is nothing like opposition to make up your mind, and now there was no doubt in his about his course in life.

Then the staunch ally and great friend of Tshekedi's, chief Bathoen of the Bangwaketse, rose to his feet. He was a small man, with flashing eyes and a determined jaw, and was much loved by the journalists for his poetic utterances. "I said you fear the chieftainship," he said to Seretse, "and I say so again. Nobody can cast fire among people whom he loves," and he warned Seretse that the tribe would scatter from him. "If the people go from here, would you be chief of these poles?"[45] – a reference to the crescent-shaped, stockaded kgotla.

A blind, old uncle, his hair white with age, his dignified face lined and sad, rebuked Seretse for his marriage against all tribal laws. "If he wanted to marry and light the family fire, it must be done according to custom," he said.

"But Seretse has broken the family water pot."[46] A murmur of assent rumbled through the kgotla.

Then it was Tshekedi's turn to rise to his feet, and in a manner typical of him, he aroused the ire of the British officials present by thanking the district commissioner for attending the kgotla as follows: "When I invited him to this meeting, he did not refuse to come nor did he plead government business … mostly they (the district commissioners) stay apart, not knowing how we speak, how we act, and feel."

The chiefs of the Bamalete, Bakwena and Bangwaketse were addressed next: "A fire is burning in the Bamangwato, and you have come to pour water on it, so, I thank you."[47]

Now it was Seretse's turn to be addressed, and the highly-strung, nervously intense uncle, so different from his outwardly laconic nephew addressed the latter as a child. And in the long hours that ensued, the twenty-seven-year-old law student was not allowed to forget that he was a child, listening to his father. Tshekedi probably destroyed most of their filial relationship that hot day, in the kgotla, under the mokala trees.

Tshekedi reminded those present of custom. "When a new chief is to be installed, I call to you to say he has arrived. Then there is a time to teach him his duties, after which I must call you again to hand over the power to him. After that I can give him a wife, after having secured him in his position."[48]

Tshekedi took the British to task, the irritation clear in his voice as he said, "There is a special law for royal marriages. Had I had proper help, he would have been prevented from marrying before we could speak together." As Seretse heard those words, his mind flashed back to his abortive wedding day and to Ruth's frustration and great misery, and he thought again of the enormous contrast in their lives, and how hard it would be for her to imagine her humorous, witty husband being dressed down in his African village and reduced to the status of a child.

"I do not want the woman; if she comes, I go," cried the impetuous Tshekedi.[49] The district commissioner, despite his ticking off at Tshekedi's hands, had sympathetic words for the regent and the tribe in their great trouble, and he said he would refrain from asking them to join in the celebrations at the birth of Princess Elizabeth's first-born son, Prince Charles.

"The history of the Bamangwato tells of troubles from time to time, but I doubt if there was ever such a one as now," said the district commissioner, referring to the dynastic feuds that characterised the Bamangwato. "To you, Seretse, one word of advice. You have heard your fathers speaking to you. Do not disregard them," he concluded.[50] He wired the high commissioner shortly after the large assembly broke up, to inform him that although the kgotla wanted Seretse as chief, it had refused to accept Seretse's wife.

But Seretse was not entirely alone, for the good friends of his youth stood by him, although they were frightened of Tshekedi. Fear is a word that was often and is still often used to describe the regent, but the use of it should also be seen in terms of African culture, for in it fear and respect were synonymous, and they sprung from the belief that children should submit themselves utterly to a parent's authority with unquestioning, unanswering obedience. Out of this practice of complete submission gradually evolved something more than mere respect – almost holy awe for superiors.

This fear of the extraordinarily strong, autocratic, and at times ruthless Tshekedi, who had ruled the tribe for twenty-three years, did not easily allow rebellious thoughts, but a group of young lions was forming who were to call themselves the Sons of Sekgoma (a reference to Seretse's father), and in time they would make their voice heard. Now was not the time, for it was overwhelmingly clear that, while the tribe wanted Seretse for its chief, they did not want his wife.

It was a dejected Seretse who mentioned to the district commissioner that he thought it might even be an advantage as far as the women of the tribe were concerned for him to have an enlightened wife. How prophetic his words were that hot November day, for in time Ruth was to have a most beneficial effect on the women. But Seretse was not to know that then and, dismayed and disappointed by his reception, he could only suggest at that stage that he would take Ruth to Serowe as an experiment, and if she could not tolerate conditions he would allow her to return to England.

Seretse's ambivalence about the chieftainship had vanished completely after the kgotla meeting.[51] His view had been that hereditary chiefs were not necessarily good leaders and that they often abused their autocratic powers. He felt they did not rule democratically. But now he felt that, if there was to be a chief, and the tribe clearly wanted him to assume his rightful position, then why should he not bring an enlightened rule to his people? The deep-thinking, disturbed chief designate retired with some of his young friends to a cattle post, to rest and get away from the press, the tribe and his uncle whilst he waited for a second kgotla.

Meanwhile back in foggy London, the press was fascinated by a story which had for them all the ingredients of a pot-boiler: "Handsome black chief marries pretty white typist, but wicked uncle rejects the marriage."[52] It sensed there was even greater drama waiting in the wings, and it set up watch on the "pretty young typist", to monitor her reactions to the strong words emanating from the kgotla.

"Our bedsitter was in one of those old-fashioned houses which had a common front door that everyone had a key to, and then you went upstairs to your own bedsitter," said Muriel. "We would always make sure the door was locked, but the press bribed people in the building to open it, and we'd suddenly find them outside our room."

The young bride was pestered almost daily during the kgotla for her views on what the speakers had said. There was no time for Seretse's explanatory letters to reach her, the wires hummed across oceans and continents, and the nervous young woman, with no informed husband to guide her, took the safest way out and repeated constantly, "No comment."

The press was not happy. "What do you think about this? What do you think about that? When are you going to Bechuanaland? Have you had a letter from your husband today? What is your opinion of the uncle?" it pestered.

Having no luck, it tried Mr and Mrs Williams. The reluctant father-in-law who suddenly found himself front page news was absolutely appalled. The marriage had been bad enough with only a few friends knowing about his "shame". Now Britain knew. Naturally he had nothing to do with the press, but his friends were intrigued, everyone was intrigued, and still he refused to say a word, not even to his closest friends.

"I think that he still, in a way, had a persecution complex. I think he was quite disappointed that people didn't cut him dead, it just wasn't what he had figured out at all," said Muriel. "And yet, his friends wanted to sympathise with him, for they put themselves in his shoes, and they knew that they too would have been shattered by the experience of a daughter marrying a black man."

It was, quite simply, a nightmare for the whole Williams family. Ruth felt desperately lonely without Seretse and anxious that his feelings towards her might have changed during his absence. She wondered if Tshekedi and the tribe would be able to persuade him to give her up. As the slow days passed, she lost weight, and her pale face grew more and more tense. Those close to her knew how anxious she was feeling, by the way she rubbed her fingers nervously together and patted her hair in her customary worried gesture. She and Muriel discussed endlessly what they would do if Tshekedi cut off all Seretse's income, and they agreed they would club together and pay for his return fare.

They agonised over how to get rid of the press and were stunned when they returned to their bedsitter one evening to find a reporter waiting there. Furious, they told him to get out, and the nosey little man who had been ferreting around in the flat, and who had discovered Ruth's air force issue pyjamas said, "Oh, I could write an article about the man's pyjamas you've got in your house while your husband is away." Ruth blazed, "Go right ahead. But get out first." Seretse's warm, loving letters were the only things that saved her sanity during those agonising weeks.

While she battled on in London, and Seretse conferred with his friends at the cattle post, the vigorous Tshekedi was not idle. He realised after the first kgotla that Seretse was not going to give up his English wife in spite of massive tribal opposition, so he hotfooted it down to his lawyer in Cape Town. He faced a battery of reporters and cameramen as he stepped off the train in his summer suit, trilby hat and bright tie, but he was embarrassed by the attention and refused to answer questions. A few days later the resident commissioner wrote to the acting high commissioner, Sir Walter Harragin (who was standing in for Sir Evelyn Baring who had gone home on leave) that it appeared Tshekedi was planning to challenge the legality of Seretse's marriage.

His lawyer, Douglas Buchanan, had suggested that the marriage might be dissolved on the grounds that one of the parties came under Tswana law, the other under English law.

A few days later Ruth received a letter from Buchanan, saying that it was possible the marriage could be annulled. Frightened and alarmed by what she considered to be an intimidating letter, she rushed off to see Seretse's friend, Charles Njonjo, who was also a law student, and he was able to reassure her. "We seemed to be handling crises from minute to minute, but we just struggled through them, and it wasn't until much later that we realised how nerve-wracking it all was. But then it was too late, and it had taken its toll on Ruth," said Muriel.

Realising the marriage was legal and could not be dissolved or annulled, Tshekedi and his lawyer drew up a memorandum[53] presenting their position "in the political crisis occasioned by the marriage of Seretse Khama to Ruth Williams in England."

In it, Tshekedi asked the British yet again to keep Ruth out of Bechuanaland, saying they knew of no instance, "where an alien was permitted to force itself into a tribal society without the consent of the chief and tribe."

And he pointed out, a little petulantly one senses, that it must have been much more difficult for the government to exile a chief from his tribe (which was the treatment that had been meted out to him), or to remove a "European-born in a tribal area" (the treatment meted out to the young man flogged by Tshekedi), than it would be to remove Ruth.

Seretse was most unhappy when he returned from the cattle post and saw Tshekedi's memorandum. He complained that Tshekedi was holding secret meetings behind his back and said he wanted the memorandum confirmed by a full tribal meeting. The district commissioner, worried about the fast-deteriorating relationship between uncle and nephew, called a meeting of the three of them, at which Seretse expressed his dissatisfaction at the way the first kgotla was held. He said that Tshekedi, who held very strong views on the matter of his marriage, both personal and political, presided at the kgotla enquiry but could not possibly be impartial.

Seretse believed that Tshekedi was holding secret meetings to urge people not to accept him as chief. Tshekedi, enraged by the accusations and the implied flouting of his authority, hit back hard, and in his usual fiery manner suggested there could be political unrest and warned of a country rent by civil war. This was very strong talk indeed.

Seretse, who had been keeping his anger about the autocratic manner in which he had been treated by Tshekedi to himself, now reminded his uncle that he was not his "natural father" and therefore could not treat him in the way Khama III had treated his son Sekgoma. He pointed out to the now furious Tshekedi that he was after all only regent, and then tackled him about his property. This was to result in a civil action later, and so the property issue should be explained.

There were two sets of property in dispute,[54] that of Khama III and that of Sekgoma (Seretse's father). In view of Sekgoma's banishment, the Great Khama left his property in his will to his second son, Tshekedi. The will was made before Seretse was born. After Sekgoma died and Seretse was declared chief designate and Tshekedi became the regent, the latter called his tribal advisers and said he would regard Khama's property as belonging to Seretse, for he was after all the son of Khama's eldest son and could not be chief without property. He said he would not claim it, although it had been willed to him.

And so Tshekedi mingled the smaller herds of Sekgoma's with the great herds of Khama, and from that came Seretse's allowance. Now in his anger, Tshekedi threatened to claim the Khama property, and furthermore, to cut off Seretse's income altogether if he insisted on returning to his wife in England.

It was against this distressing background that a second kgotla to discuss Seretse's marriage was held after Christmas, on the 28th and 29th of December.

Although the tribe was still opposed to Seretse's marriage, some of its censure had lost its bite, and in some quarters the view was being heard that the marriage might even be pardonable if the tribe would in this way gain their rightful chief. Rumours had begun to circulate that Tshekedi was fomenting tribal dissatisfaction over the marriage, so that he could be made chief in Seretse's place.

People who were there at the time – members of the tribe, traders, administration officials – argued passionately one way or the other about Tshekedi having designs on the chieftainship. Some were quite adamant that the regent acted only in the interests of the tribe, and yet the other camp was equally adamant he was motivated by self-interest.

Whatever the case, the fact is that many in the tribe were tired of Tshekedi's dictatorial rule, and this began to emerge at the second kgotla. They were opposed to his use of the regiments to build roads, dams, schools and particularly Moeng College. They resented the levies they paid which financed these projects, and it would only be later that they would realise what an enlightened and progressive leader he had been.[55] The feeling of the second kgotla was perhaps best illustrated by an elderly headman who said in Setswana, "I thoroughly disapprove of the marriage – it is a bad thing – but I see what it all means. You want to destroy the marriage, which will require money – that means another levy. Let the wife come, let the wife come."[56]

People always tire of old leaders, particularly when they are as autocratic as Tshekedi was, and Seretse, sensing this, decided to play for time. He proposed to return to his wife and his studies in England, to which the tribe agreed. They suggested he report back in six months' time when they hoped he might have overcome what many of them considered to be an infatuation. Tshekedi and Seretse parted with cold, formal words.

Said Tshekedi, "I do not believe he will come back." And Seretse replied, "I am going to return soon." He left the tribe in no doubt about his sentiments. "Don't talk about me," he addressed the kgotla, "talk about me and my wife. If she is not acceptable, I will not come back." Tshekedi retorted, "If she comes, I go."[57] It was a deadlock.

Ruth had spent a miserable Christmas on her own, hiding from a press that continued with its unwelcome attentions. Here is an example of one of its distortions. One newspaper reported that Ruth had made some fatuous remarks, implying the high commissioner, Sir Evelyn Baring, who had returned to England on home leave, had in fact gone to Britain with the express purpose of intervening in her marriage.

What happened was as follows: the press told Ruth they had heard Baring was going to try and persuade her to give up Seretse, and they asked what her reaction to that would be. She had replied, somewhat naively, that she would be rude to anyone who tried to break up her marriage, and the subsequent headline ran, "Ruth Khama says 'I will be rude to Sir Evelyn Baring'." It was incidents such as this that resulted in both Khama's refusing for over a year to talk to anyone from the press.

Seretse returned to England on 6th January 1949, about ten weeks after he had kissed Ruth goodbye, and his overjoyed wife was waiting at the airport to greet him ecstatically before driving him home. When he walked into the flat, he was astonished to see it hung with Christmas decorations. Ruth, who had refused to celebrate it without him, had put up the festive bunting as soon as she heard he was returning. She had been through a desperately lonely time, for Muriel was torn between her sister and her parents, and they had decided she should spend Christmas day with her parents, and Ruth went to friends. With Seretse's return, things seemed to Ruth to improve, for he took a firm hand with the intrusive press, booting out an individual Ruth had dubbed "creeping paralysis".

"I'd go to my front door and find him sitting at the top of the stairs. The way he used to creep up them and give me a fright because I hadn't heard him was horrid," said Ruth. Seretse was, however, a light sleeper, and when he heard the creeping one night, he opened the door and sat there, waiting for his man, who, thinking he had reached his target safely, was startled out of his wits to hear a deep, quiet voice saying, "Yes? My wife told me about you!"

The next break in the clouds hanging over Ruth's life came when her mother asked Mr Williams if Ruth could come home when he was out. She had never hidden her meetings with Ruth from him, and after a lot of humming and hawing he agreed.

"He still refused to see Ruth, but I think he was almost African in his reaction. He didn't want to lose face, you see," said Muriel. And so Mr Williams went out if he heard Ruth was coming home, and then one day, Mrs Williams said to Ruth, "Why don't you just come home when your father is there, and let's see what happens." Ruth did so, and her father was terribly overcome and overwhelmed to see the daughter he loved so dearly. He clasped her slim frame in his huge embrace, and there were tears in both their eyes as they hugged each other.

"He hadn't realised how much he had missed her until he saw her. Whilst she was there, he would be warm and friendly, although of course Seretse was never mentioned, and then after she had gone, he would exclaim, 'Oh why, oh why did she have to do it', and he would go on and on about it," said Muriel. But the main thing as far as Dorothy Williams was concerned was that her darling daughter and her husband were together again.

A measure of calm, therefore, settled over the stormy lives of Ruth and Seretse.

EIGHT

The growing storm

In the two and a half months that Seretse had been in Bechuanaland, Ruth had lost four kilograms from worry and nervous tension, and one of the first things the couple did on his return was to catch a bus to the West End to have a celebratory dinner. They naturally had a lot to tell each other, and so involved were they in earnest conversation that it was some time before they realised they were the subject of curious glances.

In the period Seretse had been away, the constant photographs of them in the press ensured that on his return they would be easily recognisable. This isn't surprising, for they were both striking people, and although they might slip by unnoticed individually, at the time mixed marriages were infrequent in Britain. When they were out together, people glanced at them curiously at first, and then with growing attention.

Post from all over the world, simply addressed to "Ruth and Seretse Khama, London", started arriving soon after their marriage hit the headlines. People, it seemed, had a lot to say to the Khamas about their marriage. A large percentage of the letters were sympathetic and supportive, but, as anybody who had been in the limelight knows, there are lots of cranks who have little better to do than write silly letters. Some of them expressed disapproval of the marriage, and yet others contained offensive sexual remarks. Ruth soon learnt to look for a signature before bothering to read a letter – anonymous ones she discarded without a second glance. Before Seretse's return, Muriel would help Ruth open them, and she used to hide the ones which she considered distasteful and then burn them. Commented Muriel: "Until you get caught up in a situation like that, you don't realise how many unbalanced people there are around."

Seretse, who had been able to elude most of the press in his own country, now found he couldn't get away so easily, and although he was normally the most forbearing of people with his humour and generous smile, he grew irritated by the constant attention. One reporter who visited them described the couple as follows: "While he (Seretse) leaned against the doorway of this modest, two-roomed flat on the top floor of an old-fashioned mansion, his wife, trim and pretty in a dainty white apron, cooked a meal in the tiny kitchen. Tired of all the publicity her marriage has brought, she shut herself in and let her husband do all the talking."[58]

Yet another reporter asked them how Ruth would feel about, "digging potatoes and mealies, and working in the fields as a woman of the tribe?"[59] With some asperity, Seretse remarked, "It is not true to say she will dig potatoes. We don't grow them. She will not have to dig anything." And Ruth, who laughed at the reference to working in the fields, added, "It is a good job that I have a sense of humour."

This she had, although as some individuals and reporters soon found, it could be quite sharp when directed against them. Ruth knew her mind, and she knew whom she liked and whom she didn't, and those who found disfavour were not left long in the dark about their standing.

A short while after Seretse's return, the couple moved to a large flat, in the north of London. 34 Adolphus Road, Manor House was very different from the cramped bedsitter. For a start, it was clean, "beautifully kept," said Ruth, to whom the middle-class virtues of cleanliness and neatness were always so important. It was a ground-floor flat, in one of those lovely old houses that had been divided up into apartments, and it boasted not only its own bathroom, but a spare bedroom, sitting room and a spacious kitchen that Ruth, who continued to enjoy cooking felt she had room to move around in. A feature of it that particularly pleased her were the French doors, opening from both kitchen and lounge on to a small, walled garden.

Seretse continued with his law studies, working towards his exams in May, after which he planned to return to Bechuanaland to establish finally whether the tribe would accept him with Ruth. But studying hard wasn't easy for him with the constant press interruptions, and the disturbing letters from his friends back home in Serowe containing reports of Tshekedi's plots to keep Ruth out and to litigate against Seretse.

Tribal factions and feuds – going back nearly 100 years to the time when Khama III fought his pagan father so that he could practise his Christianity, and which had split the tribe then – had never stopped simmering below the surface of tribal affairs. The two opposing sides became known as the Sekgoma (Seretse) and Khama (Tshekedi) factions, and British administration officials who said they knew about what went on beneath the polite facade of the average Bamangwato, wrote official memorandums warning that the marriage was becoming of secondary importance. Ruth was emerging as a mere pawn in a game in which battle lines were being drawn to establish a new power base. One official believed that to the Sekgoma faction, "this marriage is made in heaven," for opposition to the marriage gave them the opportunity they needed to pose as champions of legitimacy, of laying the foundations of their own future prosperity and of paying off old scores.

And while there was no doubt about the existence of the factions, the result of the third kgotla was not their work. But we shall return to that aspect of the whole affair later. We will leave Ruth and Seretse now, in their roles of student and housewife in the cold of a London winter, and return to hot Bechuanaland, where Tshekedi was raising a great deal of dust, both literally and figuratively, as he tore about the country making his plans.

Tshekedi fired off a series of letters and memoranda to the administration in such quantity that he appeared rather like an embattled general, firing missiles frantically in the hope that some would reach its target. He continued with his efforts to have Ruth officially prevented from entering the Bechuanaland Protectorate and suggested that an alternative might be a temporary order until he had brought a court order declaring that she was not the "queen elect" and that children born of her marriage to Seretse would be incapable of inheriting the Bamangwato chieftainship. The desperate regent did not hear until April 1949, when he met the high commissioner Sir Evelyn Baring, that the administration would not comply with the request to exclude Ruth from the territory. His extreme bitterness against the man he called his son emerged when he pointed out to Baring that Seretse had shown himself incompetent to ever be chief, and that if he wasn't chief he could not live in the Bamangwato Reserve as a private individual. It was at that meeting that he asked Baring for a third kgotla to be held, which he said would show once and for all that the tribe did not accept the marriage of Seretse to Ruth.

Baring agreed to the kgotla, and Tshekedi hurried back from Cape Town to Serowe to tell his followers. The engine of his car was hardly cold before he dashed into the district commissioner's office to inform him that if Seretse announced at the third kgotla that he planned to take Ruth to Serowe, he would not hand over the chieftainship but would make Seretse fight him for it. Tshekedi was in fine fettle, for he added that he would not go into self-exile as he had said he would earlier on, but he would remain in Serowe and "resist everything that Seretse does to the end."[60] Note this last claim of his, for he would change his mind again before the year was out.

Tshekedi's lawyer wrote a frightening memorandum[61] to the administration for his client, in which he talked about the necessity for arresting Ruth on arrival, about armed camps and civil war. One of the factors which was undoubtedly adding to Tshekedi's fury was Seretse's (not surprising) lack of letter writing. "Seretse is corresponding with a number of his friends, but never writes to me,"[62] he complained to the resident commissioner in Mafeking, It was from this town outside the protectorate borders that Bechuanaland was administered.

A month before the vital third kgotla, Resident Commissioner Anthony Sillery assessed the situation for Baring as he perceived it in Serowe.[63] He could not have been more disastrously wrong, for he believed the bulk of responsible opinion in the tribe was still opposed to the marriage.

There was a lot of excitement in Serowe in the days that preceded that kgotla, and obviously some of Tshekedi's prognostications of doom hit their mark, for the security measures taken to control the passive tribe during the tribal assembly would have been far more useful three years later when that characteristic passivity turned to violence.

All police leave was cancelled, an intelligence system was set up to establish the identity and plans of potential trouble makers, the hospital was alerted there might be riot victims, the sale of arms and ammunition was prohibited, and the possibility of evacuating "European inhabitants" from Serowe if the situation called for it was considered.

In addition to all this, tear gas bulbs and cannisters were obtained from the Union of South Africa's Defence Force, and the commissioner of the Basutoland Mounted Police was requested to return the two Bren light machine guns lent to him the previous year.[64]

By 14th June 1949, a week before the kgotla, the tension in the rocky village was electric.

Due to Seretse's lack of correspondence with Tshekedi, nobody knew quite when he was due to return to the protectorate. Baring now shared Tshekedi's view that Ruth's presence could be inflammatory, and wrote to the Commonwealth Relations Office, asking them to get hold of John Keith of the Colonial Office, who had established a rapport and trust with Seretse, to ask him to approach Ruth with a request not to accompany Seretse to Bechuanaland. On the 1st of June, Keith succeeded in his task.

The tension proceeding the third kgotla was given a further edge by the ill health of the district commissioner, whose doctor advised that his nerves were in no condition to cope with a crisis, and that he must stick to his plans for overseas leave which was due to commence shortly after the tribal meeting.

A week after Ruth was persuaded not to go to Serowe with Seretse, he arrived back home. He had written his exams but was to learn later that he had failed them. It was about this time that the first rumours that Ruth was pregnant began to appear on newspaper front pages. This was not true, and she later exclaimed, "They had me giving birth from the Cape to Cairo, almost from the day I married." For the second time in eight months of marriage, the young bride had to wave a sad and apprehensive farewell to her husband. It was ironic that she was assuming all the characteristics of the war bride she had so determined in the past she would not be. Her thoughts were in turmoil as she waved Seretse goodbye. What sort of a reception would he get? Where would they live if she was rejected a third time? Next time she saw her husband she would know their future.

Seretse arrived back in Serowe without incident and prepared himself as best he could for the vital kgotla that would decide the course of his life. Two telegrams, written before the kgotla, serve to illustrate the contrast in style and manner of Seretse and Tshekedi. They were in response to one from the high commissioner, appealing to them both to ensure calm during the momentous proceedings. Tshekedi's cable went:

> Your personal telegram to Seretse and me received, for which I tender my humble gratefulness. I wish to assure Your Excellency that it is my life's purpose and motto to work selflessly for the good and growth of the Bamangwato people. To this end my expressions in attitude, action and talk will be directed in the present constitutional crisis. If and when matters are referred to you, may God guide you to offer lasting solutions which will maintain intact Bamangwato tribe.[65]

Seretse's cable went:

> I appreciate very much your personal message and Your Excellency can rest assured that I will do everything in my power to ensure that proceedings at forthcoming meetings are decorous and well conducted. My main consideration is for the welfare and prosperity of Bamangwato tribe.[66]

Accounts vary as to how many there were at the kgotla, for some newspapers estimated it to be 6000, others 9000 and the administration officials at between 3500 and 4000[67]. Most of those present were seated on stools, chairs or on stones, said a police officer who was on the lookout for any objects which could be used as weapons. His search proved fruitless – the tribe had made its way on everything from donkeys to trains from all corners of the vast reserve to talk, not to fight.

The kgotla lasted from the 20th to the 25th of June. Tswana tribal tradition allowed a chief to have several wives, but the one who was to bear the future chief had to be chosen by the royal family, and the status of the wife was of paramount importance. She became the Great Wife, displacing in seniority all other wives, regardless of the length of their marriages or number of children. The Great Khama, having abolished polygamy when he embraced Christianity, ruled out the possibility of Seretse taking another wife more senior to Ruth who could bear the future heir, and that's why the tribe's consent to a wife was considered so important. But as Seretse had already pointed out, both Tshekedi and the Great Khama had married wives without tribal consent.

Now the question that faced those thousands of men was: would they have Seretse as chief with Ruth, or would they give him up because of her? He had returned from England to hear the tribe's answer. He was resolute. Under no circumstances would he give her up. Now the young man wanted a clear decision one way or another. While he was in England, close friends had kept him in touch with the affairs and mood of the tribe, and Seretse was aware of the widespread dissatisfaction with Tshekedi's increasingly autocratic rule; with his imposition of levies and the use of the age regiments. He was aware too that Tshekedi had said he would no longer go into exile if Ruth were to be accepted by the tribe, but that he would stay and fight Seretse to the end. It irked Seretse that Tshekedi refused to deal with him on a man to man basis but continued with his paternalistic approach.

As the two estranged men took their seats side by side in the kgotla – the highly-strung uncle and the outwardly laconic nephew – and gazed at the upturned mass of faces, the people shuffling in the dust to get comfortable on a box or on the ground, both their pulses raced with alarm and anticipation. Present at the kgotla were chiefs from other tribes, administration officials, the first assistant secretary in Mafeking, Mr Vivien Ellenberger, who observed proceedings for the high commissioner, the wives of some administration officials, and traders who were curious to know the outcome of the extraordinary affair. And there too, of course, were newspaper reporters from all over the world, sent by editors who were fascinated by this story of love and power unfolding on the edge of the Kalahari Desert.

The kgotla went on for five days. The image that remained in the minds of those who attended it, was of a dominant Tshekedi, legs apart, standing over the squatting tribesmen, and of Seretse, confident with his British education, speaking calmly to the confused men. The talk of the first two days was mostly of a skirmishing nature, with an occasional stinging attack which elicited a sharp retort. At noon on the third day, Serogola Seretse, who had often acted as Tshekedi's deputy, rose to his feet and put the arguments in a nutshell. "The talk is no longer about the wife but about the chieftainship. Sekgoma's son, not Khama's, is the chief. Seretse is the chief. I say, let the woman come and their child shall succeed."[68] A subdued rumble of approval emanated from thousands of throats.

On the fourth day, Tshekedi accused Seretse's supporters of using the young man to further their own ends. And then he made a tactical error, for he called to his side senior headmen who supported his view of the marriage. Mary Benson, Tshekedi's sympathetic biographer, writes:

> Even his friends were dismayed by the increasingly arbitrary manner in which he was handling the kgotla. Perhaps he felt exhausted by the immense strain. At all events, at this point he proceeded to announce a recess for tea, and this turned out to be a second error in tactics.[69]

It gave Seretse time to work out his response to Tshekedi's calling of loyal men to his side to show his support base, and he determined to follow his uncle's example. As soon as the tribe had settled down again, he said, "I should like to see which of the seniors are agreed that my wife and I should come."[70] Seventeen of the royal "uncles" came forward for him. Seretse took a deep breath, and then quietly asked those who were against him and his wife to stand. Forty men rose to their feet, their eyes on Tshekedi while Seretse counted them.

"And now," he said, sensing success, "now, stand up those who want me and my wife," and with a tumultuous roar like a desert wind before a storm, nearly everyone present rose to their feet, raised their hats in the air and shouted, "Pula! Pula! Pula!" The sound rose and fell on the hot, dusty air, and all the village heard it, for it went on for ten minutes, and during it the desolate Tshekedi realised he had outgeneralled and overreached himself in his frantic attempts to prevent the acceptance of the marriage. His friend, Chief Bathoen of the Bangwaketse, was appalled at the turn proceedings had taken, for he believed that by tradition no one but the presiding chief had the right to put questions to the tribe.

When the shouting had subsided, and the men sat down, smiling at the stunned but happy Seretse, Tshekedi rose slowly to his feet. His fierce words rang out through the kgotla, "If this white woman comes, I go. My nephew has killed us. I warn you my nephew, son of Sekgoma, they are not speaking truly. They are using you as a tool." He emphasised that he would be leaving the Bamangwato Reserve as a free man, free to return when he liked, and said he would often be seen in Serowe.

Mr Ellenberger, in summarising for his administration the overwhelming change of tribal opinion in six months, listed some of the reasons for it as follows:[71]

1. The issue before the tribe was not Seretse's marriage but the succession. The innate attachment of Africans for the chiefly blood is well known, and when Seretse bluntly told the meeting that he would not stay if his wife could not live with him, they accepted his wife, rather than lose Seretse.
2. Tshekedi handed the opposition a powerful weapon when he said that if Seretse did not break off the marriage, he would not hand over the chieftainship or Sekgoma's estate; and then went further and challenged Seretse to wrest the chieftainship from him.

At the close of the meeting, Mr Ellenberger told the tribe that he would inform the British Government of its decision, and that until it had signified its approval of it, the administration of the tribe's affairs should continue as it had before the kgotla.

Seretse's jubilant friends clapped him on the back and clasped his hands and hugged him, and it was with difficulty that he made his way to the small, picturesque post office with its veranda supported by wooden poles, on the other side of the kgotla hill, to wire Ruth his exciting news.

In the days that followed, families were split as sons took sides against their fathers and husbands against their wives over the issue, for Tshekedi had called to those loyal to him to follow him into exile. He planned to go to the south, to the senior tribe, the Bakwena, ruled by Chief Sechele, and to build a village at Rametsana, on the border of the two tribal reserves. Dr Chiepe, a former cabinet minister told me, "Some people took the affair very seriously, they took everything. My uncle was one of those who went. You got a wife going to Rametsana and leaving her husband behind, and a husband going and leaving his wife behind, and parents going and leaving sons and daughters behind. You were either for Tshekedi or against him. He was that sort of person."

The implications of that tribal decision shook southern Africa and consequently the British Labour government of Clement Attlee. The South African Nationalist government that had swept the moderate United Party government, headed by the famous Field Marshal Jan Smuts, out of power the year before, was busy enshrining apartheid. Under Prime Minister Dr D.F. Malan it became the only country on earth brazen enough to entrench apartheid in codified law. And one of the cornerstones of that monstrous system was the Mixed Marriages Act, which prohibited marriage between black and white people.

Ironically Ruth and Seretse had married in the very year in which the Nationalists swept to power, but it was to be some years before the world would repeat the word, "apartheid" (separateness) and know the full horror of it.

For it broke apart families, and sometimes white people who broke the Immorality Act killed themselves in shame when they were discovered.

In June 1949, the very idea that the chief designate of the most powerful tribe, living in a territory the South Africans had long regarded as potentially theirs, should marry a white woman and be recognised as chief by the British, was totally unacceptable to the Nationalists. It flaunted the very basis of their existence – the separation of the races. The Bamangwato had no idea when they yelled "Pula!" and accepted Seretse with his white wife, that they were adding fuel to the fire of a dispute over the territory of Bechuanaland that had continued for nearly forty years between the Union of South Africa and Britain.

To understand the sequence of events immediately after the third and decisive kgotla (for what happened next baffled people for years and years afterwards) we must take a brief look at the history of requests for the incorporation of the three British territories of Bechuanaland, Basutoland, and Swaziland into South Africa.[72]

The granting of British protection in 1885 to Bechuanaland at the request of the three paramount chiefs did not mean their country was safe for all time. When the constitution of the Union of South Africa was drawn up in 1909 (the South Africa Act), the possibility of handing over the three territories was contemplated on the assumption that the Union of South Africa would remain an integral part of the British Empire.

The act made it clear that the protectorates could not be subordinated to the Union government unless the British king, acting on the advice of the Privy Council and following on addresses from the Houses of Parliament both in Britain and the parliament of the Union of South Africa, agreed to the transfer of the high commission territories to the Union Government. A memorandum attached to the act made it clear that the British Government undertook to consult native opinion in the territories before any transfer could take place. But the widely held view in 1909 that transfer would take place eventually was to be a source of continual diplomatic dispute, and from that time onwards, South African prime ministers – General Louis Botha, General J.B.M. Hertzog, and Field Marshal Jan Smuts – regularly requested transfer.

World War II postponed further discussions of transfer, but when Sir Evelyn Baring arrived in South Africa in 1945 as British high commissioner, both to that country and to the three protectorates, he learnt from Smuts that the Union of South Africa would ask for the three territories once the war was over.

The British were in a difficult position regarding Smuts, for he had stated publicly that he would ask for the protectorates; and he was being watched closely by the Nationalists, who were bent on gaining office. Smuts had been a staunch ally of the British during the war, and they did not want to put him in an embarrassing position. Added to this was the fact that Bechuanaland was at the economic mercy of the Union of South Africa, and its dependence on the union markets and transport system was almost total. As mentioned earlier, about sixty percent of adult Batswana went to work in the mines, households and on the farms of the union.

The South Africa Act had, however, stated that the wishes of the tribal inhabitants of the territories would be considered. Naturally they had escaped the colour bar regulations introduced in the union in the 1930s, which meant by the end of the war there was a distinct difference between the rights of the black people in Bechuanaland and their counterparts in South Africa. British officials had to report regularly on the attitude of the Batswana to incorporation, and there was never any doubt about their feelings on that score.

This was the situation when Prime Minister Malan's National Party came to power, and the British waited for his first demand for transfer of the territories. Sir Evelyn Baring regarded the question of transfer as his most important work in South Africa, according to his biographer Charles Douglas-Home,[73] and he was surprised the Nationalists did not make demands immediately after they gained office.

But the questions of transfer and the economic dependence of Bechuanaland on the Union of South Africa became a lever in South African protests to Britain over the recognition of Seretse as chief, as we shall soon see. Only five days after the third kgotla, the South African high commissioner in London, Mr Leif Egeland, called on the secretary of state for commonwealth relations, Mr Philip Noel-Baker, on the urgent instructions of Prime Minister Malan. Mr Egeland stressed that his representations were on an unofficial level. Note this, for it was to cause both governments grave embarrassment eight months later.

Mr Egeland earnestly requested the British Government not to recognise Seretse as chief of his tribe, and based his government's request on three main points:

1. It believed the repercussions in the Union [of South Africa] of a white woman becoming the chieftainess in an African tribe would be extremely grave. People of all races in the Union [of South Africa] would condemn the marriage and would think it a grave infringement of a basic principle.
2. Ruth's arrival would break up the Bamangwato's tribal tradition.
3. The resignation of Tshekedi would be a serious loss to both Bechuanaland and to Africans in general in view of his vision and statesmanship.
4. The future of the new white chieftainess would be very sombre. Coming from an English home, she would find it extremely difficult to settle down to the kind of accommodation and living conditions which Seretse could offer her. She would be not only lonely; she would be isolated in every way. No one of any race would visit her or give her any social life of any kind. She would certainly not be able to stand the strain of such an existence.[74]

Mr Egeland told Noel-Baker that he would wage a large sum of money that Ruth would not last six months, and at the end of that period the situation might be very different and the after-effects of the whole episode lamentable.

The National Party's view was telegrammed to Baring, who was being subjected to a great deal of pressure by the South Africans in Pretoria. But in the days immediately following the kgotla, there seemed to be no reason why Seretse should not be recognised as chief. The report of Resident Commissioner Anthony Sillery[75] stated that the kgotla had been a fair one; the district commissioner in Serowe urged recognition of Seretse, "to allay the suspicions" of the tribe; the resident commissioner recommended recognition; and there was no doubt about the general feeling of satisfaction amongst Bechuanaland administration officials and the majority of the tribe at the thought of having a pleasant young man in power as opposed to the demanding, aggressive Tshekedi.

Baring asked for both Seretse and Tshekedi to see him, and Seretse left immediately for Pretoria. There he was cordially received by Baring, who said he would welcome some indication of Seretse's plans and policy if his chieftainship was confirmed. Baring's advice to Seretse to heal tribal rifts and so on was qualified, but there was no doubt in Seretse's mind that it was a matter of weeks before he would be made chief, for why else would the high commissioner bother to give him advice on how to run the tribe? He left the office walking on air, and cabled Ruth that it would not be long before she would be able to join him in Serowe. Seretse's view that he was about to be made chief is confirmed in a letter[76] that was written by Baring to the Commonwealth Relations Office in which he said his first reaction had been to press for an early confirmation of Seretse's appointment by the secretary of state.

But there were powerful political forces at play that would see the cup of success dashed from Seretse's lips before the month of July was out. Events happened so fast, and telegrams and letters flashed at such a rate between Serowe, Mafeking, Pretoria and London, that it is no wonder many people were totally taken by surprise by the British Government's eventual decision.

Tshekedi did not take long to recover from his lonely hour of defeat in the kgotla. He knew the value of a sympathetic press, and he took them to the Khama Memorial, with its stupendous view over the undulating village to the great plains beyond, and he spoke of his disappointment at the dashing of his plans to help his tribe to progress.

"The thing that cuts deep into my heart," said Tshekedi to Noel Monks, *London Daily Mail* correspondent, "is that this tribe of ours is heading for disintegration. My work goes overboard because of a white woman, almost 10 000 kilometres away, who has never seen Africa in her life."[77] He took Monks to his lolwapa (yard) and explained that his wife's daily duties entailed listening to the problems of people who trekked hundreds of kilometres through the bush to meet their chieftainess. How could Ruth possibly do the same, was the question that Tshekedi posed.

Margaret Lessing, correspondent of the London *Daily Herald*, a cheerful, motherly soul, was so touched when Tshekedi, with tears in his eyes, said to her, "You talk of a white man gone native – my son has gone white," that she flung her arms around him.[78]

Tshekedi decided to play for time, and instead of leaving the reserve immediately to go into his self-imposed exile, he hedged about his plans for handing over the tribal and chiefly duties to Seretse. He was hard at work plotting a new way of keeping the reins of power out of Seretse's hands. Mary Benson, Tshekedi's biographer, described him as being in a highly-emotional and frustrated state at the time, and of not showing his usual discernment. It was one of the occasions when, having fixed on something in his mind, he would pursue it to the end, even if, as on this occasion, some of his friends tried to dissuade him.[79]

On the 5th of July, Tshekedi and forty-two headmen drew up a petition[80] in which they requested that a judicial enquiry be held, "to declare once and for all the final position as regards Ruth and her children." In it, they warned that unless their request was approved, continuous trouble would lead to the complete disintegration of tribal administration, compelling the British Government to forgo their declared principle of indirect rule and forcing them to introduce direct administration. The result, they prophesised dramatically, would be the end of the Bechuanaland Protectorate.

It is a measure of Tshekedi's desperation that he, to whom interference in tribal affairs was anathema, was asking the British to do just that, and he took the petition to Pretoria, along with his legal adviser, when he went for his interview with the high commissioner on the 7th of July.

That same day, the Southern Rhodesian parliament was debating the Seretse affair as a matter of urgent public importance, and the next day Prime Minister Sir Godfrey Huggins wrote Baring a second letter on the matter.[81] In his letters he pointed out that, "an official Native-European union in Bechuanaland would increase our difficulties here and add fuel to the flames of the fire kept burning by our fortunately diminishing band of anti-Native Europeans."

In South Africa, the official mouth organ of the ruling party, *Die Burger*,[82] said, "… the Union Government cannot stand impartially to one side when such developments as this (marriage) occur on our borders." And the powerful Afrikaans Dutch Reformed Church passed a resolution asking for recognition of Seretse to be withheld on the grounds of his marriage to a white woman.

At the same conference a policy of racial separateness for "non-whites" was accepted as being in line with the principles of Christian trusteeship and ethical values.

From Britain, Sir Percivale Liesching, permanent secretary at the Commonwealth Relations Office, suggested to Baring that the powers and functions of the chieftainship might temporarily be exercised by a council including neither Seretse nor Tshekedi.

In his reply of the 11th of July 1949, Baring[83] advocated the British Government accept Tshekedi's suggestion of a judicial enquiry, as he suggested this would enable them to play for time.

Baring had been subjected to great pressure from the South African apartheid government. It had informed him that the political consequences of recognition by the British of Seretse would be used by the extreme right wing of the National Party as an excuse for establishing a republic outside the British Commonwealth. The nationalist extremists argued that South Africa could not remain associated with a country that officially recognised an African chief married to a white woman.

In his memorandum to the Commonwealth Relations Office,[84] Baring wrote that he had been informed that some proposals for defence cooperation between Britain and South Africa might be jeopardised by the affair, and that Dr Malan's distress showed something more radical than a fillip to the campaign, for transfer of the territories was in the air.

Added Baring, "The mere residence of Seretse and his wife in Serowe without official recognition is objectionable to them (the South Africans) … but it is the recognition of Seretse as chief which will be the match to set off the gunpowder. As regards the Union [of South Africa], the situation is the gravest which has faced us since I first came to this country." While Baring realised that to refuse recognition of Seretse would lead to accusations of British acquiescence to the union's demands, he felt that to completely reject Dr Malan's representations would lead, "to a head-on collision with the union." This was something he felt was best to avoid, if possible, when the territories were so economically dependent on South Africa: "To argue that this incident on the edge of the Kalahari might lead to the complete secession of South Africa from the [British] Commonwealth may seem far-fetched, yet (it) … has the ring of truth." Baring believed that a small committee of enquiry would enable the British to play for time and would help them avoid a confrontation with South Africa.

It seems from Baring's letter that he, as well as Tshekedi, hoped that Ruth would not be able to tolerate life in Serowe. He went further, "Seretse himself might become tired of her, the Bamangwato might change their minds, or the enquiry might disclose reasons to refuse recognition," wrote Baring.

There is no doubt he was in a difficult position, for he was both high commissioner to the three protectorates and to the union. At times he must have felt he was walking a tightrope.

The British Cabinet was now in a dilemma. How was it to justify refusal to recognise Seretse on the grounds that he had married a white woman – a decision that would appear to be aimed at appeasing the South African Government? And yet, Baring's warning of a confrontation with the union could not be disregarded. Maybe a judicial enquiry would provide the breathing space they needed.

In London, Sir Percivale Liesching met the chief of the South African Defence Force, General Beyers, for lunch, and later reported that the general believed that recognition of Seretse would light a fire throughout the British colonial territories in Africa which would not soon be quenched. "He said," wrote Liesching,[85] "that the very existence of white settlement in these territories depended, in view of the numerical inferiority and defencelessness of the white population, upon the principle that the native mind regarded the white woman as inviolable."

Liesching added his own comment to the report[86], in which he said that although he was doctrinally as correct as all those in Britain who strongly disapproved of discrimination based on race, he did not believe that many who were of this persuasion, "would, if confronted with this matter in personal terms, view with equanimity, or indeed without revulsion, the prospect of their son or daughter marrying a member of the negro race."

Liesching continued,

> I mention this controversial topic in order only to argue that if this is true of people whose habitation is in this country (Britain) where they are not in a minority and where the problem does not present itself except in terms of visiting students or half-domiciled diplomats, it is overwhelmingly more true of European populations inhabiting areas where they are constantly in contact with a coloured majority.

His sentiments are so akin to those of Ruth's father, you could almost imagine the two of them had been commiserating with each other over their problems, although this is certainly not the case. What it illustrates is that Mr Williams's views were like those of many others in Britain.

Ruth was of course totally unaware of the direction in which events were moving in the corridors of Whitehall, so close to her home, and yet so far removed from her in its thinking. In Serowe, Seretse was beginning to suspect that Tshekedi's frantic activities, which were known to him, might bear fruit. On 18th July several heads of the Bamangwato tribe loyal to him wrote to the district commissioner in Serowe, underlining the tribe's acceptance of Seretse with his wife, and asking the government to recognise their rightful chief.

But Baring had made up his mind. On 11th July he wrote a lengthy top secret and personal letter to Liesching,[87] advocating a judicial enquiry: "We should defer the recognition of Seretse as chief until we are sure that (a) the tribe really want him and (b) he is himself fit to be chief."

Baring wrote that it was the recognition of Seretse as chief, "which will be the (British) match to set off the (SA) gunpowder."[88] He was referring to the political consequences in the union of recognition of Seretse which, he envisioned, could stir up nationalist Afrikaner emotions. This might result in South Africa's voting for the severance of its commonwealth ties.

Baring argued, "We should do everything we can to avoid a collision on this issue with the Union [of South Africa]."

On 20th July, he sent another request to the Commonwealth Relations Office to appoint an enquiry saying, "by a false move we might damage both our case for retaining the high commission territories and the cause of all Africans in South Africa."[89]

A couple of days later and, it appears, before the secretary of state had approved the holding of the enquiry, Baring wrote to Resident Commissioner Anthony Sillery in Mafeking, telling him of the points he would make to Seretse in the event of his request for an enquiry being granted.

By the 27th of July, Baring had his answer from the British Cabinet, and he flew to Mafeking where he met both Tshekedi and Seretse and informed them of the British Government's decision. A triumphant Tshekedi raced back to Serowe to warn the district commissioner that he should postpone making an announcement about the enquiry until stricter security measures had been taken, for he feared violence, and especially violence directed against him.

The day before the judicial enquiry was announced simultaneously in Serowe and Pretoria (on 30th July), the Commonwealth Relations Office sent the text of the announcement to the South African high commissioner in London, requesting it be regarded as confidential until it was made public. The South Africans had indeed won the first round of the match.

The announcement of the enquiry was a shattering blow to Ruth and Seretse. They had no idea then of course of the behind-the-scenes role played by the South Africans, of their private and unofficial representations made to Baring, and of the big guns that had been dragged out to help persuade the British not to recognise Seretse as chief as long as he had a white wife.

Naturally there was speculation at the time about South Africa's role, and it was generally accepted that Dr Malan's representations had borne fruit.

But it was only years later, when the British Official Secrets Act allowed the documents regarding the affair to be made public, that the full story of the South African involvement, and of Baring's concern over and preoccupation with the issue of the transfer of the three protectorates to South Africa, put the matter in its true perspective. At the time it seemed to Ruth and Seretse, and indeed to many other people, that the British action was gross interference in the tribe's affairs, and worse, that it was interference based purely on racist grounds.

We should also remember that in 1949 relations between the British and the South Africans were very different from what they are today. The South Africans had been staunch allies of the British in World War II, and their soldiers, a high percentage of whom were Afrikaans speaking, died in the Western Desert, in the East African campaign, and on the battlefields of Europe. Field Marshal Jan Smuts, besides having taken command of the East African campaign, was admired worldwide for his statesmanship, and he and Sir Winston Churchill's friendship was well known. This has been excellently portrayed by Richard Steyn.[90]

The relationship between the South African and British Labour governments was a paradox. The Labour Party had the old tradition of being pro-Boer which it had inherited from the Liberal Party when it was in opposition to the Conservatives during the Anglo-Boer War. And as one politician commented later, "The Labour government had not yet found out how South Africa treated its black people."[91]

The terms of reference of the enquiry must have been galling to Seretse. They were twofold, and were:[92]

> 1. to report whether the kgotla held at Serowe between the 20th and 25th of June 1949, at which Seretse Khama was designated as chief of the Bamangwato tribe, was properly convened and assembled, and its proceedings conducted in accordance with native custom.

2. to report on the question whether, having particular regard to the interests and well-being of the tribe, Seretse Khama is a fit and proper person to discharge the functions of chief.

By questioning the fitness of Seretse to be chief, the British were interfering directly in the affairs of the tribe, and their action at the time seemed inexplicable in view of their strict neutrality, and what some have described as their "masterful inactivity" when the dispute over the marriage first became a tribal issue. Within a month the shouts of triumph at the third kgotla had turned to ashes in Seretse's mouth.

Ruth, happily planning a sensible summer wardrobe to take out to Bechuanaland, was stunned and furious at the turn of events. She had been on her own for nearly two months when Seretse's telegram with news of the enquiry arrived, and with trembling fingers and puckered brow she tore open the envelope, for of course the newspapers had already carried reports of the British announcement.

Let's consider what the poor woman had already endured in the short period of eight months. She had been disowned by her father; her efforts to marry the man she loved in church had been thwarted, and they had to sneak off to a registry office in nervous anticipation of being discovered; her husband had left her within three weeks of marriage to return to his people who categorically rejected her in their thousands at two kgotlas; and now the hope of settling down to a peaceful married life amongst her husband's tribe, happy in the knowledge they had finally accepted her, was cruelly taken from her. It would have broken, or reduced to a gibbering wreck, many of us. But Ruth, displaying the remarkable fortitude and courage that were her hallmarks, carried on despite her tendency to suffer from nervous tension.

The third kgotla, attended by the international press, had ensured that Ruth and Seretse were front-page news, day after day in Britain, and Ruth became the subject of intense press attention. Political reporters pondered in print how Whitehall would handle an African crisis, which on a lower scale they compared with the abdication of Edward VIII. Its possible implications, they noted, were almost unlimited, for while approval of Seretse as chief would scandalise a great many white South Africans besides Dr Malan, rejection could irretrievably offend the black people.

But the politics of the situation did not interest the public as much as the human drama of the marriage, and so editors sent their reporters to keep a twenty-four-hour watch on Ruth. Some hired rooms over the road from her flat in Manor House, Finsbury Park, and bribed those in neighbouring houses with flowers and gifts so they would not miss Ruth if she tried to slip out. It was fortunate for Ruth that the people living in Manor House with her were solidly supportive when it was necessary to shield her from over-zealous reporters, for she was genuinely terrified of saying or doing anything that could be wrongly interpreted and might jeopardise Seretse's position, or her joining him in Serowe. And while everyone understood reporters had a job to do, the intrusion by some of them into her private life went beyond the bounds of decency.

One of the many photographs which was taken of her at the time is headlined, "A queen shops" and shows her striding down a London street, golden hair streaming behind her, clutch bag clasped tightly to her side and her attractive face turned slightly away from the camera. There is a haunted look about her. No wonder. In a one-week period alone, her photograph stared at her from every newsstand she passed, with headlines that ranged from, "This girl can upset the peace of Africa", to "Queen Ruth awaits her tribal escort" and "Marriage that rocks Africa". The American magazines, *Time* and *Life*, ran articles on her. The European press followed suit.

Reporters told Ruth she would live in a mud hut, with no electric light, no sanitation and wild animals roaming nearby. "You will have to work in the fields with the native women. You will never stand the heat and the monotony," they told her. No wonder Ruth retorted in anger that she knew what to expect when she married Seretse, that she had married the man she loved and not a black man, and that the colour bar was unchristian. At one stage Ruth felt so desperate, she took to climbing over the back wall of her pretty little garden to avoid the reporters at the front, but it wasn't long before they tumbled to her tricks, and she was surrounded.

"It was dreadful, for I would board a tram or bus, thinking I had escaped, and suddenly a voice would come from behind me, 'Good morning, Mrs Khama …' They chased her down the street firing questions at her. She went to the police for help, and when that did not ease the situation, she appealed to the newspaper editors, again without satisfaction.

In desperation she resorted to playing the press at their own game. She decided to confuse it, by not leaving her flat for a solid two-week period. "My friends at Manor House shopped for me, and one of them even dressed up in my sunglasses and scarf one evening for fun and went out giggling at how she would trick the press and came back a nervous wreck. They had followed her and tried to question her before they realised they had been tricked. We enjoyed that, getting our own back on them for once."

During her two-week incarceration, the press, thinking she had slipped out to Africa, sent their correspondents in Serowe to tell Seretse she was on her way, and although he knew this could not possibly be so, he nonetheless went to meet all the trains coming through Palapye, until he heard from Ruth about what was going on.

One night, Ruth, who had not drawn the curtains of her lounge together as tightly as she normally did, looked up to find a face peering through the chink at her, which mesmerised her with fright. A light bulb flashed, and she heard the sound of a step ladder being removed from against the wall. It was incidents such as these that led to such a lack of cooperation between the Khamas and the press in the early days of their marriage, although that was later to change.

Maybe at this stage some of us might have reconsidered a marriage that had engendered such extraordinary publicity and powerful opposition. But Ruth never faltered in her belief that she had married the right man for her. It seems she was certainly given lots of opportunity to change her mind about joining her husband in Serowe, for apart from anything else, in a letter written in July by Mr G.E. Nettleton (deputy resident commissioner in Bechuanaland) to Mr Ellenberger (the government secretary) Nettleton says baldly that it would not be possible to buy Ruth off.[93] The letter, written in London on the 4th of July 1949, after a visit to her by the British official and his wife, is interesting because it shows so clearly the prejudice and preconceived notions held in Bechuanaland and South Africa at the time about the "little London typist who had hooked a big fish …"

Rumours about Ruth's background were rife and included one that had her living in a sleazy part of London with gangsters for friends. It was thought by some that she came from a working-class background and had survived a poverty-stricken childhood from which she was determined to escape. Clearly no scenario was to be discounted in trying to understand how a white woman came to marry the black chief of a poor African tribe.

Now for Nettleton's letter, in which Ruth is described as better looking than she appeared in photographs, with golden hair and tallish. "She speaks and behaves nicely, and is quite presentable, in fact in Serowe she can hold her own in the European social circle, such as it is, without trepidation. She was nicely and simply dressed and conversed freely and intelligently. In fact, she is a tougher proposition than we had hoped she might be. She will never be bought off. Our impression is a good one, but the one thing that is going to shake her is dirt, and the manner of living."

Ruth, already tired of newspaper stories describing her as a typist, had something to say to Nettleton on that score. "She says she is not a typist, but was with an insurance firm, and in fact, had her own typist. She spoke with scorn about typists, as people do. 'Typist!' said she, 'I'd rather die than be a typist.'"

And Nettleton continued, after that piece of direct quotation, "It is not going to be easy for the Europeans to turn against her – if they do, she will be an embittered woman, and could be quite a nuisance and a great influence on Seretse, which in turn means she could cause him to vent her wrath on those whom she wants to harm."

The false rumours of Ruth's pregnancy had also reached Nettleton, and he reported, "There is no sign of an heir in the near future. She says she has been so worried that she lost fourteen pounds when Seretse first went out and has lost nine pounds since he left this time. She looks rather thin, but not bad. She has a nice, neat figure, and is generally a nice-looking girl."

From chorus girl to gangster's moll, to struggling typist – in view of these interesting descriptions, it is no wonder people evinced the surprise and amazement they did when they first met Ruth, and realised she came from a good middle-class family, was raised in the best British traditions by a Victorian father and had served her country bravely and with spirit during the war.

NINE

Ruth makes Serowe her home

The high commissioner, Sir Evelyn Baring, had asked Seretse, when he saw him shortly after the triumphant third kgotla, not to arrange for Ruth to go to Serowe until his chieftainship had been confirmed by the British Government. After the announcement of the judicial enquiry, however, Seretse wrote to Ruth asking her to join him in Serowe, and she immediately set about making travel arrangements with the Commonwealth Relations Office.

Seretse, who had been living with friends of his, then set about finding a house for Ruth and him to live in, for although Tshekedi had three houses, two of which were particularly cool and gracious, relations between the men were so bad that Seretse wanted nothing to do with him. He heard of a house being built by the tribe for the agricultural officer employed by the Bamangwato Native administration, and although it was quite some distance from the centre of the village, about seven kilometres from the kgotla, he accepted the tribe's offer of the house. It pleased him that Ruth would be moving into a brand-new home, and he tackled his next task. This was to ask the wife of a Palapye trader, Mrs Minnie Shaw, whom he had known since childhood, to take in Ruth for a few days on her arrival, and to help her adjust to her new surroundings.

Mrs Shaw, who was in her early sixties, was already something of a legend amongst the Bamangwato, for she spoke their language and welcomed them into her home at a time when only the missionaries did.

She was an energetic woman with a shock of white hair, whose nimble, quick movements belied her age. She had been born and brought up in England in a strict Victorian household, and she had inherited from her mother an affinity for the Temperance Movement. She and her husband lived in a house consisting of three tin-roofed rondavels, surrounded by a cool veranda that was gauzed to keep out flies and mosquitoes. A kitchen, bathroom and bedroom led off the three rondavels, which contained a dining room, lounge and spare bedroom. I have gone into this detail because Mrs Shaw was incensed when a British newspaper, describing Ruth's arrival in the protectorate, said the house was "a hut". Minnie's brother, who lived in England, sent her the account when he read it, and she sent him photographs to disprove it.

The house was situated behind their store, which faced on to the main north-south railway line. Palapye was not much more than a rail halt in 1949. Along the line was situated a row of tin-roofed bungalows, and there was a hotel and a tennis club. The African village was on the other side of the tracks. When Khama III lived there, before he moved the tribe to Serowe, it was a bustling, thriving village, and although Mrs Shaw did not know the great chief back in those days, she subsequently became a good friend of his when he moved to Serowe. In her Khama III recognised immediately the qualities of sincerity and friendliness to all, regardless of colour. It is not surprising, therefore, that in time she became known as "Ma" Shaw, the mother of the tribe.

When Seretse, wearing his customary felt hat and jacket, knocked on her gauze door, Ma Shaw darted an appraising look at him with her sharp but twinkling blue eyes, and drew him in for a cup of tea and one of her famous scones. With her characteristic forthrightness, she said she would ask Tsheke-di's permission before agreeing to take in Ruth, and she rushed off to Serowe to do so, before acceding to Seretse's request. The Palapye locals thought Mrs Shaw was silly. "Why can't Ruth go to the missionaries or stay with the Africans?" they asked each other over sundowners and at tea parties.

In Serowe, gossip about Ruth was rife. Nobody was quite sure when she was coming, but it was assumed it would not be long before she joined Seretse.

In their dim stores, with tiny windows set high up in the walls, the traders, most of them of South African origin and many of whom were related in some way or other through marriage, wondered how they should react to her presence. Her marriage was contrary to their fundamental beliefs about race relations, but Seretse could well be chief, and it was he who gave them licence to trade. And of course their clientele was almost exclusively Bamangwato. They had to consider their social behaviour in relation to that. They were in a dilemma, they told each other. The women were in favour of ignoring Ruth totally until their husbands reminded them about the licences. The wives who often helped their husbands in the stores, rubbed their hands, chapped by the dry winter wind, pulled their jerseys around their shoulders, and huddled over coffee and cigarettes as they gossiped endlessly about Ruth, wondering what she was like and what on earth had possessed her to marry a "native".

Some of them looked suspiciously at their servants, wondering if they were "getting ideas" above their station in life, just because a white woman had married their "chief". They looked around their homes, furnished with a mixture of African and European items, and wondered how Ruth would furnish her home. There were coir mats and animal skins on their red polished stoeps, carpets and club chairs in their lounges, lace doilies on their African wood tables and cabinets, and net curtains and canvas blinds covered their windows. In summer their gardens looked pretty with flowerbeds filled with cannas, carnations, marigolds and geraniums, but in winter the lack of rain combined with the dry wind shrivelled them. Their lawns turned brown, and the slightest breeze whipped up the powdery dust that seeped into every crack and crevice and provided endless work for dusting maids.

The British officials and their wives, who lived on a long, sloping hilltop known as Nob Hill, also gossiped endlessly about Ruth. They did not have the same problem about socialising with her as did the traders, for once it became known that Ruth was going to live in Serowe, an unofficial directive was sent to them, stating there was to be no social contact with her.

It was hoped that Ruth would find life so hard, so lonely and so alien from what she was accustomed to, that she would go back home to England after a few months. It was a tight-knit civil service, and those people who thought the directive was cruel, kept their thoughts to themselves in those early days. "What can have possessed the girl to marry an African chief?" asked one British matron, in her clipped English accent at a morning tea party. "How will we command respect from our servants if they think that we white women are going to marry their black men, that's what I'd like to know?" asked a worried, timid little woman. "Imagine only having black friends and relatives around you," murmured another. Their horror was mixed with disdain at the thought that one of them could have let the side down in such a manner.

They sipped their tea, ate their scones and cakes, talked about their next home leave, the latest ritual murder and their children's health. Then, calling to the nannies to bring their children, now happily covered in dust, they rushed home to make sure the cook wasn't burning the lunch for which their husbands were due home. In the sharp, wintry evenings, as they gathered for sundowners and looked out over the thatched huts below, talk was almost exclusively centred around Ruth and Seretse. They speculated wildly about her looks, her family background and her education. Although those who knew Seretse liked him, they could not imagine that the "little London typist" had married him for anything but ulterior motives. She must be running away from something, they postulated amongst themselves.

Serowe was a huge village, but it boasted little in the way of entertainment for the white population, for it had no hotel, cinema, pub or restaurant.

The population relied exclusively on itself for amusement, and it didn't do badly. The district commissioner, who had a commanding view from his large, gracious, whitewashed bungalow over the valley below Nob Hill, invited people to play tennis on the sand court next to his garden. The latter was filled with jacaranda and syringa trees. Flowerbeds made by piling stones up one on top of another, and then filling the container with soil, looked pretty, almost English.

At the weekend, there was the sports club to go to in the little valley below Nob Hill near the dongas (dried out river gullies). It had tennis courts, a croquet field and a golf course made almost entirely of sand and dust. During the week, the administration officials' wives would walk down from the line of government houses, along the rather unorthodox golf course (the cattle used it as a path too) and through the dongas at the bottom. The cattle liked lying there under the shade of overhanging thorn trees, and every so often one would collapse and die, and vultures would flock down to tear at the carcass. The big birds ate so much, as is their wont, that they would stagger along the ground if someone approached them, in an effete, drunken dance, doing belly flops as they tried to take off.

On Saturday afternoons, the traders and the civil servants, smartly togged out in white, met at the club to play sport, and mid-afternoon there was always a splendid tea, for the wives vied with each other to see who could make the best cake. Their children played in the dust nearby, watched by a nanny per child, who ensured their young charges did not eat poisonous berries, were not bitten by snakes, and did not turn over stones and get stung by scorpions or bitten by spiders.

It might have been an isolated community, but like British colonies throughout the empire, it had its standards. New administration officials' wives were expected to call on the district commissioner's wife soon after their arrival, wearing a hat and gloves. And although the junior wives, as they were called, told themselves how silly it was to attire themselves in such fashion in temperatures that rose to over forty degrees centigrade, they kept quiet because they did not want to displease the leading wife. On the Queen's birthday, the officials turned out in white pith helmets and uniforms, and the women wore smart little hats and gloves, and got their elegant shoes scuffed in the dust. But everyday wear was sensible. The men wore khaki longs and shirts, or shorts if they were going out into the bush to visit villages and districts, and shirts with ties and cool jackets if they were working in the office. The women wore simple cotton dresses with sandals, and in winter a light jersey sufficed to keep them warm.

The village was like any other small community you will find anywhere in the world, in that it was hard to keep anything secret. If your friends didn't gossip about you, your servants told your friend's servants what was happening in your household. In addition to this, the postmaster (or postmistress) read the telegrams people wrote out in the tiny office with its ink-stained wooden counters. Only the district commissioner had a telephone, the rest of the community made their calls from the post office, and naturally there was no such luxury as direct dialling or private booths. In such an isolated community, letters, newspapers and magazines livened up what could be an extremely boring existence, and therefore the post office became a social gathering place.

Contact with the tribesfolk was limited to that between servants, gardeners, office workers and so on. Khama III and Tshekedi were obviously such outstanding, educated people, that they were welcomed wherever they went, and although Seretse had spent very little time in Serowe after the age of ten, he had made friends with the traders' sons, and those friendships remained. Due to Khama's skilful and sophisticated handling of the white people who came to live amongst his tribe, relations between white and black were generally good. The whites had the respect of their servants which they felt was their due, and the blacks were treated well, which was what the chief expected. In the village, friendly tribesmen would lift their hats to traders and civil servants, the black women gave their little bobbed curtsey of respect and the whites smiled back in return. But for all that, they lived in different worlds.

The tribe ploughed and harvested, herded their cattle, built their huts, sat in the kgotla and lived their lives according to the seasons and the rhythm of nature. The traders worked long, sticky-hot days behind the counters of their stores, and the rhythm of their lives was governed by their profits, the hunting season and visits to their relatives in South Africa. Because they lived in houses next to their stores, which were scattered amongst the tribe, according to Khama's edict, they knew and understood what was going on in the tribe far better than most civil servants. The latter, living removed from the village on Nob Hill, led lives governed by their next home leave and their next official posting. "The Afrikaners called us 'kaffir', and we knew where we stood with them," said a Botswana cabinet minister to me. "But the English would say quietly, 'the noble savage', and you never knew where you stood with them." Serowe was unique in terms of its social structure, for in the other protectorate villages the traders generally lived in close proximity to one other.

In August 1949, when it became known that the Englishwoman who had married the Great Khama's grandson was coming to live amongst them, the hilly village of Serowe was peaceful, even sleepy. After that things were never quite the same again.

Ruth's arrival was supposed to be a secret, but as I have said, there were no secrets in Serowe, and a couple of days before her arrival, the international press swooped down on dusty, quiet little Palapye. They arrived in chartered aircraft, in hired cars and by train. They filed reports describing their trek to the African interior in a manner that made the travels of Marco Polo seem insignificant. Palapye's small hotel was soon filled to capacity, some reporters had to sleep in corridors and on the veranda, and the clatter of their typewriters and their chatter in the bar provided an excitement the locals had not experienced for years, although they were careful to mention to one another how silly they thought the reporters were to make such a fuss over an Englishwoman, who after all "had only married a native".

The foreign correspondents represented British, South African, American and European newspapers and news agencies. Their editors wanted a change of diet for readers, one that didn't dish up McCarthy's communists, the fighting in China and Mao Zedong, and the fighting raging in the new state of Israel. They wanted romance, and one between a fair-skinned beauty and a handsome chief in darkest Africa was just the sort of story that sold newspapers, so senior reporters were told to "go for it" and to "get their man", and money was to be no object. The locals, however, closed ranks, as insular villagers tend to do the world over, for the subject of this intense press interest, a black-white union, shocked and embarrassed most of them.

Ruth, unaware of the waiting hordes of press in Africa, was continuing her battle with them in England. The Commonwealth Relations Office had bought her flying boat ticket under the name of Mrs Jones, and Ruth was asked to keep her departure quiet from the press, although she was offered no assistance in this regard. But her father helped her, for he suggested that Ruth and Muriel take his car. They parked it in the dark one night at the end of Adolphus Road before creeping back to the flat, hoping in this manner to escape the attentions of the reporters keeping watch from a flat across the road. Ruth had sent her heavy trunks by sea some days before, and she quickly finished packing the suitcases that Muriel would collect the next day in a taxi. It was near midnight when, clutching only an overnight bag and with no torch to light the way for it might give them away, they made their way down the road to Mr Williams's car and sped in unobserved triumph to their Lewisham home, where Ruth spent a couple of days before boarding the boat train to Southampton.

Ruth was enormously excited at the prospect of at last joining Seretse. She was pleased to be leaving London, for although it was summer, and the plane and beech trees were in leaf, softening the dismal buildings that had been shattered by bombs, life was still hard with rationing and the general economic depression that followed the war. She looked forward to the heat (she had always found the cold depressing, even as a child) and she regarded with pleasurable anticipation the wide-open spaces, so different from London's crowded streets, and the excitement of a novel way of life. She spent her last few days saying goodbye to her aunts, uncles and cousins, many of whom had never even ventured over the English Channel to France, and who regarded the adventuresome Ruth with awe and amazement. Her parents took her to the railway station and watched with lumps in their throats and tears in their eyes as the plump little schoolgirl whom they had watched grow into an attractive, independent woman chugged off on the first stage of her long journey to Africa.

Ruth's determinedly cheerful face hid apprehension about her trip, for both South Africa and Southern Rhodesia had told the British Government they would prefer her not to land in their countries. In addition to this, she was travelling alone, and it was a three-day trip. At Southampton, she was relieved when a BOAC (British Overseas Airways Corporation) official met her at the train, took her suitcase and escorted her to the flying boat. They must have looked like father and daughter, for the press who were there in force, photographing some stage personality, did not recognise Ruth at all to her amazement and joy. When she had initially caught sight of them, her heart had lurched uncomfortably, and she had panicked for a brief moment.

Her assumed name caused problems when the plane stopped for the night in Egypt, for the name and address on her ticket didn't correspond with that in her passport, and a lot of explaining had to be done. Two days later, Ruth's heart leapt with joy when she saw the spray that rises hundreds of metres into the air above the spectacular Victoria Falls, and she realised the bulk of her journey was over. The flying boat touched down gently on the waters of the mighty Zambezi and a BOAC representative soon spotted the apprehensive Ruth in her calf-length black overcoat and silk scarf and whisked her away from under the noses of a crowd of pressmen. Ruth hardly had time to glance at the swiftly flowing waters of one of Africa's great rivers, bordered with dense, tropical vegetation, before she was bundled into a car and driven across the Falls Bridge and into Northern Rhodesia where she spent the night with a British official and his family in Livingstone. The next day she boarded a single-engine plane that had been specially laid on for her by the British to fly her to Francistown. The pilot took off earlier than had been planned, probably on instructions from the British, and once again the press was foiled, arriving at the airstrip as the little craft rose into the bright, clear morning sky.

It touched down at the little airstrip outside Francistown, which was one of the largest towns in Bechuanaland with two hotels, garages, shops, schools and a hospital. Seretse, who had risen when it was still dark that morning and who had been waiting with his cousin and childhood friend, Goareng Mosinyi, strode over the bumpy, bush-dragged strip to help Ruth down from the plane and to welcome her to his country. His large face beamed with happiness as he hugged his slim wife, clasping her warmly to his large, comfortable body, and gentle, soft-spoken Goareng welcomed her in the perfect English spoken by so many members of the Bamangwato royal family. Roaring with laughter at Seretse's witty sallies and relieved that finally the young couple were together again, the three climbed into Seretse's smart 1949 Ford model car, and raced off to Palapye, 163 kilometres to the south. Seretse drove fast as was his custom, and Ruth glanced curiously at the flat landscape, covered with thorn trees and bushes, in clearings of which at intervals were huts and kraals (enclosures for goats and cattle).

Ruth's arrival in Palapye coincided with a tennis match that the village was hosting between itself and Serowe, and, unfortunately for the Khamas, all that separated the tennis court from the front gate of Minnie Shaw's garden was a few hundred metres of thorn bush and a little road. As Seretse drove down the dirt track running alongside the railway line and turned left between Mrs Shaw's house and the tennis court, his car was recognised. "Good gracious, I do believe that is Seretse with his wife," gasped one official's wife, and the players paused to catch a glimpse of the famous Ruth Khama. But all they saw was a flash of golden hair and a trim figure, before Mrs Shaw closed her gauzed front door firmly behind her guests.

Word of the arrival flashed around the village, and soon the bush in front of the white-haired, determined old lady's house was filled with the press, eager to catch just a glimpse of the couple together in order to file their first reports to a waiting world. They hung about in vain. Some of them dashed back to the hotel for dinner before resuming their watch in the chilly winter night, and others did not even do that, scared they would miss a scoop. Mrs Shaw, who was president of the Bechuanaland Temperance Society, offered her weary guests soft drinks as they sat in her lounge, furnished in heavy Victorian furniture with wood-framed pictures on the walls. Her maid, De Fly, so named because she was born the same day Sir Alan John Cobham flew over Palapye on his record-breaking flight up Africa from Cape Town to London and was therefore called The Flying Machine by her parents, served them dinner. Before it was over, Minnie Shaw had made up her mind that she liked her young guest, for apart from anything else she was as direct in her manner as was the trader's wife.

As the household prepared for the night, and Ruth and Seretse were shown to their thatched room, Ruth realised how totally exhausted she was by her experiences of the day. Her flight, the drive through the alien African bush, the shock of seeing the tennis crowd gazing at her, and the African night sounds of beetles chirping, donkeys braying and cattle lowing crowded her mind. She laid a weary head on her white linen pillow after extinguishing the paraffin light around which the moths clustered, dancing in the golden flame.

When, shortly after midnight, Mrs Shaw heard a sound that was definitely not the steam engines hissing and puffing into the station, she got up in her pyjamas to investigate. Discovering two reporters in her garden, she told them fiercely that they were on private property and she would shoot them if they didn't clear off. A little shaken, they then tried her son who lived next door to her, but they met with no better luck in their quest for information about the Khamas, for Thomas Shaw set his dogs on them.

A couple of days later, two American pressmen managed to charm a friend of Mrs Shaw's into taking them across to her. "I represent twenty-six American newspapers," said one. "I'm not interested in whom you represent," said Mrs Shaw. "I am not going to talk to you." And she closed the door in a manner that indicated that that was the end of the matter. In the following few days that Ruth spent with her, while Seretse commuted the forty-seven kilometres to and from Serowe to attend the kgotla and see how their new house was progressing, the two women formed a firm friendship that lasted to the end of Mrs Shaw's life. I met her in Palapye in 1983 when she was still living, aged ninety-four, in the same house, her quick, nimble movements only slightly affected by her great age.

A few days later, Seretse was surprised by a reporter as he was making arrangements to smuggle Ruth out of the Shaw's home and into Serowe without the press knowing of his actions. The reason for the Khamas' determination not to speak to the press was twofold: Ruth had given her word to Whitehall officials that she would not, and they both felt that the press had given them a pretty raw deal with their sensational and often inaccurate reporting. Seretse explained to the journalist that it was quite impossible to talk to him and then he disappeared. A few moments later Ruth, dressed simply in a skirt, blouse and cardigan, rushed out, and climbed quickly into the car. Seretse surprised the waiting press by literally roaring out of the Shaw's garden, tyres screaming as he turned the corner, and headed in a cloud of dust for Serowe.

The international press raced after the fleeing couple like baying hounds after their quarry. As Seretse sped rapidly along the dirt road, an aircraft buzzed low overhead, photographers hanging out of it as they tried to get one shot of the couple but captured only a speck in a cloud of dust. Press cars, doing dizzy speeds of between 120 and 140 kilometres an hour along the rough, sandy road that twisted through the dense thorn bush, could not catch the speeding Seretse. When he saw two cars carrying pressmen coming towards him from the opposite direction, he simply swung the wheel over hard and crashed off into the bush as he made a detour around them. Noel Monks, top reporter on London's *Daily Mail*, who had covered thousands of kilometres in his efforts to track down Seretse, was one of those in a plane, and he described later how he swooped low over Serowe but saw little in the dusty whirlwind kicked up by press cars.[94]

As Ruth and Seretse approached Serowe, he pointed out to her the distinctive twin hills of Swaneng on the outskirts of the village, which were always pointers to weary travellers that they were nearing home.

Seretse had done his best to describe the village to Ruth, but she said later, "How do you describe it to someone who has never been to Africa before? I never expected all those hills, it was beautiful, and when we drove through it, I felt straight away that I was going home. I felt at peace, as if I was going to belong there." And this was despite arriving in August, generally regarded as the most unpleasant month of the year in Serowe, for it is the windy month, and dust is blown continually into your face, the countryside is burnt brown in the dry winter months, and devil winds whirl through the bush, lifting papers and leaves in their path before depositing them on their hapless victims. But it is also the month when the sap rises, the sharp wintry nights suddenly turn into summer, and the promise of rain is there. Before the rains bring relief, however, the air is so dry your skin grows taut from lack of moisture and aches with desire for mists and dampness, and your hair literally stands on end with electricity.

But Ruth was too charged with her own electrical current of excitement to notice these depressing factors. She looked with fascination at the thatched huts, the smoothed mud courtyards that surrounded them, the stockaded fences, and the green rubber hedges that broke the harsh monotony of winter greys and browns. Flame lily trees lit up the rocky, boulder-strewn hillsides with their brilliant colour, and the bougainvillea and poinsettia added their own dash of light to the winter canvas. Here and there she noted the European-style bungalows with their tin roofs, their gauzed verandas, and she guessed there were hidden eyes that were sizing her up.

But that mattered not a jot to Ruth, for the welcome she and Seretse received was tumultuous. "They went mad. They rocked and hung on the car, they climbed on to the back of it. It was a little overwhelming, but it was wonderful," said Ruth.

She heard the ululating – a sound made by moving the tongue quickly from side to side in the mouth accompanied by a high, almost keening note – which Seretse had described to her in London, and understood that it was praise singing, loving and welcoming all in one. And her heart, battered and made weary for so long, rejoiced with them.

Her eyes widened with surprise when Seretse drew the car up under a rocky outcrop that seemed to hang right over the London Missionary Society's house where they were to spend the next couple of nights. The quaint old house, built when Khama III moved his village to Serowe, was perched on the slopes of the Thathaganyana Hill, and those who climbed up the round, granite rocks were rewarded with a view over much of Serowe.

The London Missionary Society's Alan Seagar was the minister in Serowe at the time, and if he climbed a little way up the slope, he could see the architectural feature that dominated Serowe – the huge church, which Khama had built of carved sandstone and where his tribe worshipped.

That night, as Ruth laid down her tired head, visions of racing cars and swooping aircraft flashing through her mind, she was lulled to sleep by the comforting sounds of the great village. Dogs barked, an occasional cowbell tinkled, children's voices rang through the night air, and women sang in their deep, rich voices around their fires. And the talk that night in all the homes, whether they were huts or belonged to traders or civil servants, was of Ruth's arrival, for despite the deserted air that hung over the village, inquisitive eyes had peeped from behind net curtains and around hut doors. By the time darkness swooped on the village, descriptions of Ruth had flashed throughout the village.

The next day Seretse took her to meet his family and friends. Outside one of the trading stores the cry went up that the wife of the chief had come. Soon thousands of jubilant, ululating women surrounded Ruth. They fell on their knees and kissed the hem of her dress, they clapped their hands and sang, and when she and Seretse went back to the car, they fell on the bonnet and ran alongside it, so happy were they to show their love for Seretse and his wife. The joyous welcome soon spread throughout the village and was so spontaneous that Ruth was again quite overwhelmed by it, for she had expected nothing of the sort. Naturally there were some Bamangwato who were deeply troubled by the marriage, but they were in the minority, and many in time were to respect Ruth for her own qualities of leadership, rather than only as the wife of Seretse. But in those early days, she merely smiled shyly, blinking in the strong sunshine with her fair skin reddening in the sun.

During the next few days, Seretse showed Ruth around the village to help her get her bearings. It was easy to do this, for the core of the village was characterised by three main rocky ridges that ran from north to south. The first of these that you saw on entering the village was the hill behind the kgotla, otherwise known as the Sacred Hill, a feature of which was the rocky outcrop situated to its north on which was situated the Khama Memorial and graveyard.

The second main ridge you encountered was Nob Hill where the civil servants lived. It sloped gently from south to north and the houses of the officials were situated along the sandy, rock-strewn road that led from the bottom of the slope. The few people who had cars drove them slowly, for stones were flung up by passing vehicles that could shatter windscreens, and the choking dust that whirled in their wake resulted in everyone rapidly winding up their windows to let it pass. There was only one road along the ridge, and it petered out into bush at the end of the settlement. The white-washed bungalows, the windows and doors of which were painted either in the dark brown or green regulation paint, were set amongst the jacaranda and syringa trees. The district commissioner's office was also on the hill, as were some of the other officials' offices, and at the end of it was the pretty little Anglican church that Ruth was later to attend.

On the third main ridge the hospital was situated, and a little distance beyond that the village came to an end in a straggle of huts. Ruth and Seretse's house was the first building you encountered on the road from Palapye in to Serowe, and it was situated in an area called Swaneng, near the identical twin hills which could be seen from some way out of Serowe. It was about seven kilometres from the kgotla, the centre of the village, and it was so remote there were no huts in its immediate vicinity, only the sweet thorn bushes with their long, distinctive spikes, the umbrella thorn trees, closely resembling their name, and the mokala (camel thorn) trees, which grow to a great height and provide lovely shade.

The first huts began a little way on from the Khamas' bungalow towards the village, and the closer Ruth and Seretse drove towards the centre, the more densely packed they became, although Serowe is a spread-out village. As they drove about, Ruth noticed the grass had almost vanished, and the pathetic tufts left were being nibbled by goats. Seretse took Ruth to the kgotla, and she was able to visualise for the first time the stormy meetings that had taken place there. She was shown the imposing Khama School where Seretse had gone as a small boy, and which was made from the same carved sandstone as the church, and near it the dam where he had played as a child.

Ruth saw Tshekedi's fine houses on either side of the kgotla hill, although she did not meet him, for he had ensured that he was not there when she arrived. At the post office Ruth telegrammed her mother to say that all was well in Serowe, and then Seretse took her past the home of Connie Pretorius, the wife of the village blacksmith. Connie was one of those tough Afrikaans women, who could sew anything, from the canvas sails for her husband's wagons to dainty party frocks for her children. She cooked the boerekos that her mother had been taught to prepare by her grandmother, and she cooked for weddings and parties in the village. One day she was to cook the food for the dignitaries who attended Seretse's funeral. Ruth noted the pretty designs smeared on the huts, and the way several huts housing all the members of an extended family clustered together in one stockade.

As they drove about, she saw women stamping corn, two to a block, their arms moving up and down in perfect symmetry. Some of the men were thatching and the others were sitting in the sun in the kgotla, talking. Little girls tended their tiny siblings, and old women, resting from their chores, raised their wrinkled faces with rheumy eyes to the sun's warmth. Boys, naked save for loin cloths, dashed about the village, tearing along the paths that wound between the huts, chasing goats and chickens and playing games.

A few days after their arrival in Serowe, Ruth and Seretse moved into their new home. The tin-roofed house was square in shape, with thick, solid walls and a veranda in front, from which vantage point Ruth looked out over a vast expanse of bush to the kgotla hill in the distance and the Swaneng hills close by. It was a typical European-style bungalow. In the front of it, steps led up to the red polished veranda, which ran almost the breadth of the house. Inside, the rooms were large and high ceilinged. There were three bedrooms, a kitchen, dining room, lounge and bathroom. There was no running water. This had to be brought in from the rainwater tanks outside, or from the dam or boreholes in the village. The toilet was outside as was the case with most of the European-type houses in the village, but Ruth, unlike her compatriots, did not have to worry about snakes and scorpions, for there were always so many Bamangwato around the house looking after her that they ensured the unwelcome pests kept their distance. The stove in the kitchen was one of those huge, black ranges that you threw logs of wood or coal into to heat up, and Ruth was relieved that Seretse had a good cook, for in summer the heat in that room was unbearable.

The couple had taken over the furniture of the agricultural officer who had been planning to move into the house. It was typical European-style furniture, some of it heavily Victorian with ball and claw feet, and they had zebra and lion skins on the floor, rush mats and carpets. Seretse's law books lent the lounge a studious air, and Ruth soon had photographs of her family and other personal belongings dotted through the house. It did not take her long to settle in, for neither she nor Seretse had anything in the way of furnishings, having previously rented furnished apartments.

The day after they had moved in, the Bamangwato arrived at the house, carrying gifts such as woven baskets, mats and clay pots to welcome the wife of their much-loved chief. They sang, danced and then sat quietly under thorn trees, waiting for Ruth and Seretse to speak to them. Ruth was both surprised and touched, despite Seretse having told her of the warmth and goodwill of his tribe.

In spite of being married to an African chief designate and living in a village amongst his tribe, Ruth's life was not materially different from that of the other white people living in Serowe. She and Seretse ate Western-type food consisting of meat, which was cheap and plentiful, and vegetables, such as cabbage, carrots, pumpkin, potatoes, spinach and onions. Ruth made puddings, bread was baked by her cook, and milk was either powdered or came from Seretse's cattle. The tribe carried water for cooking, cleaning and bathing to the house. If she needed extra water, the word was passed around the village, and through the bush, balancing buckets on their heads and singing as they walked, scores of women would go, eager for the opportunity to be near her. "They absolutely adored Seretse, and their love of him showed, I think, in their acceptance of me," said Ruth.

Hot water for her bath was heated in the donkey boiler outside, and when she rose in the morning, pitchers of hot and cold water would be waiting for her in the bathroom. The washing and ironing was done by maids, as was the household dusting and cleaning and polishing. While life in Serowe was certainly worlds apart from that in London, Ruth in fact led an existence of comparative luxury when compared to that led by her friends back home who toiled all day over household chores. True she could not run down the road to buy a dress or go to the hairdresser, or indulge herself with chocolates, magazines and newspapers. But then, none of the other white people living in Serowe had the pleasure of these daily luxuries that most Western people take for granted. Ruth did not live amongst the tribe any more than her English counterparts there did, and she did not work on the lands, tilling the fields or harvesting crops any more than they did, although of course she spent a great deal of time with the tribe, for they came daily to the house to meet her and to talk to Seretse.

Those who could not speak English either spoke through interpreters or sat shyly in the shade of the thorn trees outside and gazed with admiration at her whenever she appeared. The house, being new, had no garden, and between it and the fence consisting of thorn bush that ringed the dwelling, the ground was bare and dusty. Anyone who wanted to visit the couple had to tell a guard at the fence who they were, and then the thorn bush would be dragged back to allow them entry.

Shortly after Ruth and Seretse had settled down, the royal family, consisting of Seretse's uncles and aunts and cousins, came to pay its respects, and many of them spoke English, which initially surprised Ruth, until she learnt how many had attended missionary schools in South Africa. In time she became particularly friendly with Seretse's sisters, Naledi and Oratile, and with his childhood friend, Gaositwe Chiepe, and they taught her what was necessary for her to know about the tribal traditions and customs, although as I shall discuss later, Seretse regarded himself as detribalised and did not bother too much about the customs.

Ruth spent those early days learning to find her way around the village, meeting her new family, writing of her life to her family in England, doing the odd bit of sewing and cooking, trying to learn the language and generally adapting to her new existence. Before the rains came, the sunsets were particularly vivid due to all the dust in the atmosphere, and as the harsh light of day faded, the escarpment to the north of the village would turn a soft blue as the brilliant blue sky turned pink and then grey. Then the first stars would come out, with Venus, the evening star, brilliant in the sky. Fires began to twinkle in the yard behind her house, and in the yards of the villagers, and the night sounds of chattering around the fires, of children calling, of goats bleating and birds chirping as they settled down for the night, drifted across to the house.

It was so silent in that village at night that every sound carried on the still air. Ruth was, however, a city person, and the harsh beauty of her new country, while it impressed her, did not particularly appeal to her, for she was by nature practical rather than poetic. The burning midday sun, the harsh drying winds, the endless dust, the little insects that are a part of daily life, and the sense in an African night of the immense unknown that exists in the deep darkness, initially dismayed her as it did many others, before she became accustomed to it.

Another factor in her life in that first year in Serowe was the press, for they soon found the Khama house, and operating from their base in Palapye, for there was nowhere for them to stay in Serowe, they churned up the sandy kilometres each day, hoping that Ruth or Seretse would relent and grant them an interview. But they had to be content with the Khama visits to Palapye when they visited the Shaws to gain any real impressions of the couple. It wasn't long before the young couple made friends with Alan Bradshaw, an officer who was in charge of the recruiting centre for the South African gold-mines and his wife Doris. He was a strong character, English, as was his wife, and he was shocked to hear of the snubs and the cold shoulder that Ruth was being given by the whites in Serowe. They were determined to make up for this unkind behaviour.

Shortly after Ruth and Seretse had settled down in their new home, there was great excitement amongst the press and the Palapye locals when the word went around before one of their weekly cinema shows held in the hotel that Ruth and Seretse were to attend it. In the bar beforehand, there was brave talk amongst the sweaty, sunburnt locals about the snubbing they would give the couple, and of the offensive remarks they would make. But oddly enough, the opportunity for this never seemed to come as the couple made their way quietly through the room to sit in the empty seats kept for them by Mrs Shaw. That was the way with much of the talk in Serowe too, for there were brave words about how Ruth would be "shown the door if she dares to darken it."

There is no other way to describe it – the treatment meted out to Ruth by her own kind in that small community was cruel and not at all typical, for newcomers were always called on, invited to homes, and introduced and made welcome at tea parties and sundowners. Although the general view amongst the white population was that Ruth had "let the side down", there were those at the time who were most unhappy about their coldness and un-friendliness. Some were disgusted at the British methods of trying to make life so miserable for Ruth that she would leave Serowe voluntarily and save them more embarrassment.

As the months went by, a couple of civil servants defied the unofficial ban on inviting her to their homes, which in that tiny community took some cour-age, but that was later on. In the meantime, the traders slowly opened their homes to the brave young woman. Said one trader's wife to another in her Afrikaans accent, "Have you seen her? Man, she's that pretty. She even looks classy. Why the hell didn't she marry one of her own kind, that's what I can't understand?" Said an official's wife to her husband in her clipped British ac-cent, "I saw Ruth Khama in the village today. Why, she is beautiful. That hair, those extraordinary eyes, and that skin. It's not as if she couldn't have married any man she chose. What an enigma." Ruth wrote home bravely to her family, "You don't count your friends by their pigmentation. I have all Seretse's family and his friends."

She also had the adoration of the tribe. Dr Chiepe said, "They used to go to her house, teach her a few words of Setswana and love the couple of words she could say. They bent over backwards to show she was accepted, and they just sort of worshipped every little thing she did."

Another massive demonstration of the tribe's warmth came the first Sunday that Seretse took Ruth to the great sandstone Khama church. As she and Seretse walked outside at the end of the service, conducted in Setswana, the women milled around her, waving their hands and ululating, and dancing a path in front of the couple as they made their way, smiling and laughing to their car. When she got home, Ruth, who was fascinated by the ululating, went straight to the bathroom and laughed as she practised it in front of a mirror. It was one of the last happy things that she did before she collapsed with a nervous breakdown.

She was having lunch with Seretse and two of his cousins, when, as she stood up to leave the table, she fainted and was caught by a cousin who had seen her white face turn even whiter. She was carried to bed in a dead faint. In the days that followed, Ruth lived in a dim haze, scarcely aware of what was happening to her, or of the figures who moved with such loving concern around her bed. Later on, Seretse was to tell her that her face seemed to lose all its shape, as if all the muscles in it had collapsed. She spent a month confined to her bed on the advice of Dr Don Moikangoa, a friend of Seretse's who worked at the hospital in Serowe, and although many of the tribe knew she was ill, very few of the other people in the village did.

The nervous breakdown was hardly surprising, for months of accumulated worry and tension about her father's reaction to her marriage, the marriage itself, Seretse's leaving her alone for weeks at a time, and finally the hounding by the press had taken its toll. When Ruth recovered fully a couple of months later, the Bamangwato, who still practised witchcraft, murder and the killing of one of a pair of twins, claimed that Seretse's powers were stronger than those of any witchdoctor. They believed that a spell had been cast on Ruth and that her husband had removed the bewitchment. As Ruth got better (she was so weak initially, she had to be carried everywhere), she said to herself that never, ever again would she allow herself to worry so much that she had another breakdown.

Her family were unaware then of the extent of her collapse, for she wrote them cheerful letters that hid her true condition. A happy note at this dismal time for her was the discovery that she was pregnant. She laughed with joy as she gave Seretse the thrilling news and their mutual pleasure helped to make up for her illness.

As Ruth grew stronger, she began to try and make a garden in the space between the house and the thorn bush fence that kept out cattle, goats and wild animals. There were leopards in the hills and lions were often heard roaring in the vicinity. In bad years of drought, the lions would sometimes sneak into the village to drink at the dam. Ruth also began to learn the customs of her people and realised that the Bamangwato with their royal family were as class conscious as anyone back home in Britain. It didn't take her long to learn who were the senior uncles, where they sat, who spoke first, who was served first at a meal and so forth. But although Ruth learnt all the protocol and manners required of her, she thought that a lot of the customs were outdated and didn't bother to conform to them.

Although Seretse was regarded by most of the tribe as their chief, in spite of the judicial enquiry hanging over his head, Ruth was not expected to perform the duties of a chief's wife, which included mediating in quarrels, spending most of the day listening to problems and, when the rains came, going out to the lands to plant and harvest. As Ruth recovered from her breakdown and her natural energy and vitality began to return, she found, much to her surprise, that she had too much time on her hands. Seretse was preoccupied with tribal meetings, for he was busy getting to know his people again, and as Ruth's only friends were in Palapye, she began to experience a very real loneliness, for she had no one in those very early days with a similar background with whom she could share her problems or joys.

But none of the civil servant's wives who met her for the first time some months after her arrival, at a school handcraft display, saw any outward sign of her inner desolation. They saw an attractive, poised young woman, with hair like burnished copper and a skin so white that as she stood with her arm slipped through Seretse's, the contrast between them was breathtaking.

Seretse laughed and joked with the schoolmasters, and Ruth stood shyly but surely at his side, smiling and outwardly relaxed, although inwardly she was stiff with tension. The officials' wives were fascinated, she was quite different from what many of them had imagined, and when some of them got home, they wrote letters to their mothers in England and South Africa in which they poured out their admiration for her. One wife thought it was immensely brave of her to attend the function at all. "Going out there (to the school) was like going out to the head-hunters," she wrote. "The reaction could have been physically hostile, how was she to know any different?" Wrote another, "She was quite at ease, not at all intimidated by the service wives, and I thought what a charming young woman she was."

And what of Ruth's feelings at the time about the treatment being meted out to her? Naturally she felt the unfriendliness towards her and at the same time the intense curiosity. "They all thought I was a freak, I had to be a freak to have done what I did (in marrying Seretse). But I had learnt from my experience during the war, where you mix with all kinds of people from all walks of life who just want to get on with the job, that class and colour distinction is not important in life," said Ruth. "I felt it was a small society that I had moved into. What were their interests? The traders sat and sold all day in their shops, and the officials sat on their hill and drank tea. Was I really missing out on so much? I had my own friends," she added defensively.

As the traders' wives began seeing more of Ruth, they remarked on her humour. "She had a black chair in the lounge, and she used to say that she liked something black in the house besides Seretse. She also had a reversible bathmat – on the one side it had black feet and on the other side white feet," said one woman to her friends, who had not yet overcome their aversion to meeting Ruth.

Ruth and Seretse's behaviour was naturally closely observed by the administration officials. In mid-September, Sir Evelyn Baring wrote a report to the Commonwealth Relations Office in which he expressed concern about the declining popularity of Tshekedi amongst the tribe and the growing support for Seretse. "There is a danger that, unless the protectorate administration is extremely careful, he may even begin to assume some of the functions of chief," he warned. In this official dispatch Baring also wrote of, "a minor but troublesome matter – Seretse's wish to obtain European liquor for which he apparently developed a liking in England. The administration has been forced to point out that this is not only against the law of the protectorate, but also contrary to Khama's stringent edict against liquor of any kind which is now tribal customary law."[95]

This report, which obviously emanated from Serowe, serves to highlight the difference between the educated, Westernised young man who had spent a couple of years at Britain's most famous university, and the average young men of the tribe. Quite simply, there was no comparison. As for the official who told Seretse he was breaking the law, he was probably less educated than the man he was addressing. The affront to a man of Seretse's dignity is clear, for when a trader who was marrying his cousin asked them to the wedding, Seretse politely declined, saying the laws would not allow him to attend and partake in the spirit of the occasion. What is extraordinary, in view of the petty behaviour meted out to Ruth and Seretse, was his complete lack of bitterness or vindictiveness in later years. Ruth, however, still felt an intense resentment at the humiliating treatment meted out to her husband.

A British journalist, Margaret Lessing, who was covering the Khama story, later told me, "What upset me at the time, were the absolutely cold-blooded attempts by the British to break up the marriage, efforts that did not stop at spreading rumours of the girls Seretse was supposed to have on the side. But Ruth just went on behaving like the good, middle-class Englishwoman she was, and refused to listen to them."

One perplexed South African male journalist who thought Ruth was throwing herself away, asked her, "Can't you see the difference between me and Seretse?" To which Ruth replied, "Yes. I think that Seretse is much more handsome than you are."

Many people expressed amazement at her strength and determination, and when questioned about it, Ruth answered that only someone with strong convictions would have gone into the marriage in the first place. But she, more than anyone else, was learning just how strong those convictions had to be if her marriage was to survive.

In later years, when her sister Muriel visited Serowe, she was to express amazement that Ruth managed to adjust from her former gay and vital life in London to the limited and isolated existence she endured in that first year in Serowe. Not only was she snubbed by her own kind, but she had to get used to a harsh, extreme climate in totally alien living conditions. In addition to this, she was without the motherly, comforting support that every young woman who is pregnant for the first time in her life needs so badly. But the courage that saw her through World War II did not fail her in those hard, early months in her husband's African village.

TEN

Should Seretse be chief?

The next phase in Ruth and Seretse's life was dominated by intrigue, although this was not obvious at the time to anybody but those who were plotting it, and it was not for many, many years that the real reasons for exiling the hapless couple were made known.

September in Serowe is a hot, dry month, during which tensions mount and tempers fray easily as the temperature rises, and nature works herself into a fury getting ready for the rains. The Bamangwato had lived with this for generations and so accepted it, being as close to nature as they were; but for the whites, especially those who had recently left the northern chilly climes, this sense of waiting, of anticipation, produced in many a tremendous irritability. Some people even referred to the period during which the heat built up for the rains as suicide month. While nature threw her energy into producing great rainstorms, there were clouds of a different nature gathering over Ruth and Seretse's heads in September 1949.

Let us look first at the electrical currents flowing through Serowe society. We know about the short-circuiting of any social intercourse with Ruth by the civil service officials and their wives. But there were other electrical charges, for the relationship between Tshekedi and Seretse worsened daily, and some members of the tribe became unhappy as Tshekedi urged those who sided with him to accompany him into exile to the south, to the senior tribe, the Bakwena.

Very few responded to his call, but those who did were able tribal administrators and leaders who had served Tshekedi during his regency, and with the tremendous tribal sense of loyalty were prepared to leave those members of their families behind who had thrown their loyalties behind Seretse. Night meetings and meetings unauthorised by the district commissioner were banned to reduce tribal intrigue, but they continued nonetheless, and the police were kept busy filing reports and infiltrating meetings. At one held at dawn, Seretse told his people that the British Government was in favour of Tshekedi, and there was a likelihood that he himself might not be made chief.

Sworn statements alleging intimidation were made by both Seretse and Tshekedi supporters, and an uncle of Seretse's, Peto Sekgoma, took the police to his hut to show them where a shot had been fired at him through the window. The police were inclined to disbelieve this and were angry when newspaper reporters picked up the story. The police officer commanding the district, who had had to deal with a reporter demanding verification of the story, filed the following report to his superiors, "I denied that Peto had made a statement, and (I) turned the subject to foot-and-mouth disease (this affects cattle). I informed the (*British Sunday Express*) reporter that it was hardly likely that he would obtain information from the local inhabitants, as printed reports were usually distorted and utter nonsense."[96] The local administration's contempt for reporters who were after all just doing their job increased along with the growing tension in the tribe and led later on to bad relations between press and officials.

While the Serowe police collected evidence of secret meetings, Sir Evelyn Baring was collecting evidence of a different kind. He wanted to know from liberals and blacks in the Union of South Africa and the blacks in Bechuanaland what they envisaged the consequences would be of the recognition of Seretse as chief while he had a white wife. According to Baring's biographer, Charles Douglas-Home, he found support from a totally unexpected quarter: Father Trevor Huddleston, who later became the president of the Anti-Apartheid League, but who was then widely known for his work amongst the black people in Johannesburg's Sophiatown. "When I put to Trevor the point whether it would be immoral to refuse to recognise Seretse, because by this action the break-up of his marriage would be brought nearer, he brushed it on one side, and is very strongly against recognition," wrote Baring.[97] This letter is also significant because it appears to show that Baring was so keen to resolve the problem of a chief with a white wife on the South African borders that he even envisaged the break-up of the marriage.

Quintin Whyte, director of the South African Institute of Race Relations, wrote to Baring that liberal opinion was generally that Seretse had the right to marry anyone that he wished, but that support on any issue between Seretse and Tshekedi would probably go to the latter. He did not think that concessions to the government of the Union of South Africa would prevent it continuing along its nationalistic path. He warned Baring about the rising tide of nationalism throughout Africa and pointed out that any action by the United Kingdom against Seretse could result in the young man becoming the "sacrificial leader of southern African Africans."[98] But Baring was set on his course, firmly believing that it was worth sacrificing Seretse in order not to bedevil relations between South Africa and the United Kingdom.

Two letters written at the beginning of October 1949 indicate the definite line taken by Baring before the enquiry had made its finding. On 11th October, he wrote to Sir Percivale Liesching about the South African prime minister's anxiety that his request for transfer for the protectorate should reach the United Kingdom before the British general election to be held in February 1950. Baring was anxious that a decision on Seretse should have been taken, and publicised, before the transfer request was made, to ensure that it did not appear the British were acceding to South African pressure.

"In these circumstances I am suggesting to Harragin [the commission judge] that he should complete his enquiry as quickly as possible," wrote Baring, and he continued, "the announcement concerning Seretse might be made in January. Sillery [the resident commissioner] thinks there should be no ill result from a pause between the completion of the commission's work and an announcement of the decision."[99] The question is: what decision? Had Baring already made up his mind regardless of the commission's findings? Sillery's letter of 6th October[100] to the district commissioner in Serowe would appear to suggest that this was in fact the case, for in it he pointed out that it could do no harm if people of all races were to appreciate that the commission might not be in favour of either Seretse or Tshekedi, but that neither might rule, and the government of the tribe would be carried on without them. This is exactly the course of action adopted subsequently by the British Government. And Ruth Khama would later be of the firm opinion that the enquiry was a total farce.

Dr D.F. Malan, the South African prime minister, increased the pressure on the British for non-recognition of Seretse, by announcing at the end of October 1949, that he had made Ruth and Seretse prohibited immigrants.[101] This of course meant that if Seretse was made chief, he would not be able to visit the Bechuanaland capital in Mafeking, which was situated about thirty kilometres across the protectorate border. Neither would he be able to visit the high commissioner who lived in Pretoria for six months of the year and in Cape Town for the other six months, following the South African Government in its annual migration between its legislative and executive capitals. Malan also announced that he intended asking the Union of South Africa Parliament to send a deputation to Britain to ask for transfer of the protectorates.

The prime minister's action in publicly announcing his intention to ask for transfer shows the depth of feeling by the apartheid government towards the marriage. They would have been upset about it at any time, for it struck at the very root of their religious, social and political beliefs – but the atmosphere of fury engendered by it was enhanced by preparations for the unveiling of a huge monument to Afrikanerdom – the Voortrekker Monument outside Pretoria in December of that year. The defeat of the English-speaking United Party at the hands of the Afrikaner National Party the previous year had exacerbated the often simmering tensions between the two language groups. It was felt therefore by moderates within the country that the Khama marriage, constituting an affront as it did to everything that Afrikanerdom stood for, would widen the gap even further between Afrikaners and the English, whose country, Britain, had allowed it to take place.

It was against this background of local, national and international tension over the marriage that the world press began arriving in Serowe to record the work of the commission. In those days, all reports had to be telegraphed, and one of the busiest people in the village whenever the journalists arrived, was postmaster and telegraph operator, Joe Burgess, an ex-royal navy signaller. He provided newsmen with a table in the little post office where they could write the reports he telegraphed, and he often worked until midnight to push through their copy.

The control of the post office was a complicated one and gives some idea of the invidious position Bechuanaland was in vis-à-vis its more powerful South African and Southern Rhodesian neighbours. Joe Burgess told me, "When I was there, the telephones and telegraphs belonged to Southern Rhodesia, and we operated them on behalf of that country's authorities. The postal side was organised by the postmaster in Mafeking [in South Africa] but we were British civil servants."

The telephone lines were like an old washing line. Every time the wind blew, something would blow off, and if an ox wagon knocked over a pole, Burgess would have to go out and lash it up as best he could. To the press this was a source of amusement, to the locals it was a way of life. The locals did not escape the amusement of the press either – the insularity of the traders, the boredom of those in the civil service, and the excitement they found in seeing new faces – these were all duly recorded.

The judicial enquiry members arrived during the last weekend in October, to prepare for their sittings on 1st November, and the district commissioner threw a party to introduce them to the local civil servants and leading lights of the community. Ruth and Seretse were not invited to this, an omission that caught someone's attention, for within days of it a question was tabled in the British Houses of Parliament, asking why Ruth Khama was the only white person in the district not invited to the reception. The district commissioner's reply was straightforward – he had given an unofficial party, to which many white people in the district were not invited. This little incident illustrates the growing concern at the time amongst British Labour Party backbenchers and Independents over the treatment of the couple.

In the protectorate, some British officials were beginning to revise their opinion of Ruth, for she was courageously coping with loneliness and snubs which they knew they themselves would have had great difficulty in enduring. Baring waited in vain for reports showing that Ruth was disappointed with the tribe, or that she was piqued at not being the Indian rajah's wife she might have expected she would be, or that she was tiring of Serowe life. In fact, the situation was quite the opposite. Ruth was beginning to take a lively interest in the welfare of the Bamangwato womenfolk. She expressed concern about their hard lives and the general lack of hygiene and health education. She was distressed at the almost total absence of welfare centres and clinics outside the main villages in the Bamangwato Reserve.

And it wasn't long after her arrival in Serowe that she inquired why the trading stores were such poor-looking places, and she learnt that the traders were not allowed to buy the land, and therefore, understandably did not want to spend money on improving their buildings. Some people were fascinated by the large stores with their dim interiors, in which were stored such a vast and fascinating array of implements and foods, but Ruth was not one of them. In a typical store, bicycles hung from the high tin ceilings, and tractor parts, ploughs and great bales of brightly-coloured cloth jostled for space. Huge bins of beans and meal lined the walls, and basins of brightly coloured sweets graced the heavy wooden counters. The sight of all this, so different from the smart, neat London stores that she was accustomed to, shocked Ruth initially, and her comments according to one British official, who mentioned them in a report, alarmed some of the traders. Ruth was never one to be less than direct. If she did not approve of something, she said so, whether it was political or not.

Sir Walter Harragin, chief justice of the high commission territories, who visited in turn Bechuanaland, Swaziland and Basutoland, presided over the enquiry. He was a tall, handsome man, who had years of colonial service behind him, and he was noted for his ability to sum up long and difficult cases without having to refer much to his notes. He was a popular person on the Pretoria social scene (his headquarters were there) for he could tell a good joke and had many interesting stories to recount. His two assessors were Mr R.S. Hudson, in charge of the African studies branch at the Colonial Office, and Mr G.E. Nettleton, who was for many years an official in the protectorate service and then government secretary, before becoming deputy resident commissioner.

The enquiry opened on 1st November in a marquee in the terrible heat of a Bechuanaland summer, and no quantity of fans or mopping of sweat-drenched faces could alleviate the torrid conditions. There were 5000 Bamangwato outside that tent, seated in row after row after row on the ground, come to see that the justice the British were famed for was done to the man they wanted as chief. They waved the buzzing, irritating flies patiently away from their faces, and they silently raised their hats, with their noteworthy dignity and good manners when the judge made his way to the table, which was heavy with books and documents, and brightened with flowers from someone's hard-won garden. The hats had been whipped off too when Seretse arrived, although he had tried to make his way as unobtrusively as possible into the hearing. Ruth was not beside him, she did not attend the enquiry throughout its sitting, but despite that, her presence hung so strongly over the gathering that she might have been there physically, for it was her name that was mentioned over and over again, mentioned with love and with hate, depending on whoever was speaking.

As many of the local white population as could get away from their stores, their jobs, their children and chores, attended the hearings. In this enquiry then were met the forces of Seretse and Tshekedi; of Britain and of South Africa; of Africanism and of Europeanism. The terms of reference of the enquiry bear repeating. They were:

1. To report whether the kgotla held at Serowe between 20th and 25th June, 1949, at which Seretse Khama was designated as chief of the Bamangwato tribe, was properly convened and assembled, and its proceedings conducted in accordance with native custom.
2. To report on the question whether, having particular regard to the interests and well-being of the tribe, Seretse Khama was a fit and proper person to discharge the functions of chief.[102]

But the enquiry members had hardly settled down on their seats, when they received a petition from Tshekedi asking for it to be transferred to Lobatsi, a town situated 381 kilometres to the south of Serowe. His reason for this request was that he feared his life would be in danger in his home village.

And so the enquiry members packed up and went down south, to the pretty, hilly town of Lobatsi, where it again unpacked its books and documents, but this time in a small court house, situated close to the jail and to the district commissioner's office. Lobatsi (today called Lobatse) is about 100 kilometres from Mafeking and is encircled by hills. It was known in Bechuanaland for its plantation of blue gums, for being the seat of the high court, and for having a strip of tar road (Francistown being the only other place in the protectorate to share this distinction).

Tshekedi, tense, eloquent, verbose and emotional, spoke for hours on end as he made his points, in which he contended, inter alia, that:

> Ruth could never be queen of the tribe because Seretse had married without the consent of the chief and the family elders; Ruth's children could never succeed to the chieftainship; Seretse was unfit to be chief because he had ignored native law and custom in his marriage; at the third kgotla, Seretse had stampeded the tribe into an improper decision; Seretse was unfit to be chief, because, contrary to native law and custom and particularly Bamangwato custom, he had been drinking intoxicating liquor; the recognition of Seretse as chief would cause disruption in the tribe and would endanger the friendly relations of the Bamangwato with the Union of South Africa and Southern Rhodesia, two countries upon which the tribe was greatly dependent; Seretse's prohibited immigrant status in South Africa would make it impossible for him to carry out his duties as chief. The statutory law of the protectorate did not envisage a European as a member of a tribe.[103]

Tshekedi was certainly an embittered man to lay such dreadful charges against his nephew in front of a judicial enquiry. When he turned his attention to Ruth his bitterness turned to hatred, for he said, "I cannot accept a woman who will probably set her dogs after me when I go to her house."[104] For all his eloquence, the enquiry members were not impressed with the manner in which he appeared to regard every question that was put to him as a carefully thought out trap, which he took every precaution to avoid falling into, even where, in their opinion, the answers were obvious and simple. But they recognised him for the dynamic, shrewd, strong-minded person he was, and they appreciated the twenty-three years of service he had given to his tribe.

Once Tshekedi and his witnesses had completed their evidence, the commission returned to Serowe, to the marquee and the heat, and then it was Seretse's turn. The local populace and the commission members sat up in some surprise when Seretse spoke, for, although he did not talk as fast or as much as Tshekedi, in fact quite the opposite, for he was relaxed where his uncle was tense and his words were few and well chosen, he was clever. The commission noted how well he spoke English, how quick he was to appreciate the European point of view even if he did not agree with it. They found him, in contrast to Tshekedi, an easy witness to examine, for he immediately understood the questions, and answered them without hesitation, clearly and fairly.

And when he said, his voice ringing, even in that hot tent, "I could never accept from any tribe or nation a decision that I should divorce my wife", most of those bigoted white villagers present realised for the first time how deep the love was that bound them together, and that it was not a mere infatuation that they might grow out of as the circumstances of their life together became more difficult.

Seretse continued, "As I told my own people, 'husband and wife are one, and there is no way in which my wife can stay somewhere and I elsewhere.'" His speech was calm and slow, his words measured and thoughtful. A hushed silence fell over the tent in their wake. Some people shifted uncomfortably in their seats. This marital steadfastness of course impressed the commission, it being a far cry from heathen polygamy and much in tune with their Christian thinking and principles.

The commission members found themselves agreeing with Seretse's contention that although he had acted incorrectly in not obtaining the tribe's consent to his marriage, he had subsequently obtained their forgiveness and ratification of his action. Why then, Seretse wanted to know, should Ruth not be recognised as queen, and their children as lawful successors to the chieftainship? Later, when the time came to write its report, the members wrote, "We are well aware that in the old days this matter would have been settled quite simply by the tribe either killing Seretse or driving him into exile. In these days, Seretse has won the battle for himself and his wife, not by force of arms, but by force of votes." And the commission went further: "In our view, the matter is one for the tribesmen, and for them alone, and if they are prepared to forgive a chief who has ignored their custom, who are we to insist on his punishment?"[105]

The commission found that it also could not agree that Seretse had stampeded the tribe in the third kgotla by putting to them the question, "Who is for me?", for it was satisfied that the tribe, in voting for Seretse, knew what it was doing. After listening to evidence from members of the tribe, the commission concluded furthermore that Tshekedi was so unpopular with the tribe that it looked to Seretse as its only hope of deliverance.

And now, for the vexed question of liquor, raised by the embittered Tshekedi, who clearly was not going to leave any stone unturned in his efforts to discredit his nephew. It was stated that from the time Ruth arrived in Serowe until the holding of the enquiry, eight bottles of liquor (which included three bottles of gin and three of brandy) had been purchased by the Khama household, for which a permit had been issued by the district commissioner as was routine. As British reporter John Redfern pointed out: "Eight bottles in nearly three months would be regarded as quite a meagre allowance by some of the white people who listened, pop-eyed, to this part of the enquiry."[106]

In retrospect, it seems ridiculous and petty that a British judicial commission should question Seretse about eight bottles of liquor, but it did, and he answered frankly that he did from time to time have a drink, and to that extent departed from custom. The commission found, "We do not consider this to be an insuperable obstacle to Seretse's recognition, for it is always possible to amend the statutory laws to meet hard cases." Is there perhaps a shade of irony in this section of that report? I'd like to think so.

No wonder, in view of this sort of evidence, the Westernised young man who loved jazz and a good curry in a London restaurant, went home to his modern bungalow set amongst the thorn trees and bushes, and reduced his wife and his cousins to fits of laughter as he imitated the men who were interrogating him. "He was a very good mimic, and he used to be quite hysterical the way he captured their characteristics," said Ruth. After the laughter had died down, Seretse's face would become serious once more, and he would sit down with his lawyer, Percy Fraenkel, who came from Mafeking and who advised Seretse throughout his troubles, and they would try and work out the kind of questions he could be asked, and the answers that Seretse could give the following day.

Something that incensed Ruth at this time was the officials' "snubbing" of Seretse at tea time. "He was asked if he could supply milk from his cows for the tea of commission members and the whites who were sitting around there. But although they could drink his milk, he couldn't share their tea!" And so Ruth used to drive to the marquee, park under a nearby tree and wait for Seretse to come to her for something to eat and drink. Recalled Seretse's cousin, Goareng Mosinyi, "Yes, the government went off and had its tea, and we had ours, the officials didn't want to mix with Seretse. Ruth got angry, but Seretse could always cool her down with a joke, and they would laugh and forget it."

Someone else living in Serowe got so angry about the incident – an episode that the tribesmen sitting outside regarded as a slight to their chief – that she wrote a letter to a British member of parliament, giving him the details. And she added quite a few more, for she was scathing in her condemnation of the attitude of Serowe's white populace towards Ruth and Seretse. "The white people live by keeping shops or are in government service. The women have good Bechuana servants and spend their time in tennis and gossip. All, in fact, depend upon the natives entirely for their living, and they live well by the tribe, yet have no good word for them. It is from these people that one hears again and again, 'I shall not receive Ruth Khama.' To me it seems that it is Ruth Khama who should be in the position of saying: 'I shall not receive them,'" she wrote indignantly, and her letter was subsequently published by the British press.[107]

It seems from what I have written so far of the commission's report that it favoured Seretse, and indeed, it took a harsh view of Tshekedi, for it concluded that although the latter was one of the most enlightened and experienced administrators in Africa, the fact was that as far as the Bamangwato tribe was concerned, he had outstayed his welcome, and despite all his good work he was the most unpopular man in the tribe. The commission suggested that it was in his own interest, and in the interests of law and order, that he should remove himself from the Bamangwato Reserve (as he had himself suggested and had in fact done).

Now comes the rub as far as recognition of Seretse is concerned. Tshekedi's allegation that recognition of him would endanger the friendly relations of the protectorate with the Union of South Africa and Southern Rhodesia was accepted by the commission. It stated that it was aware of the dependence of the territory on the two countries and listed specific areas of dependence that ranged from customs to medical matters, the railway, posts and telegraphs.

"We know in what straits the Bamangwato Reserve and Bechuanaland would be if for some reason the Union of South Africa ceased to cooperate, if only to the extent of finding it impossible to supply Bechuanaland with maize during famine months," went the commission's report.[108]

The commission also accepted Tshekedi's contention that Seretse's prohibited immigrant status in South Africa would prevent him, the official representative of by far the largest tribe in Bechuanaland, from visiting its headquarters in Mafeking or going to Pretoria. "We realise that it is unfortunate that the official headquarters of the protectorate lie in a neighbouring territory, but it is a fact that has got to be faced, and we are quite unable to think of any practical way in which the difficulty could be overcome, short of moving the headquarters into the protectorate." In years to come, when Seretse became prime minister of Bechuanaland, that is exactly what was done.

The enquiry sat for a total of eighteen days, before it packed its documents into bulging briefcases and headed for Pretoria, where in the remarkably short space of twelve days it wrote its report and submitted it to the high commissioner on 1st December 1949.

Its findings were, firstly, that the third kgotla at which Seretse was acclaimed as chief, was properly convened and conducted, and secondly, that Seretse, regarding the interests and well-being of the tribe, was not a fit and proper person to be chief.

The reasons given for non-recognition of Seretse were as follows:

1. Being a prohibited immigrant in the Union of South Africa, he will be unable to efficiently carry out his duties as chief.
2. A friendly and cooperative Union of South Africa and Southern Rhodesia is essential to the well-being of the tribe, and indeed the whole of the Bechuanaland Protectorate.
3. His recognition will undoubtedly cause disruption in the Bamangwato tribe.

The commission made two interesting points that we should note well in view of the subsequent British treatment of Seretse Khama. It felt that, if conditions should change, Seretse should be allowed to assume his duties as chief, for the commission recognised that he was the lawful and legitimate heir to the chieftainship, "and save for his irresponsibility in contracting this unfortunate marriage, he would be in our opinion, a fit and proper person to be chief."

The commission members pointed out too that it was not disinheriting Seretse's family forever from becoming chief, and that it might well be that in the not too distant future Seretse could become chief. Having said that, the commission then went on to recommend drastic action for the British to take against both Seretse and Tshekedi. It suggested that they should both be exiled from the Bamangwato Reserve. A pension was suggested for Tshekedi, on condition that he remained outside the reserve.

Seretse, it was suggested, should be paid a subsidy that would enable him to, "live in appropriate style," provided he lived outside the protectorate, for his position as chief designate, with the willing (tribal) allegiance that accompanied that status, would prove embarrassing to the British administration and upset tribal tranquillity. If Seretse did not leave voluntarily, the high commissioner should think about using powers to ensure his removal.

The commission advised that the vacuum created in tribal administration, where the chief wielded wide powers, should be filled by the district commissioner in a period of direct rule. I have discussed the behind-the-scenes South African activity, which clearly had some influence on the commission's findings, and it is interesting to note here that due to the British Government's suppression of the report for many years, people concluded that it could not have been in accordance with the British Government's wishes. In fact, as we shall see, the report acutely embarrassed the British Labour prime minister when he first read it, and it was subsequently decided to suppress it and to leave out entirely any mention of South Africa, and to concentrate instead on the aspect of tribal dissension as the reason for exiling Seretse.

Six days after the members of the judicial enquiry signed the report and handed it to him, Baring wrote to the secretary of state for commonwealth relations, recommending that Seretse should not be recognised as chief, and that both Seretse and Tshekedi should leave the Bamangwato Reserve "at least temporarily". Baring was due to leave South Africa for the United Kingdom and he said he had a couple of proposals and suggestions to make, which he preferred to make orally. But the very next day after he had written this, on 7th December, he wrote a detailed memorandum on how Ruth and Seretse could be "persuaded" to go and live outside the reserve. He seriously misjudged both Ruth and Seretse, for he believed that Ruth was, "a little disappointed in Serowe" and that Seretse might, "hanker after Western ways and life in London" and might accept a reasonably generous allowance in order to live there.[109]

Baring also suggested the British Government should put the idea of self-imposed exile to Seretse in London, where he and Ruth would have the opportunity to consider the position in, as he put it, "a calmer atmosphere than that of emotion-charged Serowe."

About a week later, the secretary of state for commonwealth relations, Philip Noel-Baker, drafted a memorandum to the British Cabinet[110] in which he said that, while he did not question the finding that Seretse should not be chief, he was "considerably embarrassed" by the reasons on which it was based. And he did not know how he would be able to defend such reasoning in parliament. Noel-Baker had had discussions with Baring by then and had accepted his view that a decision to recognise Seretse would have unfortunate repercussions on the interests of Africans in the high commission territories and in the union. This view, Noel-Baker was advised, was held both by black people and by liberals in South Africa. Despite this, he felt that the United Kingdom had to avoid even the appearance of allowing its action in the matter to be dictated by apartheid South Africa. On 20th December, a highly-worried Noel-Baker wrote to his prime minister about the recognition of Seretse and described the commission's report as an "inflammable document" which, if leaked to the press, would make a difficult position even worse.[111]

Baring must have felt that his stand on non-recognition of Seretse needed bolstering, for a couple of days after Christmas he wrote to another official in the Commonwealth Relations Office, defending his views on the grounds that leading tribes in Bechuanaland, black people and liberal whites in the Union of South Africa held the same view, namely that Seretse should not be recognised. He emphasised the dissension that Ruth's presence would create in the tribe.

The reasons he gave for this included her ability as a white person to buy liquor for Seretse; the fact that the native courts could not bring a non-native under their jurisdiction; and finally, he suggested that Ruth would be unable to perform the duties required of a chief's wife.

He outdid the enquiry with all his reasons for non-recognition of Seretse, and it is worth noting that Tshekedi's arguments to the commission for not recognising Seretse are contained in Baring's memorandums. He clearly laid great store by Tshekedi's views and opinions.

It is interesting, therefore, that one of the enquiry members, Mr Hudson, felt so strongly about this matter that he wrote a letter himself, saying that he disagreed with the belief that Africans in South Africa and the protectorate, and liberals in South Africa, did not want the marriage.

The British prime minister, Clement Attlee, was clearly most worried about rushing a decision on Ruth and Seretse, for he said he did not want the matter handled precipitately, and an anxious Patrick Gordon Walker, acting on behalf of Noel-Baker who was away, wrote to Attlee that there was a sense of urgency.[112] Dr Malan was about to present his demand for the transfer of the protectorates, and much use would be made by him of the Seretse case in criticising the British administration of the territories. Gordon Walker felt it would be deplorable if the announcement of the British decision not to recognise Seretse should follow such a criticism by South Africa – a criticism that would become harsher, he said, if the British appeared unable to make up their minds.

Gordon Walker also pointed out to his prime minister that Ruth was due to have her baby in May, and that Seretse would be reluctant to leave Serowe without her: "There may be some risk in inducing his wife to travel to London, but I think we must face it, and the risk will be least if she can be brought to make the journey at once. An offer of the best medical attention in London in her confinement may prove a strong inducement," he wrote.

The prime minister replied, "This matter must come to cabinet. The document is most disturbing. In effect, we are invited to go contrary to the desires of the great majority of the Bamangwato tribe, solely because of the attitude of the Governments of the Union of South Africa and Southern Rhodesia. It is as if we had been obliged to agree to Edward VIII's abdication so as not to annoy the Irish Free State and the USA."[113]

These are laudable sentiments, but despite them and his caustic remarks, his government was within the next few months to follow exactly the course of action he so abhorred. The forces at work against the Khama marriage were eventually to overpower even the sense of outrage expressed initially by the British prime minister.

ELEVEN

A very disreputable transaction

Ruth did not remember much of her first Christmas in Africa, which is not surprising, for the mind has a way of forgetting things that are unpleasant or difficult, and life was both of these for the Khamas at that time. While Britain shivered in an icy Christmas and its political parties prepared for the general election in February, the 100 000 strong Bamangwato tribe sat around their fires on starlit nights and pondered the fate the British had in store for them and Seretse in the wake of the judicial enquiry.

Seretse had realised when the enquiry was appointed barely a month after the triumphant acclamation of him at the third kgotla that all was not well, but as he and Ruth sweltered in the blistering heat in their bungalow during Christmas 1949, neither of them imagined even remotely the shocking events that would characterise the forthcoming year for them. It was impossible to conceive that the British Government's treatment of them would be such that it would be criticised around the world.

The festive season, celebrated with as much gusto and merriment in Bechuanaland as it was in the colder climes, did not produce any thaw in the icy approach of the Serowe civil servants to Ruth. Some of them felt horrified at the way in which they were forced to snub her, but their position was a difficult one. Any overtures to Ruth would have been picked up by that tiny, close-knit community and instantly relayed to headquarters, and transfer to a less pleasant posting or some other indication of government displeasure might have resulted. Indeed, later this was to happen to three men who took a stand on the British treatment of both the tribe and the Khamas.

But the traders did not concern themselves with civil servant directives, and when Judge Harragin said during the enquiry that he thought the treatment meted out to Ruth was rather cruel, some of them took their cue from that and began to visit her. But she felt keenly the lack of contact with those who had a similar background to hers, and no doubt she heard much of the Christmas parties held up on Nob Hill, complete with tinsel, mince pies, paper hats and Christmas pudding. It did not matter to the colonials that wax candles drooped in the heat or that the bright colour of festive paper hats ran in rivulets down perspiring brows – Christmas had to be celebrated in true northern style. And if you were friendly with the district commissioner, then you could cool off in his plunge pool, the only one in Serowe. The rest of the white populace had to be content with lying in cold baths to try and cool down, but even that did not help much, for the cold water did not live up to its description, having been heated in the pipes by the sun's fierce rays.

Ruth missed the traditional English family Christmas, although she did not say as much to Seretse; she was so happy to be with him. "But we had no Christmas pudding, mince pies or turkey. Seretse was never much given to that sort of food," said Ruth. She was fast becoming accustomed to the screech of cicadas and crickets, that acutely African sound which at times can be so loud that your eardrums vibrate. Scorpions, spiders, lizards, snakes and beetles of every description were harder to cope with, and Ruth's house, like the rest in Serowe, was fitted with gauze window screening in an effort to keep the wildlife of Africa out of doors where it belonged. "It took a bit of getting used to, but we were fortunate not to have snakes in the house. Seretse particularly disliked them, and we always had so many people around us all the time that they kept them at bay," said Ruth.

But even Ruth, who loved the heat, found it trying when her face creams melted, and face powder that could keep the shine off your nose for only a few minutes at a time was a bit of a joke. In those scorching, torrid days of summer, the temperatures rose to forty-five degrees centigrade during the day, and did not fall below twenty-six degrees at night, and many a person tossed and turned and moaned with sleeplessness through the still, hot nights.

At that time, Ruth and Seretse became close friends of Alan and Doris Bradshaw. He was the mine recruiting officer in Palapye, and in the twenty-two years he had been there, he had come to understand and appreciate the Bamangwato way of life and customs. Indeed, it was part of his job to inform his superiors about their customs and traditions, for the mines were a great melting pot of tribes from all over southern Africa. Bradshaw was an Englishman with a loud voice, a robust and friendly man with a religious and political outlook that did not recognise any colour bar, in the true spirit of the British Empire.

In a letter home about that time, he wrote, "When we knew Seretse had married a white girl, we knew she was going to face many difficulties in a strange and foreign country and would need all the help and friends she could get, and we made a point of doing all we could for her."[114] And so the Bradshaw bungalow over the track from the railway line in dusty, sleepy Palapye became a haven for Ruth, although she would certainly not admit to this at the time. Gaositwe Chiepe was another good and loyal friend and a frequent visitor to the Khama bungalow. Gentle, humorous Naledi Khama, Seretse's younger sister, who nearly always had a chuckle welling in her deep-throated voice, made her home with her brother and his wife after he had asked her to leave her nursing job in the South African harbour town of Durban and join them. She was at the King Edward VIII hospital there when she read in the South African newspaper of Seretse's marriage to Ruth, and she was so agonised at the thought of how they would be treated that she became ill. She was teased mercilessly by the mainly Afrikaans-speaking staff, and it is to the credit of the Afrikaner matron that when Naledi complained to her she told her staff that any further such behaviour would result in expulsion.

Shortly after Naledi returned to Serowe, Tshekedi asked her if she would accompany him into his self-imposed exile in Rametsana, a village he had hacked out of the bush just over the border from the Bamangwato Reserve. When she declined, there were no harsh words from her uncle. They were fond of each other, for Naledi had grown up in his care as did Seretse.

But her allegiance lay clearly with the brother she loved. Two of Seretse's cousins, Lenyletse Seretse and Goareng Mosinyi, laid the foundations of a life-long friendship with Ruth at this time. Lenyletse was large and well-built with a slow way of speaking, and in later years Ruth would go horse riding with him in the hills of Serowe. Goareng was charming and good-looking with his laughing eyes and attractive, amusing personality. Both men helped Ruth to ward off the press, who in the new year renewed its efforts to obtain the "inside story" of her marriage to Seretse. It sensed the drama – electric as the thunderstorms that crashed through the hot summer days – that lay ahead. Whether or not the British recognised Seretse as chief, there was a good story to be had in the decision.

Life magazine sent Margaret Bourke-White, the world's most famous female photographer, to Serowe. Her previous assignments had included photographing the Indian leader Mahatma Gandhi and the Russian dictator Joseph Stalin. No wonder she had earned a formidable reputation, for she succeeded in getting into the Khama bungalow and taking domestic pictures of Ruth and Seretse which no one else had managed to do. She subsequently gave Ruth two kittens which Ruth, with her sharp wit, immediately named

Pride and Prejudice. A story, probably apocryphal, which did the rounds at the time, was that Bourke-White, who had had the devil's own job of getting her pictures of Stalin, cabled *Life* when she succeeded with the Khamas: "It was worse than Uncle Joe."[115]

Alan Bradshaw featured prominently in some of those pictures and indeed, his discretion and his loyalty to the Khamas is all the more noteworthy in view of the constant pounding on his front door by the media, who envied his access to Ruth and Seretse. Swedes, Americans, Canadians, Frenchmen, South Africans, Britons and Germans all took turns in filling his glass in the Palapye hotel bar, to no avail.

While the Khamas and the press languished in the Serowe heat, the high commissioner and the British Government put their heads together in White-hall to work out the best way of getting Ruth and Seretse out of Bechuana-land with the least possible publicity and fuss. Baring had made up his mind that Seretse must leave the protectorate, whether he did so voluntarily or not, and he had all manner of plans for bringing about his removal. But the British Cabinet hoped that Seretse could be persuaded by the secretary of state for commonwealth relations to resign the chieftainship voluntarily, and to that end, they wished Seretse to travel to London for talks. They also hoped Ruth would accompany him, for then they would have removed them both from the protectorate without having to serve them with deportation orders in the full glare of world publicity and under the angry, rebellious eyes of the tribe. It is interesting that at that stage (the end of January 1950) the British Cabinet had not yet reached a definite decision to withhold recognition of Seretse if he should refuse to resign the chieftainship, although it had almost decided not to publish the "inflammable" report of the judicial enquiry.

Resident Commissioner Anthony Sillery, acting on instructions, asked Seretse to meet him in Lobatsi. During their official talks, and later over lunch with Ruth and Seretse, he told them of the secretary of state's wish to hold talks in London with Seretse, and their hope that Ruth would take the opportunity of seeing her family again. Sillery later described his "tentative impressions" of that meal. He described Ruth as being "gay and excited" at the thought of the journey and being able to shop in London, while Seretse who was engrossed in his own thoughts, "had a poor appetite and showed curiosity about [the] return journey." On the latter score, Sillery wrote, "We parried his questions."[116] And in this manner was begun the extraordinary bungle the British made over getting the Khamas out of Bechuanaland, and their unkind and cruel treatment of them when plans went awry. Both Sillery and Baring seemed then to believe that Ruth and Seretse, struggling financially and socially, would welcome a British-assisted return to London life. They were as wrong about that as they were about the intense loyalty of the tribe towards the couple. On their return to Serowe after the meeting with Sillery, Seretse immediately called a kgotla to tell the tribe of the British invitation. The upshot of days of discussion by several hundreds in the sweltering heat was that the tribe decided that Seretse should go to London alone. It could not understand why Ruth should also have been invited and they feared (rightly so as it later transpired) that it was a trick to get the couple out of Bechuanaland.

A deputation of Seretse's supporters visited Sillery and asked him for a guarantee that Ruth would be allowed to return. It was one he was obviously unable to furnish, and Ruth, who had become as suspicious as the tribe was of British intentions, decided to stay behind. Again, Sillery misjudged her, for he believed that she had only come to her decision due to pressure from the tribe and against her personal wishes. She had no doubt been initially excited at the prospect of seeing her family and London again, and who wouldn't have been under such lonely and miserable social conditions? But she was a person of principle and courage, and although she longed to be with her mother, as does any woman pregnant with her first child, her first loyalty was to Seretse. And so Sillery had to report, "Ruth has jibbed at the last minute," for the administration had already booked two passages on the BOAC flying boat.

A letter written by the tribe at the time to the secretary of state for commonwealth relations, Philip Noel-Baker, is a good illustration of the way in which the traditional trust of and loyalty towards the "great Queen across the sea" was becoming strained by suspicion. It began, "We regard this [the invitation to Seretse] as an honour and [...] as proof that the government of the United Kingdom will always act in accordance with the spirit intended when our country was first proclaimed as a protectorate."[117] The tribe regretted their "queen" could not, in view of the lack of guarantees, make the journey to England, but said that their distrust flowed from the strong objections by the union and Southern Rhodesia to their "chief's" marriage. "Throughout our history," went the letter, "both these countries have sought to dispossess us of our land and our rights, and it was on account of this very apprehension that we originally sought the protection of Great Britain." And the tribe requested that the "present controversy be examined and handled with care, so that it may in no way impair the trust, confidence and understanding that exists between England and ourselves." It was a far-seeing, almost prophetic letter, recognising as it did the role played by South Africa and forecasting the betrayal by the British of their trust.

When Baring heard that Ruth had turned down the British invitation, he was furious at the upset of his plans. He urged the Commonwealth Relations Office to inform Seretse, as soon as he got to London, that it insisted that Ruth attend the discussions about their future. The depth of Baring's feelings on the matter is made clear when he advises the government in case of further requests for guarantees of Ruth's safe return, to say "orally" that their return would not be prevented, but if their presence proved a danger to peace in the protectorate, then they might have to be "removed".

As Seretse kissed his now visibly pregnant wife goodbye for the third time in their short-married life, she clung to him, wishing in that sad, lonely moment that she had agreed to accompany him whatever the consequences. Her eyes misted with tears as she watched him drive away and turned slowly and heavily towards the house. She would have been even more miserable if she had known that instead of a couple of weeks, it would be two months before she would next see him, and that it would be under the most traumatic of circumstances. To the press clamouring for some comment on the tribe's wish that Ruth stay behind with them, Seretse said, "They like Ruth, and she likes them. We both do. She is quite at home in Africa," and with that the large, well-built young man, attired in flannel jacket and trousers and wearing his customary sunglasses and the broad smile that hid his deep feelings, flew off to England.

A perceptive article written at the time by Noel Monks of the *London Daily Mail*, warned the British Government of the fervent support of the majority of the Bamangwato for their chief and Ruth.[118] He mentioned the growing sympathy of some white people in the protectorate for the couple and pointed out that Seretse was no longer his own master, able to make his own decisions, for now he belonged to and was responsible to the tribe. If the British at that early stage had recognised the strong commitment of the tribe and the Khamas towards each other, it is possible some of the subsequent misery and drama could have been averted. But it would seem that a London journalist had his finger more on the pulse of the tribe, than did the British administration officials on the spot, although as is the case in most administrations and governments, there were doubtless officials who had their own views which they either suppressed or which were disregarded by their seniors.

When Seretse arrived in England, he was rushed by car from Southampton straight to Whitehall. There he was cordially received by the undersecretary of state for commonwealth relations, Sir Percivale Liesching. After some preliminary skirmishing about the tiring journey, the tough-minded, square-jawed Liesching pointed out that the secretary of state felt it was in the interests of Ruth, Seretse and the tribe that his wife attends the talks in London with him.

"I paused for some reply," said Liesching later, "but none came. It was not that we had not succeeded already in putting Seretse at ease, or that he looked dour or obstinate. In fact, he looked quite relaxed and cheerful."[119] It is possible that if he had known more about Seretse's personality, he might have been aware that this external appearance of Seretse's habitually hid deeper feelings.

Seretse's deliberate silence unnerved Liesching, who decided it would be unwise then to press him about Ruth's presence, and in this manner, a young man inexperienced in the politics of duplicity outmanoeuvred the undersecretary. The next day, Philip Noel-Baker fared no better with Seretse on the subject of Ruth, and he had to give up the plan to get her out of the protectorate by devious means. He then plunged into the heart of the matter by asking Seretse, in view of the "dangers of disintegration and faction within the tribe", to voluntarily relinquish his "claim" to the chieftainship.[120]

In spite of his suspicions, this must have come as a great shock to Seretse who no doubt saw in a flash the direction the British were taking him. Noel-Baker told him that the government would also exclude Tshekedi from the reserve and would also not allow him to be chief. He explained that in the absence of both Seretse and Tshekedi there would be a period of direct administration of the tribe by the protectorate administration. An incredulous Seretse emphasised the extent of the support he enjoyed in the tribe and put his finger on the raw nerve of the whole affair by saying that the British Government was refusing to recognise him as chief due to their fear of annoying the union. And he added that the government obviously felt it was better for it to annoy the tribe than to annoy Dr Malan. This was of course exactly Baring's point of view, but naturally the secretary of state stated categorically that it was not United Kingdom policy to placate the union at the expense of Seretse or the tribe.

He was able to add, quite truthfully this time, that the vitally important question of relations between Africans and Europeans was one of the United Kingdom's main considerations, for Baring believed that recognition of Seretse would lead to pressure for incorporation of the three protectorates with unhappy consequences for the inhabitants; and that it would result in the secession of South Africa from the British Commonwealth, which he believed could not improve the lives of the black people living there.

At one stage, the British Government considered that it might be possible to confide in Seretse their concern about what would be the effect of recognising him on race relations in the union. But this possibility was rejected. When Seretse had recovered a little from hearing Noel-Baker's suggestion of voluntary resignation, he put a counterproposal to him that the government could not refuse outright to consider. Seretse's proposal was that he be made chief for the period the British contemplated imposing direct rule on the tribe. Seretse added that if his chieftainship proved unsatisfactory, only then should direct rule, which he believed would be disastrous, be introduced.[121]

The government was nervous that Seretse would return immediately to Serowe if it did not hedge, and it asked him to remain in London until later that month before it gave him an answer to his proposal. During this time, it was hoped that Seretse would reconsider relinquishing the chieftainship and would accept the British offer of 1100 pounds yearly allowance, provided he lived in England.

In the two weeks that followed Seretse's meeting with the Whitehall officials, he hung around in a chilly, grey London that was wrapped up in general election fever. As the weeks progressed, he became increasingly bored, depressed and homesick. He asked his lawyer, Percy Fraenkel, to join him in London after those initial meetings with the secretary of state. While he waited for Fraenkel, he confided his fears and his loneliness to John Keith in the Colonial Office. The latter, in all his dealings with both Ruth and Seretse, had found them both reasonable, sensible people. Seretse told Keith that he was adamant that he would not allow Ruth to join him in London, but that he, despite this, could not stand to be away from her much longer and that he intended to go home immediately after his next meeting with the ministers, "no matter what happens."[122] This caused some alarm in the corridors of Whitehall, for it was realised that Seretse could not legally be detained in London.

Seretse explained to Keith that he could not possibly take a decision on his own about the chieftainship, which might disappoint the tribe, but that he was prepared, after talks with his people, and if they were willing, to compromise and to accept the British Government offer. How right Noel Monks was about the commitment of the tribe and Seretse to each other. At least Seretse had one strong supporter in government, for Keith thought him a "gentleman with great moral courage"[123] and he wasn't afraid to describe him thus to his superiors.

While Seretse waited for his lawyer and the general election and grew more homesick and worried about Ruth as the days passed, Ruth was equally miserable as she waited impatiently for his return in her thorn-fenced Serowe bungalow. Her pregnant figure was seen daily at the post office, waiting for a cable or letter from Seretse, and the locals noted how the reporters swarmed hungrily around her. "She looked so calm in spite of all that attention and harassment," said one official's wife, who secretly admired Ruth for her dignity and strength but didn't have the courage to walk up to her and say so. Although Ruth was living on her own as far as the white populace was concerned, in a lonely bungalow on the fringes of both Serowe and their society, she was far from alone, for Seretse's cousins and friends and members of the tribe lived with her. They camped in the large, dusty yard and kept watch over her for Seretse.

She sat inside the hot bungalow and knitted and listened to the radio and thought over the names she and Seretse had decided on for their first child – Jacqueline for a girl and Seretse for a boy. The evenings were the hardest for her. She would watch the sun's rays disappear behind the kgotla hill and the escarpment turn deep blue, before the sudden blanket of blackness that is night in Africa descended. Then melancholy filled her soul and she longed to hear his rich, deep voice calling to her. Behind the house, golden leaping flames from campfires broke the intense blackness, and the fragrant smell of burning wood filled the night air.

The press had thought, as everyone else had done, that Seretse would return to Serowe within a couple of weeks, and as the time dragged by without him, their enquiries about his absence grew more and more insistent. But with typical British reserve and cool, the administration officials dispatched the reporters with "no comment". The British had not taught their civil servants much about public relations, and after all, they were acting in the officious manner most officials did the world over. From then on, however, there was a steady deterioration in the relationship between administration and the press, and in the end a press officer was appointed by the administration to try and improve matters. As Doris Bradshaw wrote in a letter to her sister in England, "Some of the reporters have come from America, Amsterdam, England and South Africa to hear, 'Our lips are sealed.' It has become a big joke here."[124]

March arrived. In London, a few brave daffodils and crocuses made their appearance and waved gracefully in the cool winds. In the general election the Labour Party was returned with a very slender majority. There was a cabinet reshuffle, and the secretary of state for commonwealth relations who had been handling the Seretse affair, Noel-Baker, was replaced with the liberal and intellectual Patrick Gordon Walker. It was a far more conservative government than the one that would follow it in later years, and the foreign secretary, Ernest Bevin, was particularly conservative, for it was under him that Britain took such a hard line on allowing the Jewish refugees into Israel before it was proclaimed a state by the United Nations. Sir Winston Churchill, who was then in the opposition, did not have much time for Prime Minister Attlee, for he growled, "Mr Attlee is a very modest man. Indeed, he has a lot to be modest about."[125]

On 3rd March 1950, Seretse had another meeting at Whitehall, which was as unsatisfactory as the first, for his suggestion that he be given a trial as chief and that direct rule be abandoned until it was proved he was unsuitable, was rejected. His lawyer's contention that Seretse enjoyed tribal support throughout the protectorate did nothing to change the grave look on the secretary of state's face, for he had hoped to hear of Seretse's voluntary resignation. Three days later, on 6th March, Seretse found himself back in the same office for another meeting. But this time he heard the stunning news that he was to be exiled for five years. At the end of that period, said the secretary of state, the position would be reviewed, and the government would be able to ascertain whether the tribe had settled down. A shattered Seretse reacted with totally uncustomary fury and bitterness to the announcement.

"Am I to understand," he enquired incredulously, "that I am being kicked out of my own country? This seems to me to be a very improper proceeding."[126] The secretary of state pointed out that the British Government had the power to exclude anyone from the Bechuanaland Protectorate. Replied Seretse, "I am quite aware that you have the power to exclude me, but I feel strongly that I have been tricked into coming here and am now not being allowed to return." Why had the government extended the invitation for him to go to London at all, he demanded to know. If they wished to exclude him from the protectorate, they could have done so whilst he was there. He felt bitterly disappointed at the way he had been treated. The feeble excuses made by the secretary of state about the necessity of his trip to London did not impress Seretse at all, and in the heated exchange that followed, his legal advisers repeated continually their contention that it was South Africa that had made up the government's mind for it. They did not believe for one minute that tribal dissension was the real reason for exile. Seretse was angry that Tshekedi was to be allowed to live next door to the reserve, while he would be forced to live almost 10 000 kilometres away from his home. When he pointed out that his uncle had returned to Serowe despite his self-imposed exile, he was assured that Tshekedi would be kept out in future.

When Seretse was told that he would be "removed" if he returned to the protectorate, he raised the question of the legal dispute with his uncle over his cattle, which was due to go to court in Lobatsi the following month. This made the government pause awhile, and finally he was given permission to return for the court case. Seretse was then asked for his views on the government's suggestion that Ruth be provided with an air passage to Britain (with every possible attention given to her during the air journey). The poor chap replied that it seemed there was no option but for him to agree to the suggestion.

There must have been some red faces and uncomfortable government officials in that Whitehall room at this stage, for Seretse was then told that if he insisted on Ruth staying in Serowe until the baby was born, his wish would be respected. The unhappy meeting ended with the man who was being kicked out of his own country, being told that he was to say nothing about their discussions until 13th March when a simultaneous announcement about the exile would be made in the British Parliament and in the Serowe kgotla. After the announcement, Seretse was informed, he could say what he liked.

Ruth described the meeting as ending with an offer to Seretse of a glass of sherry by Gordon Walker. "And of course, Seretse told him, 'You know what you can do with your sherry'." The angry man who seldom showed his feelings, went straight from that meeting to call his first press conference. Totally disregarding the governmental instruction to keep quiet, he declared he had been tricked. He cabled Ruth, "Tribe and myself tricked by British Government. Am banned from whole protectorate. Love Seretse." The British decision made front page headlines around the world and unleashed a storm of disapproval about their treatment of the couple. Two days later, when Gordon Walker, easing himself into his new position, announced the five-year term of exile in the House of Commons, Sir Winston Churchill attacked him.

He described the invitation of Seretse to London without telling him he was to be exiled as a "very disreputable transaction".[127] Gordon Walker was asked in the House of Commons if the South African Government had communicated with the British over the matter. His answer was that there had been no representations and no consultation over it. It was a deliberate lie and his answer to parliament was to have repercussions later that month.

The overall reaction in the British press was one of dismay at the government's actions. Political commentary in *The Times* declared, "If the Bamangwato do not object to a white consort and the prospect of a half-breed succession, it would not seem to be for the Imperial government, pledged before all the nations to respect the equal rights of all races, to overrule them in their own domestic concerns. There, should be an end of the argument ... [transfer considerations] are acutely perplexing to HMG [His Majesty's government]. But they do not touch the rights and wrongs of the case. No good can come of compromise involving injustice to individuals if its aim is to blur the outline of the truth."[128]

The Guardian wrote, "Whatever Mr Gordon Walker may say in his diplomatic efforts to avoid a collision with Dr Malan, we can all guess that Seretse would be recognised as chief today if more white people in South Africa thought differently about race relations."[129] Even the South African press, except for the National Party mouthpieces, thought the British had handled the affair deplorably. But the National Party newspaper, *Die Transvaler*, rejected all suggestions in the British Parliament that the ban on Seretse had not been related to the attitude of South Africa. It said, "While trying to prop up with words the whitewashed face of liberalism, the British Government has had in practice to concede to the demands of apartheid."[130]

For those people who were not particularly interested in politics and who saw the affair in purely human terms, the British Government action meant that a pregnant woman, living alone in a strange and totally foreign country, who was being cruelly ostracised by her own kind, was now to be separated from her husband and the father of her child. What enraged many was that not only had he been tricked away from his home, but he had then been exiled for no apparent crime at all, beyond that of having married a white woman and taken her home to live with his tribe. The British public, with its sense of fair play, decided it was not cricket. Ruth's family were shattered. "I remember Seretse ringing me up at home at 6 a.m., and you know how early that is in England, and saying, 'I've been banned, I've been banned.' We couldn't believe it – not at the hands of a Labour government," said Muriel.

In South Africa, the Barings were visited at their gracious Cape Town residence by Field Marshal Jan Smuts. According to Baring's biographer, Charles Douglas-Home, Smuts told Baring he had written a private letter to Churchill telling him not to play with dynamite. He warned that if Seretse were recognised it would be the end of the British Commonwealth as far as South Africa was concerned, and there would be a united and overwhelming demand for the territories which would be extremely difficult to withstand.

In a telegram on the 8th of March to the Commonwealth Relations Office, Baring suggested that if Seretse did return unexpectedly to the protectorate, he could confine him to Lobatsi. The extent of his anxiety is clear in his suggestion that he could serve a similar order on Ruth "simultaneously, if not earlier, for she has just announced to the local press her intention to 'stay put'."[131]

Baring, however, did not want Ruth and Seretse in Bechuanaland at all, for he felt their presence would embarrass the local administration. He suggested, therefore, that if Seretse resisted attempts to move him, he could be put into jail, but added, "If it came to this, a suspended sentence might of course suffice."

He was desperately keen to get rid of Ruth and hoped that Seretse would be persuaded to ask her to join him in London, and that he would leave her there when he flew back for his case against Tshekedi. But Baring had grave doubts about the Khamas falling in with his plans, for he said, after reading press reports, that he thought Seretse "would prove difficult" and might try to make as much trouble as he could. "Ruth seems to be playing the same game," he added.

Some people have found it extraordinary that Baring, who was so involved in the Khama affair and the effect that their marriage was having on his deliberations with the Union Government about transfer, did not during this whole troubled period travel to Serowe to meet Ruth or to ascertain the situation at first hand. And although he was undoubtedly in a difficult position with the South Africans, the tone he adopts in his letters regarding treatment of the couple seems particularly insensitive, if not downright cruel.

In the wake of Seretse's first press conference in London, Ruth threw open her home to the press in Serowe, for in view of Whitehall's trickery, she did not feel she was bound any longer by its rule of silence. She and Seretse realised for the first time the enormous value of a sympathetic press when it comes to lobbying for a cause. And so the special correspondents flocked to

Serowe, and the postmaster Joe Burgess became a busy man again as he battled to telegraph their copy all over the world. When the writers ran out of space in his little post office, he offered them his dining room table, and as his wife Monica told me, "Our lounge looked like Fleet Street. And our garden! They pitched tents and slept there and cooked their food over fires they made in our yard."

Ruth's lounge was seldom without a journalist in it in the wake of the banishment. It was a welcome change for her to hear first-hand news reports from all over the world. The socially lonely life she had been leading suddenly became a full and intense one at times. But there are all sorts of journalists, and when Ruth was confronted with highly personal, sometimes aggressive questioning, she threw up a barrier of reserve and caution which irritated some of them. "One of them asked me how I could be bored when I had all Seretse's lawbooks to read, and then he went off and wrote an article which began, 'I do not like Ruth, and the more I saw of her, the less I liked Ruth Khama'," Ruth told me in one of our many interviews.

Overnight Ruth became one of the most publicised women in the world. She was featured in *Time* magazine, and she appeared for a second time in as many months in *Life* magazine. Some journalists wrote that all the attention had gone to her head, but maybe they were the ones who, finding that Ruth was out when they called, simply sat themselves down in her lounge where she would find them waiting on her return, to her intense resentment. "I wasn't used, coming from England, to people being rude and not having manners, and saying that if I wasn't nice they would write something horrid about me," she said. Other journalists such as Margaret Lessing, who was as direct as Ruth, John Redfern and Noel Monks, made friends with her and they sympathised with her. They were always made welcome by Ruth's staff and let through the thorn-fence gate by her tribal protectors.

In those early weeks of March, as the correspondents from all over the world poured into Serowe, they learnt with interest that Baring was going to Serowe at last. A kgotla was organised on his instructions, where he planned to announce both Seretse's five-year term of exile and tell the tribe of the introduction of government by direct rule. He also intended to see Ruth, and he sent a message asking her to meet him.

Serowe was galvanised into action, two sorts of action: those preparing for the kgotla, and those intending to boycott it. Normally a kgotla addressed by the representative of the great protecting power across the sea was an occasion marked by pomp and ceremony which was much enjoyed, both by the tribe who loved the sense of grandeur, and by the white populace who had the opportunity to turn out in their best. The kgotla was to be held on Monday, 13th March, and the preceding week, the Bechuanaland Protectorate police, dressed in their Victorian uniform of dark brown khaki tunics, helmets, jodhpurs and riding breeches, rode their horses in practice formations up and down the kgotla. The British with their flair for ceremony, prepared for a show complete with white uniforms and pith helmets, swords jangling and flashing in the sun, fluttering plumes and sparkling medals. The red polished floors of the district commissioner's bungalow were given an extra shine, and the large garden swept in preparation for the high commissioner's arrival.

But the tribe had other ideas. They were angry, extremely angry, at the way the British Government, whom the Great Khama had approached for protection all those years ago, should now trick his grandson, their chief, into leaving his wife and home. Seretse's followers, who had organised themselves into cells and held secret night meetings in their huts to formulate strategy, had tuned into the wavelengths of the police radio and knew all about the reasons for the kgotla called by Baring. They prepared, therefore, to deliver one of the greatest snubs to a representative of the Crown in British Africa that had ever been witnessed on that large continent. They went for help to the white man who spoke their language and knew their feelings, the mine labour organiser Alan Bradshaw, who gave them all the advice of which he was capable. First it had been Seretse, then Ruth, and now it was the tribe, who learnt the value of a good press in a cause, and the boycott organiser Peto Sekgoma went to the hotel in Palapye one evening and, with his eyes flashing white in the night light of the hotel stoep, he told those members of the press who were having a drink there of the planned boycott.

There were two reasons for it, he said. The first one was that a kgotla could not be called by anyone but the chief, and how was the tribe to welcome anyone of such distinction as the high commissioner without their chief? Secondly, the tribe knew already that the British had exiled Seretse. They did not need to be told again.

The press subsequently told the administration of the intended boycott.[132] Baring, who was informed about it shortly before he was due to leave Mafeking in his special coach on the night train, asked the district commissioner by wireless to take immediate steps to make it known that he could not accede to the tribe's request to postpone the kgotla in Seretse's absence. He ordered the district commissioner to "pursue energetically" arrangements for a good attendance. Having given his orders, he then chugged off into the velvet night, the steam engine flashing sparks from the fire in its belly as it tore along the single track that traversed the huge, empty country.

But when Baring was driven into Serowe on Monday, 13th March, he learnt that many of the people who had made their way into Serowe for the kgotla from their lands and cattle posts and from outlying villages had already begun to disperse. Some officials in the administration could not believe that what they had regarded as the lazy, disorganised black man could manage a total boycott. They felt sure that at least a few hundred tribesmen would be present, and so the preparations for the kgotla continued.

The stamped ground of the crescent-shaped kgotla was swept, and lines were drawn with whitewash to demarcate the places where the police would stand and where the guard of honour was going to be. The police reported that the boycott organisers had been traced to five people, who had in the past few months set themselves up as Seretse's chief advisers and lieutenants. Baring immediately ordered that the five men be interviewed, and that they were told to ensure that the tribe attended the next day's kgotla.

Baring subsequently learnt that at the time the five were being interviewed, regiments of young men were being given last-minute instructions on how to picket the kgotla the next morning. Early the next day, the police reported the presence of two pickets turning back people who were making their way along the winding sand paths to the kgotla. Officials dashed in alarm from their hill, down to the village where they found not two, but large numbers of pickets, posted tactically on all roads and paths leading to the kgotla.[133]

There was no violence, despite subsequent reports of intimidation, for all that was needed to turn back the tribe, was the use of the magic name Seretse. The appointed time of the kgotla was 10.30 a.m. Usually when a meeting was called, the wide-open space started filling from dawn, but by 8.30 a.m. there was not a soul present. And at 10 a.m. the village near the kgotla was strangely lifeless and deserted.

Undeterred, Baring continued to put on his uniform, and the white populace dutifully took up their places in the sun. One black man strolled into the kgotla and sat down; it was Peto Sekgoma who with his mischievous sense of humour decided that, as he had organised the boycott, he should attend it to ascertain its effectiveness. There was also the press, some of them highly

182

amused at the abortive proceedings. But Nicholas Monsarrat, who had travelled overnight with Baring as his aide and information officer, surveyed the empty ground with dismay. And five minutes before the appointed time, he sent Baring a message telling him that there was no point in leaving the district commissioner's house. Up on the hill, Baring put down his plumed hat and removed his grand uniform. Down in the kgotla, Monsarrat told the press that Baring would address them up at the residency, and then he turned to British journalist Margaret Lessing and confided, "Oh Margaret, I've just written a bestseller," she told me in an interview. She had roared with laughter – not knowing that he had been trying to write one all his life. She was not to know that the book was *The Cruel Sea* and that it would indeed be a bestseller.

But Baring was not finished with the tribe yet and, trying to salvage something from the wreckage of the meeting, he asked the district commissioner, who was acting as native authority in the absence of a chief, to deliver written instructions to twenty-four headmen to appear before him later in the morning to listen to him deliver the secretary of state's parliamentary message. Police trucks tore through the quiet village, dispensing the message, but not one of the recipients of it obeyed its command. The boycott was a total success.

Baring had therefore to content himself with holding a press conference under the spreading branches of the jacaranda and syringa trees in the pretty garden of the district commissioner's residence. And there he hinted at the improvements he intended to make in the system of tribal administration, where a native authority more representative of the tribe than the present chief, he said, would operate with a council.

But the press was not going to let Baring off with statements about improvements to tribal administration (in the absence of its chosen chief). He was asked if Seretse had any knowledge that he would not be allowed to return if he left, and Baring admitted he was given no sort of assurance.

When questioned if there was any evidence that Seretse would imperil peace and order if he returned to Serowe, Baring hinted that the feud between Seretse and Tshekedi might worsen.

When a South African journalist asked if Seretse would have been chief already if he had not married a white girl, Sir Evelyn responded that the question was too hypothetical.[134]

As he spoke, down in the village Seretse's advisers were drawing up a manifesto stating that the tribe would not obey any further instructions from the local administrator or pay any taxes without Seretse's authority. It was the beginning of their non-cooperation campaign and what they referred to as the "struggle", one that did not end until Seretse's return in 1956.

Down in the village, a policeman, sub-inspector Graham Russell, was dispatched to organise the obliteration of the whitewashed lines and the evidence of the British humiliation. Determined the job should be done right the first time, he grabbed a brush and demonstrated the correct action. How was he to know that Margaret Bourke-White would photograph him at that moment, being watched by puzzled black policemen who were not used to their superiors doing that kind of physical work.

Baring suffered another failure during that trip – he was unable to meet Ruth, for when he sent a message to her home to arrange a time that would be convenient for her, the messenger returned empty-handed, saying that she had left for Palapye the previous day. She had gone to stay with the Bradshaws, and when she was asked later if it was coincidence that she was out of town the day that Baring arrived, Ruth told me she merely replied that she had responded to an invitation. Monsarrat subsequently suggested to newsmen that Ruth and Noel Monks might have organised the boycott, which amused them both enormously.

But Baring was not amused, for on his return to Cape Town he reported to Whitehall, "An unsavoury aspect of the affair is the participation (in the boycott) of certain local Europeans. The most important is the representative of the Native Recruiting Corporation [NRC] … I am told both by officials and by journalists, he had participated very actively in anti-government activities including the organisation of the boycott. When passing through Johannesburg I asked formally for his transfer and was told that this would be arranged at once."[135]

It was. Less than a week after the abortive kgotla, a stunned Bradshaw was told he was being transferred to Vryburg, a dairy centre in South Africa, just over the border from Bechuanaland, noted for its large Afrikaner community. Baring must have known that in removing the Bradshaws, he was inflicting a double punishment, for Ruth's reliance on their close friendship was known to all.

In a letter home to England, written from Vryburg on 1st April, Doris Bradshaw commented, "Now of course, people who were inclined to be friendly to Ruth are afraid because of what has happened to us. So she is completely isolated."[136] And Doris continued, "When Ruth heard we were going, she said that we must stay, and the tribe would look after us, and several headmen said the same thing to Alan, but the tribe have enough troubles and fights ahead without the expense of keeping us too." Alan Bradshaw, in one of his letters, explained his role in helping to organise the boycott. "I certainly advocated to the sub chiefs and the headmen passive resistance – what else can they do? I was asked to be their introductory agent to the press when they decided what they would do."[137] And in their letters to Doris's sister in England, both Bradshaws encouraged her to stir up as much trouble for the British Government as she possibly could, on behalf of the Khamas. One of the Labour members of parliament, Fenner Brockway, who was later to play a leading role in agitating for an end to the Khamas' exile, subsequently asked informed and difficult questions in the House of Commons.

But that of course did not return her friends to Ruth, and as her loneliness returned and grew, she came to rely increasingly on the friendship of journalists, who were shocked at the British Government treatment of her. It seemed nonsensical to them that the government was exiling a man on the grounds that he would cause dissension in a tribe that they had seen not once, but twice, overwhelmingly demonstrate its support for him. And the continued social ostracism of Ruth appalled them. It appeared to them to be horribly cruel, and many of them refused to accept the government's reasons for its actions. Furthermore, the suppression of the judicial commission's report caused great suspicion, both in England and in South Africa.

On 20th March Mr Sam Kahn, the South African Communist Party member of parliament asked Prime Minister Dr D.F. Malan in the house whether the Union Government had made any representations to, or communicated with, the United Kingdom Government in the matter of Seretse Khama's marriage and subsequent developments in Bechuanaland. Malan gave an evasive reply that did not answer the question at all, and he contacted South Africa House in London, asking his high commissioner there to warn the British about what might be coming.[138]

This alarmed the secretary of state, Gordon Walker, for when he had been questioned in much the same manner as you will recall in the House of Commons on 8th March, he had stated categorically that there had been no representations between the two governments over the Khama affair. Gordon Walker therefore asked the political secretary at South Africa House, Mr Anthony Hamilton, to see him and help him clarify whether the representations made to the British the previous June by the Union of South Africa's high commissioner, Mr Leif Egeland, were official or not.

For three hours, four men pondered how best to extricate both governments from a tricky situation, and a detailed examination of files and documents revealed that, although Egeland had been sent by Dr Malan to see Noel-Baker, the latter had recorded Egeland having said that he was making only, "semi-official or private representations".[139] This appeared to them to let them all off the hook and to clear up any misunderstandings the two governments might have had about their respective actions. A telegram was drafted to Malan,[140] the general text of which was that the British Government was embarrassed by the whole issue. Hamilton, who dictated the telegram to Liesching's secretary, gave him a copy of it before returning to South Africa House to send it off.

Baring was sent a copy of the telegram to keep him *au fait* with the troubled situation but was instructed on no account to disclose the text, "in order to protect Egeland."[141] It was during this tense time that a group from the Parliamentary Empire Association was being shown around the Tower of London. It included Hamilton and Gordon Walker's wife Audrey. "Poor Patrick, he'll probably be immured here before long," she murmured to Hamilton, who told me this in an interview. And indeed, if it had been established in the house that Gordon Walker had misled it, he would have had to resign his seat, and it is not too improbable to speculate that, with the Labour government's extremely slender majority and the general outcry at the treatment of Seretse, the government could have fallen.

It is Hamilton's view that Malan emerged as an "absolute gentleman" in refusing to say anything that would compromise Britain in the South African parliament in spite of the determined probing by the member of parliament Sam Kahn.

Gordon Walker was not the only one who thought his head would roll over the Khama affair. According to Douglas-Home, Evelyn Baring's biographer, the high commissioner thought privately at that time that he might get the sack for his handling of the Khama affair, "and he appeared to his wife to be more worried … than he had ever been about anything before."[142] This gives you some idea of the magnitude of the drama of the matter, when you consider that Baring had been governor of Rhodesia and subsequently became governor of Kenya.

But Baring, in spite of his anxiety, was a man who stuck to his principles, and he believed he had acted correctly in advising the removal of Seretse. When he received a telegram from the British Cabinet suggesting that Seretse return to Bechuanaland for his lawsuit against Tshekedi and for the birth of his child, Baring advised against return. He was prepared to resign if the government, which was under severe pressure from all sides in Britain, reversed its decision to withhold recognition of Seretse.

And although the government did stick to its non-recognition of Seretse, it did not, however, take Baring's advice to keep Seretse out of the protectorate. The young man was told he could return both for the birth and for the lawsuit. But he was to be confined to Lobatsi, where he would be limited to a ten-kilometre radius of his quarters there. Seretse therefore made his plans for his return to Bechuanaland. The world was about to witness, through the eyes of the media, yet another case of appallingly insensitive treatment of Ruth and Seretse at the hands of the British.

TWELVE

A shameful period

Seretse cabled the news of his return to Ruth immediately he heard it, but her face, which had lit up with joy at the first sentence, clouded when she read of his exile to Lobatsi, 380 kilometres to the south of Serowe. "How can my own people do this to me?" she asked herself wretchedly, looking up blindly from the telegram, to find a crowd of women from the tribe watching her in concern as she stood outside the post office.

Ruth made her way slowly past the women to her car, trying to smile, but feeling miserable and lonely. As she was driven home, she thought to herself that having Seretse in the protectorate was certainly better than being separated from him by thousands of kilometres of continent and oceans, but she felt a surge of bitterness and anger well up inside her that was so intense it frightened her for a moment. She clenched her hands and muttered, "I won't let them break me. I will do what is best for Seretse and the tribe."

"Seretse is coming back, but not to Serowe," she told Naledi and his cousins. "I wonder how and when I am going to see him?" Will they let him come home to see me for a while before they insist on him going to Lobatsi? she pondered to herself.

But no official came to tell her of any meeting with her husband, and she waited uncertainly and anxiously for news. It was Noel Monks who told her of Seretse's impending arrival. The cheery, well-built *London Daily Mail* reporter, who always managed to look neat and tailored in his cream suits despite the heat, and who sympathised with Ruth over British treatment of her, drove over to her bungalow when he heard that Seretse would be landing at the Victoria Falls before changing planes and flying on to Gaberones, a village situated on the railway line seventy-two kilometres north of Lobatsi. Monks told Ruth that his newspaper would like a good photograph of her reunion with Seretse, and she asked him to let her know when and where that meeting would take place, for she had still not been told anything about Seretse's return.

Monks flew up to the Victoria Falls along with other pressmen who had hired planes specifically for the event. And when Seretse stepped from the flying boat on to the launch pad on the Zambezi, Monks told him of Ruth's agreement to a photographed reunion, and it was decided in consultation with the pilot who would be flying Seretse that he would touch down in Mahalapye, 114 kilometres to the south of Serowe, for refuelling. The bitter and angry Seretse rejoiced at the thought of seeing Ruth again after seven weeks of separation, for he had worried ceaselessly about her in her pregnant condition, and longed to comfort her in her loneliness. The journalists who heard of Monk's plan were pleased they would be getting a good story and photographs. Monks therefore telegraphed Ruth: "Be [at] Mahalapye airfield at noon tomorrow." But Ruth was being subjected to intensive attention by the police, who had been told to keep the administration informed of her activities as well as those of the tribe. And so she wasn't the only person to read Monks's cable. In his autobiography, *Eyewitness,* Monks writes:

> Somewhere along the line, an administration official, who saw my telegram through service channels, had a brainwave. There was a plot afoot to kidnap Seretse! Else why should Ruth want to go all the way to Mahalapye. This stupid construction on a perfectly innocent and legitimate telegram was fed to the South African press, with the prompt result that, just before we took off, we learnt that Seretse's pilot had been ordered not to land at Mahalapye. Faced with the wrecking of my plans to get a picture of the reunion between Seretse and Ruth, I planned afresh. It was too late to stop Ruth making the hard drive to the Mahalapye airstrip now, but the pilot of Seretse's plane saw no reason why, while not actually landing, he couldn't fly low enough for the two, at least to see each other.[143]

An excited Ruth, totally unaware of the forthcoming drama, woke at the first sound of birds chirping in the thorn bush outside her bedroom window, and moving slowly with her pregnancy, padded quietly around the bungalow, getting ready to leave. She didn't tell Seretse's cousins that she was going anywhere in particular. "I didn't want any excuses, I didn't want anybody to know that I was going to meet Seretse, so that nobody could breathe a word of it, and destroy the plan." And so she slipped quietly away from Serowe with her driver. Poor naive and gullible Ruth was shocked when she drove up in her car, to find hundreds of Bamangwato waiting at the Mahalapye airstrip. They too had their inside information, and their means of disseminating it, and they wanted to see their chief.

When the three light aircraft carrying the press arrived ahead of Seretse's plane, they were as surprised as Ruth to see all those people and the well rein-forced police waiting on the strip. But few knew Seretse was not going to be allowed to land. Monks, whose plane was much faster than Seretse's, landed some twenty minutes before Seretse's was due. He leapt out of his plane as soon as it landed and strode quickly over to Ruth, who was holding an um-brella to ward off the burning sun and waiting near her car. Her face crumpled with sorrow at the news that Seretse would not be allowed to land, but she resolutely pulled herself together, hiding her misery and desolation. "Come now," said Monks, "Seretse will be here at any minute."

And Ruth, holding on to Monks's arm, walked a little way away from the crowd on to the strip. Soon they heard a dull drone and when the tiny speck grew larger, and the plane began to come in low as the pilot had promised, Monks left her there, for this was her "private" moment. As the Rapide came down to make a pass in front of Ruth, she ran forward, waving, waving vigor-ously, searching the small plane desperately for a sight of the man she loved so much. She saw for a moment his face pressed against the tiny glass window. He saw her heavy figure, her face raised to the sky and her scarf fluttering in the breeze, and his heart contracted with longing.

Then Ruth's vision blurred with tears and suddenly all around her everything darkened, and she thought, "I'm going to faint. How awful! There will be pictures of me splashed all over the world lying on this strip in a dead faint and they will be seen by Seretse and my parents and my sister." All this flashed through her mind in a few seconds while the world tumbled and heaved around her, and at that moment the perceptive Monks reached her side and offered her his arm.

"I walked in blackness, holding on to his arm as tightly as I could. Without his support I would have fallen, have gone. But he didn't know that. He never knew how close I was to total collapse that day," said Ruth, whose eyes filled with tears as she recalled the intensely painful episode. "I suppose if I had fainted, all those newsmen would have loved it, it would have been perfect, wouldn't it?" she asked me.

But the photographs are poignant enough as it is, for there is a heavily preg-nant Ruth, bareheaded in the hot African sun, waving her scarf over her head at the plane skimming a few hundred metres above the bush that surrounded the airstrip. When the craft began to gain height and to disappear into the intense blue sky, the disappointed crowd, realising they were not going to see Seretse after all, shouted "Pula! Pula! Pula!" loudly after it, as if they hoped the man they wanted for chief would hear their anguished cry. Ruth, dark glasses hiding her brimming eyes, murmured, "I hardly saw him," and then, "he's gone."

Her shoulders sagged, and her head swam as she leaned momentarily against the car. With a deep sigh she allowed her driver to help her get into it. "Then I had to drive all that way back to Serowe," said Ruth, whose head throbbed with the sudden events of the morning. "You shouldn't have gone without us," reproached Seretse's concerned cousins, as they helped her gently out of the car in Serowe. "We knew where you were going, please don't ever go without us again," they murmured solicitously as they poured her tea, and made her eat.

"I felt terrible, just terrible. I felt a mixture of anger and sadness and of wanting of course to go hot-footing it up to Lobatsi," said Ruth. "But everyone said to me, 'you mustn't, you mustn't. This is just what they want you to do, and once you leave Serowe they will never let either you or Seretse back again.' And so I stayed."

The enormous courage and strength of purpose that Ruth displayed in that lonely hour of decision, when every nerve in her body screamed to be with Seretse, is one that was eventually admired by even her few detractors.

The British reported the non-meeting as follows: "Seretse's arrival on 31st March was without incident, but it appears that this was so largely because administration was a step ahead of the press."[144] What cold words to describe such an emotion-charged incident.

After his aircraft had flown over Mahalapye, Seretse was taken on to Gaberones, and there too crowds of Bamangwato who had travelled in every conceivable type of conveyance were waiting in their hundreds for him. As Seretse stepped out of the plane, a great roar of welcome rose from the crowd lining the fence, and under the watchful eye of police drafted in from Serowe, the men flung their hats in the air and shouted "Pula!" repeatedly, while the women ululated shrilly. Seretse, dressed in grey jacket and brown trousers, looked surprisingly calm in view of his emotional glimpse of Ruth at Mahalapye. Carrying a bundle of books under one arm, he walked forward to shake hands with four headmen who had been allowed by the police on to the strip. He told reporters before leaving with his lawyer, Percy Fraenkel, that although the British Government had said to him in London that only the Bamangwato were supporting him (18 000 out of a total Bamangwato Reserve population of 100 000), "I was pleased to see representatives of every sub-tribe in the reserve waiting to greet me here."[145]

Later that day, out of the glare of photographers' flash bulbs and the emotion of his tribe, in a small Gaberones office, he was served with orders confining him to the Lobatsi district.

The news of the couple's abortive meeting was flashed around the world at about the same time that the British Government tabled a White Paper in parliament in which it stated that the judicial enquiry's report would not be published. There was a fresh outburst of condemnation of the handling of the whole affair. Amongst the many voices raised in protest was that of the Church of England, which carried this comment in its newspaper, "Who would have believed that any government would have been capable of such a mean, petty and utterly despicable trick as to deprive Seretse of the opportunity of meeting his wife, who had travelled 250 miles [more or less 400 kilometres] through tropical country just to have a little time with her husband."[146]

The left-wing liberal organisation, Americans for Democratic Action, which had a chain of branches throughout America, and which exercised considerable influence on public opinion, wrote to the British Government, "It would be difficult to exaggerate the repercussions of the Seretse affair among some quarters here. Some of us like to think that the Labour government policy is pretty free of the common stultifications of American racial attitudes. The negro press, which is a highly influential medium, is full of the Seretse debacle."[147]

The secretary of the League of Coloured Peoples in Britain questioned the intervention by the British in a domestic tribal affair and expressed concern at the attitude of the Union of South Africa over the affair. The secretary warned the British of the dangers of "detribalising" the administration of the Bamangwato and emphasised the emergence of nationalism in the colonies.[148] Among the many organisations that protested, were the Seretse Khama Fighting Committee, the African League and the West African Students Union. The government was told that extremists in the Seretse Khama Fighting Committee advocated chartering an aeroplane to fly Seretse to Serowe where he would be dropped by parachute; organising an army to prevent Seretse and Ruth's removal to the United Kingdom; and the boycott of British goods and the shooting of British officials throughout the empire.

March 1950, a protective hedge of thorns surrounding the grounds of the six-room bungalow in which Seretse and Ruth resided during the controversy over their mixed marriage.
(Photo by Margaret Bourke-White/The LIFE Picture Collection/Getty Images)

March 1950, Ruth listening as tribal women who have come with gifts sing "Our queen will come with rain" as they take shelter on her porch during a thunderstorm.
(Photo by Margaret Bourke-White/The LIFE Picture Collection/Getty Images)

A pregnant and anxious Ruth awaiting the return of her husband from London on 29 April 1950. Original publication: Picture Post, *The Rights And Wrongs Of Seretse Khama*, 1950.
(Photo by Bert Hardy/Picture Post/Getty Images)

29 April 1950, Ruth on the porch of her and Seretse's Serowe bungalow. Original publication: Picture Post, *The Rights And Wrongs Of Seretse Khama*, 1950. (Photo by Bert Hardy / Picture Post / Hulton Archive / Getty Images)

August 1950, an exiled Seretse and Ruth walk from the giant flying boat that took them from Bechuanaland to England. An airways officer carries their baby Jacqueline in a travel cot, and following behind is Naledi, Seretse's sister. (Photo by Getty Images)

At last their six-year exile over, Seretse and Ruth relax in the garden of their Surrey home with their two children Jacqueline, 6, and Ian, 3. Seretse had renounced any claim to the throne for himself or his children.
(Photo by Getty images)

October 1956, Seretse heads for the airport surrounded by Ruth, Jacqueline and Ian. Also seen is friend Clement Freud and behind little Jackie is Ruth's sister Muriel.
(Photo by Brian Seed/The LIFE Images Collection/Getty Images)

Seretse lost no time in leaving London after his exile ended, ensuring there was no last-minute change of mind. Ruth followed a few weeks later with the children.
(Photo by Brian Seed/The LIFE Images Collection/Getty Images)

Their affection for each other is clear in this picture of Seretse and Ruth attending a garden party in Lobatsi around the time of Independence.
(Photo by Terence Spencer/The LIFE Images Collection/Getty Images)

Ruth was a relaxed and clearly confident personality at Independence in September 1966.
(Photograph from the author's private collection)

Lady Khama wearing a striking red dress for the Independence ball in Gaborone on 30 September 1966. With her are Sir Seretse, Princess Marina, later known as the Duchess of Kent, and Deputy Prime Minister Quett Masire.
(Photo © Tiso Blackstar Group)

From exiles to first couple of the new Botswana, Sir Seretse and Lady Khama in front of State House, Gaborone in 1966.
(Photo © Tiso Blackstar Group)

The Khama family on 24 September 1967. Ruth and Seretse with their daughter Jacqueline, son Ian and twins Tshekedi and Tony.
(Photo © Tiso Blackstar Group)

Sir Seretse and Lady Khama greet
Kenneth Kaunda, president of Zambia,
and his wife on their state visit to
Botswana on 22 May 1968.
(Photo © Tiso Blackstar Group)

Ruth and Seretse in a festive mood in
late 1972. Ruth always looked elegant
no matter what she wore.
(Photo © Sunday Times)

Ruth had amazing energy and
never stopped working for
the causes she supported.
(Photograph from the author's
private collection)

Ruth in her office. Her work
with women's and children's
organisations was extensive
and highly valued.
(Picture by the author in 1976)

The grief Ruth suffered after
Seretse's death in July 1980 is
clearly evident in this picture,
taken a few months later by
the author, on the Khama
farm.

Ruth Khama was staying with the author at her home when this picture was taken in 2000.

Ian Khama, pictured here on 5 November 2009 in President Barack Obama's Oval Office, was elected the fourth president of Botswana on 1 April 2008 and served until 1 April 2018.
(Photo by Ron Sachs-Pool/Getty Images)

But the British stuck to their course, although much anxiety was expressed about it in government circles.

When Seretse reached Lobatsi with his cousin Goareng Mosinyi and his lawyer Percy Fraenkel (who was charged with seeing that his client went straight to the little town) he found he was to be quartered in a typical government bungalow off the pretty tree-lined avenue that leads to the hospital. It was situated outside the centre of the town, on the slopes of a hill where most of the administration officials and their families lived. "They gave Seretse a house with two tin mugs, two tin plates, two beds and an ordinary wooden table that wasn't even polished or varnished," said an indignant Ruth. She was incensed by what she considered the discourteous treatment of Seretse by the British.

"After all those years as a colonial power, they should have realised that other people have as much respect for their own royalty as the British have for theirs. His cousins and some Bamangwato who were living in Lobatsi went out and bought him china and some linen and proper knives and forks and they said, 'This is our chief, and this is not how our chief lives.'" After Seretse became president of Botswana years later, he said with typical humour to Ruth on a visit to Lobatsi that they should make the house a national monument. As usual, there was no trace of bitterness in him, just amusement, as he looked back on an unhappy period in his life.

As soon as he arrived at the five-roomed bungalow, which had a breezeway separating the living and sleeping quarters to keep the house cool, Seretse asked for permission to go and see Ruth in Serowe. He was, in terms of the British restriction order, only allowed to move around an area within the confines of Lobatsi, about a ten-kilometre radius, and he was terribly anxious to see Ruth after their weeks of separation. He had hoped to leave almost immediately for Serowe, but after some days had passed, he was told that any applications for him to leave the district had to be in writing, stating the destination, purpose of the visit, and its duration. The high commissioner had not wanted Seretse to return to Bechuanaland, and it appears that he was going to ensure that every move Seretse made there would be as difficult as possible and bound up with red tape.

Baring was not the only one who made life difficult for Seretse, for the largely South African population of Lobatsi, a fair proportion of whom were Afrikaans speaking, were not at all happy to have the famous black man quartered there. Some hotheads spoke of "smoking Seretse out", but if they had gone to the bungalow in order to do so, they would have got the surprise of their lives, for when the Bamangwato heard that their chief was not going to be allowed to go to Serowe, they went to him. Soon the garden was filled with his tribesmen who camped there, cooked his food, cleaned the house, and did whatever they could for his comfort. When they had done all there was to be done each day, they just sat and watched the young man that many of them idolised.

Gaositwe Chiepe, who was working in the nearby village of Kanye, went to visit him one day, and found herself being screened by the royal Bamangwato who were there. "There was an outer and an inner gate where you had to say who you were and what you wanted, which was natural. But sometimes, they, well … they overdid it a little. I remember speaking to the man at the outer gate, and was busy with the one inside, when Seretse saw us, and said, 'Come on, don't be silly, don't just stand there'," Gaositwe Chiepe told me in an interview and concluded, "he was never keen on self-aggrandisement despite his obvious dignity and chiefly bearing."

And he always had a soft spot for anyone down on his luck, such as the young student who was so keen to see Seretse that he caught the train to Lobatsi, but had no blankets or money, and so Seretse gave him his coat, and his people were aghast, asking how he could share his coat with a nonentity. "But somebody needed a coat … and so off went his. That was what Seretse was like," said Gaositwe.

As Seretse waited for permission to visit Ruth, he whiled away the days talking to his tribe, receiving deputations of headmen from the sub-tribes, and when there was not much else to do, he and his cousin Goareng would buy the newspapers and go to the nearby blue gum plantation and lie there reading. When they got back in the evening, they would find the yard lit with fires, the smell of cooking meat wafting on the evening air, and later his tribe would settle down in their blankets and sleep under the stars.

The only contact Seretse had with Ruth was the letters they wrote to each other and which, according to Ruth, were smuggled through roadblocks by Seretse's uncle and cousins, who commuted regularly between Serowe and Lobatsi and who gave the couple details about each other. "I was definitely lonely and out on a limb, no doubt about that. And there was also the language problem, although I was lucky to have friends, and Lenyletse, Goareng and Naledi. And Dr Chiepe used to come and keep me company quite often and help me make baby clothes. And friends would bring me nappies from South Africa," said Ruth.

The rains continued late that year, well into April, and Ruth, as she lay in her bed at night, would hear the drops drumming on her tin roof. Sometimes she sat on the veranda in the front of her house in the evenings and watched the sun's last rays dip over the horizon and light up the hills and thorn trees with their golden light. On the clear evening air, she could hear the sounds coming from the village of cow bells tinkling as the cattle were driven to water before nightfall, of birds calling before they went to sleep, of children's playful voices and adults' commanding ones.

She no longer had the Bradshaws to visit, and so relied on the traders and on journalists. The latter were divided into two camps. One went to Lobatsi to be with Seretse and the other one remained in Serowe with Ruth, although some commuted regularly between the two. On Nob Hill, many who wouldn't admit publicly to it had a great admiration for the woman, who although heavily pregnant and deeply in love with her husband, stuck it out on her own, in her miserable isolation. Many thought they would never have had the courage to remain in Serowe in similar circumstances, and to those who said as much in later years, Ruth replied, "Oh but you would have. Seretse would never have got back to the Bamangwato if I hadn't stayed, which would have been bad for him, and I knew that. I don't think you would have leapt into a car if it meant your husband couldn't see his people again. And you see, his family were so good, they never left me alone. And there was my doctor, Don Moikangoa, whose support was quite marvellous. And don't forget, you are fighting for a principle anyway ..." Ruth always had, quite literally, the courage of her convictions.

But that didn't stop her from waking each day, desperately hoping that it would bring news of Seretse's return. Coffee would be brought to her, and she lay drinking it, watching the sun's early morning rays dancing on the ceiling. Then she rose slowly, feeling with joy the baby moving within her and imagining how Seretse would have loved to share the precious moment with her. She often went to the post office, hoping for a letter or cable, and always had a cheery word from postmaster Joe Burgess, who was able to ignore to a certain extent the ruling that they were not to fraternise with her.

"I thought she was a beautiful woman, and my comment at the time was that she would have made any chap a proud man," he told me in an interview.

Monica Burgess was at more or less the same stage of pregnancy as Ruth, and although she couldn't go and call on her, she gave Joe any literature she could lend Ruth. "I felt very sorry for her out at Swaneng, so far away from the rest of us, and unable to speak the language of the people with whom she had most contact," said Monica.

One administration official was so distressed at the ostracism, that he and his wife discussed at length how they could circumvent it. And another, a bachelor, said openly that he thought Seretse was being badly treated. But an official's wife that I spoke to but who did not want to be named, said that when she heard this at the time she spluttered indignantly, "I thought the British were treating the couple too well."

Ruth was as much the subject of police intelligence surveillance as was Seretse, and one policeman who was part of it but who did not want to be named, said that at times it was done quite openly so that Ruth should not feel at home in Serowe. "We would follow her wherever she went in the village. It wasn't pleasant duty." Seretse, although not under guard in a "gentlemen's agreement", was nonetheless visited frequently by police officials who were detailed to keep a watchful eye on him. Naturally the isolated communities of the protectorate seethed with gossip over the latest state of affairs, and perhaps one of the unkindest comments came from a nurse in Lobatsi who said that if Ruth entered the hospital where she worked, she would not help her at all in her confinement.

As Ruth grew more miserable by the day, she decided in her resourceful way to do something about it. She asked her doctor, Don Moikangoa, to tell the administration that she would have a nervous breakdown if she didn't see Seretse. And although he was a good friend of Seretse's, and sympathised with them both in their predicament, he was too honest to do anything he felt was not ethical, and so he refused Ruth's request. Undeterred, she tackled the problem from a different angle. "I asked the cook to leave me a flask of coffee each night, and then for several nights I kept myself awake." At the end of that time, Ruth was so exhausted she could hardly stand up, and when she went to see Dr Moikangoa her condition reminded him of the bad nervous breakdown for which he had treated her on her arrival in Serowe. It made him terribly anxious, and he informed the administration that he could not be responsible for her condition unless she saw Seretse.

The government response to this was to send the Director of Medical Services, Dr M.L. Freedman, up from Mafeking to see Ruth, and on 14th April a message was sent to Ruth, informing her that the director would see her at any time and place convenient to her. Ruth replied, "I cannot encourage you in your racial prejudices, I have got my own doctor." He, poor man, being a civil servant, was in an awkward spot, but despite his efforts to persuade Ruth to see the director, she adamantly refused, saying it was a trick on the part of the government. She produced a telegram from Seretse stating that she was not to submit to any medical examination. And so the matter became a battle of wits between Ruth and the administration.

News of her unhappiness at being separated from Seretse and of the strain on her health soon reached London, where the member of parliament, Fenner Brockway, wrote to the secretary of state, Patrick Gordon Walker, begging him "to remove all impression of an absence of human approach" and taking him to task for not allowing Seretse to visit Ruth. He also expressed concern at the "humiliating conditions" under which Seretse was living, saying, "one gets the impression that the whole approach to him is unsympathetic and unappreciative of his sensitiveness to any indignity." And he finished his letter with a sentence that alarmed Gordon Walker, "I am doing my utmost to bring about an agreement between Tshekedi and Seretse and this looks promising."[149]

The secretary defended his actions by saying that it was due to Ruth's determination to remain in Serowe, when she was free to join her husband in Lobatsi that kept the couple apart. He was clearly peeved at Ruth's obstinacy. He wrote:

> Suggestions have been made in the press that owing to the state of her health and the conditions of the local roads, it would be unreasonable to expect Ruth to make the long journey. But it is worth noting that she recently made a motor-car journey of about 160 miles [more or less 250 kilometres] on the off-chance that Seretse's plane might land at Mahalapye for refuelling. In order to get to Lobatsi, she would only have to make the much shorter road journey to Palapye, where the remainder of the distance to Lobatsi could be covered by railway.[150]

It is of interest that Gordon Walker, while lauding any efforts to end the uncle / nephew feud, pointed out that any reconciliation between the two men would not necessarily remove the "anxieties and misgivings which led the government to withhold recognition of Seretse." And while he stuck to the White Paper for his reasons for this, we now know that of course any reconciliation between Seretse and Tshekedi and resultant peace within the tribe would not have made South Africa happy at all.

And so the war of words continued, between Brockway and Gordon Walker, between Ruth and the administration, and Seretse and the administration, and with the Seretse Khama Fighting Committee threatening to take the issue to the United Nations Trusteeship Committee. Rumours were also being spread around that Ruth was going to invite her sister and a friend out to stay with her in Serowe. News of her threatened nervous breakdown was soon picked up by the press which banner-headlined it, "Mrs Khama on verge of breakdown", and "Mrs Khama's doctor to appeal to officials".

Ruth told me that she accused the authorities of conducting a "war of nerves." She told reporters that before Seretse arrived from London, an official government spokesman told the press that after four or five days he would be allowed to go to Serowe. Later the high commissioner confirmed that Seretse's application would be given urgent attention. When Seretse had been in the country for ten days there was still no sign of him being allowed to leave Lobatsi.

She was not the only one who wanted to see Seretse. As soon as the tribe had heard of his return to the protectorate, they began flocking into Serowe, leaving their lands and cattle to be looked after by their women and children in the hope of seeing their "chief". It was at this time that a Tshekedi supporter, trying to leave Serowe with wagons and cattle to join the ex-regent down south at Rametsana, was stopped by a crowd of Seretse's supporters, and in the ensuing riot, the police resorted to tear gas and arrested eleven alleged ringleaders.

Subsequent press reports described Serowe as an armed camp, patrolled by tin-hatted police, armed with rifles and heavy batons. A couple of days later, the ox-wagon convoy was escorted out of the village by troopers on horseback carrying rifles, and armed police marching on either side of it. Three trucks filled with police followed, and the impressive procession, equipped with radio, was a spectacle the whole village turned out to witness.

The upshot of that was a British statement that the government might reconsider its decision to allow Seretse to be in the protectorate, and Gordon Walker said in parliament, "We are not going to be intimidated by violence or threats of violence. Seretse's return to the protectorate is on condition of his own good conduct, and (also) that order and good government of the tribe are not disturbed."[151]

But despite its threats, the government, painfully aware of the attentive press that was shocked at the way the authorities were keeping the couple apart, decided that it would lose more than it could gain by continuing to withhold permission for Seretse to visit Serowe. A decision was therefore taken to allow him to return for a specified period under certain strict conditions.

But in the meantime, Seretse, growing impatient at the delay and unaware of the government decision, was busy planning a clandestine visit to Ruth.

He sent her a secret letter with his uncle, Peto Sekgoma, telling her he planned to go to her for a weekend, and asking her to ensure that nobody would visit her during that time. His cousin Goareng was not at all happy about the plan. He was desperately worried that Seretse would be caught and he tried to dissuade him, but to no avail. A determined Seretse filled up his uncle's truck with petrol and was busy with final preparations for his journey when he received a request from the Lobatsi district commissioner to see him.

"You have permission to go to Serowe for a few days," said the official to an astonished Seretse, who almost blurted out that he was going anyway.

When the district commissioner in Serowe visited Ruth to give her the news of Seretse's visit, she stared at him silently for a moment in her surprise. The conditions of Seretse's visit were that he was not allowed to go to the kgotla, hold any meetings or address his people, and was to be accompanied by a government official.

Seretse set off on his journey north on Saturday afternoon, 15th April.

It was more than two weeks after his return from London, and nearly nine weeks since he had last seen Ruth. His cousins Goareng and Lenyletse accompanied him in the truck, and following him were the United Kingdom information officer, Nicholas Monsarrat, and several reporters. "When we got to Mahalapye where we had to stop because we were not allowed into Serowe before midnight, Leny was covered in blood. Seretse had hit a small buck in the road, and Leny, despite Seretse's requests to leave it, insisted that Ruth should have venison, and he picked it up and put it in the truck," Goareng told me, roaring with laughter.

The British did not laugh. They considered Seretse had broken one of his conditions by attending a meeting of supporters in Mahalapye, while Monsarrat, whose car had broken down, was having it fixed. The district commissioner was to take Seretse to task for his breach of conduct when he got to Serowe.

While Seretse smoked a cigarette with his friends and family in Palapye, Ruth, like women all over the world who know their husband or boyfriend is going to see them, got ready by washing her copper hair, manicuring her nails and having a nice dress ironed for her. When dusk fell, she was ready, and she sat down to wait for Seretse with a group of newspaper correspondents. They had a drink and then dinner was served. After it, they sat around talking in desultory fashion until someone suggested playing cards. Every time the sound of a vehicle was heard the chatter would stop, in spite of them all knowing that Seretse could not appear until midnight. Into the silence would fall the sound of the hissing pressure lamps and occasionally the cry of a jackal howling across the plains.

Ruth found it harder and harder to concentrate. She walked about the room restlessly, wondering what cruel trick of fate might now prevent her from reuniting with her husband. She rubbed her hands together nervously and had yet another cup of coffee. She was tense and keyed up, straining her ears as the night wore on to distinguish the sound of a truck against the night chorus of croaking frogs and chirping crickets. As the clock ticked off the hours, the village sounds grew quieter and the singing stopped. It was almost midnight, and Ruth was sitting at the bungalow window, when through the still night she heard the sound of an approaching engine and, instinctively knowing it was Seretse, she leapt up from her chair and ran out into the night with the press hot on her heels. Nimble feet flying, she raced down the bush-lined sandy track for several metres before the bright lights picked up her pregnant form from a distance. "Stop!" ordered Seretse and flung himself out of the truck.

They ran towards each other down the road, arms outstretched, hands reaching for each other. It was a minute after the allotted time of midnight, and if anybody had tried to stage-manage a more dramatic meeting between the world's most famous couple, they would have been hard put to outshine that one. Ruth, in trying to outmanoeuvre the press and greet her much-loved husband alone, had by her wild action added an even greater sense of tension and emotion to the whole affair.

As she felt Seretse's warm arms enfold her, her tense body relaxed, and he drew her heavy form within his powerful embrace, wondering as he did so at the growth of their child in his absence. Ruth's eyes filled with tears of joy as they clung to each other. Here at last was peace. Here was rest and love and security. They remained clasped silently to each other, oblivious for a few seconds to the waiting figures in the darkness. The press caught its breath at the sight of the reunion, and they felt a sense of intrusion and a pricking of their eyelids as they witnessed such intimacy. Then the night exploded with flash bulbs, as one after the other they lit up the bush, the road and the happy couple. After a while, Ruth climbed into the truck with Seretse and, surrounded by a few ululating women and men shouting "pula!", they drove slowly to the bungalow.

They walked up the steps to the veranda hand in hand, and there they posed briefly for those photographers who, fumbling in the dark with their equipment, had missed the poignant moment. Seretse said a few brief words about being pleased to be back, and then he and Ruth walked into their house and closed the door on the watching world.

A government official (not Monsarrat) who had been detailed to ensure that Seretse kept to his conditions, later described the meeting; "You could see," the official told me, "by the way they flung themselves into each other's arms, what a great and incredible love it was between them. Nothing and nobody mattered to them but each other. It was a humbling experience."

Early the next morning, the groups of Bamangwato who had gathered the night before outside the house and who had slept in the bushveld, began to assemble silently in the yard behind the house, and when Ruth and Seretse peeped out of the kitchen windows at breakfast time, they saw a crowd of several hundreds waiting for them. They decided that they must report to the district commissioner as agreed to by Seretse, and they drove through crowds so wild with happiness at Seretse's return that time and again the car came to a complete stop. "The people went mad, they flocked around us, they fell on the car, it was like a circus," said Ruth. The women danced and sang, arms outstretched, feet tapping the earth rhythmically, and the men raised their hats and bowed in their customary gesture of respect. By the time that Ruth and Seretse drove into the gracious grounds of the residency, the district commissioner noted that it was 11.20 a.m. In his view Seretse had not only been tardy in reporting his arrival but had broken one of the conditions for his visit while in Mahalapye. Before he could say anything, however, Ruth snapped, "The prisoner comes to report." No doubt the official felt a little uncomfortable after that, especially when Ruth declined his offer of a cup of tea.

The report and ticking-off over, the couple drove back to the village through the singing, laughing crowds. Chickens squawked wildly as they scurried out of the way of the oncoming mass, and goats, waiting lazily until the crowd was on them, leapt nimbly to one side. All of that Sunday the royal Bamangwato went out to the isolated bungalow to pay their respects to Seretse, and on

Monday, when people began to gather in the kgotla in the hopes of seeing Seretse, they were told by his supporters that he was not allowed to appear there. And so they walked the kilometres through the bush to his house.

It seemed churlish not to say anything to the hundreds waiting so patiently and silently outside, and so Seretse with Ruth at his side told them he had been exiled by the government because they feared his presence would cause dissension amongst them and retard their progress. He mentioned that in spite of there being no trouble whilst he and Ruth had lived amongst them, he would need to comply with the orders. At that, the women uttered their high keening sound and voices were heard saying that without Seretse and Ruth the tribe was finished. After this demonstration of loyalty, the crowd dispersed, and Seretse was called before the district commissioner later that day and warned that his visit could be curtailed if he repeated his disobedience, and further, that any future visits to Serowe might be jeopardised by his action.

"What was he supposed to do?" asked Ruth, "hide in the bath when people came to visit him? The administration made that weekend miserable for us, it was horrible. They were embarrassed by his warm reception. And despite Seretse telling the people he could not talk to them, they just stayed at our house, they camped there. They came with their food and their wood and their cooking pots and brought their blankets and they settled down in our yard. And Seretse went out and said to them, 'I have been told to tell you to go. I have been told that I am going to be responsible for riots.' And they just laughed … and they stayed."

But the authorities gave Seretse a third ticking off when a couple of days later, schoolteachers who supported him paraded many of their pupils before the house to give him a choral welcome. Ruth and Seretse sat on chairs in front of the singing crowd, and when they had finished, he rose to his feet, and a little awkwardly, for he was becoming nervous, he thanked them, and said he was not allowed to address meetings. The district commissioner, however, still regarded this as a further breach of confidence, and he again warned Seretse. But in a fit of magnanimity, he decided that the occasion was a bad one on which to force the issue and curtail the young man's visit.

Seretse was angered by the treatment of him, but as usual did not show this, and only Ruth and his friends and family were aware of his fury. "He had a cold sort of anger which is worse than outbursts, because when you can let go, you feel much better. But he could be very cutting without losing his temper. I wish I had that gift, because I often lost my temper, but in keeping his cool as they say today he was much cleverer and much, much more effective," said Ruth.

Their parting a few days later was naturally an extremely painful one. Ruth was greatly tempted to climb into the truck and snuggle up next to Seretse and forget about principles, and just be close to the man she loved. But she stuck bravely to her decision to stay behind. She waved until his vehicle disappeared in a cloud of dust, and then turned slowly and forlornly climbed the red polished stairs back into the house. Ruth didn't realise that the next time she would see Seretse would be after their baby's birth, for she thought he would return to the Bamangwato Reserve to gather evidence for his lawsuit against Tshekedi.

However, people on all sides were trying to reconcile uncle and nephew so that they could present a united front to the British and obviate the necessity for exile. It seemed possible that the dispute over Seretse's inheritance could be settled out of court and so Seretse did not go north again. He remained in exile in Lobatsi, a frustrated man who longed to be with his wife and his people.

In her letters to him, Ruth spoke of her increasing tiredness and heaviness. She went to bed earlier and rose later. Her pregnant body, tired by all the tension, was reacting and demanding rest. The arrival of Ruth's baby took everyone, including her, by surprise. The agreement between Seretse and the British Government had been that Seretse would be allowed to return to the protectorate to attend his wife's confinement, but Ruth and her doctor, Don Moikangoa, had somehow got their dates wrong. They expected the baby at the beginning of June. And so when Ruth was awakened one night in the middle of May with cramps, she groaned, thinking it must be her stomach and, not wishing to tramp outside to the toilet in the dark, she turned over heavily in bed, and hoped that the cramps would go away. Each time a new cramp woke her, she turned over and determinedly went back to sleep.

But when she woke in the cool light of dawn, the cramps seemed to her then to be a little less like a tummy problem and, alarmed, she went off to see her doctor. He thought it was probably a false alarm, but suggested she return a couple of hours later at 9 a.m. By then there was no doubt at all about Ruth's true condition, for she was already in second stage labour. The administration was informed, but by the time that Seretse received the message in Lobatsi, it was lunch time; he had to wait for his uncle to return with the truck, and then all the garages were closed. Seretse fumed with impatience as he waited to fill up with petrol. He roared out of Lobatsi at a furious pace and after several kilometres of tearing at wild speeds around bends and crashing through potholes, he realised he was driving stupidly and stopped the vehicle to let his uncle take over.

But he could never have hoped to make the birth, for Jacqueline Tebogo Khama made her appearance at 1.15 p.m., a healthy baby, weighing seven pounds and four ounces. She was born at the Serowe hospital, named after Seretse's father Sekgoma. When Jackie, as she was known later on, was born there, it was like a cottage hospital or large house, set in spacious, tree-filled grounds with a tin roof, and dressed stone forming the base of the building. The matron in charge of it was known as "Peps". "Pepper by name and Pepper by nature," said Miss Pepper, who kept it in immaculate condition, for everything from the red polished floors to the ceiling gleamed.

It was in one of the private wards at the front of the hospital that Jacqueline Tebogo (the second name was her grandmother's) was born in a straight-forward, uncomplicated birth. Ruth of course had no mother, and no relatives on her side of the family to provide the sort of support that a woman having her first baby needs so badly, and she kept asking her doctor after the birth, "When is Seretse coming?" And instead of falling asleep after her exhausting experience, she lay in bed, wide-eyed and tense, calling over and over for Seretse, who was tearing through the bush towards her, knowing how desperately she needed him.

As night fell, Ruth's doctor, conscious of Ruth's exhaustion and nervous disposition, and worried that his patient had had no rest after what is one of the most physically gruelling experiences there is, said sternly, "Enough is enough. You have not slept since this child was born, and I am now going to give you something to make you sleep." Ruth sat up in bed and glared at him.

"No, I am going to be awake when Seretse gets here," she said defiantly. But despite her protestations, she was given an injection with a powerful sedative, and she concentrated all her efforts in fighting the waves of sleep sweeping over her with every nerve and muscle in that determined body of hers.

Seretse arrived in Serowe an hour before midnight, and after knocking on Dr Moikangoa's door, was given permission to go and see Ruth, who the doctor fondly imagined would be in a deep, deep sleep until the morning. Seretse roared up the dusty slope to the hospital and jumped out of the truck, slamming the door behind him in his haste. Ruth heard the sound and knew instantly that it was him. She sat up, joyfully calling his name, her face alight with love, although her head was swimming. Happiness transformed the white face, drawn with tension and exhaustion, and Seretse saw only the most beautiful mother in the world holding out her arms to him. Now he thought, as he held her close, now we will not easily be separated again, and he kissed and soothed her, stroking her face and hair.

Then off he went to see his sleeping daughter. "Won't she ever look any prettier than that?" he asked Ruth on his return, who gave the warm little chuckle that those who knew her well, loved about her. Then she fell at last into a deep and satisfying sleep, content that the three of them were together. The next day her doctor was astounded that she had been able to sit up and greet her husband, for the injection he had given her was so powerful it normally knocked people out completely.

Matron Pepper had to use all her fiery qualities in the following days to keep the press and the tribe from the hospital door. She stuck up a notice at the entrance asking tribal deputations not to try and see Ruth, and she took a firm denial from Ruth to one reporter who was offering her 1500 pounds for an exclusive photograph of Jacqueline. "I don't go in for that sort of thing," explained Ruth.

The world press which had planned its moves according to Ruth's inaccurate dates, descended in droves on the village, by plane and by car. Said one, "The black women flocked around with gifts for Ruth, but the British officials' wives just didn't dare." She was wrong there, for at least one – my mother Mary Cardross Grant – sent Ruth a jacket she had knitted for the baby. She had invited Ruth to tea at my father's suggestion on the day Jackie was born, and Ruth had accepted, not dreaming she would be in hospital. Ruth, with her extraordinary sense of loyalty, never forgot that gesture of kindness in a period of such unkindness towards her.

When she left hospital a week later to return home with Jackie, journalist Noel Monks wrote, "I have never seen Ruth look prettier or happier. The marriage that rocked Africa seemed to be making out fine."[152] As Ruth carried her baby nestling in her arms to Seretse's car, tribal women flocked around her, gazing at the sleeping child of their "chief". The road to the bungalow was lined with singing, waving tribesfolk, and Ruth returned their love with warm smiles. In the days that followed, gifts from the tribe of goats and sheep arrived along with crocheted shawls, smocked dresses and booties from Khama supporters all over the world.

In the manner of all new mothers, Ruth fussed and worried about how she should rear her newborn baby. But she had the clash in cultures to contend with too. At the time of Jackie's birth in 1950, the practice in Western countries was to leave a child to cry, whereas African culture demanded that babies be picked up and nursed whenever they cried.

Ruth was fortunate to have Seretse's sister Naledi living with them, for her nurse's training and her warm comfortable nature were great assets. Several books on childcare made their way to the Khamas' house through Joe Burgess's office – there is nothing like the common experience of birth in helping to break down barriers.

But the trauma of the preceding year had taken its toll of Ruth. "My doctor said it would only be after the birth that I would be able to see the damage that had been done by keeping Seretse from me. My nails kept splitting and cracking, my hair looked dreadful and immediately after I had given birth, I got back into the clothes I had worn before I fell pregnant. I was terribly thin, and dreadfully anaemic," said Ruth.

Back in England, Ruth's mother, who had worried ceaselessly about her daughter being left alone without her husband in a hostile white community in a strange country, was naturally thrilled when she learnt the birth had been an uncomplicated one.

"My parents had been out visiting friends, and when they opened the door, the telephone was ringing, and there was a telegram on the floor. So, one of them ripped open the cable, while the other heard the news of the birth from a reporter," said Muriel, who was immediately telephoned at her office by her mother. "I remember leaving the office that night, and during my ten-minute walk to London Bridge to get my bus home, I think that nearly every poster I saw on the way there proclaimed, 'Ruth Khama – a daughter'. I was still amazed at all the publicity she was receiving," said Muriel.

In the same month that Jackie was born, the district commissioner in Serowe, Forbes Mackenzie, who had been appointed by the British Government as the native authority in the absence of a chief, went to the kgotla to address the tribe. He was shouted down in a display of anger and defiance unparalleled until then, for the generally docile and friendly Bamangwato had enjoyed a good relationship on the whole with the government for whose protection it had asked so many years previously.

Now the policy of indirect rule by that protecting power was being changed to direct rule in what the British described as "a development fully in accordance with His Majesty's government's policy today of affording the mass of African peoples a fuller say, and more direct participation in the conduct of their own affairs."[153] Those were laudable sentiments, and the irony of the situation was that in years to come, as the country moved towards independence, and away from the system of tribal courts and the great powers of chief, Seretse would endorse them. But in 1950, the right moves were being made for the wrong reasons, and a more sensitive and informed administration would have been aware of the fierce loyalty commanded by a chief, and of the vital and pivotal role he played in tribal affairs.

When that chief was Seretse and the affair was complicated by a "wicked and unpopular" uncle, the moves to replace the rightful chief became even more abhorrent to the tribe.

As early as May 1950, the tribe began to resemble a vessel drifting rudderless and without a captain on a wild sea. Their proud customs and traditions were subjected to abnormal strains, and in the absence of a chief, there was growing lawlessness in the Bamangwato Reserve. Police patrols increasingly broke up secret meetings, and policemen had the unpleasant task of marching into villages and knocking over beer stills in a display of strength. It was the beginning of troubles with the tribe, which had decided that if it was not to be allowed to have Seretse, it was certainly not going to allow anybody else to take his place.

THIRTEEN

Ruth and Seretse go into exile

Ruth and Seretse had spent only three weeks together after the birth of their daughter when they were told that Seretse's permit to remain in the Bamangwato Reserve would soon expire, and he would have to return to Lobatsi. Ruth, apart from being angered by the exile, which she had hoped would somehow not be enforced, was also sad that she could not adhere to Bamangwato custom in which no fuss was made over a newborn child until the mother had completed three months of seclusion. The period varied according to the wealth and rank of the family, with poorer people generally staying at home for a shorter time than others. According to Tswana law and custom this postnatal seclusion was regarded as necessary, because of the weakness caused in the woman by labour and its after effects and was also held to give the baby time to grow stronger.

But when it became clear that Seretse would have to leave Serowe in terms of his exclusion order, the couple decided there was no point in being separated again, and that they would leave together for Lobatsi on the first stage of their trip into exile. Members of the tribe, who since Seretse's return had been walking regularly through the bush along the footpaths to the Khama bungalow, continued the practice in greater numbers when they heard their chief was leaving. Every day, when Ruth rose, she would see these patient groups of bewildered people who could not understand how the man who was by birthright their chief could be taken from them. And so they squatted in the dust, talking quietly to each other, making gestures of anger and despair. If Ruth emerged with Jacqueline, they would cluster around her, gazing with love and fascination at the little mite.

Ruth was feeling exhausted, due partly to the effects of the tension of the months without Seretse and her severe anaemia. She was therefore both surprised and grateful when Jackie cried in the night to hear Seretse tell her to stay where she was while he attended to his daughter. "It surprised me because many fathers even today won't do this. And he would also come and talk to me when I bathed her," said Ruth during one of our many interviews.

The couple left Serowe on 12th June 1950. It was an emotional time for both, for Ruth, in her tumultuous year there, in spite of the ostracism of the civil servants and the loneliness of being separated from Seretse, had grown to love the people and the village life. London with its lights, theatre, ice skating and dancing seemed remote and unimportant compared with her new life and the challenge it presented; and the quite extraordinary acceptance of Ruth by the tribe with their demonstrations of loyalty, love and respect touched her deeply.

Often the women on seeing Ruth would fall to their knees and touch the hem of her skirt in respect, and there was virtually nothing they would not do for her. And although she was wont to say, "They do it out of love for Seretse," they had grown to admire Ruth for her own qualities of loyalty and courage. The exile of Seretse from the place of his birth and childhood, from the pretty hills and great plains, from his rightful seat in the kgotla, and from his close friends and family was a traumatic experience for him.

The day of departure dawned bright and cold, for June is the month when chilly winds blow, and people do not go out much at night, but huddle for warmth around their fires. They did not waste time sitting around their breakfast fires that morning but made their way over the dusty hills and along the sandy paths to Ruth and Seretse's house. Some of the tribe had slept there, keeping watch on the last night, and in the early light of dawn they doused their fires with sand and wrapped up their blankets. When the time came to leave, there were so many people present that they could not all fit into the Khamas' yard and so they spread beyond it around the perimeter.

The crowd bowed their heads when Ruth and Seretse appeared on the veranda, and prayers were said for a safe journey and for a speedy return. There was silence after the last prayer, and into the heavy sorrow of the moment fell the sweet chirping of birds sitting in the thorn bushes, and in the background was the cooing of the rock pigeons. Many of the women cried, tears pouring down their faces, but this was done silently and with dignity. It was quiet, intensely quiet as the wintry sun rose high over the bushveld and began beating down on the tin roof of the house and on the bare heads of those who prayed.

With a sigh the crowd rose to its feet, and the bustle of departure began. Seretse's friends and family who were going with him to Lobatsi packed their luggage into trucks and cars. The cats given to Ruth by Margaret Bourke-White were put in too, and then Jackie was brought out. Ruth could not say a word because she was so overcome with emotion, and as their car pulled away, the bungalow where she had suffered a nervous breakdown and to which she had brought her first child, became a blur, as did the mournful faces around her. An administration report filed on the departure, described the village as deserted, which gives the erroneous impression that nobody turned out to bid Ruth and Seretse farewell. It stated baldly: "No one attended departure of Seretse and his family from Serowe."[154]

The 380-kilometre drive over dusty, pot-holed roads to Lobatsi was an exhausting journey at the best of times. "Thank goodness I was breastfeeding. Can you imagine travelling over those roads with bottles and sterilising equipment?" Ruth asked me. They were quartered in the same house Seretse had been in prior to his return to Serowe, and Ruth was surprised to find curtains, a settee and chairs there. Also there, however, were the tin mugs and plates that had so incensed her when she first heard about them and which feature again later in this chapter. Lobatsi can be quite cold in winter, cold for Bechuanaland that is, not cold when compared with a northern winter. But then you are not prepared for cold in a country that is extremely hot for much of the year.

And so Ruth, who loved the heat, simply froze at night and recalls lying under as many as six blankets trying to keep warm.

Lobatsi, as already described, had a lot of South Africans living there and was situated on Crown land. It, along with Gaberones (later to become Gaborone) and Francistown, were once described as "white enclaves, whose settlers spent their time toying with the idea of moving away from the government shadow of the Bechuanaland Protectorate and of becoming incorporated with South Africa or Rhodesia."[155]

That will give you some idea of the kind of reception she could expect from the white populace of Lobatsi. But to Ruth's surprise, it was not all bad, and as she walked down the tarred main street to the big trading stores, she was the subject of tremendous curiosity and sometimes of warmth too. She began to be aware that people like her father, who were in principle opposed to mixed marriages, were so incensed by the way in which she and her husband were being treated, that they sympathised with them. "My father never accepted our marriage, but he also said that it was immoral the way we were made to suffer. Therefore, some of the locals were quite friendly, but others said openly, 'Well, it is just what they deserve, good for the British.' But of course they never said that directly to me, and if they had, I would just have laughed. It used to infuriate people when I laughed at their prejudice." But for all Ruth's bravery, she confessed to a very real feeling of persecution at the time.

The British, it appears from reports and telegrams sent at the time, were not all that sure about their stated intention to exile the couple, for when Baring returned to the United Kingdom in June, he was asked to submit a report justifying his assertion that good government in the Bamangwato Reserve was impossible as long as Ruth and Seretse remained in the protectorate. And so Baring telegrammed the British High Commission Office in Pretoria and asked: "What proof have we of the use by Seretse for personal purposes of money from levies? What proof have we that Ruth openly threatened future action against those who did not regard Seretse as chief?" And he added, "great importance is attached to this."[156]

The British must have felt they would need all the ammunition they could lay their hands on, if the public outcry when the Khamas returned to London became overwhelming.

An impressive description of the tribe's refusal to cooperate with the administration resulted from Baring's request, for it emerged that the tribe would not attend meetings, and the Serowe district commissioner had to broadcast regulations regarding the control of foot-and-mouth disease by loud-hailer from a moving vehicle; a headman who had been sent word that he should call a meeting replied through a representative that he was too ill to even read the district commissioner's telegram; no taxes were being paid voluntarily in Serowe; and no one would serve on finance, school or livestock committees.

The frustrated administration, not believing that the tribe could act without Seretse's help, felt that he was directing the campaign of non-cooperation from Lobatsi, and was surprised when the campaign continued during his exile when he was thousands of kilometres away in England.

Ruth was not excluded from allegations of trouble-making, for rumours that she would wreak vengeance on those who had been unfriendly to her and that she would force traders to erect proper stores when Seretse became chief were rife, and while it is true that she was not impressed with most of the stores, her behaviour after her return to the protectorate never supported these allegations.

But the determined, strong-minded Ruth was clearly a source of irritation for the administration. She was no blushing English rose as far as it was concerned – much more akin to a Kalahari thorn. "It is becoming clear that

Seretse is prepared to go quietly, but that Ruth may make herself the focus of future trouble," complained the acting resident commissioner.[157] If Seretse went to London and Ruth returned to the Bamangwato Reserve, she would most likely be set up by Seretse's supporters as the tribal titular head, he claimed. The image of an English woman ruling one of Africa's large tribes is an interesting one. Thus, armed with information about the disquieting effect of the Khamas on good government, the British loaded their guns and waited to see what Ruth and Seretse would do when permission for Seretse to be in the protectorate expired at the end of the following month (July).

Before then, however, Seretse was given permission to return to the Bamangwato Reserve with Tshekedi in order for his uncle to formally hand over to him the cattle that formed the inheritance from his father, Sekgoma. This was done according to Bamangwato custom, and Seretse and Tshekedi therefore left their respective lawyers behind. However, they were not alone, for they were accompanied by a government official whose job it was to keep an eye on Seretse. According to Ruth, whenever the party stopped for the night, each of the three men had his separate camp, and Tshekedi resented any inference that he had to be watched too. "Seretse is your prisoner, not me," he remarked testily to the official, recalled Ruth. "Everybody was being difficult at the time, and the British were being the most difficult of all," Ruth commented.

As Seretse and Tshekedi counted the cattle and relaxed in the country they both loved, their great anger subsided somewhat and a little of the former warmness of their relationship returned. They took longer and longer over their meals and when the official urged them to hurry up, Tshekedi remarked, "Now this is Bechuanaland meat and it doesn't cook in one hour, it takes at least four," which gives some indication of what made the Westernised official so impatient.

It was while Seretse was away that an incident occurred which made Ruth furious. She was invited by some friends and journalists to have lunch with them at the Lobatsi hotel, and it was while they were having a drink in the lounge beforehand that the group was informed by hotel personnel that Ruth could not be allowed to have lunch there, but that her friends could remain if they so wished. The reason given for exclusion was that Ruth was no longer a member of the "European community" and therefore not entitled to enjoy the hotel's facilities. (At that time, black people were not allowed into hotels in the protectorate.)

"Of course, it made a marvellous story for the journalists," said Ruth bitterly later. "But we all went back to my house for lunch instead." It was treatment like this that scarred Ruth.

A couple who subsequently took over the hotel and who were very friendly with Ruth and Seretse were Sydney and Doris Milner, who at the time lived on a farm outside Lobatsi to which they invited the Khamas at weekends. When Seretse was away, they kept a friendly eye on Ruth which was comforting at a time when so many people in the little town were ostracising her.

It was shortly after Seretse's return from the reserve, and after he had settled his dispute over the cattle inheritance out of court with Tshekedi, that Ruth met for the first time the man who had caused her so much trouble and heartache. They bumped into each other in a Lobatsi store when she and Seretse were out shopping together. "Well, it was gorgeous, for everyone around us knew that we had not met, and of what had been going on between us," said Ruth.

She was buying something at a counter, when the crowd in the dimly-lit store suddenly hushed their chatter. Seretse turned and saw his uncle silhouetted in the light from the door, smiling a little nervously as he came towards them. The crowd thickened and pushed closer in anticipation as Seretse, taking Ruth's arm, said, "This is my uncle." She did not react immediately, for as she told me, "I had met so many uncles. But then of course when I looked closer, I realised that this was *the* uncle." In spite of her anger at the bitter, hurtful things he had said about her, Ruth extended her hand, and greeted him courteously for Seretse's sake, and they invited Tshekedi back to their house.

Ruth was to comment later to a British official that she had been "charmed" by Tshekedi and that he had been very nice about Jacqueline. "Well, of course my own father was against our marriage for much the same reasons that Tshekedi was, and so I could understand his position to an extent, and we got on very well after that."

At the beginning of July, the administration was starting to hope that Ruth and Seretse might leave Bechuanaland quietly, without any deportation order having to be served on them. But while they hoped that this would be the case, they also made provision for their forced removal if necessary, organising police reinforcements, including policewomen from Southern Rhodesia, to be at the ready. When Ruth and Seretse began to make inquiries about travelling to

Britain, the hope they would go voluntarily was reinforced, and in an effort to induce them to leave with the minimum of fuss, it was suggested that certain "concessions" be made. These included paying the air passage for Seretse's sister, Naledi; arranging an import permit for their South African assembled Chevrolet and organising for all their luggage to be shipped without delay.

However, Ruth and Seretse were not going to leave the country they both loved so much without a fight. On 3rd August, when two officials went to see them, to ask them if they were prepared to comply with the government's wishes, they said they were not, and deportation orders were promptly served on them both. Ruth told me that Mr W.A.W. Clark, chief secretary to the high commissioner, who served the orders with another official acting as witness, later described the circumstances of the interview as "trying". In view of Ruth's description of the meeting, this would appear to be a typical example of British understatement.

Before they arrived, she said to Seretse, "The first British official that crosses the threshold of this house is going to have those two tin mugs." There was a hatchway between the living room and the kitchen, and Ruth put it up telling the cook to put the two tin mugs on the tray when he served tea. Seretse, who had heard Ruth, asked the cook to remove the mugs, whereupon the excitable and angry Ruth exclaimed, "Let them have the tin mugs. They will probably be most uncomfortable with china, and after all, they must be used to them or they wouldn't have expected you to use them, now would they?"

Ruth roared with laughter as she described a Laurel and Hardy type scene, in which she rushes to the hatch, lifts it, tells the cook to replace the tin mugs, and when Seretse countermands the order, she rushes back and so on and on.

When the confused cook finally did appear with the tray of tea, he looked appealingly at Ruth, for the tin mugs were absent, and she and Seretse, in spite of the gravity of the situation, wanted to explode with laughter.

"When these two lovely creatures [officials] arrived, trying to be friendly, I was determined not to unbend, not after all we had gone through, and so I wouldn't even stand up to greet them. I was behaving really badly, but I was young and determined not to make them feel welcome."

Ruth's two semi-Persian kittens, Pride and Prejudice, were lying on the settee, and as there was nowhere else for the officials to sit, Seretse asked her to remove them. Ruth replied, "Oh, I think they are quite comfortable here." And so the two officials who didn't want to sit down on the beautiful, playful kittens, stood there, hat in hand, while an embarrassed Seretse demanded they be removed.

"Prejudice come off there, come on Prejudice," called Ruth, thoroughly enjoying the look of discomfiture on the men's faces. "Do have a seat where Prejudice was lying," offered Ruth.

"Normally Seretse used to get very angry with me when I was impossible, but on that occasion he didn't really mind, in fact he thought it was very funny," said Ruth, who was well aware that it is one thing for officials sitting in offices to issue orders, but quite another to have to go into someone's home to serve them.

"Seretse accepted his banishment papers," said Ruth. "He was a gentleman. If someone offered him something, he would take it. I refused to accept mine, and so our lawyer had to take them for me." Ruth told me that she thereupon commented to Clark that the deportation order was the first direct step the government had taken against her, and that she was surprised that a woman could be regarded as a danger to peace.

The next obstacle that she threw into the path of the officials was the yellow fever vaccination for Jacqueline, a requirement for those travelling through Africa. The officials said they would ask a doctor from the nearby hospital to do the vaccination, but Ruth retorted, "Oh no! I can't have a government doctor; I couldn't guarantee that you wouldn't tell him to give her something that would kill her. I will have to write to my doctor in England and ask if it is safe." And Ruth explained to the officials that, in view of the treatment meted out to her and Seretse by the British, she believed they were capable of anything.

"They squirmed. They were embarrassed, but why make life easy for people who are making it so difficult for you?" asked Ruth. When it was pointed out to her that those not in possession of a valid yellow fever certificate were likely to be detained in Egypt, Ruth remarked, this time with a twinkle in her eye that, "other distinguished exiles have lived there before now." The upshot of her stubborn behaviour was that Dr Don Moikangoa had to make the journey down south from Serowe to administer the vaccination, and by then Ruth had run out of ideas for making life difficult for the British.

In view of her description of that meeting at the beginning of August, it is a little surprising to read Mr Clark's report, for in it he writes, "I was compelled to some admiration of Ruth, whom I had not met before. She has obviously been through a lot, including loneliness, but she was neat in appearance and composed in manner. She displays a quick but limited intelligence and a ready wit. She undoubtedly has courage."

And more surprising still, Clark wrote of that meeting: "I may be wrong (so many guesses have been wrong over this business), but my impression was that Ruth feels the protectorate episode is nearing an end and that she will be quite glad to get back to London. But Seretse feels that he would lose face by meekly complying with the government's wishes; he therefore wants to force government to compel him to leave. Ruth acquiesces in this. Seretse undoubtedly feels very sore; his often-lethargic manner cloaks deep feelings."[158]

The British were soon to learn that the lethargic cloak hid more than they imagined, for Seretse subsequently bowled them two balls they had an enormous amount of difficulty fielding, and one of them landed on the British prime minister's desk. Seretse decided to contest the validity of the deportation orders, but not only that; he also applied for leave to contest in the high court of the protectorate the legality of the high commissioner's action in refusing to recognise him as chief.

The line which Seretse intended to follow in his proceedings against the high commissioner was that the judicial enquiry, set up by Baring to determine whether he was a fit person to be chief, was wrong according to the law, since he was already chief when it sat. Seretse claimed that he had been chief since the appointment of Tshekedi as regent when he was a little boy, and that therefore, no question of further designation, recognition or confirmation was required. When the third kgotla in June 1949 terminated the regency by its acclamation of Seretse, he had become chief without the need for any confirmation of this, he said, and thus Baring had acted ultra vires.

When the alarmed secretary of state for commonwealth relations heard of Seretse's intended action, he called in his legal advisers who suggested that if Baring had no legal right to withhold recognition from Seretse on the grounds he had set down, Seretse might nevertheless be deposed under a new 1950 proclamation. But it was soon pointed out that it was one thing to withhold recognition from a chief, but quite another to depose him as an afterthought when it was found that action in withholding recognition had been illegal.

Seretse's intention to contest the validity of the enquiry worried the government, for when the top British legal brains investigated the matter, it appeared that the high commissioner's action might well have been ultra vires. The prime minister was told about the matter when it appeared that if Seretse

216

instigated proceedings against the high commissioner, the latter might lose the case. This could happen either in the high court of the territory or, if there were an appeal, in the Privy Council.

Doubts were also raised at the time about whether the high commissioner had the power under the protectorate's deportation proclamation to exclude Seretse from the territory. There was considerable difference of opinion amongst the government's legal advisers on this, some arguing the power was sufficient, and others holding the opposite view.[159]

The problem that faced the government was whether to proceed with their deportation of the Khamas if Seretse should only institute legal proceedings about his non-recognition as chief, and not contest the validity of the deportation order. It was felt that deportation in that instance would seem to be an oppressive act on the part of the British, for Seretse would in all fairness need to be in the protectorate to instruct his lawyers and to retain control over his case. And so it was decided that if he did institute proceedings about the validity of the judicial enquiry, his deportation would be delayed a few weeks until the matter went before the protectorate's high court. If, however, he contested the validity of the exclusion order, it was decided he would not be removed until a ruling had been handed down.

In the event, Seretse withdrew his intended action on both counts just before he left the protectorate, and Baring and the government sighed with relief, for their record of insensitivity did not need further tarnishing by court procedures that might show they had acted ultra vires. It was only years later, said Ruth, that they found out what the British were doing then was, as she claimed, "illegal as well as inhuman".

The second ball that Seretse bowled the British, was a reconciliation between him and Tshekedi – and he hinted broadly of this to Clark during the meeting at which he and Ruth were served with the deportation orders. The upshot was a worried Baring, to whom a reconciliation order spelt disaster for the British, and he sent an administration officer to pick up Tshekedi in the middle of the night and rush him through to Pretoria where he asked him what was going on between him and Seretse. To his alarm Tshekedi replied that they were contemplating a joint statement both renouncing firmly their claims to the chieftainship, which would also include their children.

Baring spelt out to Tshekedi the consequences of such action, pointing out that such a statement might well remove all the grounds set out in the White Paper for the exclusion of Ruth and Seretse from the protectorate; and that the course of action contemplated could well result in Seretse's early return to the Bamangwato Reserve and his establishment as chief which, stressed Baring, "would inevitably arouse passions again in the Union [of South Africa]."

Baring, who had always had a high regard for Tshekedi's administrative abilities, then hinted to him that in view of his correct conduct throughout the Seretse affair, he could yet play a big and valuable part in the protectorate. During his lengthy conversation with the ex-regent, he established that Tshekedi's attitude towards the Khama marriage was still unchanged, and he urged him to include this in any announcement. By the end of their meeting, Tshekedi who had suggested that he should visit London to discuss developments with the British Government, accepted Baring's suggestion that no joint announcement of renunciation of the chieftainship should be made by him and Seretse, until such discussions had taken place in the British capital.[160]

An admirable plan by Seretse and Tshekedi to demolish the case the British had against allowing them to return to their tribe was cleverly and wickedly scotched in its infancy by Baring. It came at a time when its announcement would have had a devastating effect on the British Government, for it would have been hard put to justify the exile if the British touted reason for it – dissension in the tribe due to the marriage – was suddenly nullified.

The real reason was the British Government's desire not to upset the new apartheid government in South Africa by allowing such an internationally famous mixed-colour couple to live on its borders.

And so Baring suggested to Tshekedi[161] that he should confine himself to a joint call with Seretse to the Bamangwato to cooperate with the authorities and to restore an administration run by the tribe, and this is the general line that the uncle and nephew subsequently took in their joint statement. But Tshekedi's pleas to Baring not to enforce Seretse's exile met with no success, and he returned to Lobatsi to continue his talks with his nephew.

When the administration heard that the two were working on a text along the lines mentioned in the above paragraph, they agreed to a postponement of the Khamas' departure, although only for twenty-four hours.[162]

Tshekedi had hoped to have several days with Seretse. Ruth told me that Seretse had said to her – and he also remarked to the press – "I expected postponement for life – not twenty-four hours."

The press, who had begun to pour into Lobatsi to cover the departure of Ruth and Seretse, now became a problem for uncle and nephew, who despite Baring's strictures, were working on a secret aide-mémoire. In this, they agreed they would give up all claim to the chieftainship for themselves and their children; that they should take up with the British Government their case to live in the Bamangwato Reserve; and that their views would not be published without mutual consultation. The idea was to pass on their aims to people best able to lobby the government at an opportune time, and they did not want to lessen the impact of their agreement by having the press get hold of bits of it and upset their coordinated campaign.

Ruth and Seretse's departure date was now set for 17th August, and when Clark flew to Lobatsi in Baring's plane on the afternoon of Tuesday, 15th August, to supervise the departure (for the nervous administration could not be sure that there would not be last-minute dramatic hitches) he was relieved to learn from Seretse that he was withdrawing all legal proceedings against the government. This was in line with the sentiment which he expressed two days later in his farewell speech that he was not abandoning any of his legal rights, but he was postponing legal action in the hope that in the near future he would return as chief, after reconsideration in calmer and under more peaceful circumstances.

That Tuesday evening, Clark called on Ruth and Seretse at their home to give them the final details of their journey, and to tell them that the government had organised hotel accommodation in London for them until they found a flat. Again, Clark left with the impression that Ruth was "secretly quite excited at the prospect of seeing London again."[163]

Although she was obviously looking forward to seeing her family again, this did not mean that she was happy to be leaving Bechuanaland. But British administration officials obviously found it impossible to believe that a Londoner could happily make her home with an African tribe.[164] This view – that she was pleased to be returning to Britain – appeared in several press reports, and made her angry, for she retorted to local pressmen the next day that she had still not packed her clothes in the hopes of a last-minute reprieve.

Reported Clark: "Their departure was in doubt up to the last minute, but Ruth had had all their effects, including refrigerator, packed and dispatched in advance and appears to have taken the line, 'where my refrigerator goes, there will I follow'."[165] Although the administration regarded Ruth as the "more dangerous" of the pair, it seems nonetheless it could be flippant about her when they so chose.

The last two days before the departure were filled with tension and drama. The government organised a fleet of trucks, cars and jeeps to collect headmen and tribesmen to hear the joint statement of Seretse and Tshekedi which they were to deliver at Gaberones a few hours before Ruth and Seretse flew out. As the vehicles tore along the dusty roads, dashing into villages up to 1400 kilometres away from Lobatsi, Seretse and Tshekedi had a tough time hiding from the press. At one stage, according to Ruth, in their desperation to be alone, they sent a decoy off in their car, and they climbed into a battered old truck and set off in the opposite direction, straight into the bush. Tshekedi loved the sense of drama involved in all this, and thoroughly enjoyed playing the elusive quarry.

But their evading tactics delayed work on their aide-mémoire and joint statement, and when by nightfall on Wednesday they were still not finished, they borrowed lamps, typewriter, paper and carbon from the administration, and disappeared with their followers to another hiding place in the bush and only emerged at 11.30 p.m. to hand Clark their joint statement.

It was a weary Seretse who arrived home that night, and an equally tired Ruth who met him, for in addition to caring for Jacqueline and doing last-minute packing when their departure seemed inevitable, she had had to contend with the press who had set up their typewriters on the veranda of their house. They were, however, a generally friendly crowd, and one journalist had given Ruth a carrycot in which to take the baby into exile. Ruth hurried out when she heard Seretse's car tyres crunch on the gravel driveway, but he brought no news of a last-minute reprieve. Depressed, they walked hand in hand into the lounge where all was silent save for the hissing noise made by the pressure lamps.

Seretse could not have had much sleep that night, for long before the chilly, wintry dawn broke, he and his men were up and heading for the hills just outside the sleepy little village of Gaberones where hundreds of tribesmen were waiting for him. They had slept the night in the open, and in the blue air of early morning their wood fires glowed bright as they huddled around them for warmth. They drew their heavy greatcoats around them and, exhaling their pungent tobacco smoke, they cooked their breakfasts of porridge and coffee. These were the smells, sights and sounds of Africa that Seretse so loved, and his weary eyes dimmed with the painful knowledge that it might be years before he turned his back on the drizzle and the tarred streets of London and again breathed in the scents of his country.

By 7 a.m. Tshekedi had joined him, and they delivered their joint statement to the tribe. In this, in an attempt to ease the way for a reconsideration of their exile, they asked their people to cooperate with the government while discussions continued on a system of tribal administration run by the tribe. Seretse and Tshekedi had already asked the government to promote consultation between themselves and the tribe in the interests of good administration, for without it, the uncle and nephew had pointed out, secret contact would result.

They told the hundreds of silent men that they had written a government joint letter to the high commissioner in which, inter alia they called upon their people to cooperate with the government whilst discussions continued on the required restoration of a system, "of native administration acceptable to and run by the people themselves."

To that end the uncle and nephew wrote, "We humbly wish to point out that today we are perhaps the only two people of the Bamangwato tribe who have made a study of the British Colonial administration as practised in the other colonies, and we feel that it would be in the interest of the tribe for the British Government not to deny us an opportunity to assist both in the creation of a system of administration and in participating thereto."

They concluded their extraordinarily perceptive joint statement by asking the government to appoint a council of experts (both African and European) "to consult with our people in their own country regarding the formation of a workable system of tribal administration."[166] The attentive men, like everyone else close to the Khamas during those last few days before exile, had hoped Seretse would bring news of a change in government plans, but they were disappointed. Seretse rose heavily to his feet when the time came to make his farewell speech, and he said, "I wish you to know that I leave you unwillingly and because me and my wife have been served with an order to leave the country."[167] He was leaving at a time, he said, when he was convinced that the Bamangwato nation was more united than at any time in living memory.

"Hard words have been spoken, misinterpretation and misconception have taken place, and injustices have resulted. Let us call a temporary truce," he advised. And he gave credence to his plea, by asking the tribe to pay their taxes; to obey all lawful orders given to it by the government and, "above all, pay due homage and remain loyal to His Majesty King George VI."

It was a remarkable speech for a man in his miserable situation, and it demonstrates yet again his tremendous capacity for putting the welfare of others before his own. The tribe took their leave sadly from the man, who by inspiring such loyalty had united them. Then the two men whose differences had resulted in such unhappiness shook hands and hoped they would soon meet in happier circumstances.

The press, which had been excluded from the meeting, had deduced from the frantic activity of Seretse and Tshekedi and from the rushing about of important administration personnel that something big was afoot. It was therefore with considerable disappointment that they read Seretse's farewell statement,[168] for they had thought it highly probable that due to the reconciliation between uncle and nephew that Seretse would be granted a last-minute reprieve. Indeed, some had even written reports to that effect. And of course, if Seretse and Tshekedi had stuck to their original plan, the smooth departure might not have taken place after all.

Ruth had risen early in their Lobatsi house, and she shivered as she dressed in the cold dawn and thought to herself that she wouldn't miss the little town or its inhabitants. It was quite a procession that wound its way through the Lobatsi hills, for the people who had been camping in the Khamas' grounds followed Ruth as did the local district commissioner. Ruth drove their new Chevrolet, with Naledi and Jacqueline as passengers. As they entered the village of Gaberones, seventy-two kilometres away, scores of people who had gathered outside the general trading store on the main road surrounded the car and clamoured to see the baby. Ruth arrived at the airstrip fifteen minutes late, noted Clark, "for she insisted on driving in her own car, which had not yet been run in."[169]

He had also had an extremely early start, leaving Lobatsi at dawn to check security arrangements at the grass airstrip. But after breakfast, convinced by then that the departure would take place according to plan, he arranged for the police to make themselves scarce, and noted later that the press could not hide their disappointment at the trouble-free farewell.

"The absence of the police from the scene, apart from a few on the airstrip perimeter to control cattle grazing in the vicinity, was not according to their expectation," he later informed his superiors.[170] He was also pleased that he managed to keep the presence of the three policewomen brought in from Rhodesia – in case of a forced removal of the Khamas – secret from the press.

When Ruth and Seretse arrived at the airstrip, they both looked exhausted and showed signs of the strain they had been through. Lined up on the field in front of the plane were headmen, and behind the fence lining the airstrip were the tribe. Seretse first shook hands sadly with his headmen and then with the administration officials. He then joined Ruth, and between them they carried the sleeping Jacqueline in her cot to the aircraft. As they turned to look once more at their people, the headmen bowed and the tribe shouted farewell a couple of times, but apart from that the air was quiet and heavy with emotion.

Tears glistened in both Ruth and Seretse's eyes, and they were not alone, for even some of the administration officials' wives were overcome by the sadness of it all, and one police officer muttered, "Poor devils." But there were those of course who were thrilled to see the last of the couple whom they considered had brought only trouble and unrest to the country.

Ruth paused at the top of the steps before disappearing into the plane. Seretse followed her after taking a last look at his country, and the door was fastened behind them, the engines roared into life, and the RAF plane took off. It made a farewell sweep over the heads of the crowd who shouted a farewell before it straightened up and headed north for Francistown and Livingstone. A low sigh rippled through the crowd as it watched the craft disappear.

British information officer, Nicholas Monsarrat, was on the plane too, and he asked the pilot to fly over Serowe, so that the Khamas could see it for the last time – a request that Ruth said annoyed Seretse and infuriated her. Ruth later commented, "We had put up with enough as it was, and then this final blow, of having to be escorted by Monsarrat."

Sir Evelyn Baring was naturally one of the people happy to see the last of Seretse and Ruth. According to his biographer, Charles Douglas-Home, he wrote to his wife that he had had, "one hell of a time. For the moment everyone is so relieved at the complete absence of a row, that I have had a row of congratulations. Malan and I are now practically blood brothers."[171]

The administration had succeeded in dispatching Ruth and Seretse with a minimum of fuss under the circumstances, and this was acknowledged by Clark who said, "I am grateful to Mr and Mrs Khama for their propriety, in making a task which could not be pleasing less difficult for me."[172] But the non-cooperation of the tribe and its deep anger at the British for its treatment of their rightful chief was not of a transitory nature. Some of those same officials who waved the Khamas off in such relief later came to think that their exile might after all have been a ghastly mistake.

FOURTEEN

The first year in exile

As Ruth and Seretse flew away from the troubled world of the Bamangwato and up the continent of Africa on a BOAC flying boat, they flew into a world that had troubles of its own, for the Americans and the Russians were both trying to assert their supremacy in moves which resulted in the Cold War. Conflict erupted in Korea and it wasn't long before the Chinese became involved, and American fears grew that the Far East would slip away from their influence.

But when you are being sent away from the home you love, and your emotions are a jumble of anger, resentment and sadness, you tend to dismiss the larger issues and the world around you and concentrate as Ruth did on simply getting through each day. "It was pretty grim, but sitting and sulking and so on isn't going to get you anywhere, so we just took each stage as it came," said Ruth. They flew via Uganda which thrilled Ruth with its scenic beauty, and as the flying boat, which took four days to get to England, touched down each day in the early afternoon, they were able to see the Kabaka of Buganda, a university friend of Seretse's. They had dinner with King Freddie, as he was known, one evening in Kampala and it is interesting that within three years the kabaka was also to find himself exiled by the British from his country. He too was to live in England.

Ruth and Seretse availed themselves of the opportunities to go sightseeing wherever they touched down, and by the time they arrived at Southampton, on a mild, midsummer's day, they were not as exhausted as today's jetsetters often find themselves. There waiting to meet them were Ruth's mother and sister, who had made the journey down with an official from the Commonwealth Relations Office. "It was exciting to see Ruth again, but of course with all the reporters there, we had to be very British and not show too much emotion," said Muriel. Mrs Williams, after hugging her daughter, rushed over to see Jackie and bent happily over her granddaughter, exclaiming at her likeness to Seretse, before welcoming him with equal warmth. In the short time she had known her son-in-law, she had come to like and to admire him. One person missing at the quayside was Mr Williams who could still not bring himself to meet Seretse.

Jackie, at three months of age, was beginning to take a lively interest in what was going on around her, for she was a bright, intelligent child. Her proud aunts, Muriel and Naledi, carried her between them in her cot to the waiting car, which took them all to London. Naledi was of course a double boon in those early days, for besides playing the important role of the person chosen to accompany the chief into exile (a chief does not travel alone) she was, with her nursing experience, a great help to Ruth during the upsetting, troubled time. She was a big woman, with a deep voice, rich sense of humour, and a gentle, unhurried manner, and she liked both Muriel and Mrs Williams immediately. And so the family, which came from worlds apart and which would grow so close together, entered London as a unit.

As they arrived at the Grosvenor Court Hotel near Oxford Circus in the West End, a group of Londoners who were waiting outside came forward to greet them. "They came to give us encouragement; I think they were ashamed at the way we had been treated, and we thought it very kind of them," said Ruth. A reporter presented Ruth with a bouquet of flowers, and Jackie was surrounded by photographers and journalists, all wanting to record her arrival and their impressions of her. And although the press in the days that followed their arrival did not haunt and harass Ruth and Seretse in the way they had before their departure for the protectorate, Seretse nonetheless took the advice of his lawyer and appointed an agent to handle any queries from the press and to distribute press statements from the Khamas.

When the press asked if they were pleased to be back in England, Seretse replied, "No, I cannot say that", and Ruth in her fiery manner said she wanted to return to Bechuanaland as soon as possible, adding, "I don't want to live in England." She clearly did not want there to be any doubt about where her loyalties and sentiments lay.

On the day of their arrival, *The Times* of London, commenting on the efforts towards reconciliation by Seretse and Tshekedi, wrote, "The evidence given by the new agreement [...] should persuade Downing Street to receive sympathetically the proposal for a reconsideration of the case." It described the blow to the Bamangwato of having been deprived of the two men, of greatest mark among them.

That both this proved leader [Tshekedi] and the young man [Seretse], on whom the inherited loyalties of the tribe converge, should be simultaneously exiled, is a blow to the political and social order of the Bamangwato. The government has surely underestimated the force of this. They would be wise at least to study carefully the opportunity which may now have opened of healing the wound.[173]

And in South Africa, the liberal *Rand Daily Mail*, took the National Party newspaper, *Die Transvaler*, to task for its peculiarly sharp admonition to Britain – amounting almost to an order – that "it must know that there is no room or role for a native with a white wife and coloured child in the territories surrounding the Union [of South Africa]." And the *Rand Daily Mail*'s perceptive editorial continued:

> The issue, therefore, is now perfectly plain, in spite of the bungling way in which the whole matter has been handled by the British authorities from the start – and it is difficult to remember any occasion on which so important an affair has been more maladroitly managed. It is not, essentially, Seretse's marriage to a white woman. It is not the effect of that marriage on the tribe, or Seretse's inherent fitness or unfitness to lead his people. It is quite simply the question whether South Africa is to have the deciding voice in the control of major policy in the territories surrounding the Union [of South Africa] or not.[174]

The reports must have given Seretse and Ruth new heart, as they settled into their seventy pounds a week rooms (with meals) at the expense of the British Government. Seretse was hopeful that his and Tshekedi's aide-mémoire would pave the way for a return to the protectorate before the five years of exile expired, and the Khamas' spirits rose a little as they took their daughter for walks during summer days in the lovely London parks.

Shortly after their arrival, Ruth had decided that she was either going to go home with her husband and baby to see her father, or she was not going at all, and Mr Williams accepted this. "I think that he really wanted to see us all anyway," said Ruth. And so one evening, Ruth, Seretse and Jackie went to have a meal with Mr and Mrs Williams, and as so often happens in such cases, Seretse and his father-in-law liked each other immediately, for they were alike in many respects, both being big men with a rich sense of humour and both interested in politics and economics. Naturally they were wary of each other initially, but the tension was broken by having Ruth's aunt and uncle from Norfolk present, for they immediately turned it into a lively party.

"Of course, Dad was fascinated by Jackie and at the same time appalled that she was coloured. But she was such a charmer and made such a fuss of him, that I think he was secretly rather flattered that she seemed to be so fond of him," said Muriel. Comfortable Mrs Williams, fussing around her family, was thrilled to see them all getting on so well together and to see the balding, sandy-haired head of her husband's bent close to Seretse's dark one as he listened intently to the young man telling him about his country.

"My father thought the British were crazy to have treated us the way they did, it was a big mistake, and it was one that had turned Seretse into a hero. And although he liked Seretse and couldn't have liked anyone more for they had so much in common and were on the same wavelength, my father maintained right to the end of his life that he was against the marriage because he did not believe in mixed marriages," said Ruth. As she and Seretse drove back home, up the hill past the bus stop where they had hidden from Mr Williams when they were still a courting couple, they rejoiced that Seretse and her father had got on so well together.

"My family were of course quite fascinated by my accounts of life in Bechuanaland," said Ruth. There was many a Sunday lunch and an evening during which all the aunts and uncles listened avidly to her accounts of village life, of the heat and violent rainstorms, of the tribe and their customs, of the royal family of the Bamangwato, of the administration officials who lived on Nob Hill, and of the traders and their stores. Most interested of all was Muriel, whose hankering to go to Africa was as strong as ever, although it was still to be some time before she got there.

Ruth and Seretse had begun flat hunting immediately as they arrived in London. Finding somewhere to live in post-war Britain was still not easy in 1950, due to the shortage of accommodation. But now, instead of finding the door closed in their faces when they applied for a flat as had happened when they married, they were instantly recognised, and the price of the flat rocketed. "When they heard the name Seretse Khama, we were told an incorrect figure had been advertised in the newspaper. The landlords were convinced that this man [Seretse] had got a fortune," said Ruth.

This might have had something to do with the fact that the British Government allowance to Seretse of 1100 pounds annually, had been so widely reported. Finally, after weeks of searching, they found a comfortable furnished flat in Chelsea, with three bedrooms, a sitting room, dining room and big rambling kitchen. Ruth was happy to move out of the hotel for it was not easy living in one room with a child. She loved the Chelsea flat, and was most disappointed when after six months, the lease ran out, and they had to move again. "We seemed to be moving every six months, but we didn't mind really, we used to get bored. I think it was a reaction to our being exiled, that we felt we couldn't settle anywhere and we were hoping we would be allowed to go back to Serowe. And so we just moved from one rented place to another, not buying a house until much later on," said Ruth.

They moved next to a flat in Albany Street, just behind Regent's Park, and Ruth was pleased to be near the park where she could take Jackie for walks in her pram. Naledi, who worked as a nurse at Hammersmith Hospital, also used to take the baby for walks in the park on her weekends off. The big, comfortable woman would sit on a bench and rock the pram and dream of a land where the sun always shone, and no one was a stranger. "Seretse missed the sun too, but the strange thing is that he didn't mind the cold. In fact, if there was a fire burning in a room, he would always move away from it, so that he didn't get too hot," said Naledi to me in an interview. The Hammersmith Hospital staff were surprised that she spoke the good English she did, for they imagined she would only be able to talk Setswana. Naledi's sacrifice in going to England with her brother was all the greater when weighed against her dislike of the cold, wet weather, and it is an indication of her desire to fit into English society that she envied the girls their trim figures and began dieting and smoking. Her body stood the strain for three years and then she became ill with tuberculosis and had to return to the dry, warm air of her home.

Naledi was fond of Ruth's father, "He was a very charming man and liked playing jokes on people, as did Seretse, and sometimes they would get together and play jokes on the rest of us," said Naledi. And although Seretse was depressed about being in exile, he managed to hide this most of the time, and to keep up a cheerful exterior presence which hid his deep anguish at being separated from his people and his family. To this was added his concern over the growing unrest and lawlessness in the tribe.

He was a great practical joker, teasing those around him whenever the opportunity presented itself. "He had one of those rubber pens that is impossible to write with, and once my father was writing out a cheque and ran out of ink, and Seretse said, 'here, use mine.' My father tried three times to use the pen before he realised it was made of rubber, and of course he and Seretse had a good laugh about that," said Ruth. Although Seretse used props such as invisible ink, and mustard jars that figures jumped out of, he was always very subtle in his use of them, and he amazed people who didn't know him with his wit and humour.

Something that George Williams and his son-in-law did not have in common was a liking for fish. As you will recall from an earlier chapter, Ruth's father was particularly fond of it, while Seretse, who had grown up in a dry, landlocked country, noted for its meat, had no taste for it at all. "We were always eating out because my father loved good food and his favourite place was a West End restaurant which only sold fish," said Muriel. "We would start with a dozen oysters, and then go on to crab, or lobster or sole, and we, having been brought up on fish, just loved it. On one occasion during Ruth and Seretse's exile, my father took us all there, and Seretse nobly had fish, and although Ruth and I knew how he felt about it, we all managed to cover up," said Muriel.

Seretse and Ruth, not surprisingly, were usually recognised wherever they went in London, and he was often asked for his autograph, "although he was usually rather embarrassed by such attention," said Ruth. "Once when we went to see the West Indies play cricket, little boys came running up to him with their pens, and he was surprised, thinking they had mistaken him for one of the players. But no, they insisted they had not."

Ruth and Seretse were living near Regent's Park when Jackie turned one year old on 15th May 1951, and Ruth had a birthday party for her. To this she invited her many aunts and her mother, and a nephew of Michael Manley (later to become prime minister of Jamaica), as well as several other children of Jackie's age. Seretse, who wasn't all that keen on hanging around parties for the very young, stayed for the cake cutting and candle blowing and then left for a meeting he had with King Freddie of Uganda. It was in the middle of the noisy, cheerful party that Ruth heard the front door bell ring, and when her mother answered it, there on the doorstep stood the alarming uncle Tshekedi, smiling a little nervously. He was ushered into the roomful of women and children who stared at him in astonishment. Ruth, in the silence that followed, whispered to Naledi to make her uncle at home, but she stubbornly refused to do so, and indeed, such was the resentment towards Tshekedi that only one aunt offered him tea and sandwiches. "Jackie would have nothing to do with him at all. She just pushed him away with her hand, you know how children can be, it was dreadful," said Ruth. She rushed off to telephone Seretse and asked him to rescue his uncle from all her aunts. The tea party continued in spite of the tension, and when Seretse arrived, he and Tshekedi went off to discuss their affairs.

Tshekedi had gone to London to try and get his banishment order revoked. To understand all the events that led up to the resentment his presence caused and the uneasy meeting with his nephew, we must go back a little, to the time when Tshekedi shook hands with Seretse in farewell on that chilly morning the Khamas left Bechuanaland.

As Seretse flew thousands of kilometres away from his people, his uncle returned to his place of exile, a little village he had hacked out of the bush with about 450 of his followers on the fringe of the Kalahari Desert, just over the border from the Bamangwato Reserve. The contrast between the two exiles' mode of living was as great as the contrast in their characters, for while Seretse settled into a furnished Chelsea flat, Tshekedi built a village of mud huts, surrounded by a stockade of poles, on top of which were at least twenty lion skulls, remnants of the animals they had shot whilst moving in.

"Tshekedi had set up a rondavel as his study, and it was lined with his books, his rifles and his elephant guns," Dr Alfred Merriweather, the world-famous Kalahari missionary who visited him at Rametsana, and who has himself been the subject of many articles and features, including a half page in *Time* magazine, told me in an interview. Shortly after Tshekedi went to see Kgari Sechele, chief of the Bakwena (the senior tribe in the protectorate) to ask him for permission to live in his country, he visited Dr Merriweather who also lived in Molepolole, and asked him to hold monthly clinics at Rametsana.

"His wife Ella cooked the most amazing meals for us in the middle of that thick bush, and we used to see his teenage sons riding around on their horses. Tshekedi was a proud, hard man with enormous energy. But he was very good to his people and used to pay for their medical care for which we charged a minimum. But at the same time, he was hard, he flogged and punished his people, and they feared him. They also respected him, for in African life, fear and respect go together," Dr Merriweather told me in an interview.

And when they sat around the fire at night with Tshekedi, he would speak of his disappointment at Seretse's marriage to a white woman. "He was never disparaging about Ruth, but said that he was against the marriage, not because of it being mixed, but because Seretse was chief and the chieftainship must be kept pure," said Dr Merriweather. It is interesting that the Rametsana people loved Seretse and accepted him as their chief, despite their loyalty to Tshekedi.

The situation in the Bamangwato Reserve where a tribe, used to strong leadership, was drifting slowly into chaos without either Seretse or Tshekedi resulted in both men feeling extremely worried and frustrated. They felt that these circumstances, if they were allowed back, would return to normal.

In October, a couple of months after Seretse's departure, a hut belonging to one of his supporters was burnt down, and a rumour circulated that one of Tshekedi's supporters was responsible. A few days later, the official house of the chief near the kgotla, which Khama III had built and which Tshekedi had lived in until his exile, was set alight. Furniture, photographs of Khama III with Queen Victoria and other bits of family and Bamangwato tribal history and treasures, including a Bible which Queen Victoria presented to Khama III, were destroyed. Incidents such as these added to the growing tension and unhappiness, both in the tribe and in Seretse and Tshekedi.

At the beginning of November, Tshekedi became very agitated on receiving what he said were reports from England telling him that people there were campaigning for Seretse's return as chief. He assumed they were doing this with Seretse's help and approval. In this he was wrong, for although there were members of parliament who were asking for Seretse's return as chief, the latter had not instigated this. But Tshekedi with his highly-strung, volatile temperament, rushed into print with an accusation that Seretse's supporters had stood by while his nine-roomed house burnt. He then followed up that hasty action by breaking the joint agreement between him and Seretse not to publish their secret aide-mémoire. Tshekedi's biographer, Mary Benson, writes that Tshekedi had sent Seretse a letter warning him of his intention to publish the memoire and that this was delayed in the post.[175]

It was a factor beyond their control, which she says might have prevented the renewed rupture between nephew and uncle. The first that Seretse heard of Tshekedi's action was from a reporter who, after telling him about the memoire, asked for his comment. Seretse denied the reason given by Tshekedi for publication, namely that he was trying to return as chief, and said that he was surprised the aide-mémoire had been published. Ruth told me that Seretse told the press: "The statement of Tshekedi's has confused the whole issue. We shall probably have to start negotiating all over again." He must have been both saddened and angered by his uncle's precipitous action, for it closed an avenue he hoped would pave the way to the negotiations with the government for the return of them both to the Bamangwato. Baring's nefarious role in the breakdown of the relationship between uncle and nephew was clear, for Tshekedi said that his decision to publish the aide-mémoire was taken after several meetings with Baring, and naturally it was not in the latter's interest to have the two men come together again.

Before Seretse had left Africa, the arrangement between him and Tshekedi was that the latter would join him in England in talks with the Commonwealth Relations Office about their return home, and in Seretse's last communication to his uncle before the rupture, he had asked him when he was to make the journey.

In the wake of the publication of the memoire, Tshekedi had decided that he would fight his battle to return to Serowe on his own. He postponed his trip to London when he heard that Patrick Gordon Walker was to visit the protectorate as part of an official visit to British Africa, early in 1951. It could not have been a happy Christmas for Tshekedi, boiling with anger in the hot African sun in his bush village, or for Seretse, frustrated and sad amongst the tinselly celebrations in cold, wet London.

When the news of Gordon Walker's visit and of the kgotla that would be held for him to address the tribe was announced in Serowe, some of the tribe thought optimistically that he would bring Seretse back with him. But far from doing that, the secretary of state told the estimated 10 000 Bamangwato who had turned up in response to the district commissioner's summons that nothing would be done by the government for the five years of exile, and that the whole question of it would be re-examined only then.[176] Who knows what impression those sorrowing tribespeople made on the secretary, as one by one the representatives from the districts rose to their feet, approached the latest piece of technology to come their way – the megaphone – and pleaded for the return of their chief.

A new element at this meeting was the appearance of women for the first time in the kgotla, for by custom they never appeared there unless they were involved in a case. But they had been playing an increasing role in the tribe's reaction to the Seretse affair, and had begun to hold their own meetings, for they felt the men were not doing enough to get Seretse back. When women became involved in tribal affairs in this manner, it was a well-known barometer of feelings and nearly always spelt trouble, as it did later in the affair. But the warning signs of unhappiness went unnoticed for the most part, and the vast crowd which had welcomed the secretary with their customary warmth and dignity, trudged back to their huts, their lands and their cattle posts, carrying a new bitterness, anger and resolve in their hearts.

The secretary departed for Cape Town, where he was entertained at a banquet by Prime Minister D.F. Malan, who again demanded the incorporation of the high commission territories – a request that was yet again turned down by the British.

But before Gordon Walker left Mafeking for the Cape, he met Tshekedi, who made an impassioned plea to be allowed back into the reserve as a private citizen and for his knowledge and experience in the fields of administration, education and animal husbandry to be put to use by the government. The upshot of that meeting was an invitation by Gordon Walker for Tshekedi to go to London, at British Government expense, for further discussions.

The ex-regent sailed from Cape Town at a time when coloured people marched through the city in protest against a union government bill that would take their vote from them. The march was peaceful, but gained them nothing, for they were later disenfranchised.

When Tshekedi arrived in England, his friends advised him to contact Seretse, for they were able to see clearly the advantage of a joint nephew and uncle agreement to renounce their chieftainship and to work together as private citizens in the new tribal councils proposed by the British. Tshekedi, still suspicious of Seretse and feeling that he as the elder and therefore senior man should be welcomed by his nephew, hedged before agreeing to send an invitation to Ruth and Seretse for dinner. The couple accepted it, but at the last moment sent a telegram cancelling, because according to Tshekedi's biographer, Mary Benson, Seretse had a suspicion that Tshekedi and his friends were engineering something.[177]

For the second time, Tshekedi decided he would go at it alone in trying to convince the government that he should be allowed back into the Bamangwato Reserve, and he met Gordon Walker for talks on 3rd April 1951.

Ruth's feelings about Tshekedi at the time were mixed, for always at the back of her mind was the knowledge of her father's reaction to her marriage and the subsequent good relationship he had with Seretse, and so she always kept an open mind on that score. But she also believed that if Seretse had been exiled because it was feared there would be tribal dissension, then Tshekedi should share the same fate.

The suspicion and tension continued between uncle and nephew, despite attempts by Tshekedi's friends and advisers in April to persuade him that the most sensible course of action would be an agreement between him and Seretse. He was not prepared to make the first move, and so the chasm between the two remained. At this time, Tshekedi was fairly hopeful of gaining generous concessions from the secretary for visits to the Bamangwato Reserve. But on hearing of this, two administration officials from the protectorate, one of whom was the resident commissioner, flew to London to protest, for they feared that Tshekedi's return would herald serious disorders. They explained to the government that friction between the supporters of Seretse and Tshekedi was continuing, as was the policy of non-cooperation with the administration.[178]

On 11th May, the British Government presented Tshekedi with a new set of proposals which dismayed him, for all the previous generous concessions they had intimated they would make were missing from it.[179] Tshekedi would only be given permission to visit the reserve in the most exceptional circumstances. He decided that he would reject the government's terms, but during the period before he announced this at a press conference, Tshekedi caught that taxi to Jackie's birthday party to meet Seretse and met him again in Hyde Park on 25th May to tell him that he intended to fight the government by lobbying members of parliament for support. At that stage the Labour Party Government had the slender majority of six, and a few rebellious backbenchers could have toppled the government.

On 15th June, Seretse joined Tshekedi in battle by asking the government to allow him to go home for a trial period, something he had asked for when he was initially told of his banishment. He warned the government there would be trouble within the tribe if he were not allowed back. He dismissed the argument that dissension would grow with his and Tshekedi's presence in the reserve, saying that the opposite would be the result.

Events supported his contention, for in Seretse's absence unrest had indeed worsened. And he pointed out that if the government was going to work out a new form of tribal administration, consisting of councils in the place of chiefs, then the traditionalist Bamangwato would need him to inspire them and to help facilitate the changes. His plea fell on deaf ears, for the government had decided to send members of parliament as observers to the reserve to assess the situation there and to report on the attitude of the tribe to Tshekedi's return. However, the government was experiencing problems, for the opposing Conservatives and the Liberals would not agree to nominate people for the observer mission.

On 26th June, Tshekedi's request to be allowed to return to the Bamangwa-to Reserve was debated in the British House of Commons and was defeated. The following day a call for the return of Tshekedi and Seretse to the reserve was debated in the British House of Lords. British newspapers carried editorials on the subject and the British Government's treatment of the Khamas was discussed endlessly in gentlemen's clubs and around dinner tables.

Two weeks after the parliamentary debate, the disorders that Seretse had been warning of, broke out in the reserve. For those who were attuned to what was going on in the tribe they came as no surprise, for the dangerous vacuum in leadership, compounded by a revival of disputes that went back generations in certain leading families and the imposition of direct rule by the administration were all ingredients in the seething cauldron of discontent, and it needed only a little fanning of the flames to make the pot boil over. The main ingredient in the discontent was a fear that Tshekedi would return to the tribe as chief, for reports of his activities in London made their way back to the unhappy village of Serowe, and it was deduced that he, having disposed of Seretse by calling for a judicial enquiry, was now planning his own return.

The troubles started[180] when Rasebolai Kgamane, Tshekedi's friend and chief lieutenant who had followed him into exile, returned to Serowe to live in Tshekedi's house there and to look after his cattle and property. A tall, large and dignified man of few words, he happened to be in Serowe when a tribesman said in the kgotla that Tshekedi was returning to the reserve to claim the chieftainship. There was an outcry, and about fifty Seretse supporters went to Tshekedi's house and told Rasebolai and his people to leave Serowe. This they refused to do.

A couple of days later, scores of Seretse supporters attacked the house, bundled Rasebolai's people into a truck and were in the process of grabbing him too, when the police intervened, picked up Rasebolai and tracked down his abducted followers. They were put into the police camp for protection, and the next day 200 Southern Rhodesian policemen were flown in as reinforcements.

But this formidable show of force did not have the desired restraining effect, for young men gathered in angry knots around the village, rushing restlessly from one point to another, and not only shouted abuse at Tshekedi supporters but for the first time at white people too. Servants disappeared, some for only a few hours, others for days. The feeling of tension grew as road blocks were set up, and villages were raided. Riots broke out and the angry black people, armed with sticks and stones, faced armed police.[181]

The patient and generally accepting tribespeople had lost their temper, and the women who as mentioned earlier had begun to take an active part in kgotlas and in drumming up support for Seretse, now resorted to quite unprecedented behaviour by drinking in public. Khama III's strict laws, upheld by Tshekedi, had precluded any such activity for nearly seventy years.[182]

Armed with sticks, stones and hatpins, the women joined their men in the riots, and being the big, tough people they were, used to physical activity such as planting and harvesting, they were indeed a formidable sight. Three hundred screaming women, their clothes torn in their fury, stormed a police camp at Mahalapye, and shouted, "We want our chief Seretse", as they flung stones at the police. The women tried to retrieve men arrested in earlier disorders from the police, but without any success.

The riots, which were the most serious since the British had arrived in Bechuanaland, lasted for about ten days, and although no one was killed, sixty-five people were arrested. Police officers and administration officials did not get much sleep for days, and the peace that ensued was an uneasy one. The riots were all the more disturbing when you consider that the average Motswana was a quiet, law-abiding individual who did not possess the aggressive, war-like instincts of many of his Southern African counterparts, and they demonstrated clearly the depth of feeling engendered by the forced removal of Seretse.

Seretse was naturally greatly distressed, and his feeling of frustration grew when, on hearing of the riots, his offer to help the government restore law and order was summarily rejected. He publicly disclaimed any responsibility for the riots, which, he said, were the result of a growing sense of uncertainty and helplessness in the tribe. On 17th July, Seretse warned the government that his position as chief of the Bamangwato would enable him, and him alone, to solve the issues without the use of force, and he added prophetically, "events will prove that I am right."[183]

Seretse managed to hide his feelings even at this time beneath his casual exterior, but when he got home to Ruth, she who knew and loved him so well, he showed his despondency at not being able to help his people.

"He wouldn't say much, he would just stare out of the window into space. But I knew what misery he was going through and where his thoughts lay," said Ruth.

FIFTEEN

Tribe without a head

The three observers appointed by Gordon Walker to assess the feelings of the Bamangwato on the return of Tshekedi to the reserve, had a mission that was doomed before it started, for the tribe on hearing of it refused to hold a special kgotla, saying that only Chief Seretse was able to hold one. The three men arrived to find a sullen, uncooperative tribe, and their attitude seemed to affect even the observers, for they were to quarrel in public before their quest was over.

Let us look at the situation which confronted the men who have been variously described as the "Three Wise Men" and the "Three Marx Brothers", and of whom one journalist wrote, "They came, they saw, they quarrelled."[184] That the tribe was divided into Seretse and Tshekedi factions no one disputes, but what some people argued about is whether or not the faction leaders wanted the chief designate or the ex-regent to return, for in their absence they were able to enjoy a power that would otherwise have been denied them. The tribe, as we have already seen, had a long history of disputes and factions. When the Great Khama quarrelled with his eldest son Sekgoma and exiled him, the latter naturally gathered around him people who were sympathetic to him. The great chief of course had his advisers and men who occupied positions of trust and power in his administration.

Khama III died after being reconciled with Sekgoma. But the latter was chief for only a couple of years before he too died, during which his followers assumed positions of influence. Tshekedi, who followed strictly in his father's footsteps while he was regent, brought back into power the friends and advisers of Khama III, and Sekgoma's followers had again to take a back seat in tribal affairs. Some people believe that the divisions in the tribe caused by Seretse's marriage to Ruth and the subsequent rift between him and Tshekedi were seized upon by some as a marvellous opportunity for furthering their own ends. How much value can be attached to this view I do not know, but what is certain is that the love and loyalty towards Seretse was so widespread and striking that many journalists, who often seemed to be more in touch with what the tribe was feeling than were some administration officials, commented on it in their reports. And that loyalty was so powerful that the British had eventually to reassess again and again their approach to tribal affairs.

That is one aspect of the tribe; another increasingly important one was the role that the women played in its affairs, for although they had always toiled alongside their men in the fields and had built their own homes, they did not play a big part in tribal politics. The riots in June 1951 changed that, and the following month, for what was believed to be the first time in tribal history, the Serowe women called a kgotla of their own and invited the only newspaperwoman in Serowe, Margaret Lessing, to attend. They asked her to let it be known that if the British Government wanted the troubles to end, it had only to return to them their chief and their queen. Ruth's interest in the welfare of the women in the short, troubled year she had spent amongst them had been appreciated by them, and their gestures of respect in falling to their knees in front of her and kissing the hem of her dress were also genuine displays of affection.

Said Dr Chiepe in an interview: "The women were very angry. They said the men had failed in their efforts to get Seretse and Ruth back, and that they wanted to take over. The women felt the men were not expressing themselves effectively, that they were cowards and were not facing up to government." A middle-aged Afrikaans woman, who had trekked north from South Africa into the protectorate with her hunting, storekeeping brother, knew the tribe and its customs well. She was discussing the tribal disorders with a civil service wife one day who later told me she had said to her, "There is no need to worry ... yet. We only do that if the women get involved." Her words would be remembered later on.

It was the end of July when the three observers arrived in the reserve, and let's take a look at Serowe through the eyes of these Englishmen, one of whom was a former president of the Trades Union Congress, Mr H.L. Bullock; the second was Professor W.M. Macmillan, director of Colonial Studies at St Andrews University, and the third was Mr D. Lipson, a former member of parliament. They had arrived at the beginning of the dusty season when the chilly winter winds blew the powder-fine soil into their eyes, noses, even ears, and the air was so dry that when jerseys or jackets were pulled off at night, they crackled with electricity. It was the season for hunting, and strips of raw meat hung drying in the sun, both at the cattle posts and in the yards of Serowe huts, and once seasoned and dried out, became biltong. For those who first saw a village such as Serowe, the initial impressions were of little boys, naked save for a loincloth, driving cattle along the thick, twisting sand roads; of goats nibbling ceaselessly at the dried vegetation; of chickens squawking and clucking around the stockaded yards; and of course, of waves of thatched mud huts, swimming up and down the many scenic hillsides.

The three observers had between them travelled thousands of kilometres over spine-jarring roads, one of which was impassable at a certain juncture, resulting in a delay that gave rise to the story that Professor Macmillan was, "missing in Bechuanaland." Such was Gordon Walker's irritation on hearing of this that he wrote to Mrs Macmillan assuring her of her husband's safety. "He is likely to be staying for the rest of his time there in an air-conditioned rail coach. I can personally testify to the comfort of this, since I have stayed in it myself," he said in his letter.[185]

Macmillan, slightly balding, pipe-smoking, with a domed, professorial head, was often seen in khaki shorts with a sweater round his middle to guard against lumbago. Lipson, a former schoolmaster, mayor and member of parliament, was usually impeccably dressed, even in the dust and dirt, in pale, impractical colours. Bullock who was stocky and homely wore a tweed cap.

He was described by the London *Daily Telegraph* in the following terms:

> Mr Bullock repeated for the tenth time his entirely unappreciated jest
> about being the "only bullock in the reserve on two legs." Mistaking
> the dignified salutation "pula" for some kind of war cry, he persisted
> in shouting it from the platform like a cheerleader at a cup-tie, to the
> evident consternation of the tribesmen.[186]

The observers ran into trouble before they had even started their mission, for on the day they were explaining their objective to the tribe at Palapye the Bamangwato learnt that Tshekedi was to return to the reserve for their enquiry, and they accused the Englishmen of breaking faith by not telling them of Tshekedi's impending arrival. The British administration subsequently kept Tshekedi out of the reserve when it was realised how strong the feelings were. It wasn't long before the three observers realised they would not be able to hold a special kgotla but would have to accept the tribe's invitation to attend district kgotlas, held in different areas of the Bamangwato Reserve.

This was because districts had their own kgotlas whereas the chief's kgotla in Serowe was the "royal" kgotla, and only the chief – in this case, as far as the tribe was concerned, Seretse – could call it.

There was much talk of intimidation, of Tshekedi supporters not being allowed to speak at various district kgotlas, and at some meetings the kgotla would not start until his supporters had left. One such meeting was at Palapye where the three observers argued publicly amongst themselves, for when a headman complained of the presence of five Tshekedi men, Lipson suggested they be allowed to stay, to which the headman retorted, "If they stay, no kgotla." Macmillan and Bullock, taking the line that some sort of meeting was better than none, sided with the headman and angry words were exchanged between Bullock and Lipson.[187]

But the kgotlas that left the observers in no doubt about public sentiment regarding Tshekedi and Seretse were held in Serowe at the end of their trip. At the first one, when Lipson asked whether Tshekedi would be accepted in the reserve as a private citizen, 4000 booing and yelling tribesmen shouted, "No! No!" And one after the other those men rose to their feet, pulling their woollen headgear or felt hats off in gestures of respect, before disregarding the mission's objective, and pleading eloquently for the return of "The Absent One", or "The Chief." Later that day, 2000 women held their own separate kgotla which was historical in itself, and before long, the observers noted to their acute embarrassment that tears were pouring unhindered down hundreds and hundreds of cheeks. Soon the babies who had been happily playing in the dust joined in, and one woman who found it hard to hear the interpreter through the sobbing, called for silence.

Said one woman of Tshekedi, "We hate him! Our fowls, our goats, and the mice about our corn bins – all hate him!" Said another, "Even the goats cry all night since Seretse went away. Since he left, we have been a dead people." And a third, speaking for the 2000 women, said it was contrary to the tribe's custom for the chief's daughter to be brought up in a foreign country.[188]

The language that the Bamangwato use is rich and evocative and we shall hear more of it before this tale is through. But the observers probably found it too rich, accompanied as it was by such emotion, and they gave up trying to tell the women that they had not come to hear about Seretse but about Tshekedi, for in the remarkable display of mass emotion Seretse was the name that was used again and again. The observers flew out of the protectorate and back to Britain with the cry "We want Seretse" ringing in their ears, and when a couple of months later their findings were published in a White Paper, Lipson wrote a separate report that differed from Bullock and Macmillan's. But they agreed that Tshekedi could not, in the absence of Seretse, return to the Bamangwato Reserve.

Shortly after the three observers left Bechuanaland, nearly a hundred chiefs, headmen and tribal advisers met and issued a vote of no confidence in British policy in Bechuanaland. The meeting expressed extreme dismay at the dictatorial handling of the Bamangwato tribal dispute, protested that neither Seretse nor Tshekedi had been able properly to put their sides of things, and even blamed the protectorate officials for provoking the Bamangwato to acts of violence.[189]And, declared the kgotla, the Bamangwato dispute was no longer a question of the internal affairs of the Bamangwato tribe itself, but had been converted into a conflict between the entire Bechuanaland leadership and the British administration.

Colin Legum, an experienced Africa watcher and senior writer at *The Observer* in London who attended and reported on the meeting, commented that the South Africans, "contrary to their normal practice of exploiting every apparent British failure and difficulty in Africa," have significantly refrained from making any public comment throughout the controversy. "This silence is not accidental, it is strategic," he wrote.[190] He commented that leaders in the apartheid government were pleased at the recent developments in Bechuanaland, for chaos in that country would enable Malan to accuse the British of being incapable of maintaining orderly development in one of their border states.

Concern about the South African attitude was reflected in a British Government document written at the time,[191] which stated that the primary object of government policy was to avoid doing anything which would arouse such adverse reactions in the union that continued administration of the high commission territories became untenable. It pointed out that there had been abundant evidence that Seretse's return to the reserve as chief while still married to Ruth would cause such consequences.

The document written at the end of August reflects the views of Baring who, having finished his term in South Africa, went home to Britain and wrote a report which shows that his attitude towards Seretse had hardened to the extent that he would advocate his exile for life.

Baring, who was influenced by Smuts in this regard, wrote in a memorandum:

> The plain fact is then that if we are to maintain our rule over these three enclaves in South Africa, we cannot recognise an African chief with a white wife. The evidence is very strong that if we did so the Union Government would turn the economic screw. I have equally little doubt that in the end our present government would give way under economic pressure from the Union [of South Africa]. But I fully realise the bad results of a refusal to recognise. The marriage of an African chief to a white woman in a small territory dependent upon rich and powerful neighbours where the ruling people are fanatically opposed to mixed marriage is to present a choice of evils. Refusal to recognise is, I think, the lesser evil, but it is still an evil.[192]

Baring's recommendation was also influenced by the criticism with which South Africa reacted to a British Government statement envisaging the Gold Coast's independence. The decolonisation of Africa took place so fast during the 1960s that today we often forget the alarm with which many whites who lived in Africa viewed the winds of change.

In October 1951, a couple of months after the return of the three observers from Bechuanaland, the Conservatives regained office. "I remember we waited until after midnight to hear the election results, we were so excited about a possible change of government," said Ruth. "We were standing at Piccadilly with thousands of others, watching the results flash up on a board and when we heard it was the Conservatives, we were enormously thrilled and filled with anticipation. For after all it was Tory leader Churchill who had described Labour treatment of us as a 'disreputable transaction'."

The excited Khamas returned to their new home, a double-storey house in the country situated near the village of Chipstead in Surrey, and they discussed endlessly whether the Tories would put into action their fierce criticism of the Labour Party's handling of the tribe and of them. And they began to speculate on a shorter term of exile and even an immediate return home.

But as so often happens, what politicians say from an election platform, or whilst they are on opposition benches, can be vastly different when they are faced with the realities of power. We must also remember that Smuts had written to Churchill about the National Party's attitude towards the Khama marriage, and of the possible consequences in South Africa of British recognition of Seretse as chief while married to a white woman.

Tshekedi, on hearing the election results, left almost immediately for London where he met the new secretary for commonwealth relations, Lord Ismay, who had been military secretary to Churchill during the war. After discussions, Lord Ismay told Tshekedi that he would be given increasing freedom to look after his cattle in the Bamangwato Reserve and, if all went well, that he would be able to return to his home as a private citizen who would, however, be excluded from participating in politics.[193]

Lord Ismay then spoke to Seretse about renouncing the chieftainship, but the chief designate pointed out, as he had done when the government first asked him to resign in February 1950, that he could not do so without first returning to Bechuanaland to discuss it with the tribe.[194] The Conservative government was not prepared to accept this.

It was a little while earlier that Sir Roy Welensky, then leader of the Unofficial Members of Northern Rhodesia Legislative Council, and later prime minister of the Federation of Rhodesia and Nyasaland, said that he had been struck by the contrast between the treatment meted out to Seretse, and to the Duke of Windsor when he decided to marry the woman of his choice: "Edward VIII when faced with broadly similar conditions made his decision and accepted the consequences. Seretse should have been placed in the same position. People who hold high office have great privileges, but equally great obligations are placed upon them."[195]

People were fond of comparing Seretse with the duke, but whilst there are similarities, there are also many points of difference in their cases.

The observers' report[196] was published on the same day that the British Government announced that Tshekedi would, under certain circumstances such as seeing to his cattle, be allowed to return to the reserve. This made a mockery of the report, for in it Bullock and Macmillan said it was impossible to conceive of Tshekedi as a private citizen if the Serowe kgotla was the dominant factor in Bamangwato politics.

Lipson, in his separate report,[197] had admitted there was a substantial majority against Tshekedi and that most of the tribesmen would accept him back only when Seretse was chief. But clearly the Tories had been impressed by Baring's description of Tshekedi as "the flower of the tribal administration." Naturally this turn of events bewildered and angered the Bamangwato, for they had left no one in any doubt about their feelings towards Seretse and Tshekedi.

Now it seemed to them that the British, whom they had regarded as the protecting power, were behaving quite out of character in their treatment of them.

Early in 1952, Tshekedi returned to the reserve to visit his cattle posts and whilst there was no trouble, as he had predicted, there was enormous resentment that he was being allowed back while Seretse remained in exile in Britain. The year was to prove a most unhappy one for the Bamangwato and they began it filled with uncertainty, puzzlement and frustration – sentiments that to a certain extent were shared by Ruth and Seretse.

They however still believed the Conservatives would, in view of their record in opposition, adopt a different approach to them from that of the Labour Party. Towards the end of March, the government made it known there would be an announcement on the Seretse affair in parliament. British newspapers began speculating on a possible shortening of Seretse's exile.

He was approached for comment on what he would do if his exile were to end suddenly, and he said, "I would take the first plane to Bechuanaland." Ruth added, "and I would too."[198] In Serowe the tribe was told that an important announcement was to be made to them by the resident commissioner, and the traders shut their stores early to ensure as many people as possible attended the kgotla.

Seretse entered the famous Houses of Parliament on 27th March 1952, filled with nervous anticipation, while Ruth, tense and hopeful, looked after Jacqueline at home. In London spring was evident everywhere with daffodils waving in the chilly March winds, and in Serowe, although summer was drawing to a close, the sun beat down fiercely on the heads of the tribe as they made their way to the kgotla.

It was a shocked and horrified Seretse who heard the bespectacled, slightly stooped secretary of state for commonwealth relations, Lord Salisbury, pronounce a life sentence on him. He declared that Seretse would never be allowed to return to the Bamangwato as chief, and that the tribe would have to choose an alternative chief to both him and Tshekedi.

Seretse was stunned. "It was awful, just too ghastly after all we had hoped for," said Ruth who in all the years I knew her always found the emotions that recalling that day evoked were so powerful that her eyes filled with tears. Despite his shock and anger at the government's decision, Seretse did not rush out of parliament and deliver a broadside to the waiting press.

"His immediate reaction was usually that he would sleep on a thing, think about it and then say something the next day," said Ruth to me. "The only time he didn't stick to that was when they banished him initially and he called a press conference immediately."

That night Ruth needed all her strength of character to maintain her determined optimism in the face of Seretse's anguish and despair. "He used to have terrible fits of depression at times, it was extremely hard for him and I would say to him, 'don't worry, we'll get back,'" said Ruth, whose courage was as necessary in this crisis as it had been in the lonely days in Serowe.

"We were absolutely shattered and felt a sense of total despair," Ruth told me. "Our only ray of light was the number of Labour MPs who said they were determined to make their party agree that when they got back into power they would allow us to return home."

The government's decision to permanently bar Seretse from the chieftainship made front-page news in most national British papers, with *The Times* taking the government to task. It did point out, however, that the opposition Labour Party had no room to adopt a "high and mighty" attitude, for the premise of Conservative Party policy was the same as that chosen by the previous government.

In a lengthy editorial *The Times* wrote that whilst the Labour government had put off a final decision, hoping that during the five years of exile the chieftaincy could be replaced by the development of new representative councils, the Conservatives had recognised that without a chief, settled conditions and satisfactory administration were impossible.

"Unless there is some dramatic shift in the strongly traditional views of the tribe, no successor is likely to be generally accepted unless he has Seretse's blessing. No one will wish for more trouble among the Bamangwato; and the possibilities of wider trouble in Africa arising out of his affair have always been evident," went the editorial.[199] It proved in time to have been a prophetic one.

The *Daily Express* delivered a bitter attack on the Marquis of Salisbury, "…his deed is a bad, mean deed which should arouse shame and anger throughout the country. Why does he pursue a vindictive and unjust policy against a man who has done no wrong and against whose personal integrity not one word has ever been said? Why above all does he choose this moment of tension in Africa as the time to issue a statement which can only further inflame existing passion?" asked the newspaper.[200]

In a heated debate in parliament the following day, the role of South Africa in the Seretse affair was raised repeatedly with categorical denials of that country having had any influence in the matter. Mr Anthony Wedgewood Benn, then a Labour MP, who was to fight the Khamas' cause for them, said that Africa was facing a choice. It was either going the way of apartheid, which Dr Malan was trying to force on South Africa, or towards a period of cooperation.

The government was derided for an offer of a post in Jamaica that it made to Seretse at the same time the permanent exile was announced, for while some believed the intent was a kind one, others said vehemently that the government was trying to move Seretse as far away as possible from South Africa in accordance with that country's wishes. It strained the credibility of those who pointed out that Seretse had been declared unfit to be chief, and yet here he was being offered a post in which he might rise to the rank of assistant secretary.[201]

The offer was immediately rejected by Seretse who pointed out that although he would like to serve the Jamaican people, his own developing people needed him more. "I should like to serve the Jamaican people, but I cannot take bread out of any Jamaican's mouth," he said.[202] The tribe, which had given the resident commissioner a lively reception with boos and shouts when he announced the news of Seretse's permanent exile in the kgotla, had decided early in 1952 when they heard of the relaxation of Tshekedi's banishment order, to send a delegation to protest about it. And shortly before the tribe heard the devastating news of Seretse's exile for life, they were told the government would not receive the deputation, for it would serve no useful purpose. Lord Jowitt (of the Labour Party) described the government snub as the greatest blunder in the affair. When the tribe refused to take no for an answer, Lord Salisbury capitulated and said that he would see the delegation as a matter of courtesy.[203]

The six members of the delegation arrived on 9th April 1952, led by the African authority Keaboka Kgamane and although the inclement weather, the underground railway system, the sights, sounds and smells of London staggered these men of the desert, they acclimatised in a remarkably short space of time. Shortly after their arrival, they caught the train down to Chipstead in Surrey where they were given a warm welcome by Ruth and Seretse, and spent the day with them, recounting the events that had transpired in the reserve since their departure. They brought a breath of dusty Bechuanaland air with them that was as painful for homesick Ruth and Seretse as it was joyful. And they brought with them two pieces of kaross (animal skin) which they had had mounted and framed as gifts for their chief and Ruth. Jacqueline was nearly two years old and captivated them with her friendly manner and bright-eyed ways.

A couple of weeks later they were permitted to see Lord Salisbury who interviewed them in his rooms near Downing Street. They pointed out to him that the tribe considered there was nothing wrong with Seretse's marriage in terms of Bamangwato law and custom; that the Bamangwato did not appoint chiefs, for their position was hereditary; and that the British Government had shocked Africans in the Union of South Africa and throughout the continent by its latest decision on Seretse. And now the Marquis of Salisbury was also subjected to the rich imagery of the Bamangwato. Said a delegation member, "We ask for bread and you give us stones! Release our chief!" And after a second meeting with the unbending patrician, another member sadly muttered the Setswana saying, "The chief never dies."[204]

But Lord Salisbury and the government did not budge an inch, for they were determined that the chieftainship of Seretse was dead, and all that was needed to bury it was the election of another chief. As Ruth commented, "You would think the British of all people with their own royal family would understand that kings and chiefs are not chosen but inherit their positions."

It was while the delegation was still in London that Seretse made his first public speech delivered from a platform on which sat his tribesmen. It had been organised by the Seretse Khama Fighting Committee – comprised of various unions, councils and leagues that were created to fight issues of race and colour. He appealed to the British people not to let their government destroy the faith of the black people of Africa in British justice.

"Don't let your government teach us racial prejudice," he urged. "We don't have it. We don't want it."[205] And motioning to the delegation he pointed out that it was composed of simple men whose only concern was whether the people they were dealing with were sincere or not. Referring to the rioting in the reserve in his absence, he wondered if his request to be allowed to go back and stop it was refused because some people were afraid that he would succeed where others had not. The frustration and disappointment of Seretse are clear in these few words of his.

But at the end of April in yet another House of Commons debate, the government reaffirmed its decision, and a few days after the delegation had arrived back home, the government secured an Order in Council, the effect of which was to extinguish the birthright of Seretse. As the order was revocable only by the King of England, it meant there could be no petitioning on Seretse's behalf to the high court of Bechuanaland. The level of misery and anger rose both in the Khamas' Surrey household, and in the hearts of the tribe in Serowe.

When the district commissioner Mr Gordon Batho called a meeting at the kgotla at which he tried to announce the terms of Lord Salisbury's reply to the delegation and the government's future policy, he was howled down by the crowd, and when he tried to get the members to talk about their discussions with Lord Salisbury, tribesmen said they knew about them already. The tribal authority and leader of the London delegation, Keaboka, wrote to the new high commissioner, Sir John le Rougetel, after their return to Serowe, stating their refusal to accept any other kgosi than Seretse, and announcing a fresh campaign of non-cooperation.

Shortly after this, on 31st May, the kgotla was closed and all gatherings there were banned,[206] which was a fairly drastic step in view of the enormous importance attached by the Bamangwato to this meeting place. Many people regarded Batho's handling of the tribe then as insensitive, and it is possible that someone else who understood them better might have averted the subsequent disaster. Batho also announced that Khama III's old law restricting the brewing and consumption of liquor would be strictly enforced.

On the afternoon of Batho's announcement, there were a couple of attempts by the tribe to defy the ban on gatherings, but these were successfully circumvented by the police. However, the next morning (Sunday) after church, administration officials who went to the kgotla found the tribe having a prayer gathering there. The women sat peacefully singing hymns, and it was naturally rather difficult to put a stop to such praiseworthy activity. But at the end of it the district commissioner issued instructions through a loud-hailer that the kgotla had to be cleared. What he did not know was that the many women present had carried stones to church under their shawls, for there were no stones in the immediate precincts of the kgotla. He was also not aware that there was not a hatpin to be bought in Serowe for they had purchased the lot to use as weapons.

After clearing the kgotla, the officials returned home for lunch. The people of Palapye had travelled to Serowe for a weekend of sport. As they were playing both tennis and golf matches against Serowe that weekend, much of the chat was about who was up to par and on form, and no one really thought very much about what might be brewing in the village below. But the assistant district commissioner, Dennis Atkins, who loved his sport, regretfully told his wife Joan that he would have to return to the kgotla in the afternoon. "Well, you're not going in that awful old gardening jacket," she declared, and she made her jovial, good-natured husband change, an act she told me that she later regretted.

The golfers returned to their tees, the tennis players to their courts. The district commissioner, some administration officials and eighteen policemen returned to the kgotla which they found deserted, and they threw a cordon across the two entrances in the stockade to prevent anyone returning. "It clearly wasn't going to be an easy task, so Gordon Batho and a policeman went off to collect the rest of the security force and I was left holding the fort with the rest of the policemen," said Dennis Atkins.

The tribe returned, and a good percentage of their number was made up of women who, when they saw their way blocked, began reaching for their stones, and the men gripped their sticks more tightly. Atkins, noting this, climbed on to the thatched platform where small meetings were held, and through an interpreter said, "Come on, this is a lot of nonsense, getting unruly isn't going to do you any good."

Said Atkins to me in an interview, "It was amazing really because it was still quite quiet. I suppose things always start in a spontaneous sort of way, these chaps hadn't really got their hearts in it because as they started breaking through this cordon of police, we said, 'Emang. Stop.' And they did. There was a wave of people coming into the kgotla which suddenly stopped, and then they must have thought, 'to hell with it', and they started throwing stones."

The two kgotla entrances and exits were just over one metre wide, and when the police realised how serious the situation was becoming, they made for these exits, and under a devastating hail of chunky stones they escaped to the kgotla hill and made their way up it and over to safety on the other side. But some of the policemen who had been drafted in from the other two high commission territories of Basutoland and Swaziland and who had not yet got their bearings, broke round the edge of the kgotla and ended up in the village where they were chased by the crowd, now totally out of control, whose shouts of anger rose and died on the wind.

Particularly vicious attacks were made on those who became separated from the main force. Three black policemen were stoned to death that Sunday afternoon. One of them rushed panting into a hut and dived under a bed for refuge where he was found and killed. Another was clubbed, left for dead on the ground and picked up by a rescue party. And the third ran for a mile, twisting through the huts and courtyards before the shrieking crowd got him and clubbed him to death.

Meanwhile back in the kgotla, the numbers were clearly so against the police and the two administration officers – 800 to about eighteen – that the police retreated to the two exits but found their way blocked by the mob. "I stood outside one of the exits, I couldn't do anything inside the kgotla, and I thought I'd tell these chaps to stop their damn nonsense as it wasn't helping anyone, and then another wave of rioters came through, and they chucked stones at me," Atkins told me.

As the security forces withdrew up the hill, leaving the tribe in possession of the kgotla, a few stones were hurled after them in a desultory fashion and then they were left alone.

The traders heard the ugly sounds that a rioting mob makes from their homes dotted throughout the village, and they were not all that surprised by it. Speaking the language as they did, and sitting in their shops day after day, they were aware of the intense unhappiness and frustration of the tribe. Nonetheless they were horrified to see groups of men and women, armed with sticks and stones, pursuing fleeing policemen wildly through their carefully cultivated gardens.

One of the Serowe traders, Chum Blackbeard, who was respected by tribe and administration alike, was asked to fetch a doctor who lived on the opposite side of the village from the hospital. As he neared the kgotla which he had to pass to reach the doctor's house, he was stopped by the rioters but got out of his car and said very firmly, "Look, I am not playing with you people, I am going to go and get the doctor," and he was allowed through, his brother Dennis told me in an interview.

Dennis, hearing the shouting coming from the kgotla, decided to investigate, and grabbing his binoculars, climbed the kgotla hill from which vantage point he observed the entire proceedings of that sad afternoon. By early evening, although the rioting had stopped, a siege mentality had gripped the village, and it was divided into two camps. The tribe was in possession of the kgotla and the village, and the British evacuated the security camp situated over the hill from the kgotla and withdrew their forces to the district commissioner's office on Nob Hill.[207]

Details of the riots were sent in morse code to administration headquarters in Mafeking, but a telegraphist in Johannesburg somehow picked up the message too, and early the next morning, after driving all through the night, pressmen appeared in the troubled village, much to the annoyance of the administration officials.[208]

Urgent messages calling for police reinforcements were dispatched by the officials on the afternoon of the riot. The first of these arrived from Gaberones as darkness fell and were assigned to guard duties outside the district commissioner's office.

The traders were of course even more vulnerable, dispersed as they were by Khama's edict throughout the village, but although many of them were anxious, some even frightened, they felt they knew and understood the tribe and would therefore be safe.

It was a tense and miserable night in Serowe. Everyone, including the Bamangwato, was shocked by the violence. When Batho, his black eyes dramatic in his pale face, asked the postmaster why he couldn't get through on the direct line to the security camp in nearby Palapye, Burgess discovered the lines had been cut, and early the next morning said he was prepared to try and mend them, but it was decided that it would be safer to wait for reinforcements. The latter arrived within a couple of days by air and road from Basutoland and Southern Rhodesia and set about restoring order with a vigour that alarmed some people who said they were being too tough. "I thought all the tearing around and show of self-importance was a bit farcical. After all, most of us had just survived a horrible war," Monica Burgess told me.

After the Serowe riot, there were sporadic outbreaks of violence in other villages, which were soon quelled by the police, who rushed about the reserve with pistols, steel helmets, mesh-wired lorries, tear gas and batons. They were told to stop all beer-brewing and drinking in the Bamangwato Reserve as a punitive measure. "We would walk into villages and kick over beer gourds and stills. It was very tense, and the raids were an excuse really for house to house searches. I was bending down to go into a hut one day when I was hit on the back of my head with a knobkerrie," said one policeman, who did not wish to be named. He felt embarrassed by the order to stop beer drinking, and felt it aggravated the situation.

A sub-inspector in the police force, Graham Russell, recalled one riot when the women charged them with long hatpins. "They held them in both hands and made a jabbing motion at our faces. We were worried there would be people lying behind us as we retreated who would trip us up and we would lose face," he told me.

"The latter was not allowed, for although we might get fall-down drunk, the police did not trip." Russell bore for life the scars of the stoning he endured in one riot when he was knocked unconscious.

In a debate on the riots held in the House of Commons a few days later, the undersecretary of state for commonwealth relations, the Oxford University educated John Foster, said that the rioting was the result of a deliberate attempt by a small fraction of the Bamangwato tribe to flout the authority of the government: "Only a minority of the tribe took part in the disturbances – a maximum of 800 out of a total population in the reserve of 100 000."[209] Mr Foster also said that a considerable proportion of the rioters were under the influence of drink, and that women took a very active part in the demonstrations. Almost all the officers and police who were involved in the Serowe kgotla riot were injured, twelve of them seriously. One hundred and thirty people were arrested, amongst them the former tribal authority Keaboka Kgamane, and Peto Sekgoma, Seretse's uncle who was looking after his cattle. Mr Foster said the police had acted with commendable restraint and there would be no enquiry into the riots. Opposition members of parliament felt the administration had acted high-handedly by closing the kgotla and attacked the government for denying free speech. They also emphasised that while Ruth and Seretse were living in the reserve there had been no disorders. As in previous debates, their teeth were drawn by the original action of the Labour government in exiling the Khamas.

As Serowe began to return to normal, the traders removed the shutters from their shop windows and opened their stores, the administration wives came down from their hill, and friendly, although cautious greetings were once again exchanged between blacks and whites. It was a time for assessment, and as the traders and officials met up at the post office, waiting for the mail that arrived three times a week, they recalled what they had been told earlier about the role played by black women in times of trouble.

But there was another side to the picture, for some people ascribed the growing tension and friction between the tribe and administration to the enlarged police force, which was made up of men from different tribes. The Bamangwato had a history of tribal warfare with the Matabele from Southern Rhodesia, and the Great Khama had led several expeditions against raiding forces from the north. Old wars die hard, and an ancient black woman with no teeth or hair, who was allowed to fetch water from the postmaster, Joe Burgess's house, was so frightened of the Matabele police who were guarding the nearby district commissioner's office, that she crawled on her hands and knees up the side of the Burgesses' fence, dragging her bucket behind her in order to avoid detection.

Most of the administration officials who had worked with the Bamangwato were shocked and surprised by the rioting, for there is no doubt at all that it was totally uncharacteristic. But the removal of Seretse and Ruth, the allowing back of Tshekedi after the three observers had been told in no uncertain terms of the resentment towards him, the imposition of direct rule, the extinguishing of Seretse's birthright, and then the order that they should choose a new chief were all factors which led to the riots.

Dr Chiepe who was in Serowe at the time, stressed how shocked the tribe itself was by the killings. "They would never set out to kill anybody. They were very sorry that people had died, but they blamed it all on the government. They brought in police who behaved very differently from our own and the people didn't like it. They were rough. If you were going somewhere the police thought you should not be, and if they were near enough to hit, they would hit you," Dr Chiepe told me.

Goareng Mosinyi, Seretse's cousin, who said he was number five on what he called the administration's "trouble list", escaped the riots and almost certain arrest because he was in Johannesburg posting letters to Seretse, giving him information about what was happening in the reserve. He told me that, "Our post was opened, and so I used to travel all over the place, to the Union, to Southern Rhodesia, to mail letters in which we included the latest information on tribal events for Seretse."

The riots were yet another blow for that beleaguered man and his wife, and the enormous frustration he experienced as he heard of the dreadful occurrences in his once peaceful village was indescribable.

But Seretse was not alone in his unhappiness. There were rumblings from some administration officials in Serowe who were so disturbed by the insensitive treatment of Ruth and Seretse, by the way the tribe was being treated, and the relaxation of Tshekedi's banning order, that they wrote a letter of protest to the secretary for commonwealth relations. This had to go through the resident commissioner who tried to persuade them to withdraw it, saying it could adversely affect their careers, but the three persisted, which, in view of the anger of the British Government then towards the tribe, was a brave action on their part. The three men were consequently split up and posted to different villages.

One of them, my father district commissioner, Peter Cardross Grant, said later: "In spite of what happened to us, I am sure that if a number of such letters had been written by district commissioners to the Commonwealth Relations Office they could conceivably been somewhat more enlightened."

In the absence of a chief and in the wake of the riots, the tribe that had been so disciplined until Seretse's exile became increasingly disordered and unruly. They began to keep the administration officials awake, especially on moonlit nights when they would sing and dance, blow whistles and horns and use tea chests as drums. The listless tribe no longer took pride in keeping their village clean and neat and the general breakdown in tribal law and custom saddened many of the older people. They recalled that the last time the Bamangwato had known such bad times was before Khama III began his rule in 1875.

SIXTEEN

Six years of waiting

Ruth and Seretse spent six years in exile in Britain, from August 1950 to September 1956. These were six frustrating and often sad years, and yet in retrospect, they had their bright side. For one, Seretse's health, which had been such a source of worry to his uncle when he was a child was, according to Ruth, probably the best he ever enjoyed in his life, for in later years it was to become not only her concern, but also that of their nation.

Seretse, unlike his sister Naledi, didn't mind the inclement English weather, and in fact preferred the cold to heat. He would go through an English winter seldom wearing gloves or a top coat, and rarely wearing a jersey, and in later years when he returned home he would look forward to the winter during which Ruth, who after all had been born and bred on that chilly, drizzly island, always suffered. "In England we were always having a battle over the heater. I would turn up the central heating, and then when he came in he would immediately turn it down. People used to think that we did this deliberately, as some sort of gimmick, which was nonsense of course," said Ruth.

It is interesting that in later years Seretse told senior British administration officials with whom he worked that his time in exile had been valuable to the extent that he had been able to observe the British political system at first hand. If he had not spent the many hours he did sitting in the visitors' gallery in the Houses of Parliament, listening to debates on whether or not he should be allowed to return to the Bechuanaland Protectorate, he might not have seen the Westminster form of parliament in action before his country adopted it at Independence in 1966.

These small advantages cannot, however, be weighed against what seemed to both him and Ruth to be interminable years of waiting that were characterised by a sense of futility and emptiness. They were restless years in which they waged a ceaseless battle to be allowed to return home, and during which they felt they were suspended from daily living and existed in a state of limbo. By 1952 they were living in the Surrey countryside, and it is not hard to imagine Seretse waking early as is the custom in Africa, and on hearing blue tits, starlings and cuckoos, wondering when he would hear again the wild cackling of guinea fowl in the dry bush. The magnificent roar of lion had been replaced by the growl of traffic, and instead of brilliant, star-studded night skies, he had to be content with neon city lights. The violent, tree-bending electric storms that flash and crackle across vast plains in Africa were replaced by a steady drizzle from unexciting leaden skies.

The years in exile were naturally not as hard on Ruth as they were on Seretse, for whom the call of Africa was like a fever. Ruth after all had only spent one year away from England in her entire life, and she had all her family living nearby plus her schoolfriends and relations. But this is not to say that she too did not wish ceaselessly that there would be a change of heart and that they would be allowed to return to the village she had grown to love in her short time there. Ruth's support, encouragement and understanding helped Seretse enormously during those lonely years away from his people.

They had been living in London for nearly one and a half years when Seretse suggested they move to the country to be closer to nature. They rented a furnished house (for their only furniture was a refrigerator) in Chipstead, Surrey. The double storey house was situated in a country lane, about one and a half kilometres from the nearest railway station, and was so quaint and attractive that people used to call it the doll's house. The large garden had pear, apple and apricot trees, and the Khamas might have bought it if it hadn't been so small, with only two bedrooms. "It was glorious there for most of the year, but winter was a bit too bleak," said Ruth. "Once we spent three days trapped in the house by snow. We couldn't get our car out, and the tradesmen couldn't deliver because the snow was so thick." There was one little village store, and what Ruth couldn't buy there she went further afield for, and in such a small community they soon made friends. When the Khamas first returned to London, rationing was still in force, and coming from a big meat-eating country, this was naturally a little hard for Seretse who liked good food. "But Seretse had many friends who were sorry for him being exiled, and they had ways of showing it," laughed Ruth. He often used to go into the kitchen to find out what she was cooking, and at times even pottered around there himself. He loved curry, as mentioned earlier, and since Ruth loathed it, he found someone to teach him how to make it. Occasionally they would go to London for dinner, to their favourite restaurant in Shaftesbury Avenue, and friends were always making the one-hour trip down to them by train, so they led a lively social existence.

Ruth and Seretse were often recognised on outings to theatres and restaurants and were sometimes even cheered by the audience and fellow diners. "There were a few boos too, but people were mainly sympathetic, and Seretse was always being asked for his autograph. Sometimes people who disapproved of us would turn around and try to attract our attention to show us they didn't like us. The obvious thing here of course is not to allow your eye to be caught," said Ruth. "You act as if nothing is going on, as if they don't exist. But such behaviour was the exception."

One can imagine the feelings of Ruth and Seretse when a couple of months after the riots in which the three policemen were killed they heard that Tshekedi's banishment order had been revoked and that he was free to return to the Bamangwato Reserve as a private citizen, provided he played no part in tribal politics. Tshekedi did not however move back into Serowe, but built yet another village, this time at Pilikwe in the Tswapong district, about sixty-seven kilometres to the east of Serowe. There, in a slightly wooded area, his followers again erected their thatched mud huts and he built a brick bungalow, in front of which he planted a rose garden and behind it fruit trees. The British Government again suggested to Seretse that he renounce all claims to the chieftainship, but as the Order in Council had already extinguished his birthright, he could not see what would be gained from such action and refused.

At the beginning of November 1952, a petition signed by 6000 people urging the return to the Bamangwato of their "accepted Chief Seretse Khama", arrived at the Commonwealth Relations Office. The petition, delivered by a deputation from the Seretse Khama Campaign Committee, accompanied a request for an interview with the secretary for commonwealth relations, Lord Salisbury. He declined the interview, and a few days later the undersecretary Mr Foster announced in the House of Commons that the British Government would not review its decision to ban Seretse.[210] It was at this time that the British administration called several kgotlas in Serowe in order to get the tribe to choose another chief, for it was obvious from the continuing disorders and non-cooperation that direct rule was not working. But on the eve of one such kgotla in November 1952, 1000 tribesmen declared they would have no leader except the deposed Seretse.

"We can only have a chief who is born a chief," said their spokesman. "The government changed its mind and let Tshekedi come back. We will wait until it permits Seretse to return."[211] The kgotla was unique in Bamangwato history, for never before had the tribe been asked to choose a chief. The next-in-line had always been designated, and the administration, anticipating trouble, had established radio communication between the security camp and the kgotla, and the police were issued with Sten guns, tear gas and armoured cars. The two-day kgotla proved a futile one for the administration, for the tribe refused to designate anyone else for the chieftainship. When the district commissioner, Gordon Batho, refused to accept Seretse's nomination, he was booed, an action that would have been unthinkable before the disorders in the reserve. Seretse supporters protested that, as long as Seretse lived, his successor could rule "only with spears".

Pleaded a prominent Serowe tribesman, Owabone, "Kill me and let Seretse come back. Better we live like wild animals than under another chief while Seretse still lives."[212]

Rasebolai Kgamane, Seretse's cousin, who was a great friend of Tshekedi's and had followed him into exile, was next in line for the Bamangwato chieftainship, but in view of the strong opposition to any chief but Seretse, and possibly stung by charges that it was trying to force a chief on the tribe, the administration did not persist in its efforts to force a new chief on the tribe for the time being.

But it reintroduced the thorny subject in May of the following year, and it is somewhat ironic that in the interim a child whose life would be affected by the kgotla deliberations was born to Ruth and Seretse. Ian Khama was born on 27th February 1953, in an auspicious year for the British, for two days after Edmund Hillary and Sherpa Tensing conquered Mount Everest, the young Queen Elizabeth II was crowned in Westminster Abbey. It was also the year that food rationing ended in Britain, and the world's first jet airliner, the Comet, flashed through English skies.

When Ruth's labour pains started in the middle of the night, Seretse drove her through the cold, wet dark to the nursing home in York, about ten kilometres from their Chipstead home. There, at 5.30 a.m. on 27 February 1953, Ian made his appearance to the great joy of his proud parents, and who can guess at the thoughts of Seretse as he held in his arms the handsome little baby who, in spite of British action, would one day be chief. Seretse was not present at the confinement for he was extremely nervous when all his children were being born. Ruth didn't have any profound thoughts about the chieftainship as she looked at her sleeping baby, "I just thought, thank God it is all over." She found her pregnancies uncomfortable, and the anaemia from which she always suffered worsened during and after them.

Naledi, Seretse's sister who had been such a help to Ruth when Jacqueline was tiny, was ill in hospital when Ian was born on her birthday. But despite Naledi's absence, Ruth was not exactly the stereotyped harassed British housewife and mother, for she had an English nanny for her son as well as a maid to clean the house and a gardener. Ian was christened Seretse Khama Ian Khama. "Seretse wanted him named after himself, and so we had to have the two names; Seretse and Khama, and then we had to have something to put between the two Khamas, so we called him Ian," said Ruth. The little chap was eight weeks old when the Council for the Defence of Seretse Khama held a press conference at the House of Commons, and among those who attended it was Canon Paul Collins of St Paul's Cathedral, and Labour MP Fenner Brockway. A message was sent from it to the heads of the Bamangwato in which it stressed its strong determination to continue efforts to secure the return of Seretse to Bechuanaland.[213]

Within three months of Ian's birth, the Bamangwato were again asked by the administration to choose an alternative chief to Seretse and Tshekedi, and to short circuit the proceedings of the November kgotla, the district commissioner reiterated at the end of April that neither Seretse nor any of his children would be eligible for the chieftainship, by order of the Queen of England. The government was faced with a dilemma for it wanted to end direct rule, but that necessitated a chief and it had promised not to impose one.

For the second time in six months the tribe refused to select a chief to replace Seretse, and for four days 3000 tribesmen sat in the dusty Serowe kgotla under the huge mokala trees, listening to one speaker after another express his views in the rambling, unhurried manner that often exasperated British officials. Gordon Batho gave up the attempt to get the tribe to designate a chief on the fourth day when he realised he was getting nowhere, and he interrupted the kgotla by saying: "You have failed to appoint a chief. You may now all go and reap your crops."[214] His words were greeted with prolonged applause and the kgotla dispersed. But their jubilation turned to ashes one week later, for on 13 May 1953 the British Government announced that Seretse's cousin Rasebolai Kgamane was the new native authority, instead of the district commissioner.

There was immediate criticism of the appointment, both in the protectorate and in Britain, because Rasebolai was Tshekedi's friend and had worked closely with him during the ex-regent's administration. And although the big, measured man of few words was highly respected for his leadership amongst the high commission territories' troops in difficult conditions in the Middle East during World War II, it was feared that his allegiance to Tshekedi and the latter's proximity to Serowe would enable the ex-regent to influence tribal affairs.[215] Some people even suspected that Tshekedi would work his way back into the chief's chair, with the help of the administration. Apart from all this, however, the arbitrary action of the British government was criticised as another example of its insensitivity in dealing with the tribe.

During Seretse and Ruth's years in exile, several committees were formed to fight for their return to Bechuanaland. Among them was the Council for the Defence of Seretse Khama, chairman of which was Fenner Brockway, and its treasurer was Anthony Wedgewood Benn. Muriel Williams kept the books. Another was the Seretse Khama Fighting Committee, and several organisations provided a platform at intervals for either Seretse himself or for his supporters. Naturally the Conservative government was not pleased about the continued campaigning and lobbying that went on, and on at least one occasion it called for a report on the activities at some of the meetings. The disdain of one official, who attended a meeting called by the Committee for Racial Unity is clear from the following: "The meeting was attended by 184 people, eighty percent of whom were female. The feminine portion of the audience was divided into roughly fifty percent tense bobby-soxers, and fifty percent elderly suburban matrons, half of whom wore coloured scarves as head coverings and the others a bewildering and staggering array of Lady Baldwin specials."[216]

The meeting thus described was in marked contrast to a meeting held in May 1952 in the Birmingham town hall which was attended by 2000 people, and where Seretse spoke so movingly, said Ruth, that people were reduced to tears. Chairman of that meeting was Mr D. Lipson, one of the three observers sent to the Bamangwato. In his speech Seretse said, "I have been here two years now and I have been a very good boy. But where has that got me? If it is true, as it has been said, that I am not fit to rule, that I am irresponsible, how can I hope to serve ably and properly the Jamaican people? If I am fit to be the assistant governor of Jamaica, I think I am more fit to be the ruler of my own people."[217]

His suspicion of the role played by South Africa in his exile is clear from his questioning whether the British Government was prepared to sacrifice the friendship of sixty million Africans for the doubtful friendship of Union Prime Minister Dr Malan. His not infrequent public attacks on the government were clearly not appreciated, for one senior Commonwealth Relations Office official said with reference to Seretse's talks, "He comes dangerously near breach of the conditions attaching to his allowance." But he added pragmatically that he thought it best to give him a "lot of rope and think of intervening only if he offends outrageously." And yet another official, who had studied reports of the meetings and speeches, noted that Seretse was "obviously being very careful."[218]

And so, for the main part they left him alone, although Ruth says that he was warned at one stage that his allowance would be withdrawn if he continued to attack the government, and he apparently took a fairly defiant stance on this, saying that all he was doing was talking about the British treatment of him, and about British colonialism in Africa.

Seretse, it seems, was never bitter, but understandably in some of his speeches he almost sounded it, for when he spoke at an "Africa Must Be Free" conference, organised by the Congress of People Against Imperialism in London, which was attended by 100 delegates from political parties and trade unions, he said, "It is not only the Russians who send exiles to a Siberia. There are many Africans in Britain who cannot go home. The Africans do not hate white people, but we certainly detest the policy of administration in our part of the world."[219]

And he continued, "It is being said that next to the donkey, the African is the most patient animal in the world. But perhaps our patience is not so elastic as that." The previous year, the world had been shocked by reports of the Mau Mau rebellion in Kenya, and during discussion at the meeting on the subject, Seretse said that he hoped the Mau Mau would not spread to other parts of Africa, for he said the continent was being destroyed by both black and white people.

Seretse was a marvellous orator, a gift that stood him in good stead later in his life, but which was appreciated even at that early stage in England. He could speak without notes, in fact he was usually better without them, and was clever at assessing his audience and tailoring his speech to their specific interests. And although he was witty and amusing, he could when the occasion called for it be extremely sarcastic, especially when he was quoting some of the statements made by the British Government.

Seretse also did some lecturing for Foyles Book Club. "He was supposed to lecture on 'The Life and Customs of My People'," said Ruth with a laugh, "but it was mostly on his own situation." He toured the whole country, including Scotland and Wales, giving talks. Ruth accompanied him when she was able to leave the children with someone trustworthy, and occasionally she too gave talks, although hers were not political and concentrated on life in Bechuanaland. "When you are brought up in a place like England, where you flick a switch and the light always goes on; where you turn the tap and there is always water; and where you open the front door and there is a bottle of milk always there, you do not realise how easy life is. People were interested to learn that in other countries you do all this yourself, you have an engine to generate electricity (if you can afford it); you put down a borehole to get water and you make milk from dried milk powder."

Ruth also joined a group fighting for women's rights called the Six Point Club where she not only learnt a great deal about rights, but also about committee procedure, which was to stand her in good stead when she returned to Bechuanaland and became involved in organising committees and meetings.

But if this makes her appear an extremely confident, almost militant sort of personality at that stage, it would be wrong, for then she was quite shy, almost diffident in public, although she did have strong views and could be outspoken amongst family and friends.

It was round about the time that the Bamangwato were told Rasebolai Kgamane was to be the tribal authority that Ruth and Seretse finally bought a home, in Addiscombe, one of the best suburbs of Croydon, to the south of London.

Situated on a large corner stand in Maple Dale Avenue, it was a big, double storey, five-bedroomed house with lounge, study and dining room. Ruth had daily help and a gardener to keep it in the neat and tidy manner to which she was accustomed. Addiscombe did not have the village atmosphere of Chipstead, it was a commuter suburb, the sort of place where doctors and stockbrokers lived. But the large garden had a fishpond, an abundance of fruit trees, and in the summer they grew their own vegetables. The station was less than a kilometre away, and after having breakfast with Ruth, Seretse would often get the train up to London to the Inns of Court for he was still busy with his law studies although he did not have the same heart for it as he had when he first met Ruth. She no longer had a nanny, as they were expensive and hard to come by, and so she had a busy day, feeding, cooking and shopping, and as

Jackie got older, taking her first to nursery school and then to school at Addiscombe College.

The children, whose early years were spent in exile, were naturally unaware they were any different from the other families living around them, and they led the mischievous, fun-filled existence of many of their contemporaries, loved by their doting grandparents and adored by aunts and uncles. Ian was particularly fond of his granddad, and enjoyed playing pranks on him, such as tying his shoelaces together and then pulling him to his feet with a command to run. "Of course my poor father played along, but sometimes he nearly fell on his face," chuckled Ruth. Ian was an extrovert, and Jackie was an extremely independent little girl who didn't easily give her affections to anyone. "But she was terribly close to her father, like his shadow. Nobody could do anything better than her father could." For example, Mr Williams could carve meat beautifully, an occupation Seretse loathed, and Jackie would say, "You know, Grandpa, my father is the best carver, he can carve better than anybody else," Ruth told me, adding, "And she would know it was completely untrue."

Naturally when Ian was born, Jackie experienced the jealousy with which a firstborn regards an intruder, and her aunt Muriel was sensible enough when Jackie showed resentment of the fuss another aunt was making of Ian, and demanded to be a baby again, to play along by putting her in a pram and pushing her up and down the garden next to Ian.

He was an extremely lively child, for one day he resented being put to sleep in his cot while everyone else was having fun in the garden below, and he rocked the cot over to the window and climbed out on to the sill. Seretse looked up at that moment and rushed into the house and grabbed him. On another occasion he climbed out of his cot and somehow managed to cover the heater with his bedroom curtains. Ruth said it was sixth sense that made her go into the room just as the curtains started smoking, and she and Seretse quickly pulled them down and bundled them into a bath of water. He was three years old when he decided he should direct the traffic in the street below and a neighbour, spotting the little figure walking down the road, collared him and took him home. Ruth made her family laugh when she said that it was her first indication that Ian, who was a brigadier in the Botswana Defence Force before he became the country's president, was interested in the forces.

The children were, not surprisingly, very English and spoke it beautifully as did their parents. But they could not speak any Setswana, and whether this was due to permanent exile obviating the need for it, or because Ruth did not speak it is not clear. Dr Chiepe who was in England at university towards the end of the Khamas' exile, recalled Jackie asking to be taught "African". Naledi said that one day when Ruth was out and she and Seretse were sitting chatting in the lounge, he suddenly exclaimed, "But why are we talking English?" It had become his first language.

In the early days of their exile, Ruth liked to take Seretse to the beautiful Channel Islands, which she loved, for their holidays. "Neither of us was particularly keen on swimming and just liked to sit on the beach, but there you could find a cove and have it all to yourself which was lovely. Once we met up with some local farmers who had Jersey cows, and when they discovered Seretse was also a farmer we became good friends and one of them even wanted to give Seretse a cow! We often went to the South Coast, and if Seretse saw a herd of cattle, he would stop and gaze at them. He was besotted with cattle and farms."

Seretse would soon get chatty with the local farmer, and learnt a great deal about different breeds, knowledge he took with him when he returned to Bechuanaland and introduced some of the breeds into his own herds. They loved driving about the countryside, Ruth poring over maps giving directions while Seretse drove. As the children got older, the couple took them to the beach. Their movements were not restricted, but it was made clear to them that if they wanted to travel outside Britain, they should inform the Commonwealth Relations Office of their intentions.

The struggle to return Seretse and Ruth to Bechuanaland continued, and intensified as the Labour Party began to adopt a much tougher line on the exile issue. In March 1954 Fenner Brockway presented a petition in the House of Commons signed by 10 839 people in which they asked the government to allow Seretse to return to his tribe and to be recognised as chief.[220] In September that year a sad little story appeared in some London papers.[221] It was about an appeal made by the Bamangwato tribe to the Queen of England, and it went, "O Great White Queen, we are desperate. The Bamangwato are unhappy, and over our land there is a great shadow that is blotting out the sun. Please put an end to our troubles. Send our real chief – the man born our chief – back to us." It was four years after Seretse had been exiled and still the tribe did not have a chief, and still they talked only of Seretse.

The month before this appeal was made, Dr Malan, whose requests for the incorporation of the three British protectorates of Bechuanaland, Lesotho and Swaziland had continued unabated during the exile, asked his country to give him a landslide win in the provincial elections in order to support his plans for new "South Africa for the whites" legislation in parliament. Nobody could possibly mistake the course the South African nation was taking as long as the National Party was in power. Towards the end of 1954 Seretse's banishment became a major issue in Labour Party circles, for at the party's annual conference in September of that year, a Labour member of parliament, Mr James Griffiths, a former colonial secretary, gave an assurance that Seretse's exile was being reviewed by Labour leaders.[222] And in May the following year, the Labour Party sent its commonwealth officer, Mr John Hatch, to the Bamangwato Reserve on a fact-finding mission which would enable him to recommend to the party whether or not Seretse should return. Hatch also visited South Africa and said while he was there that he believed every black person in the high commission territories was opposed to transfer of the three protectorates. Not surprisingly, the National Party newspaper, *Die Transvaler*, described Mr Hatch as an unwelcome guest.[223] Hatch recommended to his party that Seretse, Tshekedi, Rasebolai and Keaboka should have a round table conference in London to discuss the issues involved in Seretse's return.[224]

In August 1955, five years after the Labour government had imposed its original five-year ban on Seretse, it sent a deputation to the secretary for commonwealth relations, Lord Home, to put the Hatch suggestion to him. It was rejected by the government, although it is clear from Lord Home's autobiography that he was in favour of ending the exile, for in it he writes, "I felt that exile on 1000 pounds a year in Brighton, which was the fate to which the Socialist Government had condemned him, was for Seretse Khama worse than death, and that the colour complex in reverse was nonsense. I therefore returned him to his country soon after I came to the Commonwealth Relations Office."[225]

However, it was more than a year after the Labour Party's deputation to Lord Home that Seretse's exile ended. Tshekedi, who was becoming increasingly restive about not being allowed to play any role in tribal affairs, realised when the Bamangwato refused to discuss a mining agreement unless Seretse and himself were present, that he had leverage. For the first time the Bamangwato Reserve had something to offer – minerals – that the government wanted, which might persuade the government to review their exile of Seretse and Tshekedi's exclusion from any tribal work.

When James Griffith demanded again on August 1st in the House of Commons that a conference of tribal leaders including Seretse and Tshekedi should be held in London, he added that a new factor – that of mineral resources – should be seriously considered.

The South African based Anglo-American company was showing an interest in the potential riches beneath the soil in the Bamangwato territory. But the tribe, whilst in favour of mining development in principle, insisted that no collective decision could be made until both Seretse and Tshekedi could participate in negotiations.[226]

In July 1956, Tshekedi, who was taking his two eldest sons to school in Ireland, decided to combine the trip with a visit to Seretse and to propose that they once again sign a joint statement in which they both renounced the chieftainship for themselves and for their children.

When the missionary Dr Merriweather heard that Tshekedi was planning to send his children to school overseas, he asked him whether he did not think that they too might come back home with white wives. Tshekedi's reply was that having happened once, it was unlikely to happen again, and he set off happily for London with his wife Ella, Dr Merriweather told me. When Tshekedi first saw Lord Home, the latter was noncommittal about his proposal, and Ruth said he came home in an agitated state, planning all sorts of meetings that Seretse refused to have anything to do with, for he was so determined to go back home that he didn't want anything to go wrong this time.

A determined Tshekedi, however, contacted Seretse at his Addiscombe home on August 5th and persuaded him that it was time to act. The two men were intensely wary of premature publicity which had destroyed their previous agreement in August 1950.[227]

They told nobody of their plans with the exception of Clement Davies, the Liberal Party leader in the British Parliament. For it had provided the most consistent support of both of them.[228]

Seretse and Tshekedi saw Lord Home with a signed joint statement on August 15th. In it they renounced their chieftainship both for themselves and for their children. They declared there was no longer any dispute between them and that they both wanted to live freely in Serowe in the Bamangwato Reserve with their families. They would both do everything they could to help develop a tribal council but would not dispute the right of Rasebolai Kgamane to be the "African authority".[229]

Lord Home believed Seretse should return to his people, and after cabinet meetings and various discussions the proposal was accepted. The government asked the two men to keep the news quiet for a couple of weeks, which Ruth pointed out was very difficult: "Seretse was having a series of dental appointments with someone who was a close friend of ours, and so he had to just keep on booking ahead, knowing that he wouldn't be there, it was very funny. And then somebody leaked it, I have no idea who it was, and the press got hold of it, and Seretse telephoned the government and told them it was nothing whatsoever to do with him, because he could always keep a secret, and he was nervous the government might change its mind again."

Tshekedi and his wife Ella, and their sons Leapeetswe and Sekgoma, went to stay with Ruth and Seretse to symbolise their reconciliation.[230]

"They spent two weeks with us at Addiscombe; it was the first time I had met Ella and I found her friendly and easy to get on with," said Ruth. At the end of September the government announced its decision to allow the two men to return to the reserve as private citizens in view of their formal renunciation of the chieftainship for themselves and their children. The government agreed that both Seretse and Tshekedi should be allowed to play a part in the affairs of the Bamangwato, and it announced the formation of an advisory tribal council of which Rasebolai Kgamane would be chairman, with Seretse and Tshekedi giving him their full support. And the formal announcement ended with the following words, "It is the earnest hope of Her Majesty's government that this settlement will enable the Bamangwato to forget their differences and to unite in working for the progress and wellbeing of the tribe and the whole of Bechuanaland."[231]

When Seretse first went home with the news, he and Ruth were so excited that they had a little celebration dinner all on their own. "We were bubbling with happiness; it really was jolly hard to keep quiet. I told my parents a day before the news broke in the papers and of course they had mixed feelings, for while they were thrilled for our sake, naturally they were going to miss us a great deal." The day the government made its announcement, Ruth and Seretse were interviewed by radio, newspapers and television. She came across to television viewers as a woman of poise and assurance and she made no bones about her feelings.

"I shall not miss much when I leave, except my relatives," she said. And she chatted happily to reporters of the work she hoped to do amongst the Bamangwato, and of how she planned to learn the language. Photographs taken at the time showed the lively Ian sliding down the bannisters of their home and Jackie with a schoolfriend.

As Ruth went on her shopping rounds from butcher, to grocer and so on, everyone who had got to know her, shared the joy of their return to Africa. Seretse left England within a few days of the announcement, for he wasn't taking any chances on a change of heart. "He was about to be called to the Bar, and I suggested that he wait, for after all those years of hard work and exams, it seemed sad to give it up. But he was so nervous they would change their minds, he said no, he was going. I could see his point, but I still think it was a pity. He should really have been a barrister," Ruth told me.

In the three weeks that elapsed before she and the children joined him in Serowe, she had a busy time, selling their house, their Vauxhall car, taking Jackie out of school and Ian out of nursery school, saying goodbye to all her friends and relatives. The government must have been happy to have one less problem on its hands, for the Suez Crisis was more than enough to keep them busy.

As Ruth said goodbye once more to her family and prepared to board the plane that would take her and the family out of exile and back to Africa, she had no idea it would be the last time she would see her father, for he was to die the following year. And so ended yet another era in her life.

SEVENTEEN

Your people will be my people

Seretse flew home to a hero's welcome. Days before his arrival on 10th October 1956, the Bamangwato made their way north to Francistown where his plane landed. They travelled by train, they hired trucks, and loads of singing people laughed and cheered as they tore along the bumpy, sandy tracks. Some rode on horseback, others on donkeys, and a privileged few had cars. When Seretse appeared at the door of the chartered plane that had brought him from Salisbury, a great shout went up from the tribespeople assembled to meet him. Shrill ululating filled the air and the women danced, their bare feet pounding the dust, their arms moving rhythmically above their heads.

At the gates of the airfield where most of the crowd was hemmed behind a fence, thousands of men, women and children had worked themselves into a frenzy of joy by the time Seretse reached them, and they gave him the kind of welcome that Roman generals, returning with the spoils of conquest, had received. But Seretse was no conquering hero. On the contrary, he was a worried man, for he did not want any wild jubilation or unruly behaviour to jeopardise his return. Joe Burgess, the postmaster, told me in an interview that one journalist, amazed at the screaming people, filed a report saying that the administration had to issue extra arms to police to control the people. What he had actually seen was a column of prisoners returning with their armed jail guards, who were handing in their weapons. Another journalist, Margaret Lessing, on seeing the tribe flinging themselves over Seretse's car and dancing in front of it as it made its way slowly to the district commissioner's office, said to an official, "This makes you realise what a mistake it was to exile him, doesn't it?"

Mr Philip Steenkamp, a district officer at Francistown, who was later to become the only white man in Africa to be permanent secretary to a head of state, said to me in an interview, "We had a near riot. He came down to the office, and there were thousands of people lining the route. Some people thought Seretse's return might cause problems, but he could not have been more cooperative or helpful, although later on I think he became somewhat impatient with some of the more stupid colonial restrictions."

The next day Seretse made a triumphant drive along the 120-kilometre road between Francistown and Serowe. All along the way, men and women from remote Bamangwato villages had gathered in clusters to see him, and every so often the car would stop so that Seretse could speak to them. As they neared Serowe, and the distinctive twin hills of Swaneng came into view, the crowds along the road grew thicker, until the car slowed down to a crawl, and all the way into the heart of Serowe those villagers screamed their welcome. But honouring his pledge to behave like a private citizen, Seretse made no attempt to encourage the acclamation and, preceded by seven lorry loads of elder tribesmen, he drove solemn-faced through the lines of waving tribesmen. "We went first to the Khama church to pray, and then to report to the district commissioner," said Seretse's cousin, Goareng Mosinyi to me. "Only then did we go to the kgotla where the people were packed together so tightly, you could not move an inch."

As Seretse entered the historic kgotla, a crash of thunder heralded his entrance, and moments later precious, life-giving rain drenched faces and hands raised to the sky. It was a most auspicious omen, and one the tribal prophets had predicted. "Pula! Pula! Pula!" they roared, and tears of happiness mingled with the rain on glistening faces.

During the following week, while the local gossips wondered where Ruth and Seretse would live and which school Jackie and Ian would attend, for as they pointed out there were only white and black schools, not one for coloured people, Seretse was mobbed by crying, singing and ululating crowds wherever he went. Many of those simple, devoted people simply wanted to be near the man for whom they had waited so long, and hands reached out to touch him. It was a difficult week, for the people simply could not understand how the man who was their chief, could say he was renouncing his birthright, and many said defiantly that no matter what he said, he would still be the chief. Seretse, worried by the situation, asked for a postponement of a kgotla where he would renounce his chieftainship. He called together the tribal leaders and after briefing them, sent them back to explain to the troubled, bewildered tribesmen. "Seretse is our chief. They will never dare exile him again," they repeated. Seven thousand people packed the kgotla a week after Seretse's arrival and listened in stunned disbelief as he told them that neither he nor his children would ever be their chief.

Taking off the dark glasses he was seldom without, Seretse stood calm and assured before his people as he said, "You must all know now of my promise to the government overseas. Chieftainship, with its rule by one man, has come to an end. Under the new tribal council, you can all take part in the affairs of the tribe. This has brought about a new situation and we must all study it."[232] His firm, quiet approach set the tone for the rest of the momentous kgotla, for the people, who had known no other rule but that of autocratic chiefs for centuries, were being asked to change the foundation of their society, and all who were there knew that things would never be the same again. The district commissioner, Mr James Allison, a cheerful, warm-hearted man, told me in an interview that he informed the kgotla, "You have seen a big man make a big decision, and do a big thing. He has done it for your benefit and he will expect some cooperation."

These historic events on the edge of the Kalahari Desert did not escape the attention of the South African Government, for it had received with alarm the news of Seretse's return, the abolition of the chieftainship and the introduction of a democratic form of tribal government. All this, coupled with the growing reports of mineral wealth that could be exploited with the return of Seretse and Tshekedi, resulted in articles speculating on the possibility of an independent black state on the Union of South Africa's borders. The mouthpiece of the apartheid government, *Die Transvaler,* pointed out that the new tribal administration was very different from that applied by the Union Government in South African native areas. "The prime minister has already stated that differing policies in the protectorates and the Union [of South Africa] can create an unfortunate situation, bearing in mind the future incorporation of the territory."[233] The government still had every intention of gaining control of the three protectorates, even at that late stage.

Before Ruth had returned to Serowe three weeks after Seretse, the first elections for the new tribal council had taken place, and already the kgotla had witnessed the first meetings where the wishes of the people were signified by a show of hands and not the summing up by the chief of what he thought their wishes were.

Ruth had tried to prepare her children for Africa by telling them a little bit about the village which would be their home in future, but Jackie and Ian, who had known only the lush greenery, snow, fast underground trains and the busy streets of England, were bewildered by the time they reached Nairobi. There, when Ian saw Arabs in their flowing robes, he asked his mother in loud astonishment what people were doing walking about in nightdresses, and when amused glances were directed at the bright-eyed, curly-headed, three-year-old, an embarrassed Ruth did her best to answer him. Head ringing with the warnings of his Addiscombe playmates about the lions in Africa, he grabbed Jackie's arm when he saw cats and yelled, "Do you see those lions there, do you see them?"

After a night in a Salisbury hotel suite, Ruth flew off with the children in a privately chartered plane to Serowe and arrived two and a half hours before she was expected. Ruth spent some time chatting to the newsmen and photographers before Seretse raced up in a cloud of dust and greeted his elegant wife who was wearing a green floral, glazed cotton ensemble with a black, sequin-trimmed hat and black accessories. She was introduced to the elder tribesmen lined up on the airstrip, and hugged Seretse's elder sister Oratile. Apart from the district commissioner, Mr James Allison, there were no other white people there to welcome her, and despite her brave words that this did not matter to her, it must have made Ruth's spirits sink a little.

But the tribeswomen soon made up for their chilly white counterparts, for news had spread fast through the village of Ruth's arrival, and as the family began to drive back into Serowe, hundreds of women streamed out to greet her. The roadway was soon lined with cheering people who followed the cars to the house that Seretse had prepared for her, right in the middle of the village, not far from the kgotla. This time there would be no isolated existence on the fringe of the village, for Ruth was part of the tribe.

Soon several hundred people had gathered outside the freshly painted European-style bungalow, and they shouted repeatedly for Ruth and the children to show themselves, which they smilingly did, until Seretse asked for some peace. Ruth took stock of her new home; an extremely old house that had belonged to Seretse's father, and noted with pleasure the well-carpeted lounge, the apple-green colour scheme in the main bedroom and the sunshine yellow for the children's room. She was looking with displeasure at the huge old coal stove, the type most protectorate wives struggled with, when a perspiring Tshekedi arrived, embarrassed at his lateness, to greet Ruth.

Wherever she went in the village during the next few days, happy and curious crowds followed her. Jackie and Ian stared open-mouthed at the almost naked children of their age and asked their mother repeatedly why they were not wearing clothes. They were puzzled by their inability to understand what these potential playmates were saying, and Ruth was bombarded with questions.

"Ian was terribly funny. He didn't want any milk that came from a cow, he wanted it from a bottle on the doorstep. And, pointing to a piece of coal, he asked, 'What's that dirty old stone you've got there?'" said Ruth. Jackie was fairly quiet in comparison. "Well, you can imagine, poor child, this was completely different from anything she had ever known," said Ruth.

There were myriad of new experiences for the children. For a start there was the tremendous contrast between the cold weather they had left in England and the great heat of a November summer's day. Then there were the many hands that did the washing, cleaning and ironing instead of machines. Water gurgled in rusty old pipes with airlocks. "Why isn't there tar on the roads and why does water come from a borehole at the back of the garden? Why isn't there any television?" asked the two youngsters. And they were fascinated by the pressure lamps, which every protectorate mother positioned high out of reach of inquisitive hands that could pull down the burning light. At night beetles, spiders and mosquitoes invaded their bedrooms, and they went to sleep to the singing of the villagers all around them.

For the first few days after her arrival, Ruth was the subject of intense gossip amongst the hundred or so whites in Serowe. Should she be accepted now or not? Although most of the administration officials who had been in Serowe in 1950 had moved on, as they normally did with new postings every few years, racial attitudes had not changed much during the six-year period of exile, and the prevailing sentiment was still that Ruth had "let the side down" by marrying a black person. Someone who took no notice of this whatsoever was the district commissioner's wife, Jessie Rutherford, who met Ruth, liked her immediately, and organised a tea party of welcome, to which she invited the doctor's and the policeman's wives. "I found Ruth a little shy at first, but of course when she had been out before things had been very difficult," Jessie told me in an interview. She also let it be known that anyone who snubbed Ruth would not be welcome in her gracious home again. Since that meant they would probably not be able to play tennis on the district commissioner's court and have tea under the cool Jacaranda trees, attitudes began to change.

At that first tea party on Nob Hill Jessie broke the ice with a story. She told in her soft Scots accent of the day she and a girlfriend got lost amongst the dense bush and palms, outside the little river village of Maun on the fringe of the now famous Okavango Delta. "We always went fishing on a Sunday, but on this particular day I heard guinea fowl, and we gave chase, not noticing the direction we took." Within a couple of hours the two women were hopelessly lost, and by evening, in spite of firing three bullets in succession from their .22 rifle at intervals to signify their position to search parties, they were still crashing around in the bush. Jessie decided not to tell her friend about the lions shot in the vicinity a week before, but managed to stop her singing, which she thought might attract the wrong kind of attention. They were found as night fell by a little black child who worked for Jessie and who had guessed they might follow the river. "When we got back to camp, there was dead silence. We were in disgrace all right," Jessie concluded.

The following week, Ruth wrote a note to Jessie asking her to tea at her house in the village, and so a close friendship was born. "We didn't have telephones, so we used to send notes with the servants," said Jessie. The latter was with Ruth one day when some tribal royalty visited her. "They were very shy, and although most of them couldn't speak English, their respect for her was obvious. The women went down on their knees to greet Ruth and she took their hands and smiled but exclaimed later how difficult she found it to accept this behaviour," said Jessie, who wisely counselled Ruth to accept the traditional greetings.

Ruth was in a somewhat invidious position, for she moved between two worlds that had very little in common and between which there was hardly any communication except at the level of mistress and servant. Sometimes when she accepted an invitation to tea, the servant carrying it in would drop to her knees in front of Ruth, a situation which some of the white women found awkward to handle. But if Ruth found life difficult and trying in those first few years back in Africa, she gave little outward indication of it, nearly always maintaining the dignity and composure which people were beginning to expect from her and for which they doubtless secretly admired her. The village gossips had much to thank the Khamas for, as their presence provided topics for conversation that might otherwise have been dull.

The house the Khamas began building shortly after their arrival, was one such topic. As the shell took shape, all sorts of people would wander to the end of Nob Hill to gaze at it, for Ruth and Seretse chose to situate their house right in the heart of white snobdom, at the end of the hill on which the administration officials lived, and in what is probably the most scenically beautiful spot in Serowe. The view from the house over the surrounding hills and plains was magnificent. Seretse's regiment carved a road through the bush to it, a very different occupation from their rioting during the years of exile.

The four-bedroomed house, with its tiled bathroom and shower, its modern kitchen, laundry, and terrace, and its water-borne sewage made it a dream home. For Ruth it had special significance, for now her many house moves would come to an end, she believed, and it seemed to her to be the first real home she had had since her marriage.

One problem Ruth experienced shortly after moving into her new home was establishing a garden out of the mostly solid rock on which the house had been built. In this she was helped enormously by keen gardener Jessie, who helped her build stone flowerbeds which they filled with soil. Soon walls with flowers peeping gaily out of them added charm to the spectacular if somewhat rugged view.

Less than a year after their return to Serowe, both Ruth and Seretse were involved in community projects, the largest of these being the raising of funds for a community centre, for there was nothing of the sort in the village. "It was Lenyletse (Seretse's cousin, who later became Botswana's vice-president) who suggested we build a centre, and we soon thought of ways to raise money for it. It took a long time, seven years, before it was completed, but it was worth it," said Ruth. Called the Lady Khama Centre, it boasted a clinic, vegetable garden, a large hall, a nursery school and a tennis court.

It was most unusual at that time for white women to be involved in community or welfare work, and Ruth was regarded with a mixture of curiosity and interest by the other white women. In 1957 she started one of the first women's clubs in Bechuanaland, and talks were given on hygiene, on primary health care, on nutrition and on agriculture too, for the women played such a large role in it. "Sometimes we just got together to exchange ideas, and to pass on newly acquired skills, and any money we made would go towards the community project," said Ruth. Her work at a time when self-help, now such a popular concept, was hardly heard of in Bechuanaland, is all the more praiseworthy in view of the fact that there was no onus on her whatsoever to do it, and was mainly self-motivated, although Seretse always supported her fully. Ruth was instrumental in getting a good library going during those first few years, and in the early 1960s she helped start a Red Cross Society in Serowe. By that time white women were becoming involved, and with the help of a district commissioner's wife, who was a nurse, Ruth gave first aid classes, relying on her pre-war experiences in London.

"We concentrated as much as possible on preventative measures. There were lots of accidents in the home, where small children would fall on open fires in the winter and, in addition to teaching the women how to clean and bandage a wound, we talked about preventing such accidents," said Ruth. At the cattle posts, children with festering eyes, caused by flies constantly settling on them, were a great problem, and Ruth helped teach people how to keep the flies away, to bathe the infected eyes and to keep them clean. Wounds resulting from accidents when chopping wood often turned septic. And snake bites were another major hazard. "Of course some of the old-fashioned remedies they used with herbs and roots were better than ours and sometimes we used their methods," said Ruth.

She was also involved with the Girl Guide movement, and later with the Anglican church. Some people might gasp at such a range of interests and involvement, but one of Ruth's characteristics was an inability to sit still. She would drive herself harder than anyone. Lena Mogwe, wife of Botswana's minister of foreign affairs, Archie Mogwe, played a major role in the country's largest women's organisation, the Botswana Council of Women, and she sang Ruth's praises to me: "Before we formed the present umbrella organisation, we had many clubs operating on their own in lots of little villages, and I was most impressed with the way in which Ruth so soon became one of us." Ruth would bounce through the dense bush, over dreadful roads in badly sprung trucks, to get to some of the villages.

"The women appreciated it, they would feel honoured that she ate their food (meat, mealie meal, pumpkin and melon) and they adored her. They would sing and dance, and talk to her through an interpreter," said Lena. The contrast between Ruth and these women was enormous, for she was slim, incredibly fair skinned, and inclined to be both tense and intense. She was witty, at times caustic, even sharp. She was direct, and always came straight to the point. The average Mongwato was a large, heavily-built woman, who adopted a casual approach to life, laughed a lot and had a gentle sense of humour.

It wasn't long before Ruth learnt fully about the work done by women on the lands, and she gave many talks throughout the years all over the world at women's meetings about the female role in agriculture in her country. She was fascinated by the rhythm of the seasons and the way in which it dictated the life of the villagers. When the rains came, the people went to the kgotla where the order was given to go to the lands. For the next few days the village hummed with activity as creaking wagons were loaded with beds, pots and pans, food, salt, blankets and clothing, and little herd boys rushed about cracking whips, whilst oxen lowed and grumbled as they were forced between the wagon shafts. This furious activity usually took place in October, and once the exodus was complete, the village took on a distinctly deserted air, for only old women and young girls were left behind, the former to look after the latter who were attending school. But there was constant movement between the lands, the cattle posts and the village.

"It is a hard life for the women," Ruth told her audiences. "They are growing the food they are going to live on for the next year, and if the rains don't come, or the cattle contract foot-and-mouth disease, it could mean starvation."

Life even for whites in Serowe was a source of interest to the average Westerner. The trading stores did not stock the sort of groceries favoured by the English, and so every three months orders would be posted to the highly reputable South African store of Thrupps in Johannesburg that would parcel and rail them to Bechuanaland. The women made the clothes needed by their families, or sent for some of them, as Ruth did, by mail order to South Africa.

Every so often Mr Riley from Mafeking would pack clothes from his store into huge trunks and travel the vast territory, displaying his wares in church halls or big homes. Many of the women cut their own hair, as Ruth did, and also that of their families, and in all this activity, there was much of the pioneer about their existence. People waited until they went on holiday to have medical check-ups and intricate operations, unless it was an emergency.

Ruth and Seretse became the proud parents of twin sons about twenty months after they returned to Serowe. Ruth had suspected she might be having twins, but this was confirmed by X-ray only three weeks before the birth, and the women of the tribe began frantically knitting bootees and matinee jackets to make up for lost time. Ruth's mother, who was paying her first visit to the family in Bechuanaland, was a great help with her comforting, motherly ways. But when the time came for Ruth to go to the hospital on the hill, she left her mother ill in bed with tick bite fever. The twins were born within ten minutes of each other around 2.30 a.m. on a wintry June morning in 1958. It was a difficult delivery, for the twins were big at six and a half pounds each, and Ruth lost a lot of blood. As she suffered from anaemia, this was extremely debilitating. While she lay in the picturesque hospital, trying to regain her strength, Seretse took to his bed with a bout of pancreatitis. Ruth found out later on that Seretse had been dreadfully worried the twins might be Siamese, and she attributed his illness partly to worry. Ruth, feeling weak, dragged herself home to look after Jackie, Ian and the newborn twins, and to nurse her mother and husband. Not surprisingly, shortly afterwards, she haemorrhaged twice, and Seretse insisted she go back to hospital.

"But I was a real martyr and stuck it out," said Ruth. She was also coping with an insistent press who, having been refused photographs at the hospital, now wanted to take them at home. People commented at the time of the birth how good it would be for the tribe to see its leader's wife with twins, for the practice of killing one twin was still prevalent in the remote rural areas.

Some of the women who worked in clinics would see mothers go off to the lands with twins and come back after the harvesting with only one child, something which distressed them enormously although they were always told there had been an accident or an illness.

"We decided that Seretse would name one twin and I the other," said Ruth. She chose the names Anthony Paul Toipsepinge (the latter was an old Khama family name) and Seretse chose Tshekedi Stanford, the first name in honour of his uncle. All the children's names are therefore a good mixture of English and African names and reflect the diverse cultures from which they stem.

There was great celebration in the village when the tribe heard the news of the birth, for it meant two more possible chiefs to them in spite of the fact that Seretse had renounced his birthright. "Ian is the paramount chief, but the brothers are also called nkosi (chief)," said Ruth.

The christening of the twins highlighted the conflicting attitudes of Ruth and Seretse towards the church. Seretse had grown up in "Khama's Church", as the London Missionary Society, which had converted Khama III to Christianity, came to be known. But he did not go to church that often, unlike Ruth who was a regular attendant at the quaint little Anglican Church. The tribe wanted the twins christened in its church, but the Anglicans said it should be in theirs because of Ruth. Dr Chiepe, who was in Serowe for the christening, recalled in an interview with me that the ministers from both churches "were fighting for the children. But the L.M.S. did not have a leg to stand on, for Seretse had not taken Ruth to his church, and yet they claimed him. Seretse got fed up and suggested a compromise. The actual baptism would be done by the Anglican minister in the London Missionary Society church."

The great day came, the church was filled, the congregation prayed and sang, the Anglicans did the baptism and then they walked out. "We were furious, but we decided, not in the House of God, and so we got on with the service," recalled Dr Chiepe.

There was however another drama behind the scenes. Ruth's friend Jessie, who was a Presbyterian, had agreed to be godmother, but was told by the minister she had to change her religion, something Jessie refused to do.

The twins were about two months old and Ruth was enjoying a quiet coffee with her mother one morning, when a messenger came tearing up the hill to the house with the news that Seretse had collapsed with pneumonia at one of his cattle posts, about two hours' drive away from Serowe. An anxious Ruth leapt into her car and, driving at neck break speeds along the sandy roads, got to the post in about half the normal driving time. Seretse was delirious by then, and she had a fearful drive back, wondering if he was going to survive what seemed to be a really serious attack. Seretse had already been under strict medical treatment for a serious kidney complaint, and from this time on, although he enjoyed periods of good health, his life was to become a series of illnesses.

It was while Ruth's mother was in Serowe that Seretse asked Mrs Williams to make her home with them. George Williams had died the previous Christmas (1957) of a heart attack. This had left Dorothy bereft of any immediate family, for Muriel had gone to work for the World Council of Churches in Geneva, although she was at home for Christmas when her father died. "My father's death wasn't sudden, for three heart attacks in December 1955 had left him not much more than a vegetable. We always knew there would be another stroke and it came on 26th December, and he was buried on New Year's Day," said Muriel.

"We had a terrible time trying to get the news through to Ruth. We sent a telegram and she had to drive to Palapye to telephone us, and she suggested then that my mother might like to go to Botswana for the birth of her one baby, as she thought it was at that stage. When it turned out to be twins, my mother stayed on, and when Seretse asked her to live with them, she accepted because I think she was lonely after all those years of looking after my father," said Muriel.

The comfy little Englishwoman, who had lived in London all her life, sold her home and adapted extraordinarily quickly to a strange new life in a remote African village. "I can remember Ruth saying as a child that when she grew up she wanted to live in the same road as my mother," remarked Muriel.

Dorothy Williams was a quiet soul who helped Ruth enormously but never interfered in her domestic life. "I have often thought that Ruth was lucky that Seretse's parents were dead because they can often upset mixed marriages," said Muriel. "They come and stay with you for months on end as is their custom, and they don't approve of what you do, and then they resent the relationship the black husband has with the white wife. I have seen this in Zambian marriages."

Ruth had a fairly hard time as it was adapting to Bamangwato custom, without the constant censure of difficult in-laws. Seretse being a somewhat detribalised chief, and one who had not paid much attention to what he considered outdated customs, had not taught them to Ruth, and a little while after their return to Serowe the uncles began complaining to Seretse about her behaviour. The hierarchal system was closely adhered to, and at meal times senior uncles and wives were served before those lower down the pecking order, and men were served before women. Anyone could go and see the chief, and they would line up outside the house, but if a senior person arrived he would be allowed to go in first.

Ruth transgressed when she invited some women from the sewing club to tea at home, "and Seretse's uncle was horrified because they were not high up in the hierarchy and yet not only did they drink from the chief's cups but they sat in his chair," said Ruth.

"What is Ruth doing?" Seretse was asked. Seretse, with his progressive ideas about ending tribalism and sectarianism, told the uncle that he thought Ruth had acted perfectly correct. "I am not going to stop her from doing this," he said to everyone's astonishment. "I think it is time we ended this nonsense about only certain people drinking from my cups, sitting in my chair and drinking from my glass."

There were of course many customs that Seretse thought were sensible and to which he either adhered or did not try to change. Ruth learnt quickly from observation how not to offend and practised some of the tribal customs. One that fascinated her was the dividing up of a dead animal. "In Africa, everybody gets something. The old and the young, because they have no teeth, are given the tender meat. An intestine is a delicacy set aside for the men. The head of the animal goes to the senior person present," said Ruth.

On one trip to a cattle post, Seretse, who teased Ruth whenever he saw an opportunity, said that she was not eating the same food as he was because women did not eat it. It was only for the men. "But I will get you some," he said and returned with a bowl. Ruth was tucking in happily, when Seretse asked if she was enjoying it. "Yes, it is very nice," she replied. "Good. Would you like to know what it is? That is intestine." Ruth gulped and put down the plate. "But I thought you said you wanted this food?" chuckled Seretse.

A tradition Ruth did not follow was that of going to work on the lands as the other women did, tending and harvesting the crops while the men were at the cattle posts. But she helped her husband with his farming and cattle in an equally vital manner, for she decided to use her knowledge of bookkeeping and accountancy by keeping books and records for him, something that had not been done before she arrived. This was no mean task, for Seretse was a big cattle farmer whose herds grew bigger annually due to his progressive farming methods, and he also cultivated vegetables on quite an extensive scale.

Farming was of course right outside London born and bred Ruth's experience, and initially she found the challenge almost overwhelming. "You wonder if you are going to be able to accept it, make it your life. But you make up your mind that you are going to do it," said Ruth in an extremely honest appraisal of that early difficult period of adjustment. She certainly had a great deal to adjust to, what with the tribal customs and traditions, and the initially chilly welcome from the very people with whom she had most in common.

But as time went by and people got to know Ruth and to appreciate her good qualities, she built up a circle of good friends, although it was not until the 1960s that racist attitudes and behaviour began to change. An example of the pettiness which the Khamas had to contend with was the ruling that black people were not allowed to drink liquor, not even in their own homes. "So I had to buy the liquor, because I am white, and yet of course Seretse paid for it," said Ruth. It was a law that Seretse soon rebelled against, although initially he and Ruth played along by having "orange juice" at parties, for most people thought it archaic that someone who had lived in Britain for ten years should be subject to such strictures. But although Seretse, and all the chiefs for that matter, had always been accepted in white homes, very few other black people were, and although segregation was not enshrined in law as it was in South Africa, the unwritten laws which dictated there should be no mixing between the races were clearly understood by all except for the missionaries.

Jackie and Ian encountered racism soon after they began attending the little school for whites run by the wife of one of the traders, Mrs Gwen Blackbeard. A forthright character with a warm sense of humour, she ran an excellent school although she taught children ranging in age from six to twelve simultaneously. She would give one handwork, while another did arithmetic, and another history and so on, and attendance varied between twenty and forty pupils.

Jackie, and later Ian, were the only children at the school who were not white, and it wasn't long before Jackie began asking why she had a black daddy and why her hair wasn't the same as her mother's. She had, until then, not been conscious of such differences. Ian arrived home from school one day complaining that he had been called a native. Next time, coached by Ruth, he had an answer ready: "So are you. But I am a native of England and you are a native of Africa." This sort of behaviour didn't surprise Ruth at all. "It is the way you deal with it that counts. I would just tell the children these people were ignorant, they didn't know any better."

Jackie and Ian had another problem when they first arrived in Serowe, for they could not speak Setswana and, as it was not spoken at home by their parents, they had to rely on playmates. And most of these lived in the village below the hill on which the Khama house was situated, a distance that was too great for little legs to traverse. Apart from the children of the servants, there were no other black children on the hill. Said one administration official's wife, "Jackie thought like a white child, she wanted to be white, she never played with black children. Ian and the twins played with anyone, they weren't bothered." Another officer's wife believed Ruth made a mistake "in bringing her children up as Europeans." Whatever the viewpoint, and it is always easy to judge with hindsight, Ruth was clearly in an awkward situation, for although there was obviously no colour bar in her life, from a cultural viewpoint she was English and wanted her children to have that sort of background as well as the African one.

This is one of the problems faced by those who have mixed marriages, and the confusion of cultural identity is bound to be assimilated to a greater or lesser extent by the children. In Jackie's case it was a greater extent, for although Ian suffered considerably from racist attitudes, the three boys seem to have bridged the two worlds better than Jackie did.

The twins were particularly winsome and were a popular sight as, tied to their nannies backs, they were carried from home to home on Nob Hill.

By all accounts, the four children were all high spirited, but the twins were particularly so. From an early age, they were totally absorbed in each other, not needing outside company. They spoke mainly Setswana, and there were times Ruth would have to ask them to speak English, so she could understand them. They led a free, fairly wild existence, playing for hours in a dry river-bed behind their house, and dragging their nannies through the veld on their jaunts. Tony was knocked out twice. Once he fell off his bicycle while racing down the slope from their house and the gardener carried his limp form home to a shocked Ruth. The second time he was hit on the head by a block Tshekedi had aimed in fun at his nanny's posterior.

They did not have to leave home at a fairly young age to go to boarding school like Jackie and Ian, and of course when they did they went together to multiracial schools and won hearts immediately with their mischievous behaviour and identical looks.

Jackie left home at the age of ten to attend the exclusive girls' school of Arundel in Salisbury, Southern Rhodesia. Apart from some Chinese girls, she was the only one who was not white, and as she got older and began to play in team sports, some schools refused to play against her. She started school there in 1960, five years before Ian Smith announced his Unilateral Declaration of Independence. Rhodesians were as racist, sometimes even more so, than the Afrikaners of South Africa. The Khamas were in a dilemma, for they did not want to send her to England where they would only be able to bring her home once a year, and yet they were keenly aware of her unhappiness. It was a tough situation for the little girl to cope with, and she was also subjected to conflicting social status, for at home in Serowe her father was the chief and a successful farmer. At school he was merely a black man, and the object of silly schoolgirl derision.

In the same year that Jackie went to Arundel, Seretse spent three months in Charing Cross Hospital in London, and after exhaustive tests and treatment, it was established that he had pancreatitis and diabetes. Ruth went with him to London and for three months went daily to the hospital. She had left the children in the care of her mother in Serowe. "He was sick, in hospital, you can't be divided in those circumstances." The twins had their second birthday party in their parents' absence. Jackie, Ian and Mrs Williams wrote regularly to London, keeping Ruth and Seretse in touch with home and school activities.

"It was a terribly worrying time. They didn't know what was wrong with Seretse, but he was such an incredibly patient person, he never became irritable, or depressed, or lost his temper," said Ruth. Once diabetes had been established, she had to learn how to give insulin injections, and how to prepare the food that Seretse's diet permitted him to eat.

For the rest of his life, she ensured that he did not eat anything that could irritate the pancreas. This meant fat-free cooking, no onions and garlic. "At that time, diabetics had to weigh the carbohydrates they ate to ensure it was the correct amount, and so I used to do that every day. What I had learnt about dietetics at college in London, came in useful then," said Ruth.

Seretse, who enjoyed the good things of life, was naturally irked by the strict diet he had been put on, particularly as his favourite dish, curry, was another forbidden item, and there were times when he cheated. The result was that Ruth fussed over him, to a sometimes extraordinary degree. As you can see, by this time, she had many demands being made on her with four children, an often-sick husband, a large house to run, a fair amount of entertaining to do, the accounting books of the farms to keep and her community work to attend to. But with her intense nervous energy she seemed to thrive on it all and relaxed by riding with Seretse and his cousins, who were good horsemen, having virtually grown up in the saddle. She didn't play tennis although she had been so good at it as a child because she said she had damaged a tendon in her arm. Many of the people I spoke to who lived with her in Serowe had no idea she had been so good at sport, or that she had been a competitive ballroom dancer and a competent ice skater. Clearly, she did not speak much about her past, possibly because she felt she had left the bright lights of London behind, and that a Serowe farmer's wife would do best to forget it all.

EIGHTEEN

The winds of change

The 1960s will long be remembered as the decade of revolution. While dress hems rose, becoming miniskirts, sexual taboos fell under the onslaught of the permissive society. Bob Dylan and Joan Baez wailed the protest songs that set a generation alight, and militant, long-haired students in America and Europe rebelled against the established social order. Martin Luther King led the largest peaceful demonstration in American history, during which he spoke about a dream that one day his children would be judged, not by the colour of their skin, but by the content of their character. It was a dream shared by many the world over, including Ruth Khama. Her life during the decade of change was to undergo a revolution of its own, for at the beginning of the 1960s she was still a social outcast as far as some whites in the protectorate were concerned, but at its end she was Lady Khama with the highest social standing of any woman in the vast country.

In Africa the winds of change tore through the continent, blowing away centuries of colonial rule. Tshekedi Khama, who would probably have enjoyed the excitement engendered by that change, died of a serious kidney disease in a London clinic in June 1959. Seretse flew to his dying uncle's bedside at his request and repeated his last words to the thousands of people who filled Serowe for his funeral. "Let there be peace, Bamangwato," said Seretse as the body of Tshekedi was laid to rest in the imposing, granite memorial that towered above the historic kgotla below. And there was peace. The healing process that had begun in the tribe on Seretse's return from exile, was now accelerated.

Both Tshekedi's death, and emerging African nationalism were to drastically alter the course of Seretse's life, and therefore also Ruth's. Resident Commissioner Peter Fawcus, who was later knighted for his services in guiding the Bechuanaland Protectorate to a peaceful independence, said to me in an interview that he thought Tshekedi's death, which occurred at the beginning of the talks on a constitution for the territory "was the most helpful thing he could have done at that stage. He was a very dominant, egotistical personality, and I am quite sure the talks would not have proceeded as peacefully as they did with him there." According to Sir Peter, Seretse had kept a low profile on his return to Serowe and had allowed Tshekedi to resume his dominant role in tribal affairs because of the gratitude he felt towards his uncle for playing such a big part in their reconciliation.

After his death, Seretse, who had never been the assertive, forceful character that his uncle was, immediately became much more of a force on the advisory councils that had been set up by the administration over the years. "But one had the feeling that he wasn't a budding politician, and that he enjoyed his farm and his cattle and the role he played in tribal affairs. This chap who was easy-going, amusing and affectionate did not look at that stage like becoming a political leader," Sir Peter told me.

Nineteen sixty was the year in which Britain and other colonial powers granted independence to several African colonies. It was also the year in which British Prime Minister Harold Macmillan breezed through Africa, putting into words the sentiments of many about the change taking place on the so-called Dark Continent. One of the places he touched down at on his tour was Francistown, in the north of Bechuanaland. The administration officials and their wives, standing in a reception line on the small airstrip, looked with interest at the famous patrician face, the drooping eyes and the moustache that seemed to reinforce the stiffest of upper lips.

The tour culminated in Macmillan's famous Winds of Change speech, delivered in the South African houses of parliament while the architect of apartheid, Dr Hendrik Verwoerd, listened stony-faced. That year South Africa decided to leave the British Commonwealth.

The British Empire, which according to Sir Winston Churchill had carried a greater responsibility for the lives of people born outside her shores than any other empire since the Roman, was cutting loose the apron strings. Apart from anything else, the colonies were costing the British taxpayer a lot of money. This is how the British Government had regarded Bechuanaland, for until it became clear that incorporation of that territory with South Africa was out of the question, there seemed to be no point in spending British taxpayers' money on a country someone else was going to take over.

But in 1959, Peter Fawcus was asked to formulate proposals for the establishment of a protectorate legislative council, and the poverty-stricken country took its first step towards independence. It is interesting that the impetus for political change and independence came more from Britain than from the activities of local political parties.[234] But this is not to say there was not an emerging nationalism in the sleepy protectorate, for the momentous events in Africa and in neighbouring South Africa, naturally had their effect on the territory.

In 1960, the shots fired by police at defenceless black people in Sharpeville outside Johannesburg reverberated throughout the world, and in the troubled years that followed the South African Government cracked down harshly on liberation movements, driving them underground or into exile. Refugees, some political, some unhappy with conditions in the former union, began to pour into Bechuanaland. Some asked for political asylum, others took the political refugee route north from Lobatsi to Francistown from where they travelled into Africa or to Europe. Some of the refugees belonged to militant African organisations, and their talk of African nationalism created a climate for Tswana nationalism in the protectorate. Two political parties emerged at the beginning of the 1960s. One of them, the Bechuanaland People's Party (BPP) was headed, some years after its formation, by Philip Matante, a strong personality whose sympathies lay with the South African Pan Africanist Congress (SAPAC). The BPP wanted independence almost immediately, the expulsion of white settlers, and radical social and political reforms. Its extreme nationalistic, anti-British policy alarmed both the administration and moderate black leaders, and Seretse Khama was encouraged to start a party of his own, the liberal Bechuanaland Democratic Party (BDP), together with Ketumile Masire. The aim of the party was to build a non-racial society based on equal opportunities for all – and independence from Britain. They did this towards the end of 1961, more in response to the extreme parties than any personal ambition.

The Batswana were not a politically conscious people, and Sir Peter told me, "We were pushing them, and people like Seretse. It was hard work at first. But then suddenly they became aware." Seretse's Bechuanaland Democratic Party appealed to the moderates, the professionals and the middle classes, as well as farmers and tribesmen.

The emergence of political parties, organised on a national basis, made it possible for the government to accelerate the tempo of political change. It was announced in November 1963 that the protectorate would be given a form of self-government that would lead to independence. It was a ministerial system, and the prime minister would be the member of the Legislative

Assembly who commanded the support of the majority of the assembly. The executive government would be controlled by a cabinet, presided over by the Queen of England's commissioner (formerly the resident commissioner) and composed of the prime minister and other ministers. A House of Chiefs was to be created to fill the vacuum caused by the abolition of the power of the chiefs, and it would advise the government on matters affecting Africans.[235]

The latter move was naturally not at all popular with the chiefs, who resented the removal of their traditional powers. "They accused Seretse of being like a fox without a tail, who wanted the others to cut off their tails too," said his cousin Goareng Mosinyi to me in an interview. But far-thinking people had realised how divisive tribalism could be in emergent African states, and Seretse who as you will recall had rejected the principle of chieftainship when still a young man, firmly believed that tribalism had served its purpose in Africa. Subsequent events throughout Africa with its ghastly record of tribal warfare have proved him right.

The election was set for March 1965, but first it had to be decided how people would vote. In some countries a qualified franchise based on property and education was being mooted. But in Bechuanaland the executive council decided to go for one man, one vote. "We felt we had to move fairly fast, to keep race relations happy," said Sir Peter Fawcus in our interview. "Our aim too was to break down racial barriers, for the more racial discrimination there was, the easier it was for people like Matante to flourish. It was a difficult time. As the colonial power we had to be objective and fair, and although we favoured Seretse over Matante, we had to be very careful about being seen chatting to him, otherwise we would have given him the kiss of death."

There was no statutory discrimination as there was in South Africa, but nonetheless it existed, for there were separate queues in the post office, hotels could not sell liquor to black people, there were separate schools for black and white children, and sports and social clubs were exclusively white domains. There was, not surprisingly, resistance to the social and political change taking place in the territory. For a start there were white enclaves in Bechuanaland that dated back to 1897 when the British South Africa Company built the railway line from Mafeking to Bulawayo and in exchange received grants of land around Lobatsi, Gaberones, and along the Limpopo River. In 1898 Cecil John Rhodes gave thirty-seven farms to Afrikaner farmers in the wild, remote Ghanzi area in the Kalahari Desert, and the community there spoke of joining hands with South West Africa. Farmers in the Tuli Block, Lobatsi and Gaberones had looked to the Transvaal as their natural home, and those in the Tati Concession had over the years spoken about joining with Southern Rhodesia. As the elections loomed, some whites even spoke about forming a pro-South Africa political party, although this soon died a natural death. Now we have the extremely ironical situation of the Khama marriage that had been such a bete noire, becoming the symbol of racial harmony and of white hope, and Ruth played a key role in building white self-confidence.

The pre-election chat in the country clubs and hotel bars was about Seretse's good humour, his witty quips, and the fun it was to play a game of cricket with him. His administrative abilities and his political astuteness were the subject of much comment and wonderment, and his devotion to Ruth was admired. And although the attitude towards her in some cases, even at that late stage, was still one of resentment for having contravened social mores with her marriage to a black man, word of her dedication to the Bamangwato women also began to spread through the protectorate. Cynics might scoff that this attitudinal change was both socially and politically expedient, but it is worth remembering that there was still a great deal of racism worldwide, and that it was during this period that some of the worst race riots ever experienced in the United States took place. People forget that in the 1960s President John F. Kennedy had to ask his people, "Do we tell the world we're a free nation – except for the negro?"

Seretse's party swept into power with an overwhelming, crushing defeat of all its opponents. It won twenty-eight of the thirty-one seats in the Legislative Assembly, and the remaining three went to Matante's party. Dr Alfred Merriweather, who spoke Setswana perfectly and who became the first Speaker in the House of Assembly, put the picture in a nutshell when he told me: "I remember in the first election there was a lot of talk about Matante. I asked an old man in Molepolole (his village) who he was going to vote for, and he said, 'the chief of course'. They all respected Seretse as a Khama. They said, 'Matante. Who's his mother? Who's his father? Who is his grandfather? Seretse – we know his father and grandfather and all his family.'"

This does not of course in any way detract from Seretse as a person, for Merriweather who knew him as well as anyone, having been involved with him politically and personally, as a friend and as a doctor, pointed out that in addition to his status and birth, he had both charisma and a delightful personality. "When he wanted to be, he could be strong. But most of the time he was quiet," said Merriweather.

Seretse's party's massive election win was beyond the wildest hopes of the administration, the British Government and indeed of Ruth and Seretse, and it made possible the harmonious moves towards independence. The supportive role played by Ruth during that vital election campaign was mentioned immediately when I asked people about her. It was seldom she wasn't seen at Seretse's side as he toured the thousands of kilometres in that Texas-size country.

It would have been far more comfortable for her to have remained behind in her cool, hilltop Serowe house, away from the dust, flies and heat. If she had stayed at home, she wouldn't have aroused the wrath of some of the royal family who said a woman's place was at home. But her first thought was always for Seretse, and like the intensely loyal trooper she was, she bounced through the bush and desert on those awful roads and sat day after day in temperatures that make you feel hot just thinking of them. Her loyalty was mingled with concern for Seretse's health, for in 1964, just four years after he had spent three months in a London hospital, he collapsed with viral pneumonia at a cattle post and was rushed delirious to hospital in Francistown.

When Ruth got to the little town which was like something out of the Wild West with its hitching posts in front of the roadside bars, she was so worried about Seretse's high temperature and delirium, that she moved into the ward with him, so she could be at his side day and night. "It was a terrible time. I was desperately worried about him. When he got a little better, I asked my mother to bring the twins from Serowe to see him, and he had lost so much weight that when they walked into the ward, they didn't recognise him."

"We've come to see our father, where is he?" they asked Ruth in their wide-eyed, mischievous manner. The aim of the adorable six-year-olds was to have as much fun as possible, but the sight of their emaciated father shocked them.

When the doctors diagnosed tuberculosis, Ruth took Seretse home to Serowe, from where a virus specimen was sent to Bulawayo, and the correct diagnosis of viral pneumonia was pronounced. It was suggested he go to Bulawayo for further tests and treatment. He was in hospital there for about a month, during which time Ruth supervised the sorghum and mealie harvesting during the week, and at weekends did the six-hour journey by road to Bulawayo to be with him. "I had to give him reports, tell him how the harvesting and railing was going. It was important that he had peace of mind," said Ruth, whose love and loyalty were plain for all to see.

During his spell in hospital, Seretse was visited daily by his son Ian, then at school at Whitestones in Bulawayo. He was the only child there who was not white, and he was subjected to such vicious bullying and taunting by the other boys that Ruth and Seretse removed him. The Rhodesians, alarmed by rapid decolonisation of the continent and the shouts of "uhuru" ringing through Africa, were busy working out how they could circumvent independence in their country, and the following year they made a Unilateral Declaration of Independence. This was the atmosphere in which Jackie and Ian spent some of their schooldays in Southern Rhodesia. But the vagaries of politics don't mean much to a sensitive nine-year-old. Try explaining to him why he is being called a kaffir, told to polish his playmates' shoes, and is beaten up because he isn't white.

"We were unhappy about it of course, and as soon as we heard about the marvellous multi-racial school of Waterford in Swaziland, we sent him there," said Ruth. "It affected Ian. At one time he went through a period of being anti-white and then one of being anti-black. But he grew out of it fortunately. When I approached the Whitestones headmaster he said that boys would always fight, and that they would pick on one for being dark, or being a Jew, or something," said Ruth.

Rhodesia holds no happy memories for her, for in addition to suffering with her children when she heard about their miserable experiences, she had some of her own. They arrived one day at the Bulawayo dentist with whom they had appointments and to whom they had been before, but he had been called away. When the receptionist saw them, she went off to consult with the partner, and returned to say, "Sorry. We don't do coloureds' teeth." Two little children and their mother stared in horror at the white woman, before turning and walking out in silence. Ruth seldom made a scene or argued about racial injustice, she usually suffered it in silence and counselled her children to do the same. "I can't stand the indignity of it. I am not going to lower myself to the level of small-minded people," she said.

"Come on, we'll have an ice cream instead," she said to the stunned children, clutching their hands, and they walked into a shop where Ruth ordered ice cream sodas for three. "For one," replied the white waitress. "No, I said three sodas, please," said Ruth firmly. "We don't serve coloureds," came the retort, and this time Ruth hit back. "You can keep your ice cream, we don't want it," and they marched out of the shop. Is there anything that makes a mother suffer more than to see her children publicly humiliated, and for a biological factor that is beyond their control? The confusion, bewilderment and anger that must inevitably follow in the hearts and minds of intelligent little people subjected to such behaviour is not hard to imagine.

The twins, who did not suffer the hurtful racist incidents their elder siblings did, were nonetheless also a little confused at times about where they stood. For example, as mentioned earlier, they spoke Setswana almost exclusively before they went to school. "They would only speak English to whites. People loved this of course and used to laugh about the segregation in our home," chuckled Ruth. "Seretse spoke to them in English, but they always answered him in Setswana. If they met a black person, for example an American, they would address him in Setswana, and were amazed they were not understood."

The twins had an easier time from a racial perspective for several reasons, the main one being that they were twins. They were, even for identical twins, incredibly close to one another, living in their own, happy-go-lucky world that simply excluded anyone who was unwelcome. They didn't have to cope with the enormous change involved in moving from an English language and culture to an African one. And they didn't leave home until they were in their teens, and then after a year, they demanded they be allowed to return home.

During the early 1960s, while the rapid political and social changes were taking place in the protectorate, life ambled on in its usual slow, uneventful manner in Serowe. There were a few more visitors, who were interested to see how the tribal council worked without a chief, and visiting overseas politicians liked to meet Seretse, which meant Ruth was busy at times cooking and entertaining. Journalists who had befriended the Khamas in the early days were made welcome, and one of these, Margaret Lessing, always found it fascinating that Ruth ran her home like any middle-class Londoner did. The furnishings were modern with comfortable armchairs, attractive carpets and curtains, and the occasional animal skin on the floor or walls. "Her children were always nicely dressed and beautifully behaved, although once I discovered that Ian who had been sitting angelically on my lap, had been kicking Noel Monks under the table," Margaret Lessing told me.

There was no entertainment in the village, no hotel, no pubs or restaurants. Once a week, a Serowe family projected a film against the wall in their backyard, and later on this was moved to a small hall where the projector broke down at regular intervals and where the children all went to sleep on the floor. The whites sat in the front, the blacks at the back. "We sat in the middle, I don't like to be too far forward or back, when I'm watching a film," said Ruth. At Christmas, Easter, Guy Fawkes, children's birthdays and so on, the villagers would get together for parties and often at these gales of laughter would emanate from whichever corner of the room Seretse was sitting in.

Ruth and Seretse did not enjoy the luxury of boredom. She was too involved with all her community commitments, and he was so busy travelling up and down between Lobatsi and Serowe, attending legislative and executive council meetings, that some weeks he was away five days at a time. When they went on holiday it was to their cattle posts. "This is where the Batswana have their holidays. And Seretse, having spent all those years in exile, never wanted to leave the country unless he had to, for business reasons and the like," said Ruth.

A visit to the cattle post was an exercise in logistics which might have daunted someone less determined than Ruth, for she insisted on taking beds, mattresses, tables, chairs, pressure lamps, pots and pans and so on. These were piled into trucks to the accompaniment of much whooping and yelling from the twins who usually managed to get under everyone's feet. During the long drive they would see springbuck, wildebeest, hartebeest, kudu and occasionally elephant, and at one of their cattle posts on a river, they often saw the animals drinking from water holes in the evening. But Ruth was not particularly keen on the outdoors – camping under the stars was not her idea of fun – and she preferred the outings later when fully equipped caravans were available. Seretse and the boys loved it, however, and after a day's hunting settled down around the campfire to talk. Soon the dancing flames reflected more and more faces as the word spread that the chief was there, and while hyenas howled, and lions roared in the distance, Seretse conversed as he loved doing, with his people.

As his sons grew older, he taught them to hunt, an activity that Ruth disliked intensely. When the first animal, a wildebeest, was killed in her presence and was brought into camp, she felt ill for three days afterwards.

"But I enjoyed going out there. It was so peaceful, with no telephones or people wanting this or that." Ruth had always loved reading and belonged to several book clubs. Her sister Muriel who by that time had realised her childhood ambition and was working in Africa, at the lay-training centre of Mindolo near Kitwe in Zambia, quite often accompanied the family on visits to the cattle posts.

"I have a particularly vivid memory of sitting under a mopani tree with these wretched caterpillars falling down all over us, into our hair and laps, and even down our dresses sometimes," she said. "And of course, the cattle attracted the flies and insects. But I was most interested to see how the average Motswana lives, his attachment to his cattle and the contrast between life in the village and at the remote cattle posts," she told me.

Muriel was very fond of Seretse and particularly enjoyed his rich sense of humour. He loved teasing the sisters, and Ruth in particular. On one trip to a cattle post he offered Ruth the Batswana delicacy of a fried mopani worm. When Ruth recoiled at the prospect, he roared with laughter, and said that was how he felt about eating sea snails and crabs.

It was only when independence loomed that Seretse started buying farms, for until then it was practically impossible for a black person to own one. This was because the tribal lands were communal property and never sold to an individual, and the only other land was farms belonging to whites, or Crown land.

Ruth realised early on that Bechuanaland was a man's country with its heat, dust, flies, cattle, hunting and outdoor life, and although she was involved with the farming, keeping the books and supervising activities when necessary in Seretse's absence, the gay-hearted Londoner found it a trifle wearying at times and she could be very amusing about her lack of enthusiasm. "I didn't really relish standing there, gazing at these cattle for hours on end. When you've seen one cow, you've seen them all," she used to laugh.

But despite this, Ruth was growing to love the life in Serowe where she had been accepted by all, and it came as a shock when she realised that Seretse's appointment as prime minister would mean having to go and live in the new capital of Gaborone. This little village, which back then was called Gaberones, had been not much more than a railway siding with a hotel, and a British administration camp with the usual officials. It was chosen to be the capital in the early 1960s when it became clear that independence was a few years away. It was patently ridiculous to have the capital of an independent black country in another country, and quite apart from anything else, Seretse and Ruth, as prohibited immigrants, could not go into South Africa. As it was, officials from the administration headquarters in Mafeking used to have to travel to Lobatsi for legislative and executive council meetings for this very reason.

Gaborone (the name is derived from chief Gaborone whose village it was) is set in a dusty plain and was chosen as the site for the new capital because the terrain allowed for the construction of a large dam, a vital necessity in a drought-stricken land. In the early 1960s, visitors to the sleepy village were startled to see great roads being carved out of the large expanse of virgin bush that lay between the railway line and the camp. Soon modern buildings began to rise above the dense thorn bush, and a town hall, hospital, hotel, office blocks, the Legislative Assembly, shops, and homes took shape. The progressive architects made it a town for pedestrians, with shopping malls that excluded cars, and cleverly designed pathways and bicycle tracks that enabled residents to walk from one side of the town to the other without having to battle with traffic.

Another sensible idea was to preserve all the trees and bushes possible without hampering construction, and the result was an attractive, green town. This, however, was not the way the Mafeking reserve wives felt about it, for they had been used to living in a thriving town, complete with tarred streets, traffic lights, cinemas, hotels, cafés, schools and so forth.

Protectorate gossip didn't take long to disseminate the news about the social pecking order in the new town, and Ruth heard it with a sinking heart before she and Seretse flew to Gaborone for his swearing in as prime minister. Now she was going to have to start a completely new life all over again and to make new friends in a largely alien community. "I loathed Gaborone when we first came here," Ruth told me. "I had one of the worst migraines I've ever had. It lasted for the three days I was there for the ceremony, and the minute I took off for Serowe to pack up the household, it went, which makes me think that certain migraines can be psychological."

Ruth hated the thought of leaving Serowe. It was the longest she had lived in one place since her marriage. She loved her house on the hill with its beautiful view, and she was happy and fulfilled there. "I was really miserable when we left, I struggled to adjust to living in Gaborone and I didn't know the Mafeking crowd," she said candidly.

It was naturally a time of great social change, for now there were many black faces at the Gaborone parties and the whites, who had never known much about the lives and customs of the people in whose country they were living, had to adapt.

It certainly wasn't an easy time for Ruth. She had to move the family into one house for a couple of months while work was finished on the prime minister's house, before moving again. But she came to love the new double storey house with its five bedrooms, large kitchen, cool verandas and modern bathrooms. Life became a hectic whirl of cocktail parties and dinners, for everyone wanted to meet the prime minister and future president, and the amazing woman who had married him and gone to live amongst his people in his village.

Many of them changed their minds about Ruth after talking to her and realising her sterling qualities of courage and determination. Many admired her, although there were still those who smiled at her in company and gossiped unkindly behind her back. Ruth could be sharp and distant with those she sensed did not like her, or who were plainly sizing her up. She seldom spoke about her background, leaving people free to conject about her origins.

She was attractive at the age of forty-two. She wore her copper hair short, brushed off her face with its still lovely complexion. In common with all women at the time, regardless of age, she wore her skirts short, above the knee and favoured cotton frocks or skirts and blouses. The intense slimness that had characterised her at the time of her marriage and after Jackie's birth, had given way to a slightly fuller look. She was in tune with the 1960s geometric look with her bright plastic sunglasses, but apart from that she was always a functional dresser, wearing the kind of clothes and comfortable sandals that were sensible attire for a village or a small, dusty town.

The children too had to make new friends, something the twins soon did at their school in Gaborone. But for Jackie and Ian, only coming home during their boarding school holidays, it took a little longer. They were both slightly reserved, which in view of their treatment at the hands of their schoolmates was understandable. But in time, the two relaxed and were invited to parties and film shows along with other teenagers.

The date for the granting of independence to Botswana, as the country was to be known, was set down for 30th September 1966. Ironically Ruth and Seretse's wedding anniversary was the day before, and Ruth who was superstitious about dates, figures and numbers, commented immediately on this to Seretse. As the months passed after their arrival in Gaborone and the advent of Independence celebrations approached, life became more and more hectic.

There were overseas trips, one of them to the United States where Seretse was given an honorary doctorate at Fordham University in New York, and there were increasing numbers of overseas visitors who wanted to see this African country integrating peacefully and happily. Seretse also began to apply for aid for his poor land, for before independence it was only Britain who was providing this.

A little while before independence, while he was attending one of the many meetings in London to plan the future of Botswana, Seretse was asked if he would consider accepting a knighthood. He thought about it, and then agreed, but said not a word to a soul until he got home. And then in his typically teasing manner he didn't tell Ruth outright about it. "He kept on calling me Lady Ruth. Lady Ruth do this, Lady Ruth do that. After a while I asked him what all this Lady Ruth business was about, and then he told me in his unemotional way. I couldn't believe it. Having been banned and exiled because he was not a fit and proper person to be chief, and then this ... well, it seemed ridiculous initially. It was such a contradiction," said Ruth. She regarded it as an honour nonetheless and felt that Seretse well and truly deserved it.

"He could have been such a different person with the treatment to which he'd been subjected. And yet he never held a grudge, he was never bitter, he just came back from exile and continued working both with his people and with the British," said Ruth. Many people, including Sir Peter Fawcus, thought Seretse's lack of bitterness was remarkable. "Seretse was a generous chap, both in his attitude towards his country and in the way he treated us, the British and the colonial officials," Sir Peter told me.

"I think that Seretse quite appreciated the apology the British gave him in the form of that knighthood. I think that he accepted that it was a gesture, and he always had remarkably warm feelings for the British," a close friend of his told me.

"I was very surprised because I didn't think a British title would mean much to him, but I think he accepted it because of Ruth," said her sister Muriel. "She had after all been through such a tough, rough time for his sake, enduring all that loneliness and ostracism. I think my father would have been very flattered if he had lived to see it. One of his main fears at the time of their marriage was that his friends would ostracise him, and the fact they were recognised to the extent they got a title from the Queen of England would certainly have helped him to accept the fact that now they had 'arrived' and finally been accepted. Of course my father's fears were groundless because none of his friends did cut him."

In bestowing the knighthood on Seretse, the British Government was in effect restoring Seretse, in the eyes of the outside world, to the rightful position of which they had stripped him. As Ruth pointed out, the tribe had never stopped calling him kgosi (chief) and she had her own title of mohumagadi (queen or chief lady).

The title also helped people in Bechuanaland, if indeed any help was needed, to finally accept Ruth. She had indeed come a long way from the "little London typist" that newspapers so erroneously insisted on calling her, and who could blame her if she didn't rejoice just a little in her private thoughts at the discomfiture of those who had so cruelly closed their doors in her face when she most needed their company. She was gracious, although there were a few people who had played a particularly active role during those miserable years whom Ruth did not go out of her way to welcome in her home.

The knighthood was bestowed on Seretse in a simple, but moving ceremony, in the grounds of the gracious, whitewashed, colonial Government House. There on the lawns, under the shady trees, the Queen of England's commissioner, resplendent in his white uniform, pith helmet and feathers, touched the shoulders of Seretse Khama with the traditional sword, and commanded him to rise. Ruth and the children were there to witness the historic occasion.

The Queen of England's aunt, Princess Marina, arrived at the end of September 1966 to grant the country its independence. The tall, willowy woman who, when she married the Duke of Kent in 1934, was idolised by women the world over, won the hearts of everyone with whom she came into contact during those historic few days. "When we first met, Princess Marina said to me, 'I've been looking forward to talking to you because I too lived in exile.' And she was also involved in the Red Cross so that was another point of contact between us," said Ruth.

The celebrations were unostentatious compared with those in some African countries, and this was in keeping with the poverty of the vast, undeveloped country. But this did not mean they were less impressive, for the dignity of all involved impressed the visitors, who included several African heads of state, as well as the American governor of Hawaii, and South Africa's Oxford University-educated Foreign Minister Hilgard Muller. A little while earlier, the latter's prime minister had announced that Seretse and Ruth were no longer prohibited immigrants in his country.

As the Day of Independence, the 30th of September 1966, approached, there were mixed feelings amongst Bechuanaland's white populace, for while some welcomed the new order, others were apprehensive. The newly erected stadium in Gaborone was to be the venue for the raising of the Botswana flag at midnight on 29th September. But as the afternoon wore on, anxious officials noted with alarm an enormous and ominous black cloud looming menacingly on the horizon and growing larger by the hour. By late afternoon it was apparent that a giant dust storm, the likes of which few people had seen in their lives, was going to envelop the town in its sandy grip.

But nothing was going to deprive the thorn bush town of its fun, and glasses tinkled at candlelit dinner parties and brightly coloured lights strung between garden trees lent the tin-roofed houses a festive air. The evening's events included a gymnastics display, drum majorettes, and a mock battle, the latter organised by a very stiff upper lip British army officer. As people arrived to take up their seats in the stadium, the full fury of that awesome storm was unleashed. Speech became impossible, and women who had dressed smartly for the historic occasion, in the light clothes generally appropriate for that hot climate, shivered and borrowed their husbands' suit jackets to keep warm. By the time the mock battle took place, the shrieking gale drowned out the gunfire, and nobody could see a thing through the whirling dust. They were all fighting a battle of their own to keep warm and comfortable.

The wind and dust had abated somewhat by the time Ruth and Seretse drove up to the grandstand, with the Queen of England's commissioner and Princess Marina behind them. But it was a cold wind, and the elegant Princess in her sparkling tiara and long gown was clearly going to be uncomfortable. Ruth had already lent her a fur wrap, but Seretse didn't believe in unnecessary suffering, and he sent home for some large karosses, and so the English princess and the Khamas snuggled warmly under African animal skins to watch the historic flag ceremony.

In a gale like that it wasn't surprising that the flag stuck at the top of the pole and struggled to unfurl for a while. Only the most serious could fail to be amused by the farcical situation induced by the howling winds of change. At the stroke of midnight, great fires were lit on hills surrounding the town and throughout the country, and with the soaring flames leaping into the night sky, rose the hopes that independence would bring peace and prosperity.

The next day at a formal ceremony at the House of Assembly, Princess Marina made an address from the throne and formally handed over the symbolic constitutional instruments, and that night an Independence ball was held in the town hall. Ruth made a stunning entrance in a figure-hugging red dress that left one white shoulder bare. The chiffon-covered bodice was encrusted with intricate black beading, and she wore long white gloves. Her slim figure, fair skin and glorious copper-coloured hair drew gasps of admiration from all present. Lady Khama had arrived.

The Independence celebrations were covered extensively by the South African and international press. Although Ruth stuck firmly to her policy of not granting personal interviews, this was one of the few times in her life when she didn't mind publicity. But it marked the beginning of a sometimes unhappy relationship in ensuing years between Jacqueline and the press. When they found the path to Ruth's door closed, they fixed their attention on the teenage girl. Alarmed by it, she dashed off to take refuge with her friends, who thoroughly enjoyed the fuss and entertained the pressmen whilst hiding their companion.

The celebrations provided an excellent opportunity for retired protectorate colonials to return to the country they had loved, and it is a measure of Seretse's warmth that he welcomed them back with sincere pleasure. One of these was an official with whom he had disagreed over some issue at a meeting of the Legislative Council, and the exasperated man had finally retorted without thinking, "You're the nigger in the woodpile in this matter." Seretse with his humour and generous spirit had never held the impulsive words against him, and was taking the man for a drive around the new capital when the retired official, pointing to State House which the Khamas were due to move into, asked, "What is that?" "Why, it's the woodpile," retorted Seretse according to the anonymous official.

The Independence gale, as well as blowing away tons of dust, also took with it much of the stuffy, fusty prejudice that had kept the races apart, and prevented friendships forming across the colour bar. Change from almost total segregation in the early 1960s, to total integration in 1966 had taken place so fast that some people were stunned. Nowhere was this new order more apparent than in the fast-growing town of Gaborone, for development naturally brought employment opportunities, and this appealed to those living in rural areas. Suddenly white people found themselves queueing for milk behind blacks, rubbing shoulders with them in the post office, sitting next to them in the cinema. It was a new experience, and those who didn't like it, returned to the safety of apartheid South Africa whose draconian race laws grew harsher with each passing year.

It was a formidable task that faced Seretse after Independence. The man who had unified a fragmented territory and had welded many different tribes into a nation, in much the same way that his illustrious grandfather had made the powerful Bamangwato tribe out of several little subtribes, held the reins of power in the twelfth poorest nation on earth.

There must be few countries that attained independence in such desperate straits. A drought that had persisted in some places of that vast territory for more than five years had ravaged the countryside. Hundreds and thousands of cattle, the mainstay of the economy, had died, and nearly one quarter of Botswana's people were dependent on famine relief for their basic food needs. The landlocked country's geographic position meant it was almost totally surrounded by countries that practised harsh race discrimination, for it shared borders with South Africa, South West Africa and Rhodesia and its only physical contact with "free" Africa was a ferry across the Zambezi at the point where the boundaries of four countries meet in the middle of that famous river.

Botswana's railway system was managed by Rhodesia and South Africa. It inherited a customs agreement with the latter under which it received a negligible share of South Africa's customs revenue, and employment opportunities were so scarce that a high percentage of its able-bodied men worked in the Witwatersrand gold mines. During the following troubled years on the subcontinent, with the Rhodesian war growing daily and South Africa's politically deprived black people leaving the country in increasing numbers for guerrilla training, Botswana became a haven for refugees. Seretse had therefore to follow a pragmatic line that allowed his country to exist peacefully in the shadow of its powerful neighbour while not compromising his opposition to apartheid.

"We knew Botswana would not be economically viable at Independence, but I thought it had the chance of becoming so in the following years, and I was proved right," Sir Peter Fawcus told me. Botswana had the good fortune soon after Independence to discover diamonds in massive quantities beneath its desert sands. Nickel and copper and vast deposits of coal were among some of the other mineral deposits discovered after Independence. This, combined with the healthy cattle ranching industry and beef exports, and a tourist boom in the world-famous Okavango Delta, which attracts many wealthy international visitors including Princes William and Harry, has radically altered the dismal picture that faced the new nation in 1966.

Botswana, with Seretse and Ruth at its head, was to become a shining beacon of peaceful, racial coexistence in the strife-torn years that lay ahead for the African continent. But in those early, heady days of Africa's uhuru, the once exiled chief and his much-maligned wife were not to know that in time

301

to come, their country would become one of only a couple of multiparty democracies left on the continent. Faced at Independence with the sobering picture of a drought-stricken, impoverished nation, they went forward together into an unknown future, with the same determination and faith with which they had faced the uproar created by their marriage.

NINETEEN

First lady of the land

We have seen Ruth in many roles during her eventful and interesting life. She has been a homesick evacuee in war-torn Britain, an adventurous driver of British pilots in World War II, an ostracised lonely woman living on the fringe of her husband's African village, and an angry exile forced to return to the land of her birth. Her role as wife of the president and first lady of the land, with a British title to add lustre, was one she found both challenging and stimulating. She approached it with the same zest she had tackled life in Serowe on her return from exile, although initially she was reluctant to move out of the cheerful, homely prime minister's house and into the gracious, colonial-style State House with its sweeping green lawns and high, whitewashed walls. "I thought it would be nice if we could continue to live where we were, and use State House for entertaining, and putting up visiting heads of state," said Ruth.

But the idea was considered impractical, and so the family moved into the five-bedroomed house which Ruth described as not at all homely, although it certainly was most attractive, with its circular balconies, terracotta-tiled roof, large high-ceilinged rooms, and the garden a profusion of bougainvillea, rose bushes, flame lily, and other subtropical trees and plants. The house was furnished rather like an English country house, with Sanderson linen suites, attractive linen curtains, pale-coloured carpets, and English furniture. It was certainly very different from the tiny Notting Hill Gate bedsitter in which Ruth and Seretse had started off their married life.

It was both typical of Seretse's nature and character, not to mention Botswana being the impoverished state that it was, that the Khamas did not live in the ostentatious splendour that some African leaders adopted, although their surroundings were comfortable by any standards and luxurious when compared with the lifestyle of the average Motswana. Their new position introduced a certain amount of ceremony into their daily lives, with the presidential flag being raised and taken down at sunrise and sunset to the accompaniment of the bugle, security guards manning the entrances to the large grounds and vetting visitors, and uniformed drivers and staff opening and shutting doors.

There were few people in Gaborone who did not have servants, but State House naturally had a good complement of maids and gardeners, as well as chauffeurs and bodyguards, so any family privacy was seldom possible. But as this had been the pattern of Ruth's life, with the extended family consisting of her mother, and Seretse's aunts, uncles and cousins spending a lot of time with them, it was not all that much of a departure from the norm.

Ruth could have enjoyed a relaxed life as the president's wife if she had wanted to, for she could have organised people to run State House for her and accepted nominal positions on various charitable organisations, without having to take much personal interest in them. However, she not only became president of the Red Cross Society in Botswana and of the Botswana National Council of Women, but she threw herself into organisational and committee work.

In addition to her work with the two organisations mentioned above, Ruth also started the Lady Khama Children's Christmas Fund that, as the name suggests, distributed Christmas parcels to the underprivileged. She became involved in the Save the Children Fund and continued her interest in the Girl Guide movement. "Well, I think one should be associated with something, with some organisation," said Ruth of her involvement. "You understand that your problems are nothing when compared with what other people suffer. I think it's important that you don't become an island and just worry about yourself."

Her genuine interest in the welfare of her people earned her their love and respect, and she soon won the admiration of white women for her deft handling of committee and procedural matters in the various organisations. This is not an easy task, for people who have grown up in diverse cultures naturally adopt different approaches. A woman who worked with Ruth on one committee but who wished not to be named said, "She had to deal with two Batswana matriarchs who had very strong and definite views. She was so diplomatic that she won their support, and therefore the backing of all the women. It is amazing really, for there were all the factions that you find in Africa, and here was an English girl born and bred who could understand and cope with them." Ruth soon learnt and taught her white counterparts that if you don't like something, you don't say so outright, you couch your argument in different terms.

A fairly typical day in State House began with breakfast at 8 a.m. which Ruth and Seretse liked to have with only their immediate family. Ruth then went to the kitchen to organise the menu for the day, and if there was a function that evening, she would spend quite a bit of her time during the day supervising and often cooking, which she enjoyed. She had no housekeeper, for as she said, in the newly independent country, there simply was not the skilled personnel available. The morning she spent in her office in State House, doing the accounts and books for their farms that totalled five at one stage. She ran the family businesses. A family friend who wanted to be anonymous said, "I think that Seretse would have been lost without that because he was not the sort who would sit down and do any bookkeeping. I doubt whether he ever knew how much money he had in his bank account, for she ran that sort of thing."

Ruth's work in this regard was therefore considerable, and it grew as the years passed and the number of cattle and the output of the farms increased, necessitating more staff, etc. In the ten years between their return from exile and Seretse becoming president, he had worked hard and happily on his farms and was by any standards a wealthy man.

During a typical morning in State House, Ruth would also see dignitaries or people connected to charities, or simply people who wanted to see her, for she was generous with her time. After lunch, she went back to her desk, for there was always a lot of official and personal mail, plus all her committee minutes and work. Tea was at 4 p.m., usually with homemade cakes or biscuits that Ruth would have made or taught her cooks to make. At 6 p.m. there were cocktails, and if Seretse was back from the office, friends and cabinet ministers would sometimes join them. When the children were small and there were no dinner parties or functions, the evenings would be devoted to the family, for they were a remarkably close-knit family.

Ruth, who was always gregarious and friendly and enjoyed entertaining, had more personal friends than her husband, which usually meant that most of the visitors to State House were her friends, and a large percentage of these were from the white population. This is not surprising, for Ruth did not speak Setswana. It is a complex and difficult language to master, and although she tried to learn it a couple of times when she settled in Serowe on their return from exile, she confessed she had never been good at languages and gave it up, something she subsequently regretted, she told me. If she had been able to speak it, this would undoubtedly have made a difference to those Batswana who did not speak English well. "Seretse ran the government and Ruth ran the family," said a family friend to me. "I think it was a good division. It left him free to concentrate on state matters, although he was a marvellous father, always deeply caring about his children."

Both Ruth and Seretse decided not to interrupt Jackie's schooling as she completed her A levels shortly after Independence, and then went to Belgium for a year to learn French, during which time she travelled around Europe and Britain. Ian followed in his sister's footsteps when he had completed his schooling by going to Europe, to Geneva to learn French. He then went to Sandhurst Military College in England. "He was fortunate, as his was the last intake to do academic as well as military studies, and the standard there was very high," said Ruth. The emphasis on French by the Khamas was due to the impact that French-speaking African diplomats and delegates had made on Ruth and Seretse during their travels and at the United Nations.

The twins spent more time at home than their elder sister and brother, for after completing their primary school education in Gaborone, they too were sent to Waterford, but only spent one year there. As they told me in their humorous way, "It rained too much there, we missed home, and why suffer if you don't need to?" And so they returned to the brand-new Gaborone school of Maru-a-Pula that was run on the principles of the famous school of Gordonstoun in Scotland (which was attended by Prince Philip and his son, Prince Charles).

As Ruth settled into State House and her new position, people began to conject on the amount of influence she had on her husband, and some white people believed, quite mistakenly, that Seretse held the strong democratic beliefs that he did due to Ruth's influence. Seretse's interest in a representative and participatory democracy became clear to his colleagues when he was still a student. His commitment to the rights of the small man, and to personal and political freedom, formed the basis of the remarkably free and democratic country that Botswana is today.

At Independence Botswana was listed by the UN as one of the world's twelve poorest nations and the least developed in Africa. Under Seretse's wise and careful leadership the new state began to flourish within a couple of years of Independence. He introduced the hugely beneficial Food for Work Programme. Furthermore, a major kimberlite pipe was discovered at Orapa that became, back then, the world's largest diamond mine. Between Independence and the next century, Botswana had the fastest average economic growth rate in the world of 9% each year. The resources were channelled throughout the country to benefit all the people. Furthermore, the country created levels of education and literacy as good as, if not better than, anywhere else in sub-Saharan Africa.[236]

But having said that, there is no doubt that Ruth with her strong will, determination and forthright views must have influenced him to a certain degree. "I've been there several times when she jokingly reminded him that there are women in the world, and they should have positions of leadership, and why wasn't there a woman going on this delegation, and why wasn't there a woman on some committee," said Ruth's sister Muriel in one of our interviews. "So, very quietly, but very persistently she was building up the position of women in Botswana and trying to see to it that they were represented in things pertinent to the running of the country. It wasn't that Seretse was against it, he was all for it, but even if he believed women were capable of holding certain posts, he had to convince a lot of men around him who were not as liberal as he was."

Something that always impressed Muriel about Ruth was her ability to keep a secret, and this must have been a blessing to Seretse, for Ruth said he could talk to her freely about politics and the affairs of state. "He knew I never talked, that he could say what he liked, and it stopped there. He didn't ask my advice, but he always got different viewpoints, ideas, from everyone, and then made up his own mind, and so naturally this applied to me too," said Ruth, who made a point of being up to date on world politics, and of course the situation in Botswana.

Dr Merriweather, who accompanied Seretse on many state visits abroad and in Africa, said to me that on these visits Ruth could be very outspoken and often dominated the conversation. She could be critical of the African leaders, and when she and Seretse were alone together, she would often tell him what she thought of his friends and he would often agree with her. "He wasn't easily influenced if he didn't want to be influenced. But occasionally he modified his views," Dr Merriweather told me.

The process of rapid Africanisation – which usually followed independence in the former colonies, to the extent that many countries were drained of vital administrative and other skills at the time when they were most needed – was not followed by Seretse in Botswana. Africanisation started slowly, from the bottom up, and Seretse actively encouraged British officials to stay on in their posts and was genuinely upset when people whose judgement and expertise he valued decided to retire. In certain of his key ministries he held on to his white staff, who back then had the most experience, for a long time and in so doing laid the foundation for the stable, well-run country that Botswana is today.

But any impression this might create that he was not a strong leader would be wrong. "In cabinet meetings there was never a head count, and although he always took everybody's views into account and took consensus, at the end of the meeting, what the president said was what went," said a top-ranking official who did not want to be named.

Part of the success that Botswana is today can be attributed to the controlled way the money that poured in from the mining of its rich mineral deposits was put to use in developing basic infrastructure. Tarred roads, so vital in that vast country, were a priority, and today in Botswana main roads are usually tarred – compared to only eight kilometres at Independence. The provision of electrical power, water supplies, low-cost housing, and the improvement in agriculture, the development of the cattle ranching industry, of tourism, and of course of the mines, were all pursued steadily.

Seretse did not follow the example of many African leaders and lavish vast sums on grandiose schemes that came to nothing. The corruption, so prevalent in many bloated, inefficient African bureaucracies, exists to a negligible degree in his country, and "wabenzi's", the Swahili term given to ministers who tear through poverty-stricken shantytowns in their Mercedes Benz cars, hardly exists in Botswana.

"Seretse believed in private enterprise, and that people work harder if they work for themselves," said Ruth. "He didn't think it was right that people in government should automatically receive salary increases, and he didn't take an increase at all. He said there were people out there with nothing. People would say to him, 'Ah, but you have all those cattle,' and he would answer, 'but you have your own cattle too.' He didn't like the huge gap between the haves and the have-nots. People said Seretse was rich in his own right, and he was rich, but he said he had worked for it over the years, and indeed he had," said Ruth.

Seretse's commitment to human rights was a shining light in the then gathering gloom of Africa's increasingly poor record on this score. American political scientist, Mr Richard Weisfelder of Toledo University in the United States, emphasised in research that the personality of a country's first president and how he defines acceptable behaviour are critical in determining the human rights records of African states.[237] Seretse's humanitarianism, combined with his tolerance for opposition (although at times he could be both hurt and surprised by it) and his racial tolerance, of which his marriage was an outward manifestation, all combined to make him an exemplary African leader. "You knew where you were with Seretse. If he gave you a job, along with it went the responsibility," the charismatic, lively Mr Archie Mogwe, who was Botswana's minister of foreign affairs, told me. "He didn't interfere in your portfolio without consulting you first, and if he was making a speech about your field, he would show it to you, and ask you how you felt about it, and he would change it if you didn't like it."

"He rarely lost his temper. But if he said you had done something wrong, it stung," said the highly-articulate, fast-speaking Mogwe. "He was the sort of man to put himself last. For example, he died before the road to his home village of Serowe was tarred."

Seretse's foresight in recognising the threat tribalism posed to peace and unity in Africa has been dealt with elsewhere in this book, but what is interesting is that British-born Ruth, probably out of a sense of gratitude and loyalty to the Bamangwato for the manner in which they took her to their hearts, made sure their needs were known to her husband. Philip Steenkamp, former permanent secretary in the office of the president, said, "Seretse was not as strong a Bamangwato royalist as Ruth was by any means. I think she was at times more the wife of the chief, than the chief was chief. If Seretse had liked tribalism, he would have appointed all his ministers from the Bamangwato, in the way that ZAPU did (in Zimbabwe). In fact, the only appointment from his family was Lenyletse Seretse (who was vice-president) and the president even had some soul-searching about that."

One of the anecdotes that did the rounds in Gaborone about Seretse was his attendance at the first meeting of the local Scottish society's Burns Night meeting, where they had the customary haggis, whisky and piper. The next day Seretse was asked how he had enjoyed it, and he reportedly replied, "If there is one thing I don't like, it's tribalism."

This is not to say that he was a "white African" as some people have described him, for many of his habits were particularly African, notably those regarding food. When he killed an ox he would have all the traditional dishes made for example, and he liked nothing better than to get away from State House and visit his farms and cattle and sit around a campfire, speaking Setswana to his guards and farm workers. It was one of the "nuisances" of being a president that the security that surrounds heads of state often prevented him from mingling with his people. Seretse enjoyed his early days in office, when he could walk down the Gaborone shopping mall and chat to people. He preferred that to the official cavalcades complete with blaring horns, flags and masses of policemen that swept him from one place to the next in later years.

"We had the death threats that all heads of state get," said Ruth. On one occasion they were told seconds before they were due to walk on to a parade ground that someone had threatened to shoot Seretse. "It seemed like hours, not minutes, walking down that line, wondering when a shot would ring out," said Ruth. Incidents such as this naturally intensified the security surrounding the couple, guards were increased, police escorts were enlarged, and the gardens of State House were almost doubled in size and surrounded with high, white walls.

But both Seretse and Ruth relaxed when they could. Colin Blackbeard, a childhood friend of Seretse's from Serowe, who was minister of transport and communications in the Botswana Government, recalled a tour of his district by the couple to me: "In the evening we would make camp, and Seretse would send his chair down, and come and talk to us, often until midnight, about sport, cattle, politics, farming. He liked to be able to talk to us in his own language, and he had the feeling of the people. He would say, 'I am not president now, chaps, we are just talking.' And then he would be up at 5 a.m. stoking the fire, and saying, 'What are you people sleeping for?' One evening Lady Khama was dancing around the fire, everyone joined in and she made me too, although I don't go much for dancing." It was at times like those that Seretse would look with renewed love at the vivacious copper-haired Londoner who had stolen his heart and who danced with such grace around a leaping fire on a quiet night in the wilds of Africa.

Seretse's genuine affection for his people, and their great love of him, manifested by their pouring out of towns and villages to see him wherever he went in his huge country, is well illustrated by one incident. It happened when he was in hospital, under the care of Dr Merriweather in Molepolole. A wizened old Bushman, hearing the president was nearby, told the doctor how much he would like to see him. Later that day, the patients in the old man's ward were astonished to see Seretse walk up to his bed and chat to him.

When Seretse was being driven around Gaborone, he often used to stop and pick up the children of his friends. On one such occasion, he asked a little boy if there was anything he would like to do, and the child replied he would like to get into the police car and blow the horn. Seretse granted him the wish, enjoying the child's lack of awe at being with the president, and so they rode in noisy style to State House with Seretse roaring with laughter at the escapade.

Seretse was aware even before he became president of the threat to his relations with other black-ruled countries of Africa, created by the economic dependence of land-locked, impoverished Botswana on Rhodesia and South Africa. But while retaining the respect of South Africa for his refusal to allow freedom fighters to use his country as a springboard for terrorist activities, he aligned himself with black Africa, and his implacable opposition to racism was clearly but objectively spelt out in public speeches. Seretse will long be remembered for his moderating influence on the leaders of the Frontline States (Mozambique, Angola, Tanzania and Zambia). These countries which to a greater or lesser extent also relied on South Africa for food, technology, rail and harbour facilities, to name just a few examples back then, allowed anti-South African liberation movements to operate from their territories. This in turn aroused the military wrath of powerful South Africa, and the result was a subcontinent torn by strife and upheaval, a situation not in the interests of anyone.

"Seretse was very influential, and his views amongst the Frontline States were much sought after," Philip Steenkamp who often accompanied him on trips to those countries, told me. Dr Merriweather, who went to several meetings in Africa with Seretse for medical reasons said that presidents Kenneth Kaunda of Zambia, Julius Nyerere of Tanzania, Samora Machel of Mozambique and Hastings Banda of Malawi used to joke about Seretse being their big chief. "I think that this was a combination of their liking for him, and the inborn respect all Africans have for hereditary chiefs. I think that even they felt he brought a sense of proportion to their deliberations because Seretse was never emotional, he was always matter-of-fact, quiet and logical," Alfred Merriweather told me.

Dr Merriweather recalled a Frontline meeting in Maputo, Mozambique, where a vast crowd packed a stadium in the blazing sun. Machel made one of his charismatic, excitable speeches which went on for hours and had everyone on their feet shouting, and then Kaunda followed with his tears and his white handkerchief, and he also had them all shouting, and then Seretse spoke and was very calm, and there was nothing at all excitable about his speech. "He was not prepared to say that Africans were blameless and that their lack of progress was due only to colonialism and South Africa. He said they had to shoulder some of the responsibility themselves," Dr Merriweather told me.

It is interesting that the friendship that developed between Seretse and Kaunda was initiated by Ruth's sister Muriel. She told me that she joined the president's UNIP party before Zambia became independent, and that her organisational and leadership qualities soon came to his attention. Muriel, who became a city councillor in Kitwe, at one stage held the balance of power between the parties in the council. It is fascinating that the two sisters, brought up in suburban London in a typical English family, should both end up living in Africa, playing their different roles in its political life.

When Muriel heard that Kaunda was going to some Independence celebrations she knew Seretse would be attending, she told him to look out for her brother-in-law. But it was Seretse who strolled casually up to Kaunda at breakfast one morning and said, "I've heard all about you and how wonderful you are from my sister-in-law, and I've come to see for myself if you are." When Muriel next saw Kaunda, he said to her, "I've met that brother-in-law of yours, he's quite a tease, isn't he?" Muriel told me in an interview.

"KK", as he was affectionately known by the Zambians, did not have the same relaxed manner as Seretse, but enjoyed a good laugh nonetheless and thoroughly appreciated the fund of Van der Merwe jokes with which Seretse would frequently regale him.

Ruth told me that Seretse, Nyerere and Kaunda were very close. "They had a great friendship. Julius had a very keen sense of humour and I suppose you could say it's like Seretse's, and of course you either understood Seretse's humour or you didn't." The friendship was interesting because Nyerere's socialist views differed so radically from Seretse's, "but they didn't argue," said Ruth. "Seretse would say that Tanzanian socialism wouldn't work here, and Nyerere always respected that."

Another area where Seretse's influence was felt was in the formation of SADC (Southern African Development Community) – founded to promote economic development and reduce members' dependence on South Africa's economy. But Seretse's leadership was not confined only to regional developments for he also played an energetic role in a number of international issues affecting the region. This included the negotiation of the Lomé Convention between forty-six developing countries in Africa, the Caribbean and the Pacific on the one hand, and the nine countries of the European community on the other.

Seretse travelled a great deal, and it was seldom indeed that Ruth, who was always mindful of his health and who enjoyed travelling, didn't accompany him.

Over the years Ruth and Seretse visited scores of countries, including China, India, Denmark, Sweden, the Caribbean, Switzerland, Britain, Singapore, North Korea, Canada and Europe. They travelled extensively in Africa, attending meetings of the Frontline States and British Commonwealth conferences.

At many of the meetings of the Frontline States, Ruth would be the only wife there because the other heads of state left their spouses at home. And on many of the trips, there was no separate itinerary for the wives, and so they had to organise their own amusements. Ruth was good at this, and during a British Commonwealth conference in Singapore, she would not rest until she had planned a trip of the islands.

Ruth always did her homework before setting out, reading all she could about the country and its people. "If you have any sense, you learn the names of the dignitaries you're going to meet, the names of their important towns, and where they are situated and so forth. I've sometimes been to places, I won't mention names, where they have never heard of you, and haven't bothered to look up your country on a map, which is a little bit lazy," said Ruth tartly.

She met the heads of nearly every nation on earth and learnt and digested information about other people's customs and problems.

It was while they were in Peking that 100 000 people were killed during an earthquake that measured 8.5 on the Richter scale. "With my experience of the Blitz during the war, I told Seretse to just lie down and not to move," said Ruth. Then their son Ian, who had accompanied them, knocked on their door and took them to safety, although they did not feel in immediate danger as they were about 200 kilometres from the epicentre. The following day they found the practical Chinese camping on every pavement in the city.

Ruth found a state visit to India in 1976 a nostalgic experience, for it brought back childhood memories of her father and all the romantic stories he had told her of his time there, of the gay life in the officers' mess and the social whirl, of the hunting and horse riding. "I couldn't forget how much my father loved India, but we all agreed that we wouldn't mention this, although the Indians don't resent the British, for they have a fantastic army and very good roads for which they are grateful to the colonials," said Ruth. "But we hadn't mentioned to our son that we were going to maintain this low profile, and I heard someone saying to him, 'I believe your grandfather was in India,' and he said yes, but he didn't say which grandfather it was!" chuckled Ruth.

When they got to Bombay where her father had lived, she said to Seretse, "I can feel my father's presence here." Seretse replied, "Don't be ridiculous," and then because her father had so enjoyed the social scene, he teased Ruth, asking her, "How many brothers and sisters do you think you've got here?"

"Oh don't be silly," retorted Ruth, "my father wasn't like that."

She stayed in palaces, in hunting lodges, in glorious mansions and in mud huts, and seemed to be equally at home wherever she was, for although there was a certain dignified aura about her, she was quite adventurous and enjoyed change.

On an official visit to London during the Queen of England's jubilee year in 1977, Seretse and Ruth had lunch with her at Buckingham Palace. "We had presented a picture to the Queen of a buffalo and a lion fighting, and they wanted to know from Seretse who had won the fight. But there was no answer to that one," said Ruth, who chatted about horses to Princess Anne, a passion shared by them both. A couple of years before that, Ruth and her daughter Jacqueline had been invited to Britain's Women of the Year lunch, and Ruth was placed next to Princess Margaret.

Ruth's first trip to Johannesburg was in 1967 to buy furnishings for the guest wing of State House in preparation for their first state visit, that of Kenneth Kaunda's. The South Africans were always advised of her visits, as was protocol, and she took her own security guards, although security was also provided by the South Africans. She recalled the shock she felt when she first saw the apartheid signs at the airport, in hotels, on park benches, which designated where "nie-blankes" (non-whites) and "blankes" (whites) could sit, eat, and travel. If she was with her children, these signs meant they could no longer do things together, and so she was always careful that they did not land in situations which could cause incidents or friction, for she had learnt her painful lesson about racism in Rhodesia.

If there were embarrassing racial incidents, Ruth would leave the scene as quietly and quickly as possible, and her advice to her children to do the same was for the most part followed by them. "It's not our country, why stir up trouble? If we are visitors, then we must abide by the laws, whatever we think of them." In spite of her pragmatic attitude, it naturally hurt her to see racial injustice, and her blood would boil. "You just hope that because you have a white skin, you are not going to be associated with the person perpetrating the injustice," she said.

But she had many South African friends and pointed out that it was wrong to condemn the whole country, "for there are many white people who hate the situation and are trying to do something constructive about it. You can't be against a whole group of people. Those who are racist … well, there must be something wrong with them to hate a race just because of the colour of their skin," she told me.

The South African Department of Foreign Affairs was always given her travel routes in advance by the Botswana Government when she took her children to school in Swaziland, in order to avoid any incidents. Not surprisingly, there were incidents despite these precautions, for a white woman travelling with coloured children was particularly conspicuous, especially in the late 1960s and in the 1970s. "I was always apprehensive before a trip, hoping that nothing would happen, and travelled as quickly as possible through the country to our destination, said Ruth.

On one trip to fetch Ian from school in Swaziland, she had the twins with her, and her driver, failing to see a stop sign, was pulled over by the police, who when they saw Ruth and the children demanded they accompany them to the charge office. "They told the others to remain in the car and told me to step inside. I handed the policemen my passport, told them I was Lady Khama and my husband was the president of Botswana, and asked them if they needed any more information to get in touch with their department of foreign affairs. But it made no difference, they kept me there for half an hour before they would let me go, and I smoked cigarettes and worried about the twins outside in the car. It was horrible." Ruth later described the policemen from the small town (called a dorp in South Africa) as being "dorpie people with dorpie minds".

"There were always apologies when we contacted South Africa about these incidents," said Steenkamp to me, "and obviously Seretse would get upset about it when she came back and told him of her experiences."

Another incident, in the 1960s, occurred when Ruth and Seretse flew to Jan Smuts airport in Johannesburg and boarded a plane for England. A drunken South African crowd aboard the aircraft noted the Khamas' presence, although they were not in first class with them, and began singing to the tune of a South African folk song, "Daar kom die Alabama", the words, "Daar kom Seretse Khama". "I thought it was rather funny, although no one else did," said Ruth. "The crew were dreadfully upset, and the captain told the crowd to sit down and shut up."

Ruth described herself as one of the most unobservant people she knows, saying her sons can ride past her on the other side of the road and she won't realise it. "In the past, when people were ostracising or slighting me, it was a waste of time because I wasn't noticing it." She didn't deny that she may have built a protective shell of vagueness around her to help her cope with unpleasant experiences. "I suppose one has to be a bit naturally unobservant," she said.

The Khamas tried to keep contact with South Africa to a minimum, but with Seretse's serious illnesses, there was no choice about where to go if they wanted the best medical attention, apart from flying to England of course. In 1968, less than two years after he had become president, he collapsed with cirrhosis of the liver and was rushed to Johannesburg on a mercy flight, with a doctor in attendance.

He was admitted to the Johannesburg General Hospital, and as there was no room for Ruth on the small flight, she followed later that day. "He was so ill that I would not have been at all surprised to get up there and find that it was all over with him. They were enormously kind at the hospital and told me I could sleep there if I wanted to do so. It was so terrible to see him so sick that I couldn't even sit down, I had to keep moving, doing things."

Seretse was in hospital for seven weeks, and after a while when he didn't seem to be improving as Ruth felt he should be, she enquired about his diet, and discovered to her horror that it was not fat-free. Being the direct person she is, she offered to cook his meals herself, which horrified the staff.

Traumatic events seldom happened singly in Ruth's life, for while she was hovering anxiously at Seretse's bedside, she was told her mother had died in State House. A grieving Ruth rushed home, for although her mother had not been well, her death was still a shock, and she had always been close to her. It was the severing of another link with England, for with her parents dead and her sister, by now a Zambian citizen, married and living in the country of her adoption, she had no immediate family left in England.

It was during this worrying time for her and the family that letters appeared in the Johannesburg press from the local public, attacking the Khamas for their use of South African medical facilities. The gist of most of the letters was that Seretse accused South Africa of unjust race policies while accepting the best treatment their hospitals could offer. It clearly was an invidious situation, but there was no way around it.

"He went there for treatment," said Ruth later. "This doesn't mean to say he had to like their policies. South Africans come to Botswana to hunt, and to go game viewing, yet they prefer their policies to ours."

"From Botswana's point of view, Seretse's years in office were critical and if we hadn't had him, it would have made a great deal of difference to this country," said a top government official who did not want to be named. "Ruth did a remarkable job regarding his health, although of course like anyone else he was offended when he was told he couldn't smoke or drink, and what he could and couldn't eat. It is not an easy job to do, and I am convinced with any other wife he would have been dead ten years earlier."

A woman friend of Ruth's who worked for many years in Botswana, often heard the Batswana saying that a tribal wife would not have been able to take care of Seretse in the same way as Ruth did, because traditional attitudes would have prevented them from exercising their authority in the forceful manner that Ruth could employ. "This is why Ruth went everywhere with him, because his security people and colleagues would give him anything that he wanted to eat. It was very difficult for her," she told me.

"Father was a sick man. There weren't good and bad periods, there were only the bad and the not-so-bad periods," his son Ian told me in an interview.

"My father enjoyed his food, and was like a naughty boy at times, for he would sneak off to the fridge and eat the things he shouldn't eat, say when mother was upstairs sleeping. She would sometimes find out and go at him. 'Now you know, Seretse, you know you shouldn't,' she would scold, and he would behave like someone who had been caught out. At one stage he was told to stop smoking, and then some idiot of a doctor said the situation wasn't so serious, and if he wanted to, he could smoke, and of course he did. But I got the impression that he knew his days were numbered, and he didn't see why his last years should be so uncomfortable, and why he couldn't eat the food he enjoyed." Ian spoke to me with compassion and humour when he quietly described the dietary dilemma of his much-loved father.

Seretse's diet was a strict one, for being a diabetic, as well as suffering from liver and pancreatic ailments, he was not allowed spicy, rich or sweet foods, fatty foods were forbidden, and he was not supposed to smoke or drink. But as his sister Naledi told me in her deep-voiced, humorous way, "You know what these men are like, as soon as a back is turned they take their poison."

The tales of his "disobedience" are amusing. "He was like a schoolboy sometimes," said a colleague who chose not to be named. "He was smoking at a meeting and suddenly the security guard who had seen Ruth, gave a signal, and Seretse passed the cigarette to me, saying, 'here, you hold this.' If we were on a trip, he would wait until Ruth had gone to bed, and then out would come the forbidden curry. Once there was a little left over, and he made us put it in a pot, tie it up, and put it on his aircraft, and he flew off with it to Gaborone. Everyone respected him for being so human."

Archie Mogwe recalled a banquet in Dar es Salaam, Tanzania, where the presidents were seated at different tables, and Ruth was at Nyerere's. "The presidents went to help themselves from the buffet first, and because the food was hot and spicy, Ruth was watching Seretse, saying, 'not this, take that.' Ultimately Seretse found he had very little to eat, and so finished his meal first. Someone at his table remarked on how little he'd eaten and offered to help him to some more. Ruth was busy talking and didn't notice the heavily-laden plate put in front of a delighted Seretse, who only told her the following morning of how much he had enjoyed his meal," Archie Mogwe told me.

And while the doctors who cared for Seretse, and often Seretse himself, found Ruth difficult with all her questions about his health, and sometimes interference in his treatment, they recognised too that she did know an enormous amount about his conditions. "She was so conscientious about looking after him. If I said, 'now give this pill at 7.50,' then 7.50 it was,'" said Dr Merriweather.

Ian Khama, and many others believe that Seretse sacrificed his personal interests and the great love of his life, farming, in his duty towards his country. "I think that in the first years of his presidency my father felt he would get the country on its feet and then let someone else take over. But as the years passed with all the difficulties in this region of Africa, this became harder to do. But I know that he would have liked to have chucked in the towel long before he died," said Ian.

A couple of years before Seretse's death, Philip Steenkamp suggested to him that he live on his farm in the Tuli Block, take life more easily and fly to Gaborone for cabinet and other important meetings. But the idea came to nothing, and Seretse relaxed instead either by going to one of his farms just outside Gaborone where he intended to retire, and where Ruth lived after his death, or to his favourite farm in the Tuli Block on the Limpopo River. Ruth, who had taken years to adapt to being a farmer's wife, was never at her happiest there, and Seretse was irritated by her fussing over the house, the furniture and the swimming pool, while she used to get fed up about him buying another six bulls when he had many already.

In this respect their interests differed widely, for she was not much interested in gardening, or game watching, which might have filled the gap to a certain extent, and while he was supportive and full of praise for her church and charitable activities, he would occasionally tire of hearing about them.

As a Botswana friend remarked to me humorously, "Looking at a bull was not her idea of fun, and hearing about the latest church bazaar was not his."

With this difference of interests they were like any other couple and their relationship, which survived the enormous strains imposed on it down the years – the strains wrought by loneliness, ostracism, racism, separations and illness – was essentially close and warm. They joked with and teased each other in a way that only people who are very fond of each other can do. Sometimes at State House they would put on a record dating back to the days when they had first met and fallen in love. Seretse would take Ruth in his arms, and the two of them would move gracefully and in total harmony to the old jazz music that had brought them together originally. Sometimes Seretse would put on a favourite record of his, maybe it would be Satchmo, or Paul Robeson, and he would sing to it, his rich voice ringing through the large house, while outside the security guards smiled at each other, happy that their president was relaxing. After evenings such as this, close friends of the Khamas would chuckle to themselves as they drove home and remind each other yet again of the love match the Khama marriage had been.

The couple also relaxed by playing cards. "They used to accuse each other of cheating. They both cheated actually," said Muriel. "At times, we played charades and twenty questions. Seretse especially loved the latter game."

The closeness of their relationship made it all the harder for Ruth to see Seretse suffering from heart problems at the end of a gruelling year in 1976. It was a year filled with crises for the Khamas. Apart from their exhausting trips to visit President Ford in the United States, Prime Minister Indira Gandhi in India, and Prime Minister Trudeau in Canada, they also went to China, North Korea, Sri Lanka and Great Britain, not to mention their visits in Africa.

On their return from India, in early 1976, they were met by a distraught Jackie who told them Tshekedi was lying unconscious in the Gaborone hospital after having fallen from his motorbike. Seretse was ill again, and Ruth took him home to State House. There the doctor told her that Tshekedi was more in need of her comforting presence than her husband.

So, leaving Jackie to look after Seretse, she flew to Johannesburg with her son who had torn every ligament in his knee and was suffering from internal injuries. She spent weeks visiting him daily in hospital, and it was during this time that Seretse, who had recovered, made a speech at a party rally, condemning apartheid. The next day Ruth received so many threatening telephone calls at her Johannesburg hotel that 24-hour police guards were posted outside her room and at the hospital, and the still concussed Tshekedi was moved to another area. It was an intensely worrying time for the poor woman, but her troubles that year were only beginning.

September 1976 marked the tenth year of Botswana's independence, and former colonial officials and dignitaries from all over the world attended the festivities to mark the occasion. In October, at a State House party to thank people for their help during the anniversary celebrations, Seretse was in the middle of a speech when Ruth was called away urgently by Ian who said Jackie had had an accident. She got upstairs to find her daughter with blood pouring down her face. She and her husband, Johan ter Haar, driving in at night from their farm outside Gaborone, had driven into a donkey cart that had no lights. Jackie, who was sitting in the passenger's seat, had her face badly cut by flying glass and had to have scores of stitches inserted under one eye and near her mouth. The impact of the collision was such that the Khama sons, who had gone immediately to the scene of the accident, had to shoot the donkey, and Jackie was fortunate not to have sustained even more serious injuries.

A few weeks later when Seretse said he wasn't feeling well, it was decided that the year's activities had overtired him and he was confined to bed. A nurse doing a routine check discovered that his heart was not beating regularly, and a medical team flew down from Johannesburg and inserted a temporary pacemaker that regulated the rhythm. He was then flown to Johannesburg for the insertion of the permanent pacemaker, which is usually a simple operation, but Seretse was unlucky, for problems arose during the insertion. In addition, he was also allergic to antibiotics, and when he reacted to them, the insertion had to be rushed.

"I could have cried for Seretse. He went through such an awful time, he went through far too much. You wouldn't wish that on anybody," said a distraught Ruth. "He had to have an operation every month for eight months.

We kept flying up and down between Gaborone and Johannesburg. Finally, when we went to England for the Queen of England's jubilee celebrations, the British doctors managed to get his body to accept the pacemaker." After that, Seretse, who had no history of heart ailments, took on a new lease of life.

In December 1972, Jackie, who had been working in a Gaborone office since her return from Europe in the late 1960s, married handsome, blond Dutchman Johan ter Haar who was on contract to the Botswana Government as the official responsible for the development of small industries. Jackie, who was happy to be marrying and settling down, looked relaxed and attractive. She was, at the age of twenty-two years, a high-spirited, determined individual. She adored her father, he was the rock in her life, and she loved having discussions with him about Botswana's current affairs.

Their evening wedding in the gracious setting of the State House gardens was a mixture of English and African cultures. Jackie wore a simple and most attractive white dress with a cowl hood, and Ruth looked stunning in a white evening dress, while Seretse was distinguished in a dinner jacket and bow tie. The approximately 500 guests were treated to a dinner that had been cooked by Bamangwato women in the large, three-legged cast iron pots they used in their villages, and Seretse provided the meat from his cattle herds.

Jackie had two handsome little sons, and went with Johan to live in Sierra Leone, before the marriage ended in divorce and she returned to Gaborone. This distressed both Ruth and Seretse enormously, believing as they both did that marriage is a commitment for life. Everyone had hoped that her marriage would bring lasting happiness.

Jackie's brother Ian, after graduating from Sandhurst Military College, obtained his commercial pilot's licence in Belgium, before becoming a training officer for the Police Mobile Unit in Botswana. He then joined the fledgling Botswana Defence Force and rose rapidly through the ranks to become the youngest brigadier in the world. His considered, serious approach to life was tempered by a lively sense of humour and a generally friendly, although sometimes reserved manner.

The twins' early fun-loving approach to life gathered momentum as they grew older and became the despair of teachers and friends, who while they tried to instil some sense into them, couldn't help laughing at their antics.

Ian and the twins particularly enjoyed hunting with Seretse, for when they were alone together, in the wild freedom of the bush, and sleeping under the stars, their father relaxed, letting the cares and stresses of high office slip from his broad shoulders for a while.

The twins, whose school record was undistinguished although they passed their O levels, were sent to England to do mechanical engineering, but they weren't happy away from home, and in spite of Seretse's admonishments to remain, they returned to State House.

Towards the end of the 1970s the Bamangwato tribe asked Seretse in the kgotla in Serowe to allow them to have Ian as their chief. Traditions die hard, and Seretse whom they had continued to regard as their chief, even after he formally renounced the chieftainship, was far away from them in Gaborone. Seretse, whose opposition to hereditary chieftainship had not changed over the years, conceded that the tribe could elect one of his sons, like any other tribesman, to the position. On 5th May 1979, twenty-three years after he returned from exile, Seretse saw his son Ian installed with all the ceremony and tradition that only he, in the long line of Bamangwato chiefs, had not experienced.

As Ian sat in the chief's chair, on the customary leopard skin, the irony of the moment could not have been lost on many of the crowd in the sandy kgotla, for it was in that very spot they had initially rejected Ruth and Seretse, then shouted their approval of them, and had finally been told by Seretse that he had to renounce the chieftainship for himself and his children if he was to be able to live with them again.

The wheel had turned full circle, and the chanting, singing, dancing tribe rejoiced that after thirty years they again had a chief. It didn't seem to matter to them that Ian could not give a speech in their language as he was unable back then to converse fluently in it, although he could make himself understood. He realised immediately what a severe disadvantage this was and set about learning it with determination, and today speaks it beautifully.

A few months after Ian's installation, Ruth and Seretse played host to the Queen of England, her husband Prince Philip and son Prince Andrew. Ruth, whose passionate love of altering houses – she once said that what she most enjoyed about being in State House was altering it – moved the family to a three-bedroomed cottage in the garden, three months before the royal visit.

This was to allow decorators to smarten up State House and, among other things, to repair the ceilings in the main bedroom that Ruth maintained were collapsing.

"We had to repair it before anybody else slept in that bedroom," she said, conjuring up visions of the Queen waking up with plaster lying around her ears. In twelve years of altering State House, Ruth had moved the kitchen from the front to the back of the house and indulging in her passion for bathrooms which I attribute to her Notting Hill Gate flat days, had added on six, making a total of eleven. It was by any standards a house fit for a queen.

Botswana's normally mild winter weather turned viciously cold the day the Queen of England touched down at the small international airport at Gaborone, but the genuine warmth of the ecstatic crowd soon made up for the chill. That evening she attended what was probably the first state banquet she had ever been to in a Holiday Inn, but there simply wasn't another venue large enough for it in the mainly single-storeyed town. Ruth, who had worked closely with the chef and manager, was pleased with the results. She displayed her usual cool demeanour throughout the three-day visit, although those who knew her well were able to see that inwardly she was tense, and naturally terribly anxious that everything should go according to plan.

The twins, who made a new friend in Prince Andrew, were invited by him later to attend his twenty-first birthday party at Windsor Castle outside London. The prince's sense of fun was evident from the way he flung open the windows of State House, amused that everyone was shivering in weather he considered quite mild by English standards.

Seretse who was at his most affable and charming during the successful visit, clearly kept the Queen of England amused with his humour and quips. He was as relaxed as Ruth was nervous. But it was an ill president who joined the singing, cheering throngs, in bidding the Queen of England farewell. As the royal plane lifted effortlessly into the bright blue wintry sky, the eyes of the press turned towards the smiling couple on the ground. Neither it, nor any of those present could possibly have guessed that a year later the genial president would be dead.

TWENTY

Seretse's death

Ruth spent much of her married life wondering whether Seretse would survive his latest illness. Her concern about him over the years manifested itself in tension headaches and migraines, and her at times abrupt and haughty manner hid a sensitive and worrying disposition. But his death, when it came, was sudden and from a totally unexpected cause. The man who had survived countless attacks of pneumonia, pancreatitis, liver disease, who suffered from high blood pressure, a duodenal ulcer and diabetes, and who had an irregular heartbeat, was finally to die of cancer.

"We in the family had all learned to live with Seretse's illnesses. In fact, we had all got used to the idea that he would always get over them, because when he recovered, it was usually so fast. That is why it was so hard in the end, because we were all so convinced that he would survive as he had in the past. Of course, we weren't really facing the facts," said Ruth.

Ruth was told at some stage after her marriage to Seretse that his uncle Tshekedi had said she would leave her husband once she realised what a sickly person she had married. And if she didn't leave him for that reason, she would when she realised he was not going to be chief. Her incredible devotion during his illnesses and their years of exile and hardship certainly left no one in any doubt that when she promised, "for better or for worse," she meant it.

Seretse talked increasingly of retirement a couple of years before his death. Ruth felt strongly he would have retired to Kenmuir, the farm he bought about twenty kilometres outside Gaborone. "He hated State House, he didn't like the town at all. He also felt hemmed in by that white wall around State House," said Ruth. Seretse was not keen on social activities. He would tell the office of the president to accept invitations, "for my wife, she likes going out."

Kenmuir is situated a few kilometres off the main road to the north and nestles at the foot of a picturesque little hill. Nearby is the quaint, attractive Oodi village where the Oodi weavers, famous for their tapestries, bend over their huge looms. Ruth and Seretse spent many weekends out at Kenmuir, where Seretse would inspect his cattle, check his boreholes and discuss dipping and trucking and breeding with his farm manager. The small, thatched house consisted of several rondavels, and while Seretse relaxed, reading his favourite books – cowboy and Wild West stories – Ruth would work on her plans for totally redesigning the house. Sometimes they would have friends out from Gaborone for a barbeque, and then Ruth would busy herself in the small kitchen, while Seretse supervised the fire outside and sat watching the flames while in the background guinea fowl cackled in the wild bushveld.

"I'm sure if we could have got Kenmuir ready earlier, we would have lived there, and just gone to State House during the day," said Ruth. Another place they might have retired to was one of their farms on the Limpopo River, which Seretse regarded as home. On it was a large, modern house with four bedrooms and bathrooms, and an attractive veranda, and it was there in the lush bushveld with its good cattle ranching that Seretse was happiest.

In the year before he died, the remarkably close-knit family was together much of the time, for the twins were living at home, Ian had nearly all his meals at State House, and there was seldom a day that Jacqueline, who had moved into her own house in the town after her divorce, did not take her two sons to play with their grandparents. And Seretse, who enjoyed their company, would play the jokes on them he had played on his children.

It was a lively household with the twins tearing in and out on their motorbikes, or in the new Chevrolet Kommando's their parents had given them on their twenty-first birthday in June 1979. The security guards would shake their heads in amusement at the lively pair and chuckle over their latest scrape. Quiet, gentle Ian, who respected and admired his father increasingly as the years passed, modelled himself on Seretse. And Jacqueline, who at times in her life had been interested in politics, adored discussing current events with him.

But Seretse was naturally an extremely busy and often tired man, and so it was to Ruth that the children confided their troubles and fears, and it was she who chided them and fussed over the little details of their lives. But at mealtimes discussions raged to such an extent that Ruth, glancing at her husband's often weary face, would appeal for peace. The family relaxed together at home by playing table tennis, a game at which Seretse often beat his children, and which Ruth thoroughly enjoyed.

At the end of 1979, on a visit to London, Seretse, who was suffering from increasing abdominal pain, went into hospital for a check-up, but nothing proved positive, and he was told to stick to his diet and was discharged.

"But even in mid-air on our return journey, he was in such pain I had to give him an injection," said Ruth. When the pain continued on his return home, he went into Molepolole hospital under Dr Merriweather's care. "He was there for about two weeks, and the pain used to come and go and I doubted very much it was pancreatitis as the London doctors had suggested it might be," said Ruth.

As usual she spent a great deal of time with Seretse, driving backwards and forwards from State House to be at his hospital bedside. Dr Merriweather, who as a missionary doctor believed in healing both body and mind, discussed religious faith with his famous patient.

At the beginning of 1980, Dr Merriweather returned to his native Scotland on long leave and left Seretse in seemingly quite good health. But he deteriorated fast. "I was giving him injections daily for the diabetes, and his arms were getting thinner and thinner, and he was losing weight. Then his stomach became bloated, and the doctors wouldn't touch it," said Ruth. In June when the doctors said that Seretse must return to London, Ruth suspected that he might have cancer, but said nothing, hoping desperately that she was wrong.

But tests done there soon revealed that it was a widespread cancer, and the doctors told her he had a month to live at the most and probably only two weeks. Despite her suspicions, she was totally shattered to have them confirmed and to be told that the man who was life itself to her would soon be dead. As Ruth gazed out of the hospital window, soft green plane trees rustled in the summer breeze, and the shouts of children playing in the sunshine drifted up from the street below. Amid these signs of growth and renewal, her pain and impending loss seemed all the greater.

Ian was fortunately in London at the time, as he had been invited to England by a regiment to view some military exercises, and he visited his sick father nightly. He was with his mother when she was told the news of Seretse's impending death, and although Seretse was informed about the cancer, they decided not to tell him just then how short a time he had left. When Dr Merriweather received a telegram in Scotland with the news of the widespread cancer, he went immediately to London and said to the doctors, "This man mustn't die here, he must die at home, in his own country." The English doctors said in that case he should be flown home immediately, and the British Government in a kind and extremely humane gesture, put a Royal Air Force plane at the Khamas' disposal. It was a melancholy party that boarded the plane that was to fly the ailing president home to die amongst his people. The plane touched down at Francistown where Seretse had been met on his return from exile by rejoicing people twenty-four years earlier, and an emotional Jacqueline and the twins, totally devastated by the news of their father's illness, climbed aboard to be with him on the last lap of his homeward journey.

The news of Seretse's illness had been broadcast all over the world, and when the plane landed at Gaborone, a sad and silent crowd was there to welcome him home. He was fully conscious and well enough to walk slowly off the aircraft, helped by Ruth and Dr Merriweather, and when he drove for the last time past the security guards at the gates of State House, he slowly lifted his hand in an acknowledgement of their welcome. He then walked up the wide, winding staircase to the bedroom. Ruth felt there was no point in his going into an impersonal hospital ward. She wanted him to spend his last days at home, amongst the people and the things he loved.

He lasted for two weeks, longer than anybody had expected. "He really fought that cancer," said Ruth. "Imagine if he had been told he only had days left. Once he asked Ian how long there was left, and he said we all hoped that the treatment would work, and Seretse believed that. It would have upset him too much to have known that he had such a short time." During the fortnight, medical experts from the United States and from South Africa flew in to see Seretse, but their tests only confirmed the British doctors' diagnosis.

Dr Merriweather, at Ruth's invitation, stayed in State House, and the devoted doctor hardly went out at all, spending most of the time just sitting in the room near the patient he so admired and respected. "He could talk, although in the last week he had some difficulty in conversing. But as usual, he didn't talk much. I think that he knew he was dying and towards the very end accepted that he was dying," said Dr Merriweather to me. "When the American cancer expert told him there was nothing he could do for him and that he should sort out his affairs, Seretse called the family together and spoke to them."

The entire family had gathered around the dying man, and Ruth, with quite extraordinary courage, held it together in those dark and difficult days. She took refuge in an intense need to see that Seretse was comfortable, that his treatment was right, and to give him every chance for recovery. She hoped desperately that some miracle would happen that would save him. "We just couldn't bring ourselves to believe that he was really going to leave us," said Ruth.

Her sister Muriel flew down from Zambia to be with the family, and she was met by Jacqueline and the boys and her aged English aunt, who had been living with Ruth and Seretse since Ruth's mother had died. "They told me that late each afternoon ministers and government officials as well as family and friends came in to give Ruth support, and sometimes they went upstairs to see Seretse," said Muriel. Naledi Khama, Seretse's sister, was also there. "I didn't want to nurse Seretse, though," she told me, "It's strange, but I knew he was dying."

Seretse rallied somewhat the first weekend he was home, and although July is normally a cold month, the mild winter weather with warmish days allowed the family to accede to his wishes and wheel him out into the garden in a wheelchair. There he sat in the gentle sun, with the family having tea around him and his grandsons frolicking on the grass. Later that afternoon he was feeling so much better that the whole family sat with him in his bedroom watching television. It was the Wimbledon men's singles final in which Bjorn Borg was defending his title against John McEnroe.

But a couple of days later the pain returned, and Seretse began to deteriorate fast. Philip Steenkamp, permanent secretary to the president, who felt a great sense of loss at Seretse's death to his own dying day, was called to the president's bedside a few days before he died. "Seretse said he wanted to resign the presidency, because he thought the vice-president ought to become president. I said that when the presidency became vacant, the normal procedures would be followed," Steenkamp told me. "The constitution made provision for the vice-president to do his job when he was unable to do so," said Steenkamp to Seretse. It was typical of Seretse to worry about his country and its future as he lay dying.

It was very seldom that Ruth was not with Seretse, but when she was away from him she did not sit still, for she always took refuge from misery with intense activity. She insisted that Dr Merriweather's wife Mary also move into State House, and the hospitality for which Ruth was renowned amongst her friends was greater than ever. Her children, unable to come to terms with their beloved father's terminal illness, looked to her for support and guidance, and this she gave them quite unstintingly. As her body shrank from loss of weight, her moral strength grew.

Seretse developed pneumonia a couple of days before he died, and it was obvious the end was near. On 12th July he went into a coma, and that night Naledi moved into State House to help. Ruth was totally exhausted for she had been with Seretse every night, sleeping in their bedroom and keeping watch over him. But on that last night he was so ill and she so near collapse that she went to rest in another room.

In the early hours of Sunday, 13th July, the doctor woke Ruth. "I fell into such a heavy sleep that by the time they woke me, he was almost gone, and so I shouldn't have left him to sleep," she said, heartbroken. "I should have stayed and said goodbye to him."

Muriel, who woke when she heard noises and saw lights going on, realised Seretse must have died, and with a heavy heart joined Ian and his mother at Seretse's bedside. Then they left Ruth with Seretse. Her once robust figure was slight, her famous peaches and cream skin was drawn with the pain that comes from suffering and loss, and her lustrous copper hair was listless and streaked with white.

Muriel and Jackie went downstairs to make tea, and the family, shattered by their grief, drew close to comfort each other. Ruth's aunt, who was in her nineties, and who adored Seretse, took to her bed in a dreadful state, refusing to eat or drink and asking continually, "Why him? Why wasn't it me?" She never recovered from his death, and the spritely old soul who had so impressed people with her vigour, died not long after Seretse.

The people of Botswana woke that Sunday to the sound of funeral music and the news of their president's death. For many it was a shock, for the news of his illness had only been known for about three weeks before he died, and many could not believe he was gone. The entire country went into deep mourning for a month, flags hung at half-mast and a sense of loss pervaded the land.

Ruth did not leave State House until the funeral on 24th July, as was Bamangwato custom. During that time, while the family continued to look to her for guidance and support, Ian increasingly assumed the mantle of head of the family. Again, this is custom, for the eldest son becomes the head of the household on his father's death. With two funeral services, one in Gaborone and the burial service in Serowe, lots of decisions had to be made.

Seretse's body was embalmed and taken to the National Assembly (parliament) where he lay in state for three days, and the people of Botswana queued patiently to pay their last respects to the man they loved so much. Mourning, traditionally done at the home of the deceased, was for reasons of security not done at State House, and people began gathering each evening at a little park in the centre of the town for prayers and hymns. As more and more people from around the country arrived for the funeral, a tent was put up, lights were assembled, and food was provided.

"It really was impressive how many people came, and the same people every evening," said Muriel, who went daily with the children and Naledi. The new president, quiet, likeable Quett Masire, in whom Seretse had always had the utmost confidence, was among those who attended some of the services.

Those close to Ruth who saw her in the days preceding the funeral were amazed at her strength and courage, for with his death she not only lost her husband and the father of her children, but also her privileged position as first lady of the land. "Maybe I looked so strong because I was just so numb with grief," Ruth later told me.

Dignitaries from all over the world had arrived in Gaborone the evening before the state memorial service for the president. Queen Elizabeth of England was represented by the Duke of Kent, and you will remember that it was his mother Princess Marina who had officiated at Botswana's Independence celebrations thirteen years before. Amongst the African dignitaries were Seretse's friends, the Frontline presidents, and they visited Ruth at State House the evening before the funeral. Ruth asked her sister to try and prevent Dr Kaunda from breaking down in front of her, and Muriel thought, "How do I tell my president not to cry?"

But she and Ian met Dr Kaunda at the front door and said, "Ruth's been wonderful. She hasn't broken down at all," and he got the message. Ruth received her visitors in the lounge, looking like a fragile porcelain doll. She had lost a great deal of weight, and her slight figure, dressed in black, was in striking contrast to her pale face and pale copper hair.

When Kaunda heard that Nyerere was due at State House within an hour, he stayed on to see him, and then the South African mining magnate, Mr Harry Oppenheimer, arrived at the appointed time, and Kaunda said he must stay on and see him. "We kept looking at the clock, and wondering, gosh, what's going to happen when the King of Lesotho arrives at his appointed time," said Muriel.

The result was that, instead of going in and out singly to see Ruth, these men were all with her at once. It was probably just the kind of situation that

Seretse would have enjoyed, for he used to tell jokes even at funerals. Muriel thought a remark that the extremely socialistic Nyerere made to the capitalistic Oppenheimer was priceless. "He said, 'I can't imagine there is anything in my country that could possibly interest you, but if you do ever happen to be in Dar es Salaam, do let me know,'" said Muriel.

Dinner that night, the last one that all the immediate members of Ruth's family would attend together in State House, was sad and emotional. Ruth, who since Seretse's death had been saying pathetically that maybe she hadn't looked after him well enough, retired early. In her fragile state she was like a little wounded animal, retreating into a hole where she could hide and lick her wounds. At the same time, she had to comfort those of her children who were feeling desperately emotional and were going through one of the first phases that occurs after death, that of anger. The acceptance of the death would come later, and this Ruth knew and understood, and tried to impart on them.

But the next morning everyone was up and dressed in their funeral clothes, ready for breakfast at 8a.m. as usual, and wearing their bravest faces. A Requiem Mass was held in the Gaborone Anglican Cathedral. Ruth had played a role in raising funds for this cathedral. She was dressed in black and wore a heavy black mourning veil that contrasted starkly with her white face. After the mass the bronze coffin was taken to the National Stadium in a striking black-painted military Land Rover. Draped with the blue presidential standard, the coffin was carried to the dais by cabinet members, including Colin Blackbeard, the only white member of the National Assembly. A twenty-one gun salute boomed into the intensely blue, cloudless sky, and the 20 000 people present sang the Anglican hymn, "O God our help in ages past".

Ruth, flanked by her children, Jacqueline dressed in black with a black hat, the twins in suits and Ian in his smart military uniform, maintained her incredible composure during the three-hour long service. They felt they owed it to their father to be brave and dignified, for in the centre of the stand, overlooking the arena, their every move was observed. The presidents of Zambia, Zimbabwe, Malawi, Tanzania and Mozambique and King Moshoeshoe of Lesotho, Harry Oppenheimer and the Duke of Kent were among the dignitaries who laid wreaths on the dais during the sad and moving ceremony. The Botswana and Zambian presidents delivered eulogies to the late president, and Dr Kaunda said that Seretse had demonstrated that the fears of "race and colour" amongst Southern Africans were hollow and meaningless in the building of friendships, homes, societies and nations. "He developed the life of the Republic of Botswana as a bridge between peoples and races. He loved humanity in the racially controlled south, and worked with it," he said.

Dr Masire paid tribute to Seretse's magnanimous nature when he pointed out that, "the world did not always deal kindly with Seretse Khama, but he never showed bitterness for the injustice showed to him." There were prayers and a sermon, and the service ended with the hymn, "Nearer my God to Thee, nearer to Thee!"

At the end of the service, the carriage bearing the coffin was accompanied by Ruth, her children and the immediate family, from the stadium to a military aircraft at the nearby airport, where they flew off to Serowe with it. With them went a South African cardiac specialist and his wife who had formed a firm friendship with Ruth and Seretse after the doctor had inserted the pacemaker in the president's heart. Now the specialist kept a watchful eye on Ruth whose stamina amazed him.

But it was not only the Batswana who mourned their deceased president. People all over the world were saddened to hear of the passing of a moderate, who had preached peace, and had disseminated it wherever he could.

A memorial service, given in thanksgiving for his life and work, which I attended with my family, was held in London's historic Westminster Abbey on 7 August 1980. The dean of the abbey paid tribute to Seretse for his skill, indomitable courage and the sustained moral purpose which enabled him to preserve his country's independence in an Africa divided by clashes of colour and the strife of competing political systems.

And as British Prime Minister Mrs Margaret Thatcher and the Queen of England's representative bowed their heads, the dean gave thanks for the happiness of Seretse's family life, "and the life-long affection which bound him and Ruth together in a common service freely offered."

Ruth's great role in her husband's life had been recognised by the very people who had once so misguidedly sought to prevent her marriage. It was a fitting end to a union that had endured crisis after crisis for thirty-one years.

TWENTY-ONE

Life after Seretse

When the presidents, the prime ministers, the king, the duke and the mining magnate had dispersed along with the vast funeral crowds, Ruth returned to State House, an ordinary Botswana citizen. Of course, the president's widow and the mother of the Bamangwato tribe, mohumagadi as she is called, could never be ordinary, but with Seretse's death went her exalted position of first lady, with all the privileges and status it carried. And Ruth had enjoyed her status. But more than that, it is possible that she had welcomed the opportunity it afforded her to put those who had ostracised her and criticised her for marrying a black man in their place.

She had been able to withdraw behind the high white walls of State House and keep her distance from those with whom she did not want to associate. It had also enabled her to compensate her children for the racial slights they had endured. There were times when perhaps, understandably, she herself would take umbrage and encourage the children to follow her example.

Seretse's death naturally meant an end to the morning bugle call, the saluting security guards, the chauffeurs. And whereas Seretse had disliked living in a town, and being walled in for reasons of security, Ruth had enjoyed the lively social life that went with her position. Seretse's oft repeated warning to his family, cabinet ministers and members of parliament became reality on his death. He used to say, "Tomorrow, if I wasn't elected, we'd just be ordinary people again with no status. We are only here for as long as the people want us to be." He didn't want those around him to get too used to power and privilege when it could end at any time.

Far more than social position and status, however, Ruth had lost the man she loved. People often asked her down the years why she married a black man. She always answered, "I didn't marry a black man. I married the man I loved."

But the censure the marriage attracted simply served to strengthen the commitment of both and to make them determined that nothing would break it up. And therefore, their differing interests in politics, in religion, in farming as opposed to town life, and their different personalities, with Seretse quiet where Ruth was voluble, were not allowed to endanger the marriage. Besides this, they had camaraderie and a bond of which all who were close to them were very aware. Seretse always came first in Ruth's life, she was always so terribly wrapped up in what he was doing, and in this respect, she was an interesting mixture of a modern and an old-fashioned wife. She was modern in her independence, and free thought, and yet she never allowed that to interfere with being Seretse's wife.

"When I think of what a happy marriage they had, how close they were and how they seemed to discuss everything, Seretse's death really was very hard for Ruth to take after the years she had struggled to keep him alive," said Muriel, who had spent a lot of time with the couple.

The children naturally suffered greatly too, for they had not only lost their father, but also their status as the president's children. They could do virtually anything they wanted one minute, and the next they were ordinary people.

The twins, who loved speeding through Gaborone on their motorbikes, would be severely reprimanded by their father when he heard they had broken the speed limit yet again. After his death, they were of course handed a ticket like anybody else. "What made that family different from my family, was Seretse," said a friend who did not want to be named. "This does not denigrate Ruth's role in it, for she was a very important part of it of course. But the Khama family was the Seretse Khama family."

Compounding the sudden loss was the physical break-up of the family. Before Seretse's death the twins were living at home, Ian had most of his meals there, and Jackie and her two children had moved out only a couple of months earlier.

This meant that the family spent time with each other daily, and with Seretse's death this changed drastically, for when Ruth had to decide where to live, either in Gaborone with her family, on one of their farms, or in Serowe, she chose the farm Kenmuir, which was about twenty kilometres outside Gaborone.

Having made her decision, she began frantically packing up the clothes, furniture, memorabilia collected on travels around the world, and other possessions gathered in the nearly fourteen years spent in State House. "I wanted to be out before the month's official mourning was up, but I just couldn't make it," said Ruth. She had lived in State House longer than anywhere else in her life except for her childhood home. "We had so many books, and of course I had far more clothes than I needed at State House where they were obviously necessary for all the functions we attended." Ruth was so shattered by Seretse's death and the sudden changes in her life that she simply gave away things as fast as she could, until the children stepped in and stopped her. "I believe my behaviour was quite normal under the circumstances, but I'm a little sorry now I gave away so many books," said Ruth.

Many people were surprised that Ruth chose to live on the relatively isolated farm north of Gaborone, when she could have bought a house or a flat in town. She had her reasons for doing so. With her characteristic forthrightness she told people, "Why buy another house when you've got one just down the road?" She didn't think she would have any peace in town with people constantly dropping in to see her. Ruth was also nervous about intruding on her children's privacy. "I don't want to cling. I probably see more of my children than most other mothers, but I don't hang on to them."

It is my belief that another reason Ruth moved out to Kenmuir was to withdraw from the world, in order to nurse the wounds caused by her terrible grief and, to a lesser extent, those resulting from her change in status. Out at Kenmuir, she could see whom she liked, when she liked. In a way it meant she was not available to just anyone, she was still calling the shots, which I think is most understandable. It was a place to recharge her batteries for she lost about twelve kilograms after Seretse's death. And of course, she had been used to living at a certain distance from people since she returned from exile in 1956. When they lived in Serowe, she was removed from the centre of the village there too, for it is a relatively long way from the kgotla to the end of the hill where the Khama house was situated.

But for all that, the change from the high-pressured lifestyle of State House to the intense quiet of the farm was overwhelming, and all who cared for Ruth felt intensely sorry for her in her isolated misery. She had been used to revving cars, roaring motorbikes, slamming doors, people rushing in and out all day, constantly ringing telephones. On the farm, there was silence save for the birds, the wind through the trees, the lowing of the cattle, and during the lonely evenings, the throb of the generator that provided her lighting. When she woke in the hours before dawn, the howl of jackals had taken the place of early-morning traffic.

"I felt sick for that woman during that whole period of readjustment, it must have been hell," said a woman friend of Ruth to me. "But then she immediately got stuck into Kenmuir, adding another bathroom. I wish I were English and stoic too."

To get to the farm, I crossed two dry riverbeds, which could turn into raging torrents within minutes of a downpour. On the farm a sandy track wound through the dense thorn bush where goats nibbled the grass, and Brahman and Friesian cattle looked lazily at you through their great, sleepy eyes. The thatched roofed house with its fetching front garden was in stark contrast to the farm buildings close by it, which included a reservoir, dipping trough, cattle run and petrol tanks.

The house at Kenmuir was initially four thatched rondavels. When Ruth had finished renovating, it was a three-bedroomed, four-bathroomed home, complete with library, bar, dining room, lounge and patio. When you walked into the lounge, it was like stepping into an English country house, with its Sanderson linen furniture, shantung curtains, soft gold carpet, marble-topped tables and television, hi-fi set and family photographs everywhere. French doors opened on to the front garden, and then you were in Africa, with only a bit of green lawn and a wire fence separating you from the tawny long grass, the thorn trees, goats and donkeys.

Above the bar hung two photographs, taken of Ruth and Seretse a little while after their marriage. They were so positioned that Ruth smiled up into his eyes. Also hanging there were pictures of Ian, regal in his leopard skin covered chair at his installation as chief, and a photograph of Khama III with his son Sekgoma, both tall and distinguished. In the thatched dining room, a life-sized oil portrait of Seretse dominated the scene. Photographs of the British Royal Family were interspersed among the many of Ruth's family and in her bedroom, a pot plant nestled in a Sèvres vase given to her by Queen Elizabeth. A zebra skin in the entrance hall, a leopard skin in the lounge, ivory horns, copper, wood and marble carvings, ashtrays and goblets reminded guests that they were indeed in Africa. This was emphasised when they walked out to their cars after one of Ruth's delicious dinners, and she reminded them sharply to watch out for snakes as she flashed her torch along the sandy driveway.

Gauzed doors ensured the unwelcome reptiles did not slither into the house. During the incredibly hot summer months, these gauzed windows and doors allowed the prevailing breeze to waft through, and in winter, the thatched roofs and an open log fire kept the house warm.

Tshekedi, with his kindness and his knack for finding humour in every possible situation, moved to Kenmuir with Ruth, ostensibly to run the farm. Back then Tony had bought a house in Gaborone, Ian had his house in the Botswana Defence Force camp and Jackie had hers. Although Ruth had not expected Tshekedi to work and live on Kenmuir with her, it frustrated her that the farm workers would only take orders from him.

If cattle needed dips, or vaccines, died or were stolen, Tshekedi was the one they wanted to speak to. "Well, Botswana is a man's world," said Ruth to me when I visited her there some months after they had moved in. "It is a male chauvinistic society." Driving us through the night to the farmhouse, she had noticed cattle outside the farm gate and she called the farm workers out angrily. They got into the car, their rough clothes heavy with wood smoke and tobacco. They contrasted strongly with the powerful, elegant blue saloon car, and Ruth's coiffed poodle yapped at them from the safety of the front seat.

"What are the cattle doing outside?" asked Ruth in her clipped English accent. They moved uneasily in their seats for they didn't understand her and she couldn't understand them. The cattle's eyes caught in the car's headlights, lit up like great diamonds in the black night, and matched the flash of the stone on Ruth's slender finger. As the men shooed the cattle back on to the farm, Ruth said that her goats were being stolen, and I felt immensely sorry for her. She was trying to come to terms with her new life, in a farming environment she had never particularly liked and amongst people with whom she could not easily communicate. It was ironic that after Seretse's death she chose to live the farming life he had so wanted both her and the family to enjoy with him, and she was eventually most knowledgeable about nearly every aspect of cattle farming. It was always a source of disappointment to Seretse that his children were not more interested in farming and cattle.

When we returned to the farmhouse after seeing the cattle in safely, I became the recipient of the hospitality that Ruth was noted for, and which made entertaining so easy for Seretse. Cream, bath oils and lotions, tissues and cotton wool were set out for me in the bathroom. Dried flower arrangements prettied the thatched rondavel bedroom. There was a cosy, comfortable bed for the chill, crisp night, and chocolates to nibble if screech owls or the howl of jackals woke me.

That first morning I spent with Ruth on the farm she was up at the crack of dawn, unable to sleep because of migraines that were so bad that occasionally her children had to inject her with painkillers and tranquillisers. Tshekedi had, as usual, come in during the early hours of the morning, and Ruth in a pretty, full-length dressing gown with fluffy slippers was busy baking scones and gingerbread for him. She was busy training new maids with frequent, often exasperated orders.

Over a breakfast of grapefruit and oranges from the garden, Tshekedi regaled us with a description of him teasing a cabaret star in the Holiday Inn the night before. He didn't have a hangover because he, like his two brothers, was teetotal. The Khama sons did not smoke, swear or use rough language.

After breakfast Ruth took the great bunch of keys she always seemed to have at hand, unlocked the storeroom and put out the rations of sugar, tea, flour, soap and so forth.

During the year following Seretse's death, Ruth followed custom by mourning and wearing black. Her slight figure in pleated skirt, simple blouse and sandals seemed to grow thinner each time I saw her. She rinsed her copper hair to hide the white streaks, and her pale skin at times seemed almost translucent. A few months after Seretse's death, the bodyguard she had been assigned by the government was withdrawn, and with him went one of the last trappings of her former privileged status.

The children grew even more fiercely protective of her and installed fourteen citizen band radios in all their cars, trucks, motorbikes and houses to be constantly in touch with their mother. They left them switched on nearly all the time, and Ruth consequently talked to the twins several times a day. When I was there on a visit, one conversation went as follows:

Ruth: "Those damn mice have eaten the water pipe that leads to my car windscreen. Over."

A twin: "Put down poison. Over."

Ruth: "I can't. The dogs might eat it. Over."

A twin:" Well, get mice traps then. Over and out."

Ruth always told them of her destination and route when she was leaving the farm, and if she was driving home alone at night, they talked to her all the way. The devotion of all the children to Ruth was quite remarkable, and although the family had broken up in a physical sense since Seretse's death, in some ways it became even closer in the end.

When Seretse died, he left a considerable estate and a family that was extremely wealthy. He owned five farms plus the house in Serowe, and in terms of his will the family had to sell some of the farms. This entailed a great deal of stocktaking, winding up of accounts, balancing the books, packing and moving furniture from one house to another.

Much of this fell to Ruth who, with her attention to detail and her penchant for doing things immediately, was soon both exhausted and frustrated by the vast amount of work to be done.

When Ruth first went to live on Kenmuir, she thought of giving up all her voluntary and charitable work, so she could concentrate on the farming. But her son Ian wisely counselled her to keep up the interests that had so absorbed her in State House, and later she was glad she took his advice. Certainly, in that first year of official mourning, it helped to fill the great gap in her life. The list of her organisations and involvements made me giddy just looking at it. She was president of the Girl Guides and of the Botswana Council of Women for over sixteen years; was president of the Botswana Red Cross; was involved with the Save the Children Fund, and with a time-consuming project building a children's village for orphans just outside Gaborone.

In 1981 the Botswana Government recognised Ruth's tremendous community service and her leadership in development, particularly in women's and voluntary organisations, by presenting her with an award. In 1970 she was awarded a certificate of honour and life membership of the British Red Cross Society in recognition of her services to that organisation. One of her favourite charities was the one that carried her name, the Lady Khama Children's Christmas Fund. I attended one of the gift-giving ceremonies on a hot and humid December day.

There must have been 1000 young schoolchildren lined up on that Saturday afternoon in the scorching sun behind the trestle tables that groaned under the load of sweets, cooldrinks and little presents. Jacqueline was there handing out the gifts, as was the American ambassador's wife and several other embassy wives. The present-giving over, we retired to a platform draped with a hessian covering to keep out the sun, which had been set up in the middle of the huge, sandy playground. The festive touch was provided by a picture of a white Father Christmas, and a thorn tree decorated with baubles and tinsel. The sense of anticipation as people waited for Ruth was given impetus by a storm that rumbled ominously closer. The hundreds of children milled around laughing and joking in the dust.

Suddenly a cheer went up, and soon a smart Rover driven by Ian nosed its way through the excited throng. Ruth emerged from it, dressed in black and wearing sandals. She clutched her poodle in one hand, and waved with the other, her diamond ring flashing on her hand. Still holding the poodle, she strode briskly to the microphone on the hessian-covered platform, and there she was introduced in Setswana. Her talk to the rapt, quiet children was made in English and was translated. They cheered the short speech wildly at its close, and sang and danced for her, their bright eyes and black faces gleaming with happiness. Ruth watched them intently as they sang, her pale skin whiter than ever against the black of her attire. At times she seemed remote, lost in another world. It was the first function of her fund that she had attended since Seretse's death and it was obvious she missed him, for he had made a point of always trying to be there. The storm that had been growling closer announced its presence with a peal of thunder and a wind that whipped dust and sand into all our faces. In the gathering gloom, Ruth climbed back into her son's car and drove away, leaving hundreds of satisfied little children behind her.

One of the things that Ruth had to get used to after Seretse's death was travelling alone. From the time of her marriage she had always been accompanied either by him and his entourage or some official, who had organised her ticket, seen to her baggage and steered her through passport control and customs before ensuring she was comfortable on the aircraft. In her first three years of widowhood, Ruth travelled extensively. She went to Thailand, to the Philippines, Zambia, Zimbabwe, Canada and Swaziland for her organisations, to Britain and the United States with her daughter, and to Mozambique and Malawi with her sons.

She was able to chuckle later when she spoke of her apprehension at making her first trip alone, and of the alarm with which she viewed the prospect of having to queue to get through passport control and wait for connections in crowded airport lounges. She had no such problem when she flew through South Africa, for there she was still accorded VIP status, and an official took care of all her needs.

President Samora Machel invited Ruth and the children to holiday in Mozambique shortly after Seretse died.

In Maputo they stayed in a beautiful modern house with marble floors, great windows overlooking the sea and filled with mosaics and indoor plants. The president, Mrs Graça Machel and their children joined Ruth and her sons at the holiday house on a lagoon north of Maputo, where with the exception of Ruth they spent lazy days swimming in the warm Indian Ocean.

In Malawi the Khamas were the guests of President Banda in his luxurious, rambling lakeside holiday home.

The children's sharing of holidays with Ruth was yet another indication of their devotion to her, and she was particularly aware of this and grateful to them. Ian was the most serious and thoughtful of the four children, and Ruth had come to value his opinion and advice increasingly in her widowhood.

He is articulate with a well-modulated voice and a good command of the English language, for which he can thank his father, whose vocabulary was impressive. A heavy burden of responsibility and expectation lay on the shoulders of this handsome young man with his trim, muscular figure and abstemious habits.

He was a brigadier, the youngest in the world in 1980, and was second in command in the Botswana Defence Force. And as chief of the Bamangwato, he enjoyed a considerable power base.

Back then, Ian felt keenly the pressure that came from having a famous father and great-grandfather. "I sometimes feel that if I could only be half the man my father was … I do feel I should never do anything to discredit his name or mine. It can all be a bit overwhelming at times. But a person like my father is born. If I can just be the kind of person that he would have wanted me to be, I'll be happy," said Ian during an interview with me in 1983.

He is a traditionalist and, sad that the tribal traditions are dying, he tried back then to revive some of them. There is a certain irony that this modern young man whose great-grandfather and father both played such a large role in abolishing tribal ceremonies and tribalism, sought to re-introduce some of these. Ian took a keen interest in introducing a traditional dancing group in the Botswana Defence Force, and he admired and envied the British regiments he visited who had traditions going back scores of years.

Ian was frank at the time of our discussion three decades ago about the treatment meted out to his parents when they married: "At one stage I was bitter about it. I suppose in a way I still am, for instance now when I talk about it I feel upset and annoyed. I used to dig out my mother's letters and newspaper reports about it, and I still do so at times now, I just feel for some reason I need to be reminded. But then I remember that my father forgave, and the reason he probably never spoke to me about the past was because he thought it should be forgotten."

Ian felt that his mother had had a hard life, what with her marriage and then his father's political career. "It restricted her in a sense. And then his death meant she had to get used to living alone and coping with a different status."

"Jackie was totally shattered by her father's death. She relied on him a lot," said a friend of hers to me.

Ruth worried more about Jackie's personal future than she did about the boys' and doted on her handsome grandsons. They clearly enjoyed being with "Nana" as they called her, for she was an integral part of their young lives.

Mention of the Khama twins in Gaborone in the early 1980s inevitably brought a warm, amused smile. The broadly-built, tall, good-looking men were the first to admit, in their disarming manner, that work was a bit of a bore. Not for them, their brother's suits and uniforms. Back then they were happier in open-necked shirts and slacks, worn with elephant hair bangles and medallions.

The bond between them was so strong, it was almost tangible, and one would take up a conversation where the other had left off. In spite of being identical twins, they were different in character. Tony was the quieter of the two with a steady girlfriend from South Africa whom he later married. Tshekedi also has a white wife. Before their marriages the twins on occasion swapped dates for the fun of it without some girls ever knowing.

This also came in useful at school when one had a date and a detention order that conflicted and the other would step in – and do the detention of course! They took a mischievous delight in fooling their family too. "They find it almost impossible to tell us apart on the telephone," said Tshekedi.

For all their irresponsibility, which at times made Ruth tear her hair in despair, they were gentle giants, always stopping to help people in trouble. If they found a truck broken down on the road, no matter whose it was, they stopped to help them. And their genuine concern for their mother, her physical and mental happiness, touched all those who witnessed it.

Despite them having married white wives, the twins, with the obvious exception of their father, were the closest in the family to the ordinary Batswana, speaking the language as they have since they were babies, and seldom leaving the country they both love so much.

It was the twins who Ruth got hold of within minutes of discovering her house was on fire on a cold winter's night in July 1983. She was entertaining some South African friends, and they were having dinner in the thatched rondavel dining room when a farm worker rushed into the small kitchen, yelling that the house was burning. By the light of a half-moon, he had seen smoke pouring from the thatch. "While we were sitting having dinner the ceiling was on fire and we didn't know. I have no sense of smell," said Ruth. Stunned, she and her guests rushed into the lounge where the worker said the smoke was coming from, and they found the ceiling red with heat.

Ruth grabbed her handbag, tore around turning off the gas cylinders and rushed to the car to call her sons. They answered immediately, and when they heard the house was on fire, said they would be there in ten minutes, breaking every speed limit in the book with complete abandon. They called Ian on his radio, and he tore out with a Botswana Defence Force fire engine. But in spite of a reservoir full of water, the heat was so intense that nothing could stop those hungry flames shooting higher and higher into the night sky.

"It was terrible, standing there, seeing the flames, we felt so helpless," said Tony. "They asked me what I wanted out of the house," said Ruth," and I said the oil portrait of Seretse in the dining room. But five minutes after we left it, we couldn't get back into it," said Ruth. She stood stupefied, watching the house that contained so much of her life history, and what she had left of the man she loved – his letters, photographs – go up in flames in front of her. When she heard her sons discussing going back into the burning house to save some of these precious articles, she said, "I have lost everything else, I am not going to lose you too. No one goes back into that house."

Later, as she and her guests drove to Gaborone to spend the night with Tony, she said, "A death, a funeral, is bad enough when the man who has been your life dies. But then when everything you had that reminded you of him is gone too, it just doesn't seem fair."

The fire, which was started by faulty electrical wiring, was given extensive coverage by the South African news media. In one brief and violent blaze, she lost most of the mementos of her life with Seretse, and the Botswana nation lost a great deal of history. The Khama family seemed destined to lose its heritage in fires, for when Tshekedi's house burnt down in the Serowe unrest in 1950, much of the Bamangwato history went up in that blaze.

In a three-year period, Ruth had lost her husband and her home. "If mother did not feel she had her family around her, supporting her, at the time of these two devastating events, who knows what would have happened to her," said Tony.

Ruth was superstitious about numbers. "It was the thirteenth year since we had bought that house," she said. "That number is bad for me. I had been waiting all year for something to happen. When ten cattle died in one month, I thought that was it, because that had never happened to us before. But I thought, no, there's something else coming. I just knew it."

Ruth could account for nearly everything in her life with figures. Seretse and her mother died on the thirteenth. Seretse was in his thirteenth year of his presidency, and it was the thirty-first year of their marriage, which she points out is thirteen in reverse. I saw the house about ten days after the fire. It was totally gutted, and the sagging, blackened walls contrasted starkly with the richly laden fruit trees nearby and the bright green lawn around it. Hornbills and doves called, lilac-breasted rollers flashed through the blue sky that showed through the roof, and nearby vultures flocked around a dead donkey. The pieces of burnt jewellery lying on the ground, the gold and silver threads from a party dress, a pair of binoculars and Seretse's watch were the reminders of what had been.

Ruth saved the few burnt mementos she could, wept over the ashes that had been Seretse's love letters, and with her formidable courage picked herself up and carried on. Her office in a farm outbuilding was spared, and she drove out from Gaborone daily to see to the affairs of the farm, to do the books and answer the piles of sympathetic letters that poured in from all over the world. She was already making plans for rebuilding and wondering where to site the new house when I got there. She had a strong sense of continuity, and by continuing with the everyday activities that constituted her life she was able to cope with the disasters.

Her bright little study in a prefabricated building in the grounds of the Botswana Council of Women offices in Gaborone also provided her with a sense of continuity. Sanderson linen chairs, a bright carpet, and pictures of her family on the walls welcomed her to a home of sorts.

In 1984, when I completed the first draft of this book, Ruth was living with her daughter Jacqueline and her grandsons in Gaborone until her new house was built. Her sons who pondered deeply and discussed endlessly the meaning of everything that had happened in their lives, wondered if the fire meant that Ruth should start a completely new life.

Her organisational and charitable activities were endless. Everyone in Gaborone knew that if they had a good cause, Lady K, as she was affectionately known, would assist them, particularly if it was related in some way to helping disadvantaged women and children. And she didn't simply sign cheques or sit on committees. One day she tramped several kilometres around the Anglican Cathedral in a walk to raise funds for a charitable cause.

As a widow she was still very much on the social map. Invitations from embassies, consulates, visiting dignitaries arrived almost daily, and she enjoyed the dinners and cocktail parties. Her hosts enjoyed her presence, for apart from her witty repartee, people were fascinated by the story of her life and the events that shaped it. She was always well informed about world and African affairs, for she listened to the BBC news and reviews, to the South African Broadcasting Corporation's daily actuality programme, Radio Today and to Radio Botswana.

She relaxed by riding on horseback, always a favourite pastime, through the wild bushveld near her farm. If there was a play or a musical on in Gaborone she went to see it, for she had always loved the theatre. All family occasions such as birthdays and anniversaries were spent together, and it was most unusual for the entire family not to go to Serowe for Christmas, as they had for many years. On Christmas Day, Ian, as was the custom, gave the villagers oxen which they cooked and ate both in the kgotla and up on the hill in the grounds of the Khama house. After church, the Bamangwato streamed up the hill, and settled down for the day under the thorn trees in the rocky garden, happy to be near their chief and the mother of the tribe.

At intervals during the day they sang and danced, their rich voices ringing the hymns through the rocky hills.

Dogs slept in the hot sun, and chickens and goats scratched for food nearby. Outwardly Serowe had not changed much from that first day Ruth drove through it with Seretse. The women still did most of the work while the men talked in the kgotla. They built and rebuilt the huts and the men thatched them. The villagers still waited anxiously each October for the rains that would allow them to plough and sow. The rhythm of the seasons that dictates the tempo of their lives continued.

But their social order had changed. The drift to the towns had broken up families, there were illegitimate children and unmarried mothers and the autocratic rule of the parents was increasingly challenged. Today Serowe has bottle stores as well as churches. I wonder what the Great Khama who banned liquor would think of "The Forefather's Bottle Store" which was situated near his great church. The latter did not fill as it used to before all religions were allowed to practise freely. It was a very different Serowe from the one Khama III and his son Tshekedi knew and loved.

Gaborone has changed almost beyond recognition from the new, neat little English town it was at Independence in 1966.

It will be many years before Botswana can lessen its economic dependency on its powerful South African neighbour. But today it is a country with promise. The discovery of diamonds transformed it from the twelfth poorest country in the world to one with a viable economy. Beneath the vast Kalahari sands there are believed to be many more exciting minerals waiting to be exploited. But even more than diamonds there is the hope that oil may be found, although this is still only a dream. There are vast deposits of soda ash, and of coal. And a railway line that will either run westwards from the rich coalfield near Serowe, across the untamed Kalahari to the cold Atlantic coast of Namibia, or eastwards to Richards Bay, is being investigated. If the nearly 1500 kilometres of track is laid across the Kalahari, it will be one of the world's last great railway lines and will provide access to some of the best cattle ranching in Africa.

In the years following Seretse's death, some people asked if Ruth might not return to England, and it was a question that both astounded and made her indignant. She told me, "I am a Motswana, I have lived most of my life here, my children and grandchildren are here and when I said that I was going to make my husband's country my own, all those years ago, I meant it."

The Batswana, with their tremendous tolerance and gentleness, had accepted this former Londoner as one of them, although they often did not understand her ways and didn't always find her friendly. Her inability to speak their language was a major disability and one that weighed heavily on her mind. "I would still like to be able to understand and speak it, very much so," said Ruth to me. "I think to have been here all the time I have and still not speak it, is sad. It's a shame. I know most people in my shoes would have been speaking it fluently by now, but learning languages is not something that comes easily to me." In the early Serowe days, she said she was too busy with her young children, sick husband and community work to devote the painstaking attention that she needed in order to master it.

Ruth was in many ways an enigma. British journalist Margaret Lessing, who was a friend of mine and who met her in Serowe in the 1950s told me that Ruth ran her home like any middle-class English housewife, and that she regarded Serowe in many ways as another London suburb. "She wasn't going to give up her English ways and habits because she was living in Africa," said Margaret Lessing.

That applied to a certain extent to her death in 2002. Ruth had assimilated many of the traditions and customs of her husband's people, and she set out to improve their welfare and standard of living in a manner equalled by few other white women in the country's history. No one questioned her devotion and dedication to the lot of the less privileged. And yet she clung to her English habits and ways, her homes were furnished and run like English homes, mainly English was spoken in them, and she had brought up her children as English children.

I think there were reasons for this. Ruth might have followed to a certain extent the example of the English people around her in Serowe. They did not attempt to assimilate the culture of the people amongst whom they lived, they did not for the most part learn the language, and they did not mix socially with the Batswana. And it is possible that Ruth, caught in the bewildering corridor between two worlds, clung to the life she knew as a rock or beacon that would see her through those first difficult years. Later on, it probably became harder to change.

Ruth's personality was also a study in contrasts, for she was an extraordinary mixture of kindness and arrogance, of sensitivity and tactlessness. She loved gossip and yet kept a secret better than anyone I know. She was intensely loyal, and once she became your friend, would be so for life, unless she felt you had betrayed her. She was the first to rush to a sickbed or the side of a troubled friend, but she expected the same treatment in return. She was superstitious, and yet sensible and incredibly practical. She was domineering, and an excellent organiser, yet at times suffered from an almost crippling lack of self-confidence.

The contrasts in Ruth's life – the differences between herself and her husband, between the misty island of her birth and the vast, dry country of her adoption, and between the city she grew up in and the village she regarded as home, seemed to have been echoed in her interesting personality.

She had to adapt time and again to radical changes in her life, and she tackled these with the same fortitude with which she coped with her new life after Seretse's death. Those close to her were aware of the toll her terrible and intense grief took on her nerves and her health in the months that followed his funeral, although her innate dignity and sense of pride would not let slip the model of composure she presented to the public.

Friends had feared that so much of her life had been tied up with being the president's wife and the functions that went with it that she might become depressed and bored.

Ruth told me that it took a great deal of time to accept the changes to her life wrought by Seretse's death. "I was numb for so long. You just can't absorb what has happened. You think that this person has gone on a long trip, and that he will be coming back. You cannot believe that death is possible, which is a bit stupid, isn't it," she asked me with disarming candour.

Like many bereaved people she had intensely vivid dreams in which Seretse had beaten his cancer and lived and came out of his grave to be with her. When she went back to Serowe, she climbed the rock-strewn hill to his imposing granite grave and sat there, gazing over the huts below to the vast open spaces beyond that he so loved.

"But I don't feel closer to him there than I do in other places, I just feel at peace looking out over that lovely view," she said once, so softly and quietly I could hardly hear her. It was intensely sad to learn from her that she did not feel happier once she had accepted his death. The love that brought them together in the face of such overwhelming odds and kept them together in even greater adversity had been strengthened, not dimmed, by death.

"Seretse was so loveable. He bore no animosity towards anyone, no matter what they did to him. I wish I could be like that," said Ruth wistfully. But the scars left by exile, the ostracism of her by her own people, the racial discrimination and insults she and her children suffered, probably went to the grave with her.

The big questions Ruth leaves behind her are these: What sort of life would she have led, and what sort of person would she have been if she had not fallen in love with Seretse? What legacy did she leave – if any?

People were fond of remarking in the 1950s and 1960s that she would have been a nonentity if Seretse had not married her. But isn't it just as pertinent that at a time when racial prejudice was the norm, she had the courage of her convictions to marry him? She was a strikingly attractive, vivacious young woman, who could have married any of the dashing air force officers she met during the war. But she was determined to marry someone she both loved and respected, and she found that person in Seretse.

Ruth Khama survived. Her and Seretse's marriage survived. That was her triumph.

Maybe one day her great-grandchildren will read the story of her life and shake their heads in amusement at the storm caused by the marriage of a copper-haired Londoner to an African chief.

If they can do that, the world will indeed have come a long way and Ruth Khama's wish that her and Seretse's children and grandchildren be judged not by the colour of their skin but by the content of their hearts, will have been realised.

List of abbreviations used in endnotes

BNA Botswana National Archives
BP Bechuanaland Protectorate
CRO Commonwealth Relations Office
HCO High Commissioner's Office
TNA: PRO The National Archives of Britain: Public Record Office
DO Dominions Office

Endnotes

1 Head, *Serowe: Village of the Rain Wind*, 1981: XXIV
2 See more on Seretse's childhood in Parsons, Henderson and Tlou, *Seretse Khama 1921–80*, 1995
3 Sillery, *Botswana. A Short Political History*, 1974
4 Head, *Serowe Village of the Rain Wind*, 1981: 8
5 Head, *Serowe Village of the Rain Wind*, 1981: 6–9
6 See Benson, *Tshekedi Khama*, 1960: 28–32
7 Parsons, Henderson and Tlou, *Seretse Khama 1921–80*, 1995: 9
8 For more on this history see Mockford, *Seretse Khama*, 1950, and by the same author, *Khama, King of the Bamangwato*, 1931
9 Benson, *Tshekedi Khama*, 1960: 32–33
10 See more in Head's *Serowe: Village of the Rain Wind*, 1981, and Mockford's *Khama, King of the Bamangwato*, 1931
11 ibid.
12 Head, *Serowe Village of the Rain Wind*, 1981, and also *New Zealand Evening Star*, 3 September 1936
13 Benson, *Tshekedi Khama*, 1960: 67
14 See more on Seretse's childhood in Parsons, Henderson and Tlou, *Seretse Khama 1921–80*, 1995
15 Benson, *Tshekedi Khama*, 1960
16 See more on Tshekedi's reign in Benson, *Tshekedi Khama*, 1960
17 Benson, *Tshekedi Khama*, 1960: 55
18 Benson, *Tshekedi Khama*, 1960: 32
19 ibid.
20 Crowder, *The Flogging of Phineas McIntosh*, 1988: 2–209
21 ibid.
22 From my interviews with Naledi Khama, Seretse's sister, in Serowe
23 Dr G. Chiepe told me this during our interview in Gaborone
24 Benson, *Tshekedi Khama*, 1960: 174–75
25 Seretse to Tshekedi on 14 June 1946, TNA: PRO 041953
26 ibid.
27 Sir Coupland to Buchanan, 25 July 1946, TNA: PRO 041953
28 Mockford, *Seretse Khama and the Bamangwato*, 1950: 15–16
29 Benson, *Tshekedi Khama*, 1960: 178
30 Benson, *Tshekedi Khama*, 1960: 177
31 Pilkington to Tshekedi, 27 September 1948, TNA: PRO 041953

32 Pilkington to Tshekedi, 27 September 1948, TNA: PRO 041953, and confidentail memorandum regarding Seretse's proposed marriage from R.K. Orchard, BNA S 169/15/1

33 Redfern, *Ruth and Seretse: A Very Disreputable Transaction,*1955: 37

34 Pilkington to Tshekedi, TNA: PRO D035/4113 041953 Annexure K.1

35 Buchanan to his brother, 26 September 1948, TNA: PRO DO 35/4113 041593

36 Benson, *Tshekedi Khama,* 1960: 179

37 ibid.

38 ibid.

39 Douglas-Home, *Evelyn Baring: The Last Proconsul,* 1978: 177

40 Benson, *Tshekedi Khama,* 1960

41 Report by Nettleton to British HCO, Pretoria, TNA: PRO 041953

42 ibid.

43 Douglas-Home, *Evelyn Baring: The Last Proconsul,* 1978

44 Head, *Serowe: Village of the Rain Wind,* 1981: 37–41, and Schapera, *A Handbook of Tswana Law and Custom,* 1938

45 Dutfield, *A Marriage of Inconvenience,* 1990: 55, and Johannesburg *Star,* 24 November 1948

46 Dutfield, *A Marriage of Inconvenience,* 1990: 55; and *Rand Daily Mail,* Johannesburg, 22 December 1948

47 Dutfield, *A Marriage of Inconvenience,* 1990: 55

48 Transcript of the notes of closing speeches in Serowe kgotla, 19 November 1948, BNA 1(9)

49 Redfern, *Ruth and Seretse: A Very Disreputable Transaction,*1955: 52

50 Transcript of the notes of closing speeches in Serowe kgotla, 19 November 1948, BNA 1(9)

51 Information on kgotla from Dutfield, *A Marriage of Inconvenience,* 1990, and Redfern, *Ruth and Seretse: A Very Disreputable Transaction,*1955, and also Benson, *Tshekedi Khama,* 1960

52 Ruth summarised the sensational headlines in these words

53 Memorandum by Tshekedi, BNA 1 (3), S 169/15/2

54 From Benson, *Tshekedi Khama,* 1960, and Douglas-Home, *Evelyn Baring: The Last Proconsul,* 1978

55 Benson, *Tshekedi Khama,* 1960: 184–85

56 Sillery, *Botswana. A Short Political History,* 1974, and Redfern, *Ruth and Seretse: A Very Disreputable Transaction,*1955: 48

57 Report on meeting in Serowe between G.E. Nettleton, Seretse and Tshekedi after second kgotla, 20 December 1948, TNA: PRO 35/4113 041953

58 Margaret Lessing told this to me in an interview, also in Dutfield, *A Marriage of Inconvenience,* 1990: 58

59 Dutfield, *A Marriage of Inconvenience. The Persecution of Seretse and Ruth Khama,* 1990: 58

60 Douglas-Home, *Evelyn Baring: The Last Proconsul,* 1978: 179

61 Memorandum by Buchanan, BNA 2 (8)

62 Tshekedi to resident commissioner, BNA 2 (15)

63 Douglas-Home, *Evelyn Baring: The Last Proconsul*, 1978: 180

64 Memorandum on security measures by BP Police on 24 June 1949, BNA 2(4) S 170/1/1

65 Tshekedi to Sir Evelyn Baring, BNA 2 (10)

66 Seretse to Baring, BNA 2 (10)

67 Report by Ellenberger, 29 June 1949, BNA S 169/15/4

68 Benson, *Tshekedi Khama*, 1960: 187

69 Benson, *Tshekedi Khama*, 1960: 188

70 ibid.

71 Report by Ellenberger, 29 June 1949, BNA S 169/15/4

72 See Douglas-Home, *Evelyn Baring: The Last Proconsul*, 1978: 162–71

73 Douglas-Home, *Evelyn Baring: The Last Proconsul*, 1978: 182

74 Telegram from CRO to Baring in Pretoria after representation by Egeland, 2 July 1949, TNA: PRO DO 35/4114

75 Report by Sillery, 5 July 1949, BNA S 170/1/1

76 Douglas-Home, *Evelyn Baring: The Last Proconsul*, 1978: 180

77 Monks, *Daily Mail*, London, 4 July 1949

78 Margaret Lessing told me this in an interview

79 Benson, *Tshekedi Khama*, 1960: 189–92

80 Baring to Liesching, 11 July 1949, TNA: PRO DO 35/4114 042045

81 Huggins to Baring, 7 July 1949, TNA: PRO DO 34/4114 041940

82 *Die Burger*, July 1949

83 Baring to Sir Percivale Liesching, in Douglas-Home, *Evelyn Baring: The Last Proconsul*, 1978: 181

84 Douglas-Home, *Evelyn Baring: The Last Proconsul*, 1978: 183

85 Liesching's comment on the report, in Douglas-Home, *Evelyn Baring: The Last Proconsul*, 1978: 186, and Baring to Liesching on 11 July 1949, TNO: PRO DO 35/4114 042045

86 Liesching's comment on the report, in Douglas-Home, *Evelyn Baring: The Last Proconsul*, 1978: 186

87 Douglas-Home, *Evelyn Baring: The Last Proconsul*, 1978: 180–84

88 Douglas-Home, *Evelyn Baring: The Last Proconsul*, 1978: 180–85

89 Baring to CRO, in Douglas-Home, *Evelyn Baring: The Last Proconsul*, 1978: 180–86

90 Steyn, *Churchill and Smuts: The Friendship*, 2017

91 Ruth told me this in an interview

92 Parsons, Henderson and Thlou, *Seretse Khama 1921–1980*, 1995: 90

93 Nettleton to Ellenberger, 4 July 1949, BNA: 169/15/3

94 Monks, *Eyewitness. The Journal of a World Correspondent*, 1955: 269

95 Confidential letter from Sir Evelyn Baring to CRO, 16 September 1949, TNA: PRO 16/40 II

96 Report by Kevin Lowry, 27 August 1949, BNA: S 170/1/4

97 Douglas-Home, *Evelyn Baring: The Last Proconsul*, 1978: 187

98 Letter by Quintin Whyte, BA 7 (1)

99 Baring to Liesching, TNA: PRO DO 35/4116 042045

100 Letter by Sillery to Serowe district commissioner, BNA S 170/1/4

101 ibid.

102 Report of the Judicial Enquiry into the Fitness of Seretse Khama, of the Bamangwato Tribe, 1 December 1949, TNA: PRO 35/4122, and TNA: PRO: 35/4119 041939

103 Report of the Judicial Enquiry into the Fitness of Seretse Khama, of the Bamangwato Tribe, 1 December 1949, TNA: PRO 35/4122: 10

104 Redfern, *Ruth and Seretse: A Very Disreputable Transaction*, 1995: 101

105 Report of the Judicial Enquiry into the Fitness of Seretse Khama, of the Bamangwato Tribe, 1 December 1949, TNA: PRO 35/4122: 11

106 Redfern, *Ruth and Seretse: A Very Disreputable Transaction*, 1995: 83

107 Report in the *Daily Worker*, London, 19 December 1949, TNA: PRO DO 35/4118 041939

108 Report of the Judicial Enquiry into the Fitness of Seretse Khama of the Bamangwato Tribe, 1 December 1949, TNA: PRO 35/4122: 14

109 Douglas-Home, *Evelyn Baring: The Last Proconsul*, 1978: 188–189

110 Memorandum by Noel-Baker, TNA: PRO DO 35/4 04118 041939

111 ibid.

112 Gordon Walker to Attlee, 21 January 1950, TNA: PRO DO 35/4118 041939

113 Attlee to Gordon Walker, 22 January 1950, TNA: PRO DO 35/4118 041939

114 Personal, handwritten letters from Doris Bradshaw to her sister, Hope Lovell in England, 9 February 1950, BNA 1(10)

115 Redfern, *Ruth and Seretse: A Very Disreputable Transaction,*1955: 113

116 Sillery to CRO, 8 February 1950, TNA: PRO DO 35/4119 041953

117 Telegram to CRO, 8 February 1950, TNA: PRO DO 35/4119 041953

118 Monks, *Eyewitness. The Journal of a World Correspondent*, 1955: 263

119 Liesching to HCO in Pretoria, 15 February 1950, TNA: PRO DO 35/4119 041953

120 Official minutes of a meeting at the CRO on 16 February 1950 attended by (inter alia) Noel-Baker, Seretse Khama and Liesching, TNA: PRO DO 35/4119 041953

121 ibid.

122 Report by Keith regarding Seretse, 27 February 1950, TNA: PRO DO 35/4119 041953

123 ibid.

124 Personal, handwritten letters from Doris Bradshaw to her sister, Hope Lovell in England, 9 February 1950, BNA 1(10)

125 Online: www.brainyquote.com/quotes/winston_churchill_384133

126 CRO third meeting with Seretse, London, 6 March 1950, TNA: PRO DO 35/4120 041948

127 Redfern, *Ruth and Seretse: A Very Disreputable Transaction,*1955, and *Daily Telegraph*, London, 2 July 2006, and also *Time* magazine, 30 June 1961

128 Douglas-Home, *Evelyn Baring: The Last Proconsul*, 1978: 191

129 Redfern, *Ruth and Seretse: A Very Disreputable Transaction,*1955: 118

130 Redfern, *Ruth and Seretse: A Very Disreputable Transaction,*1955: 77

131 Baring to CRO, 8 March 1950, TNA: PRO DO 35/4120 041948

132 Personal, handwritten letters from Doris Bradshaw to her sister, Hope Lovell in England, 9 February 1950, BNA 1(10), and Redfern, John, *Very Disreputable Transaction*, 1955: 123

133 Redfern, *Ruth and Seretse: A Very Disreputable Transaction,*1955: 123

134 Redfern, *Ruth and Seretse: A Very Disreputable Transaction,*1955: 128

135 Evelyn Baring to CRO, 15 March 1950, TNA: PRO DO 35/4120 0419448

136 Personal, handwritten letters from Doris Bradshaw to her sister, Hope Lovell in England: 9 February 1950, BNA 1(10)

137 ibid.

138 Union of South Africa House of Assembly Debates (Hansard), 20–24 March 1950, TNA: PRO DO 35/4121 041953

139 Liesching note, 25 March 1950, TNA: PRO DO 35/4115 041940

140 ibid.

141 ibid.

142 Douglas-Home, *Evelyn Baring: The Last Proconsul*, 1978: 191 and 195

143 Monks, *Eyewitness. The Journal of a World Correspondent*, 1955: 282

144 Telegram from HCO in Cape Town to CRO, 3 April 1950, TNA: PRO, DO 35/4120 041948

145 *Rand Daily Mail*, Johannesburg, 1 April 1950

146 Redfern, *Ruth and Seretse: A Very Disreputable Transaction,*1955: 131–132

147 Letter from Americans for Democratic Action to Gordon Walker, 28 March 1950, TNA: PRO DO 35/4125 042008

148 Notes of a meeting between the secretary of state for the colonies and the League of Coloured People, 17 March 1950, TNA: PRO DO 35/4125 042008

149 Letter by Brockway, 12 April 1950, TNA: PRO DO 35/4121 041953

150 Gordon Walker reply in parliament to Fenner Brockway, TNA: PRO DO 35/4121 041953

151 ibid.

152 Monks, *Eyewitness. The Journal of a World Correspondent*, 1955: 284

153 Telegram to CRO, 22 February 1950, BA 8(12), and TNA: PRO DO 35/4119 041953

154 Administration report, TNA: PRO DO 35/4121 041953

155 Parsons, Henderson and Thlou, *Seretse Khama 1921–1980*, 1995: 183, and Sillery, *Botswana. A Short Political History*, 1974: 113

156 Baring to the British HCO, TNA: PRO DO 35/4121 041953

157 Telegram from Clark to Baring, TNA: PRO DO 35/4121 041953

158 Clark to Liesching, 9 August 1950, TNA: PRO DO 35/4122 042045

159 Report on British legal advisers concerned its actions ultra vires, TNA: PRO DO 35/4129 042008

160 Baring to CRO regarding Tshekedi, 14 August 1950, TNO: PRO DO 35/4122 042045

161 ibid.

162 ibid.

163 CRO telegram to UK HCO in Australia, 17 August 1950, TNA: PRO DO 35/4122 042045

164 ibid.

165 ibid.

166 Joint statement of Seretse and Tshekedi to high commissioner, 16 August 1950, TNA: PRO DO 35/4122 042045

167 ibid.

168 ibid.

169 Telegram to CRO by Clark, 19 August 1950, TNA: PRO DO 35/4122 042045

170 ibid.

171 Douglas-Home, *Evelyn Baring: The Last Proconsul*, 1978: 193

172 Clark to CRO, 19 August 1950, TNA: PRO DO 35/4122 042045

173 *The Times*, London, 20 August 1950

174 *Rand Daily Mail*, 21 August 1950

175 Benson, *Tshekedi Khama*, 1960: 210

176 Parsons, Henderson and Thlou, *Seretse Khama 1921–1980*, 1995: 113

177 Benson, *Tshekedi Khama*, 1960: 216

178 Liesching to Baring, TNA: PRO DO 33/4131

179 Benson, *Tshekedi Khama*, 1960: 226

180 Benson, *Tshekedi Khama*, 1960: 209

181 Redfern, *Ruth and Seretse: A Very Disreputable Transaction*, 1955: 164–167

182 Benson, *Tshekedi Khama*, 1960: 242–243

183 Ruth, quoting Seretse, told this to me in an interview

184 *Daily Telegraph*, August 1951

185 Letter Gordon Walker to Mrs Macmillan, TNA: PRO 35/4135 042034

186 Benson, *Tshekedi Khama*, 1960: 249

187 CRO telegram regarding fight between two of the three observers, 15 August 1951, TNA: PRO 35/4135 042045

188 Redfern, *Ruth and Seretse: A Very Disreputable Transaction*, 1955

189 Redfern, *Ruth and Seretse: A Very Disreputable Transaction*, 1955: 187

190 *The Observer*, London, 2 September 1951, TNA: PRO DO 35/4135 042045

191 British draft note on Bamangwato affairs, 20 August 1951, TNA: PRO DO 35/4135 042045

192 Douglas-Home, Charles, *Evelyn Baring: The Last Proconsul*, 1978: 194

193 Benson, Mary, *Tshekedi Khama*, 1960: 252

194 Parsons, Henderson and Tlou, *Seretse Khama 1921–1980*, 1995: 119, and Redfern, *Ruth and Seretse: A Very Disreputable Transaction,* 1955: 191

195 *The Star*, Johannesburg, 3 August 1951

196 Redfern, *Ruth and Seretse: A Very Disreputable Transaction,* 1955: 192–93

197 Benson, *Tshekedi Khama*, 1960: 250, and Parsons, Henderson and Tlou, *Seretse Khama 1921–1980*, 1995: 11

198 *Rand Daily Mail*, 27 March 1952

199 *The Star*, Johannesburg, 28 March 1952

200 *The Star*, Johannesburg, 28 March 1952, quoting from London's *Daily Express*

201 Redfern, *Ruth and Seretse: A Very Disreputable Transaction*, 1955: 187–190

202 Redfern, *Ruth and Seretse: A Very Disreputable Transaction*, 1955: 192

203 Redfern, *Ruth and Seretse: A Very Disreputable Transaction*, 1955: 196–197

204 Redfern, *Ruth and Seretse: A Very Disreputable Transaction*, 1955: 199

205 *Daily Mail*, London, 16 April 1952

206 HCO to CRO, 30 May 1952, TNA: PRO Prem 11/1182

207 CRO, draft note for cabinet on Bamangwato affairs, 5 June 1952, TNA: PRO DO 35/ 4149 O42045

208 ibid.

209 ibid.

210 Redfern, *Ruth and Seretse: A Very Disreputable Transaction,*1955: 209, and Sapa-Reuter report, November 1952

211 Lessing, *Daily Herald*, 10 November 1952

212 ibid.

213 Article in Liberal Party publiction, *FACT*, January 1953

214 Redfern, *Ruth and Seretse: A Very Disreputable Transaction,*1955: 21

215 Benson, *Tshekedi Khama*, 1960: 256

216 Report of Seretse Khama meeting, Caxton Hall, 15 April 1952, TNA: PRO DO 35/4139 042008

217 *Birmingham Post*, 12 May 1952, TNA: PRO DO 35/4139 042008

218 Handwritten letter MR Clark to CRO, 2 May 1952, TNA: PRO DO 35/4139 042008

219 *Rand Daily Mail*, 28 September 1953

220 Parsons, Henderson and Tlou, *Seretse Khama 1921–1980*, 1995: 132

221 Margaret Lessing in *Daily Herald*, 20 September 1954

222 *Rand Daily Mail*, Johannesburg, 29 December 1954

223 *The Sunday Times*, Johannesburg, 3 July 1955

224 *The Star*, Johannesburg, 20 March 1956

225 *The Star*, Johannesburg, 2 August 1956

226 Parsons, Henderson and Tlou, *Seretse Khama 1921–1980*, 1995: 145

227 Parsons, Henderson and Tlou, *Seretse Khama 1921–1980*, 1995: 147

228 House of Commons Debate, Hansard Vol. 557, 1 August 1956, TNA: PRO Prem 11/1182

229 Parsons, Henderson, and Tlou, *Seretse Khama 1921–1980*, 1995: 147

230 ibid.

231 ibid.

232 *The Star*, Johannesburg, 18 October 1956

233 *Die Transvaler*, Johannesburg, 28 October 1956

234 Sillery, *Botswana: A Short Political History*, 1974: 157

235 Sillery, *Botswana: A Short Political History*, 1974: 157

236 O'Callaghan, "Botswana: Independence at Midnight", 28 September 2016, Australian Institute of International Affairs

237 *The Star*, Johannesburg, 8 August 1983

Acknowledgements

My thanks go to the following people, many of whom I interviewed for this book:

Sue Allison, Audrey Blackbeard, Doris Bradshaw, Vi Calmettes, Colin and Deirdre Blackbeard, Roy and Anna Blackbeard, Phyllis Blackbeard, Bill and Margot Bailey, Joe and Monica Burgess, Gaositwe Chiepe, Doreen Chase, Daphne Clark, Bill Craik, Pauline Cuzen, Tommy Dent, Jack Falconer, Jackie Frolich, Charlie and Doris Freeman, Hylton and Lynne Freeman, my parents Peter and Mary Cardross Grant, my sister and brother Jane and John Cardross Grant, Michael Gers, Christian Grafl, Tracy Going, Bruce Howard, Jimmy Haskins, Pauline and Peter Harrison, Jenny Hobbs, Amos Kgamanye, Ian Khama, Tshekedi Khama, Tony Khama, Naledi Khama, Leapeetswe & Seodi Khama, Sekgoma Khama, Marion Little, Margaret Lessing, Alfred Merriweather, Archie Mogwe, Hugh Murray-Hudson, Peter Mmusi, Goareng Mosinyi, Sydney and Doris Milner, Eileen Matthews, Pro and Nina Obel, Connie Pretorius, Rehana Rossouw, Jessie Rutherford, Alan Russell, Graham Russell, Philip Steenkamp, Minnie (Ma) Shaw, Muriel Sanderson, Tsogang Sebina, Peto Sekgoma, Radiphofu Sekgoma, Kate Turkington, Lynette Woodford, Billie and Paddy Woodford, Ray Watson and Muriel Whitehouse.

Michelle Walford at our Aluwani Foundation, thank you for making a sorely needed print copy of my book. Hilary Prendini Toffoli, you have supported me and this book for over three decades, wow! My publisher Nicol Stassen – you heard, you saw, you believed. Rentia Bartlett-Möhl, my firm but gentle, kind and insightful editor to whom I owe a great deal. My darling daughter Amy Marshall who insisted I persevere when I nearly abandoned this project. My gorgeous husband Don Marshall who inspired, revitalised and motivated me from the first word to the last.

If I have inadvertently not acknowledged someone, please accept my apologies.

Select Bibliography

Benson, Mary, *Tshekedi Khama* (London, Faber and Faber, 1960)

Crowder, Michael, *The Flogging of Phineas McIntosh. A Tale of Colonial Folly and Injustice, Bechuanaland, 1933* (Kingsley Trust Association Publication Fund, Yale College, 1988)

Debenham, Frank, *Kalahari Sand* (The Camelot Press, London, 1953)

Dickson. Moira, *Beloved Partner Mary Moffat of Kuruman* (Botswana Book Centre & Kuruman Moffat Mission Trust, 1989)

Douglas-Home, Charles, *Evelyn Baring: The Last Proconsul* (London, Collins, 1978)

Dubbeld, Gys, *Seretse Khama* (Cape Town, Maskew Miller Longman, 1992)

Dutfield, Mike, *A Marriage of Inconvenience. The Persecution of Seretse and Ruth Khama* (London, Unwin Hyman, 1990)

Fawcus, Peter and Tilbury, Alan, *Botswana: The Road to Independence* (Gaborone, The Botswana Society and Pula Press, 2000)

Gabatswane, S.M., *Seretse Khama and Botswana* (Gaborone, J.G. Musi and S.M. Gabatswane, 1966)

Harris, John Charles, *Khama. The Great African Chief* (London, The Livingstone Press, 1922)

Head, Bessie, *Serowe: Village of the Rain Wind* (Cape Town, David Philip, 1981)

Hepburn, J.D., *Twenty Years in Khama's Country* (London, Hodder and Stoughton, MDCCCXCVI)

Mbanga, Wilf & Trish, *Seretse & Ruth* (South Africa, Tafelberg, 2005)

Merriweather, Alfred, *Desert Doctor Remembers. The autobiography of Alfred Merriweather* (Gaborone, Pula Press, 1999)

Mockford, Julian, *Khama: King of the Bamangwato* (London, J. Cape, 1931)

Mockford, Julian, *Sereste Khama and the Bamangwato* (Staples Press, 1950)

Monks, Noel, *Eyewitness. The Journal of a World Correspondent* (London, Muller, 1955)

Parsons, Neil, Henderson, Willie and Tlou, Thomas, *Seretse Khama 1921–1980* (London, Macmillan, 1995)

Redfern, John, *Ruth and Seretse: A Very Disreputable Transaction* (London, Victor Gollancz, 1955)

Rey, Charles, *Monarch of All I Survey. Bechuanaland Diaries 1929–37* (Gaborone, The Botswana Society, 1988)

Sillery, Anthony, *Botswana. A Short Political History* (London. Methuen, 1974)

Schapera, Isaac, *A Handbook of Tswana Custom* (London, Oxford University Press, 1938)

Steyn, Richard, *Churchill and Smuts: The Friendship* (Cape Town, Jonathan Ball, 2017)

Winstanley, George, *Under Two Flags in Africa. Recollections of a British Administrator in Bechuanaland and Botswana 1954 to 1972* (Colchester UK, Blackwater Books, 2000)

Wylie, Diana, *A Little God. The Twilight of Patriarchy in a Southern African Chiefdom* (University Press of New England, Hanover and London, 1990)

Index of persons